Samuel Hirsch

Studia Judaica

Forschungen zur Wissenschaft des Judentums

Begründet von
Ernst Ludwig Ehrlich

Herausgegeben von
Günter Stemberger, Charlotte Fonrobert,
Elisabeth Hollender, Alexander Samely
und Irene Zwiep

Band 97

Samuel Hirsch

Philosopher of Religion, Advocate of Emancipation
and Radical Reformer

Edited by
Judith Frishman and Thorsten Fuchshuber

DE GRUYTER

Supported by the Luxembourg National Research Fund (FNR) (PARTIZIP).

Supported by the Institute of History (IHIST), University of Luxembourg.

ISBN 978-3-11-151859-6
e-ISBN (PDF) 978-3-11-047639-2
e-ISBN (EPUB) 978-3-11-047528-9
ISSN 0585-5306

Library of Congress Control Number: 2022935988

Bibliographic information published by the Deutsche Nationalbibliothek
The Deutsche Nationalbibliothek lists this publication in the Deutsche Nationalbibliografie; detailed bibliographic data are available on the internet at http://dnb.dnb.de.

© 2024 Walter de Gruyter GmbH, Berlin/Boston
This volume is text- and page-identical with the hardback published in 2022.

www.degruyter.com

Table of Contents

Judith Frishman and Thorsten Fuchshuber
Introduction and Acknowledgements —— 1

Part I: From Thalfang to Philadelphia: An Introduction to Samuel Hirsch's Life and Times

Christian Wiese
"An Intimate Friendship with Modernity". Samuel Hirsch's Reform Philosophy in the Context of the Ideological Controversies of the Times —— 11

Part II: Hegelian and Defender of the Faith: The Fundamentals of Samuel Hirsch's Philosophy

Gershon Greenberg
Samuel Hirsch in Dessau (June 1838 – June 1843). Freedom, Emancipation and the Christian State —— 67

Irene Kajon
Back to Mediaeval Jewish Philosophy. Hirsch's Criticism of Modern Times —— 85

Judith Frishman
Judaism Transformed and the Divine on Earth. Samuel Hirsch's Appropriation of the Hegelian Ideal State —— 99

Part III: Edifying the Congregation: Jewish Answers to Pressing Societal Questions

Laurent Mignon
The Challenges of Alterity: Notes on Samuel Hirsch's Contemporaneity —— 127

Ken Koltun-Fromm
Religious Borders of Reason and Sentiment: Samuel Hirsch and Abraham
Geiger on Jewish Education —— 145

George Y. Kohler
"Humankind is Advancing". Samuel Hirsch's Rediscovery of Messianism and
its Consequences for Modern Jewish Religious Philosophy —— 161

Part IV: **Samuel Hirsch's Luxembourg: Industrialization, Emancipation and Community**

Norbert Franz
Mid-19th Century Luxembourg. Nation Building and the Late
Industrialization —— 183

Renée Wagener
Between Recognition and Exclusion. The Effects of the *Décret Infâme* on
Jewish Emancipation in Luxembourg —— 207

Stephanie Schlesier
Between Acceptance and Aversion. Jews and Christians in Luxembourg in the
19th and Early 20th centuries —— 227

Part V: **From Luxembourg to Philadelphia. Samuel Hirsch's Transnational Reform Judaism**

Thorsten Fuchshuber
"One Always Panders to the Basest Jew-Hatred". Samuel Hirsch, *Der
Volksfreund* and *Luxemburger Wort*'s Campaign against Secularization and
Jewish Emancipation 1848–50 —— 257

Michael A. Meyer
A Sense of Loneliness. Samuel Hirsch's American Years —— 281

Bibliography —— 301

Contributors —— 327

Index of Names —— 331

Index of Places —— 337

Index of Topics —— 339

Biblical and Rabbinic Sources —— 355

Judith Frishman and Thorsten Fuchshuber
Introduction and Acknowledgements

Rabbi Samuel Hirsch (Thalfang near Trier 1815 – Chicago 1889) is one of the most important Jewish Reform theologians and philosophers of religion of the first half of the 19th century. To this day, he remains one of the key figures for understanding the debates of the time on questions of Jewish emancipation, the shape of Jewish identity, the compatibility of religion with state and society, the relationship between particularism and universalism as well as the critique of antisemitism, all of which resonate in current debates. As a "Jewish Hegelian", he debated with Ludwig Feuerbach, Bruno Bauer, Karl Marx and others about the legacy of Hegel's philosophy of religion. His writings are among the most authoritative of Reform Judaism; his influence on liberal Judaism in Europe and the USA is rivalled only by that of Abraham Geiger. Surprisingly, no detailed monograph or lengthy publication has yet attempted an overall presentation of the multi-layered significance of Samuel Hirsch. It is the aim of the present volume to fill this lacuna. The impetus for this publication was an international conference held at the University of Luxembourg in October 2010 as part of the research project "Nation-building and Democracy: The Struggle for Participation in Luxembourg from the French Revolution to the Beginning of the Second World War (1789–1940)" (PARTIZIP). The conference, jointly organized with the Leiden University Institute for Religious Studies, was sponsored by the Luxembourg Fonds National de la Recherche (FNR). Almost all those researching the life and work of Samuel Hirsch attended and their contributions are presented in this volume. These have been complemented by essays by other leading experts in the field by invitation of the editors. The result is a comprehensive portrayal and historical analysis of almost all the important aspects of Samuel Hirsch's multifaceted career. The title of the event, "Samuel Hirsch: Philosopher of Religion, Advocate of Emancipation and Radical Reformer", has been retained for this anthology. It is the opinion of the editors that this title epitomizes the significance of Samuel Hirsch's life and works and his lasting, yet often unacknowledged, influence.

En route from Thalfang via Dessau and Luxembourg to Philadelphia, Hirsch left his mark on societal, religious, and philosophical developments in manifold ways. By the time he was appointed Chief Rabbi of the Jewish community in Luxembourg in 1843, he had already written many of his most important works on the philosophy of religion. In the Grand Duchy of Luxembourg the legal and political equality of the Jews implemented in 1797 under French rule was neither revoked at the end of Napoleon's reign nor after the Congress of Vienna in

1815. In Luxembourg one of Hirsch's main endeavors was advocating for the emancipation of the Jews in Europe. At the same time, he fought against Jew-hatred, which in Catholic-ultramontane dominated Luxembourg manifested itself both in the form of traditional religious anti-Judaism and in modern forms of antisemitism. As a newspaper editor Hirsch took up his pen and spiritedly intervened in debates on social equality. When, at the final stage of his career, he moved to the USA with his family in 1866 to succeed his friend David Einhorn as rabbi of the Reform congregation Keneseth Israel in Philadelphia, his reputation as a leading figure in the Jewish Reform movement had already preceded him. In the USA, where a mass immigration of German Jews in the 19th century had taken place, he also played a decisive role in shaping Reform Judaism and was thus able to reaffirm his importance as a modernizer of Judaism.

This anthology attempts to do justice to all these aspects of Samuel Hirsch's work and to place them in their specific historical context. To facilitate reading and to make Hirsch's development comprehensible, we have divided the volume into several sections that occasionally (and inevitably) overlap thematically. The introductory section of the book comprises a detailed biographically oriented article. Tracing our protagonist's footsteps through his three cities of residence Dessau, Luxembourg and Philadelphia – Christian Wiese places Samuel Hirsch's various creative phases in their respective geographical and intellectual context, exploring how his distinctive approach to modern Judaism was shaped and developed. The four years Hirsch spent in Dessau are of particular significance for the interpretation of his intellectual growth, as Wiese explains. It was during this period of his life that he developed the central themes of his sermons as well as his primary philosophical work into an overall concept of religious philosophy. Moreover, during the Dessau period he formed his argument in defense of the Jews' participation in European society and culture that included the retention of a distinct, independent religious and cultural identity as a conditio sine qua non. He grounded these demands theologically in Israel's universal, historical mission. As for his debates with non-Jewish intellectuals, Hirsch was particularly embroiled in a dispute with the anti-Jewish attacks of the Young Hegelian Bruno Bauer that coincided with his arrival in Luxembourg 1843. Upon his arrival in the United States in August 1866 Hirsch would become David Einhorn's successor and one of the leading intellectual figures of radical Reform Judaism in the United States. While Hirsch held to the most important elements of his philosophy, Wiese notes that it is impossible to overlook the fact that the difference in conditions there contributed to a significant shift in his thinking.

The second section examines fundamental elements of Samuel Hirsch's religious philosophy in the light of their societal and political implications. Focusing on Hirsch's Dessau years, Gershon Greenberg argues that it was there that

Hirsch established freedom as the principle of Judaism. The emancipation of Jews in Western Europe opened uncharted territory for intellectual activity, Greenberg argues. It also created a stage for new and original points of departure for systematic Jewish thought, such as the principle of freedom that undergirded Samuel Hirsch's Jewish, Hegelian, religious philosophical undertaking. According to him, freedom entered history with Abraham, who instilled it in the people of Israel. Under God's leadership, Israel's history was a process of overcoming sin and realizing freedom. Drawing on *Die Religionsphilosophie der Juden*, Greenberg examines Hirsch's concept of freedom in depth. The driving force behind the religious philosopher's historiosophy was the ongoing correlation between the divine ground of freedom and the human actualization of potential freedom. This applied to the political arena as well. Even though Hirsch resented the state for not including Judaism on its own terms as an integral part of society but instead merely tolerated the Jews, he attributed the failure of emancipation primarily to Jews themselves and to Christians, as Greenberg explains. Jewish emancipation, understood in terms of the principle of freedom, was thus undermined by both Judaism and Christianity alike: they failed to foster the coalescence between the divine and human realms requisite for the state to be a vessel for a life of freedom.

In her contribution, Irene Kajon turns to the more philosophical aspects of this problem. For Hirsch, modern society and thought were unable to offer a connection between life and spirit, between the individual human being and the social whole, between history and time on the one hand, and the universal and eternal on the other. Hirsch therefore sought to find a philosophical solution to this crisis: Judaism could offer European culture and human beings a way out of their unhappy condition of oscillation between being circumscribed within their own mortality and dissipating in the All. This, however, required a turn from a metaphysics grounded in the problem of being to a metaphysics grounded in human ethical actions and divine ethical attributes, Kajon explains. Hirsch thus turned to the philosophy of Maimonides as a precursor of philosophical anthropology focused mainly on the ethical in human actions. Like his predecessor, Hirsch believed that thinking should start from a given reality – that of familial and social relations marked by justice and loving-kindness. For Hirsch, Kajon notes, the core of this philosophy is deeply meaningful not only for the Jews, but for all humans. Philosophy and religious philosophy cannot demonstrate the truth of "religious consciousness" but can only recognize it as a fact reflecting both man's belonging to nature and history and his difference from both: man as a finite-infinite being, part of natural and historical being, but able to have an ethical relationship with other human beings in the world. It is within this ethical relation that divine transcendence takes shape. Precisely because this relation finds its expression in Jewish sources, Samuel Hirsch sees Judaism as a religion of the present.

This applies also to his understanding of the role of Judaism in state and society, as Judith Frishman explains. According to Hirsch's vision of the ideal state, religion and state service are not contradictory, but complementary. Referring to the discussion on Jewish emancipation in mid-19th century, Frishman demonstrates how Ludwig Feuerbach and Bruno Bauer transformed key concepts of Christian anti-Judaism, particularly stubbornness and exclusiveness, into secular philosophical, political and material arguments, thereby contributing to the development of modern antisemitism. Frishman thoroughly examines how Samuel Hirsch engaged with the two Young Hegelians' contentions, arguing that his main goal was to secure a place for Judaism in modern society. Hirsch wholly adopted the Hegelian concept of the Christian state with the monarch – whose rule was willed by the people – as its head, and then attempted to include Judaism in that state. He emphasized the importance of religion for the universal state – specifically the transformed, ideal versions of Christianity and Judaism – rather than engaging with the Christian state's unwillingness to grant anything more than tolerance to other religions, calling for the separation of Church and State or rejecting religion altogether as did Bauer.

The third section examines the concept of education that Hirsch's philosophy of religion connotes. This is closely related to the question of the contribution Judaism can make to enable a flourishing coexistence of different social groups and religious communities. Like the aforementioned authors, Laurent Mignon turns to Samuel Hirsch's debate with Bruno Bauer. He suggests that in refuting Bauer, Hirsch sketched the possibility of an inclusive society where religious difference was not an obstacle for inter-communitarian relations. Mignon then draws attention to the fact that quite a few scholars have compared 19th century anti-Jewish argumentations like those of Bauer to current day anti-Islamic and anti-immigration discourses. While it would be wrong to postulate an equivalence between antisemitism and anti-Islamic ressentiment, as Mignon states, the two exclusionary ideologies that developed in different contexts do however share common features. He claims that the strategies of response developed by victims of this discourse are a fertile area of research that could stimulate discussions about the development of policies promoting multicultural and interreligious exchange and the countering of exclusionist ideologies. With this in mind, Mignon examines Hirsch's rebuttal of Bauer's arguments in depth. By emphasizing the need for a scrupulous and cautious approach to religion and culture as objects of study, Hirsch seems to invite us today to question the representations of Islam as an essentially different, morally, and intellectually inferior, monolithic, and static religion, Mignon concludes.

Comparing the concepts of Jewish education in the works of Samuel Hirsch and Abraham Geiger, Ken Koltun-Fromm argues that the educational approaches of both sought to secure Jewish identity in the modern world. While Hirsch produced a liberal religious catechism that offered progressive Jewish answers to pressing spiritual questions, Geiger appealed to foundational experiences and sensibilities to inform Jewish obligations. As such their educational programs were in keeping with their larger philosophical tendencies. Contrary to Geiger, Hirsch did not fear that the notion of *Weltbürgerlichkeit* (world citizenship) would separate Jewish children from their historical and local environment. Moreover, Hirsch sought to define the world citizen in Jewish terms. If Geiger worried that such a global fellowship would weaken local bonds, Hirsch responded that Jewish identity could flourish only within a broader, national community. Koltun-Fromm points to the importance of Jewish religious borders in both their concepts: while Geiger aimed to delineate these borders in order to strengthen local, sentimental ties, Hirsch desired to expand them in order to enable Jewish universal truths to become the inheritance for all. Koltun-Fromm concludes his contribution by reflecting upon how these two divergent trajectories still resonate within contemporary educational theory.

George Y. Kohler discusses Hirsch's concept of education in its relation to his understanding of messianism. Hirsch emphasizes the universal aspect of the messianic era, entailing the future unification of all humanity. For Hirsch, humankind is involved in a slow process of learning, bringing humans closer to self-betterment, for that is the historical objective set them by God. While he keeps to the idea of an individual Messiah, Hirsch wants to avoid the concept of some form of miraculous, supernatural salvation at all costs, as Kohler demonstrates. Hirsch argues that the Messiah can only bring justice there where all desire justice. Humanity therefore must first destroy evil in order to enable the arrival of the Messiah. Kohler points out that although strictly monarchist, Hirsch's messianism, as he understood it while in Europe, is not restorative; it does not constitute a simple return to some early period of a naturally peaceful, glorified utopia and original human harmony. The Messiah does herald truth and justice to a humankind ready for free judgement and is in no way defined by considerations of political power. Hirsch's Messiah is thus naturally weak and requires the willing recognition of the congregation that is able to vanquish evil on its own accord. The Messiah, therefore, cannot suddenly and unexpectedly appear as God's representative. Instead, the messianic age requires humanity to undergo a process of gaining ever increasing knowledge that will in the end lead to a universal and moral kingdom of peace.

In the fourth section, Samuel Hirsch's stay in Luxembourg and the social, political, and economic circumstances of his presence are examined in greater detail. Norbert Franz points to the fact that Hirsch's activities in both the political and religious sphere in Luxembourg transpired during a particularly dynamic phase of the country's nation building. In the mid-19th century, the first effects of modern industrialization were gradually being felt. However, it was only at the end of the century that the Grand Duchy developed into one of the leading iron producers of Europe. Franz illuminates some aspects of this social and political transition in the Grand Duchy of Luxembourg, amongst them the causes of Luxembourg's statehood formation and its continued existence. Further examining the functions of the state beyond its core governmental functions, namely law, order and national security, Franz discusses the governmental activity regarding religious communities in particular. He concludes with an analysis of the socio-economic structure of Luxembourg's urban society and the position of Samuel Hirsch's family within a model of the municipality's social stratification.

The short period from the beginning of the French Revolution in 1789 to the end of Napoleon's reign in Luxembourg in 1814 was a key period in the development of the Jewish community in Luxembourg, as Renée Wagener elaborates. Starting with a brief discussion of the situation of the Jews during the *Ancien Régime*, Wagener discusses the effects of the *décret infâme* on Jewish emancipation as part of the prequel to Samuel Hirsch's arrival in Luxembourg. While the territory of the Duchy of Luxembourg was integrated for the most part into the French "Département des Forêts", it was not until 1797 that the revolutionary French law system, and along with it the principle of equality, was implemented there. The *décret infâme* imposed by Napoleon on March 17, 1808, however, had consequences that were not merely symbolic. As a set of separate legal regulations imposed on the Jewish population, it invalidated the French Revolution's principles of equality and served as a decisive instrument for the social classification of Jews. Nonetheless its specific impact in Luxembourg remains unclear: The local Jewish community's desire to be exempt from the decree put them under pressure to conform, thus undermining Jewish particularism. Yet it was the civic rather than the social integration of the Jews that was stimulated, as Wagener shows.

In her contribution, Stephanie Schlesier explores the daily lives of the Jews who settled in Luxembourg in the 19th century, surveying their religious practices and the ways in which they were able to participate in social life. She describes the relationship between Jews and Christians as a "growing closeness". Since Jews only represented a small minority of Luxembourg's population, frequent contact with the Christian inhabitants was unavoidable, specifically in areas such as business and trade, and locations such as schools and taverns. Due to their scattered settlement, Jewish inhabitants usually had Christian locals as immediate neighbors. While the sources only permit a fragmented reconstruction of the religious life of Jews in Luxembourg at that time, Schlesier does conclude that religion occupied a very important place in the daily lives of Christians and Jews alike. Focusing on the Luxembourg Jews' religious institutions, Schlesier's research indicates that these were by and large established in the capital, and only later in smaller cities. The author also discusses Samuel Hirsch's position in the community and the role he took upon himself of ameliorator of the Jews' circumstances.

The final section of the book is dedicated to Samuel Hirsch's transition from Luxembourg to Philadelphia and his life and work in the United States. Thorsten Fuchshuber analyses Hirsch's short career as a journalist and publicist in Luxembourg. Hirsch was a founding member and almost certainly the main editor of the short-lived liberal newspaper *Der Volksfreund* (March 1848 – June 1849). In his articles, Hirsch advocated social emancipation and combatted antisemitism, as Fuchshuber shows. Engaging in fiery debates with the Jesuit-dominated Catholic newspaper *Luxemburger Wort*, Hirsch advocated against the former's attempts to repeal the emancipation of the Jews in Luxembourg. The Catholic Church's efforts to maintain power despite fundamental societal changes and the formation of the modern state provided more than just an opportunity for the articulation of anti-Judaism. Essential elements of modern antisemitism avant la lettre are recognizable in this battle against Jewish emancipation, since it was necessary to find other ways to harm and exclude Jews after they had successfully attained political and legal equality in Luxembourg. Hirsch's disappointment at this upsurge of anti-Judaism and the refusal of his fellow Freemasons to defend him was reason enough to accept a rabbinical appointment in the United States, despite his criticism of American democracy.

Taking a close look at the final phase of Hirsch's career, Michael A. Meyer points to the obstacles Hirsch faced in America. He was haunted by the fact that he had not been a democrat but a monarchist in Europe and seemed to have remained one. His intemperate relations with others and his position on the radical side of the Reform spectrum further alienated him from his rabbinical colleagues and from his own congregation. In defense of his political philosophy, Hirsch averred that he no longer believed that the king stood fully above his subjects; moreover, the law of the state was God's law only if the king acted in accordance with the constitution. Yet he remained critical of American democracy whose shortcomings included the oppression of minorities by a tyrannical majority. Hirsch focused particularly on America's history of black slavery, thus pointing to a topic that continues to unsettle society today. His stance on topics such as mixed marriage, celebrating the Sabbath on Sunday and mixed, family seating in the synagogue caused him to be numbered among the most radical of the prominent Jewish religious reformers in America, Meyer concludes.

The editors would like to thank the Fonds National de la Recherche of Luxembourg and the Historical Institute of the University of Luxembourg for financially supporting the publication of this volume. This support enabled the translation of the articles of Franz, Fuchshuber, Schlesier, Wagener and Wiese from German to English by Jessica Ring. We also express our gratitude to the staff of the Partizip research project, especially its directors Norbert Franz, Jean-Paul Lehners and Sonja Kmec, for making it possible to work on this important chapter in transnational Jewish history and the modernization of Judaism within the framework of the research project on the social, economic and political participation of Luxembourg's varied population. The editors hope that this will stimulate a more in-depth exploration and analysis of the life and work of Samuel Hirsch, including the fairly unchartered role played by his long-term membership in the Freemasons lodge as well as the systematic influence of Hegelian philosophy on his philosophy of religion in general and of Judaism in particular. The work of Samuel Hirsch still has much to offer for thorough investigation in the future.

Part I: **From Thalfang to Philadelphia: An Introduction to Samuel Hirsch's Life and Times**

Christian Wiese
"An Intimate Friendship with Modernity". Samuel Hirsch's Reform Philosophy in the Context of the Ideological Controversies of the Times

> For fifty years of active life as rabbi, both in Europe and the United States, he was the most fearless and consistent champion of enlightened liberal Judaism; and by words of mouth and pen he never tired of holding up its tenets as fundamentally the doctrine destined to be the religion of humanity, looking neither to the right nor the left, but confident of the invincible power of the truth.[1]

These are the reverential words engraved on the base of an eighteen foot high obelisk in Rosehill Cemetery in Chicago marking the grave of the philosopher and reformer Samuel Hirsch (June 8, 1815 – May 14, 1889). They render homage to one of the most important representatives of the nineteenth-century radical Jewish Reform in Germany and the United States, a thinker who occupies a lasting place among the many German Jewish philosophers who advanced the modernization of Jewish thought and practice in the wake of the Enlightenment, in confrontation as well as in dialogue with contemporary German culture and politics. He was, indeed, both a religious and a political thinker, and inevitably so. Jewish religious philosophy in the long, protracted era of Jewish emancipation in Germany, with the great hopes and profound disillusionments it entailed for the Jewish minority, was at no point a purely academic discipline. Particularly since it was – as was the *Wissenschaft des Judentums* in general – excluded from the universities and, at the same time, compelled to constantly defend the right of the Jewish community to assert its place in German society as well as Judaism's role as a legitimate element of modern European culture.[2] Jewish philosophy –

---

[1] Cited in Elmar P. Ittenbach, *Samuel Hirsch: Rabbiner – Religionsphilosoph – Reformer / Rabbi – Philosopher – Reformer* (Berlin: Hentrich & Hentrich, 2014), 104. This article is a revised and expanded version of Christian Wiese, "Von Dessau nach Philadelphia: Samuel Hirsch als Philosoph, Apologet und radikaler Reformer", in Guiseppe Veltri and Christian Wiese, eds., *Jüdische Bildung und Kultur in Sachsen Anhalt von der Aufklärung bis zum Nationalsozialismus* (Berlin: Metropol, 2009), 363–410. I would like to thank Jessica Ring most sincerely for her accurate translation of a shorter German lecture based on that article, and Judith Frishman for her careful editing of the entire English manuscript.
[2] For the debates in Hirsch's generation, see Michael A. Meyer, "Should and Can an 'Antiquated' Religion Become Modern? The Jewish Reform Movement in Germany as Seen by Jews and

from the representatives of the *Haskalah*, through the Jewish intellectuals of the early and mid-nineteenth century, to thinkers such as Hermann Cohen (1842– 1918) and Leo Baeck (1873–1956) in the late nineteenth and early twentieth century – was part of an intellectual project that fought for social, political, and cultural equality. It promoted Jewish integration and transformed Judaism into a religious tradition that responded to a diverse set of challenges posed by modernity: How to reinterpret Jewish tradition in the light of contemporary non-Jewish *Wissenschaft*? How to refute religious, cultural, and political discrimination by the dominating Christian environment and make a convincing case for Jewish emancipation by embracing contemporary ideas and values without sacrificing Judaism's distinctiveness? And how to avert the threat resulting from the explosive mixture of anti-Jewish hostility, pressure to convert or at least renounce a "separate identity", and indifference toward Jewish tradition or even internalization of negative images of Jews and Judaism? Samuel Hirsch's biographical and intellectual path – from his native village in a rural part of Germany to Philadelphia, and from the yeshivah to a leading role in the radical German and American Reform movement – perfectly illustrates the complexities of Jewish modernization and the way a specific trend within nineteenth-century Jewish religious philosophy responded to those challenges. By exploring Hirsch's thought within the different geographical and intellectual contexts that shaped his distinctive approach to modern Judaism, the following reflections will touch upon crucial aspects of the Reform-oriented theology and philosophy between the 1840s and the 1880s. These include the redefinition of the relationship between Judaism and Christianity, the interpretation of the tension between Jewish universalism and particularism, and the new conceptions of religious and ritual practice resulting from a new, historical, understanding of divine revelation.

The Years in Dessau (1838–1841/42) and the Philosophical Leitmotifs of his Sermons

> Yes, Father! You deserve gratitude and honor! […] How many good things have you offered to our Fatherland, and how many good things have you offered to us, the sons of Jacob, within this our Fatherland! Once it was gloomy and dark; it was unknown that […] 'the spirit of man is the lamp of the Lord' (Proverbs 20:27), it was unknown that […] 'the commandment is a lamp, and the law is a light' (Proverbs 6:23), destined to illuminate humankind, to banish all darkness from their heart – and it became light in our dwellings! The inhabitants

---

Christians", in idem, *Judaism Within Modernity: Essays on Jewish History and Religion* (Detroit, MI: Wayne State University Press, 2001), 209–222.

of our fatherland recognized that man cannot live by bread and the mundane alone, but that a worthy life can solely be found where one wishes to live for and from what issues from the mouth. You then gave us princes who, like the dawn, announce the day of light; you endowed us with a prince who kindled the torch of *Bildung* and Enlightenment in Germany's provinces for the nations of Germany and for us in the first place.³

With this homage to the ruling family, characteristic of German Jewish sermons of the early nineteenth century, Samuel Hirsch commemorated – in a service at the Dessau synagogue in 1840 – the one-hundredth anniversary of the enlightened prince Leopold III Friedrich Franz of Anhalt-Dessau (1740–1817), under whose tolerant reign the Jewish congregation of Dessau had experienced a period of prosperity.⁴ From Hirsch's point of view, the prince had embodied the hope that the path toward Jewish emancipation in Germany was irreversible and that events such as the Damascus Affair, which had unsettled the Jewish world that same year, would face the resistance of the European governments as well as the public.⁵ "Father Franz", according to him, had been an important initiator of equality, peace, and enlightened educational policy from which the Jewish population had profited immensely. Most notably, he had ensured that Jews enjoyed respect and that justice was done to their religious and cultural needs by promoting their synagogue services and school system. "He has built a temple for the Jews in one of his finest gardens – but he has done even more. He did not merely give them a building of wood and stone, but also elevated the Jews' temple spiritually", particularly by encouraging a reform of the religious service.⁶ Starting with this praise of the deceased prince, Hirsch next expressed his hope that the

---

3 Samuel Hirsch, *Predigt zur hundertjährigen Geburtsfeier Sr. Hochfürstl. Durchlaucht unseres hochseligen Herzogs Leopold Friedrich Franz, am 10. August 1840 in der Synagoge zu Dessau gehalten und zum Besten der israel. Franzschule herausgegeben* (Dessau: Hermann Neubürger, 1840), 1.
4 See Erhard Hirsch, *Die Dessau-Wörlitzer Reformbewegung im Zeitalter der Aufklärung: Personen, Strukturen, Wirkungen* (Tübingen: Niemeyer, 2003), 151–172; idem, "Fürst Franz und die anhalt-dessauischen Juden: 'Von der Dessauer Gemeinde ging die Emanzipation der deutschen Juden aus'", in Evelien Goodman-Thau, ed., *Zwischen Wörlitz und Mosigkau*, Dessau-Wörlitzer Beiträge 8 (Dessau: Museum für Stadtgeschichte, 1998), 11–18.
5 Hirsch, *Predigt*, 6; however, Hirsch was profoundly dismayed by "what has been written, discussed, and believed about this horrible, dreadful [ritual murder] accusation in the midst of the splendor of European *Bildung* and *Wissenschaft*". See Samuel Hirsch, *Die Messiaslehre der Juden in Kanzelvorträgen: Zur Erbauung denkender Leser* (Leipzig: Heinrich Hunger, 1843), 273. For the "Damascus Affair" see Jonathan Frankel, *The Damascus Affair: 'Ritual Murder', Politics, and the Jews in 1840* (Cambridge and New York: Cambridge University Press, 1997) and Ronald Florence, *Blood Libel: The Damascus Affair of 1840* (Madison, WI: University of Wisconsin Press, 2004).
6 Hirsch, *Predigt zur hundertjährigen Geburtstagsfeier*, 15.

protection and support the Jewish community of Dessau had enjoyed under the prince's rule would also be granted by the current ruler, Duke Leopold Friedrich (1794–1871), and his wife Friederike (1797–1850).[7]

Who was this young rabbi in Dessau, the city in which Moses Mendelssohn (1729–1789) had been born, and what was his personal and religious background? Hirsch was born on June 8, 1815 in a small village in the Hunsrück region called Thalfang, which he himself later remembered as a place characterized by peaceful and tolerant relations between the Christian and Jewish population.[8] The gifted son of Salomon Hirsch, a livestock dealer, and his wife Sara Gottlieb left Thalfang after his bar mitzvah, visiting the yeshivah in Metz led by the Orthodox Talmudist Aron Worms (1754–1836) and, from 1830, a yeshivah in Mainz.[9] After those years of training in the field of Jewish religious tradition, during which he also engaged in clandestine autodidactic secular studies, Hirsch eventually enrolled at the University of Bonn on June 1, 1835, with special permission of the Prussian authorities since he had no official "Abitur"-certificate. He studied philosophy there until the summer of 1837, attending lectures on history, literature, and even on Christian theology and dogmatics, chiefly under the tutelage of the eminent Protestant theologian Carl Immanuel Nitzsch (1787–1868), who introduced him to Schleiermacher's thought.[10] From November 18, 1837 until September 24, 1838, he enrolled in the philosophy department at the University of Berlin, where he studied philosophy, oriental and

---

[7] Ibid., 23.

[8] Samuel Hirsch, *Das Judenthum, der christliche Staat und die moderne Kritik: Briefe zur Beleuchtung der Judenfrage von Bruno Bauer* (Leipzig: Heinrich Hunger, 1843), 14. For his biography, see Heinz Monz, "Samuel Hirsch (1815–1889): Ein jüdischer Reformator aus dem Hunsrück", Jahrbuch für westdeutsche Landesgeschichte 17, 1 (1991), 159–180, and Ittenbach, *Samuel Hirsch*, 12–45.

[9] Ittenbach, 16; and see Bernhard Felsenthal, "Gedächtnisrede", in Chicago Sinai Congregation, *In Memory of Dr. Samuel Hirsch, Rabbi Emeritus Reform Congregation Keneseth Israel, Philadelphia* (Chicago: S. Ettlinger, 1889), 23–25, here 23. This information can also be found in the article on Samuel Hirsch in *Biographisches Handbuch der Rabbiner*, vol. 1: *Die Rabbiner der Emanzipationszeit in den deutschen, böhmischen und großpolnischen Ländern 1781–1871*, Michael Brocke and Julius Carlebach, eds., arranged by Carsten Wilke (Munich: K.G. Saur, 2004), 445–447, here 445.

[10] For Nitzsch, see Friedrich Schweitzer, "Kirche als Thema der praktischen Theologie: Carl Immanuel Nitzsch, sein wissenschaftstheoretisches Programm und dessen Zukunftsbedeutung", Zeitschrift für Theologie und Kirche 90 (1993), 71–86; Henning Theurich, *Theorie und Praxis: Die Predigt bei Carl Immanuel Nitzsch* (Göttingen: Vandenhoeck & Ruprecht, 1975) and Wilhelm Schneemelcher, "Carl Immanuel Nitzsch, 1787–1868", in *Bonner Gelehrte. Beiträge zur Geschichte der Wissenschaften in Bonn, 150 Jahre Rheinische Friedrich Wilhelms-Universität zu Bonn, 1818–1968*, vol. 1: *Evangelische Theologie* (Bonn: Bouvier, 1968), 15–30.

religious studies and where he was strongly influenced by Friedrich Adolf Trendelenburg (1802–1872) as well as the Hegelian philosopher Karl Ludwig Michelet (1801–1893). Whether or not he also briefly studied at the University of Leipzig remains uncertain. What is certain is that while passing Dessau on his way back from Berlin to Thalfang, he was appointed rabbi of the Duchy Anhalt-Dessau on November 18, 1838, as the successor of Rabbi Joseph Wolf (1762–1826) – apparently not without strong and enduring opposition by influential members of the community.[11] On February 10, 1839 Hirsch received his rabbinical ordination from the radical reformer Samuel Holdheim (1806–1860).

Hirsch's impressive literary debut was a bar mitzvah sermon he delivered on June 17, 1838, while still in Berlin, entitled "What Is Judaism, and What Is Its Relationship to Other Religions?" – the first reference to the topic that would engage him throughout his entire life. The intentions of the sermon were threefold and resonated with the same elements of thinking that permeated all of his work: firstly, the attempt to "obliterate indifferentism in Judaism"; secondly, the goal to unite the Orthodox and Reform interpretations of the ceremonies into "a third, higher vantage point"; and finally, the determination to convince the state that the efforts of the "more recent Judaism" were also still "truly revealed religion", bearing no relation to deism.[12] In the preface to the sermon, Hirsch criticized the inadequacy of the apologetics formulated by Jewish theologians of his era, which concentrated on refuting Jesus' miracles and the Christian dogmas of Original Sin and the trinity. He claimed that it was much more important to philosophically establish a "principle of Judaism", "which could recognize Christianity in its truth while maintaining its own validity".[13] What characterized Judaism, in contrast to Christianity, was its foundational revelation – a revelation that created the self-consciousness of an entire people, the "history of monotheism's confrontation with polytheism", which had also become the foundation of Christianity, making the latter a "flower of Judaism".[14] His crucial argument for the continuing legitimacy of Judaism's existence alongside Christianity, however, was that, contrary to the latter's claim to being the true realiza-

---

[11] For the opposition and bitter conflicts Hirsch was exposed to in Dessau, see Ittenbach, *Samuel Hirsch*, 18–21; for Hirsch's period in Dessau, see Bernd G. Ulrich, "Samuel Hirsch als Rabbiner in Dessau", Mitteilungen des Vereins für Anhaltinische Landeskunde 16 (2007), 104–132.
[12] Samuel Hirsch, *Was ist Judenthum und was dessen Verhältniss zu andern Religionen? Predigt zur Einsegnungsfeier seiner beiden Zöglinge Theodor und Oskar Heymann gehalten am 17. Juni 1838* (Berlin: Heymann, 1838), 5.
[13] Ibid., 6.
[14] Ibid., 7–8.

tion of the Hebrew Bible's messianic promises, the Jewish tradition kept alive the awareness that the victory of good over evil had yet to be won, even after the coming of Jesus. Moreover, the Jewish people, as the true Servant of the Lord, were God's instrument for the ultimate fulfillment of the universal messianic world.[15] What constituted the essence of Judaism was not a binding doctrinal theology, but rather its history: "While all other peoples still languished in the darkness of heathenism, God chose us in order to impart to us the truth of the One Holy God, of the loving Father of all creatures. He has preserved us through all the storms of time, despite all the instruments enrolled to destroy us; he will forever preserve us."[16] The people of Israel had been chosen to be the priests of God and to bring all people to God – not "by means of proselytism" or by "shouting others down", but by serving through actions as an example of virtue and morality. According to Hirsch, the ceremonies of Judaism were not a critical factor in that process but could – if understood correctly – symbolically express the great extent to which Jews were indebted to God, and "serve as a reminder of the favors our Nation has received from God". The period of "iconoclasm against ceremonies", as Hirsch characterized the debates at the beginning of the nineteenth century, had been overcome "with the blessed era of the Enlightenment": Orthodox as well as non-Talmudic Jews should now acknowledge each other as legitimate Jews and live according to God's will in order to bring about the messianic age.[17]

The four years Hirsch spent in Dessau are of particular significance for the interpretation of his intellectual growth. It was during this period of his life that he developed the central themes of his sermons as well as his primary philosophical work into an overall concept of religious philosophy. The key leitmotifs, found in varying forms throughout his works, are: the search for a philosophical "principle" or "essence" of Judaism that differentiated it from Christianity and determined its significance for the future of religion and society in modern Europe; the firm belief in the chosenness of the Jewish people and Judaism's providential role in human history; and the question concerning the appropriate valuation of Jewish rites and ceremonies in the context of Judaism's Reform movement. In 1842, before leaving Dessau, he received his doctoral degree from the University of Leipzig,[18] based on what later became the first chap-

---

15 Ibid., 9–10.
16 Ibid., 12–13.
17 Ibid., 14–15.
18 The records are located in the archive of the University of Leipzig (Phil.Fak.Prom. 00101, May 26, 1841). The documents show that influential members of the Dessau congregation encouraged him to pursue his doctoral studies and funded the costs involved.

ter (entitled "Das Ansich der aktiven Religiosität und der Abfall von ihr") of his major philosophical work, *Die Religionsphilosophie der Juden*. It was this book that made the 26 year old rabbi widely known as one of the most creative philosophers of Judaism alongside Salomon Ludwig Steinheim (1789–1866)[19] and Salomon Formstecher (1808–1889)[20] and – with Samuel Holdheim,[21] David Einhorn (1809–1879),[22] and Abraham Geiger (1810–1874)[23] – as one of the leading theoreticians of the Jewish Reform movement in Germany and later in the United States.[24]

Hirsch first formulated the theology of his Dessau rabbinate in his early sermons, which he published under the title *Friede, Freiheit und Einheit* ("Peace, Freedom, and Unity"). Obviously, he developed his thinking not merely in con-

---

19 See Aharon Shear-Jashuv, *The Theology of Salomon Ludwig Steinheim* (Leiden: Brill, 1986); Julius H. Schoeps, Anja Bagel-Bohlan, Margarete Heitmann, and Dieter Lohmeyer, eds., *"Philo des 19. Jahrhunderts": Studien zu Salomon Ludwig Steinheim* (Hildesheim, Zurich, and New York: Olms, 1998).
20 See Bettina Kratz-Ritter, *Salomon Formstecher: Ein deutscher Reformrabbiner* (Hildesheim, Zurich, and New York: Olms, 1991); Thomas Meyer, "Salomon Formstechers 'Religion des Geistes' – Versuch einer Neulektüre", Aschkenas 13 (2003), 441–460.
21 See Christian Wiese, ed., *Redefining Judaism in an Age of Emancipation: Comparative Perspectives on Samuel Holdheim (1806–1860)* (Leiden and Boston: Brill, 2007).
22 See Christian Wiese, "Samuel Holdheim's Most Powerful Comrade in Conviction: David Einhorn and the Debate Concerning Jewish Universalism in the Radical Reform Movement", in idem, *Redefining Judaism in an Age of Emancipation*, 307–373.
23 See Ken Koltun-Fromm, *Abraham Geiger's Liberal Judaism: Personal Meaning and Religious Authority* (Bloomington, IN: Indiana University Press, 2006); Christian Wiese, Walter Homolka, and Thomas Brechenmacher, eds., *Jüdische Existenz in der Moderne: Abraham Geiger und die Wissenschaft des Judentums* (Berlin and Boston: De Gruyter, 2013).
24 For Samuel Hirsch's intellectual path and philosophy, see, e. g., Gershon Greenberg, "Samuel Hirsch, Jewish Hegelian", Revue des études juives 129 (1970), 205–215; idem, "Religion and History According to Samuel Hirsch", Hebrew Union College Annual 43 (1972), 103–124; idem, "Samuel Hirsch's American Judaism", American Jewish Historical Quarterly 62 (1973), 362–382; idem, "The Historical Origins of God and Man: Samuel Hirsch's Luxembourg Writings", Leo Baeck Institute Yearbook 20, 1 (1975), 129–148; idem, "The Messianic Foundations of American Jewish Thought: David Einhorn and Samuel Hirsch", World Congress of Jewish Studies 6 (1975), 115–226; idem, "'Religionswissenschaft' and Early Reform Jewish Thought: Samuel Hirsch and David Einhorn", in Andreas Gotzmann and Christian Wiese, eds., *Modern Judaism and Historical Consciousness: Identities – Controversies – Perspectives* (Leiden and Boston: Brill, 2007), 110–144; Manfred Vogel, "Does Samuel Hirsch Anthropologize Religion?", Modern Judaism 1 (1981), 298–322; Kenneth Koltun-Fromm, "Public Religion in Samson Raphael Hirsch and Samuel Hirsch's Interpretation of Religious Symbolism", Journal of Jewish Thought and Philosophy 9 (1999), 69–105; Irene Kajon, "Hegel, la Wissenschaft des Judentums et Samuel Hirsch", in Gérard Bensussan, ed., *La philosophie allemande dans la pensée juive* (Paris: Presses Univ. de France, 1997), 115–127.

frontation with contemporary philosophy and the political discourse on Jewish emancipation but also in dialogue with his congregation, whose character, behavior, and problems challenged him to reflect on the plight of the Jewish community at the beginning of the 1840s. In his inaugural sermon on March 23, 1839, Hirsch, who felt blessed to have been given the opportunity "to work as a young inconnu in one of the larger communities in Germany",[25] invoked the Jewish people's consciousness of freedom. This freedom despite centuries of persecution, had not allowed them, as "God's chosen sufferers and fighters", to be dissuaded from fulfilling their covenantal tasks and from reconciling humankind with God. According to Hirsch, if this state of being at peace with God were to be visibly lived in the Jewish community, then Jews would be granted emancipation automatically, and the non-Jews would "accept us into the great league of humankind as brothers".[26] This, however, would only happen if the Jews managed to overcome the "wrong type of Enlightenment" that led to the deadening of religious sentiments, and aspired to be renewed and permeated by "the spirit of the divine Torah".[27]

Further elements of Hirsch's sermons consist in a justification of Judaism's religious value for human history as well as for contemporary society. The Jewish tradition, according to the Dessau rabbi, was based on divine moral laws rather than irrational dogma, which facilitated a "profound affiliation of all things human with the Divine".[28] By virtue of their divine election for this task, the people of Israel had become the "exemplary model for all nations". However, because of their historical misfortune they had, at the same time, also become a "warning sign" that would teach all the nations "that the state as well as the life of the state could only persist and achieve its goal if the mundane and the spiritual would mutually inform each other".[29] This was the divine meaning of Israel's dispersion in the Diaspora: it gave the Jewish people the opportunity to spread *Bildung*, scholarship, and the divine truth of the Holy Bible within European history. Thus, in the present, most of the nations, and particularly "the enlightened man of the German Fatherland", had come to understand that "God had but one will, and that He requires man to lead a free life, a human-divine life".[30]

---

[25] Samuel Hirsch, *Friede, Freiheit und Einheit: Sechs Predigten gehalten in der Synagoge zu Dessau* (Dessau: Hermann Neubürger, 1839), i.
[26] Ibid., 16.
[27] Ibid., 21–22.
[28] Ibid., 48–49.
[29] Ibid., 50.
[30] Ibid., 52.

As far as the actual situation of the Jewish minority in Germany was concerned, Hirsch emphasized that the state supported its citizens' religious education and assigned responsibility to the Jews themselves: The state was indeed required to recognize freedom of conscience, and the Jewish people's desire for equal participation in governmental and social life was of course justified. Yet German Jews had to "renounce that gift" if it meant abandoning Jewish tradition and identity. In their struggles for equality, if anything the Jews in Germany had attempted to conceal their religion, thus failing to convince the state they were worthy of emancipation. They could earn the trust of the state solely by living an exemplary religious life: "... then they would gladly recognize us as free men, as free men capable of leading others to freedom. Then we could enroll our power for the benefit of the state and humanity; then Israel and humanity will head toward a felicitous future, one so eloquently depicted by the prophets as the perfection of humanity."[31] The Hebrew Bible, as a testimony of the history of Israel's election for this noble task, should fill the Jews with pride and prevent the increasing indifference toward Jewish tradition, including the inclination to convert to Christianity. Hirsch's collection of sermons culminated in reflections upon "Israel's mission": While the Greeks had contributed to the history of humankind's development a sense of art and beauty, the Romans a sense of justice and law, and the Germans the "depth of soul" (*Gemüthstiefe*), Israel had given the world "the true religion".[32] The Jewish people's priestly role was, in Hirsch's eyes, the main justification for the right of the Jews to participate in the life of the European nations and their obligation to hold on to their religious lifestyle rather than simply merging in the non-Jewish society:

> Israel should be the center of all nations, the unifying link between all intellectual tendencies, the heart of all spiritual life – it should represent the realm of religion. [...] Israel represents [...] the blood of humankind, its seat of life. And as the blood perfuses all parts of the body, Israel in the Diaspora has, thanks to God's wonderful guidance, permeated all nations, all the parts of humankind's body. And as the blood again and again draws new strength from the nourishment with which the body is provided, Israel, too, appropriates each true progress of humankind and draws from it new strength for her existence and for her activities. And as the blood, while circulating through all parts of the body, should not itself be transformed into those parts, should the body stay healthy and not begin to putrefy, Israel, while permeating all nations, should not be transformed into a part of those nations, should humankind remain healthy. And as the blood should not wish that all parts of the body dissolve into the blood, Israel, too, must not wish that all human beings call themselves Israel.[33]

---

31 Ibid., 52–54.
32 Ibid., 98–99.
33 Ibid., 101–102.

Central to Hirsch's thoughts during the Dessau period was thus his argument for the Jews' participation in European society and culture while simultaneously retaining a distinct, independent religious and cultural identity, which he grounded theologically on Israel's universal, historical mission. Hirsch's motivation was twofold, i. e., an attempt to defend Judaism's religio-cultural relevance in the modern era against the manifold anti-Jewish implications of contemporary theology and philosophy, as well as the wish to strengthen the Jewish minority's loyalty to their own religion and history. These can be found in systematized form in his major work, which he had originally announced as *Das System der religiösen Anschauung der Juden und sein Verhältnis zum Heidenthum und zur absoluten Philosophie*. As Hirsch wrote to his mentor Leopold Zunz (1794–1886) in April 1841, he had ambitiously planned this work as a three-volume study, each comprising three parts ("Apologetics": religious philosophy, philosophy of religion, and historical theology; "Theoretical Theology": theology, cosmology, and anthropology; "Practical Theology": morals, ethics, and pneumatology).[34] The first and ultimately only volume of this work was almost 900 pages long and published in 1842 under the title *Die Religionsphilosophie der Juden*. It was designed to speak to "theologians of all denominations as well as to educated non-theologians", and even, as Hirsch wrote in his preface, "readers unpracticed in philosophical thoughts, although we do not want to be read with a cup of coffee on a sofa. Rather, we have those readers in mind […] for whom […] it is worth the trouble to make the mental effort to gain religious conviction".[35] The apologetic intention is obvious when Hirsch emphasizes how much the Jews felt denigrated by the enduring Christian stereotypes of Judaism and their being merely tolerated rather than accepted as an equal part of society. This despite their liberation from the ghettoes and subsequent sincere efforts to become acquainted with and embrace the German language, thought and *Bildung*. "One tolerates only what one wishes to be rid of but as yet is unable to eliminate; which is appalling and the result of the temporary imperfection of human conditions. If the state merely tolerates our religion, it feels obliged in its inner essence to bring about a time in which it no longer needs to tolerate it, i.e. in which it works toward the annihilation of Judaism. Can we, indeed, bear this any longer? If our religion means anything at all to us, are we not obligated to

---

34 See Greenberg, "Samuel Hirsch, Jewish Hegelian", 209.
35 Samuel Hirsch, *Die Religionsphilosophie der Juden oder das Prinzip der jüdischen Religionsanschauung und sein Verhältniß zum Heidenthum, Christenthum und zur absoluten Philosophie dargestellt und mit den erläuterten Beweisstellen aus der heiligen Schrift, den Talmudim und Midraschim versehen* (Leipzig: Hunger, 1842; reprint Hildesheim, Zurich, and New York: Olms, 1986), xxxii.

purge it of this disgrace?"[36] Instead of allowing Judaism to be considered a "non-divine, abnormal moment in contemporary humankind",[37] Jews – and Jewish philosophy in particular – had to engage in the noble task of defending Judaism by means of the most modern insights of *Wissenschaft*, demonstrating its divine character as well as its cultural contribution to modernity.

In his *Religionsphilosophie*, Hirsch further developed his intellectual justification of the Jewish religion,[38] arguing against Hegel who, in his *Vorlesungen über die Philosophie der Religion*, interprets the supposedly exclusive "spirit of Judaism" and its "particularistic God" as an outgrown stage in the unfolding of the divine spirit.[39] Hirsch placed special value on demonstrating that Judaism was capable of generating a systematic religious philosophy based on its own religious sources, including the Bible, the Talmud, Midrash, and the commentaries. It would incorporate Hegelian thought but would at the same time subversively turn it on its head, refuting particularly some of Hegel's assumptions and conclusions regarding Judaism, especially his famous statement: "The belief in something divine, in something great cannot live in excrements. A lion has no room in a nutshell; the infinite spirit has no room in the dungeon of a Jewish soul."[40]

---

36 Ibid., vi.
37 Ibid.
38 For Hirsch's *Religionsphilosophie*, see Hans Joachim Schoeps, *Die Geschichte der jüdischen Religionsphilosophie in der Neuzeit*, vol. 1 (Berlin: Vortrupp-Verl., 1935), 93–132; Nathan Rotenstreich, *Jewish Philosophy in Modern Times: From Mendelssohn to Rosenzweig* (New York: Holt, Rhinehart & Winston, 1968), 120–139; Julius Guttmann, *Die Philosophie des Judentums. Mit einer Standortbestimmung von Esther Seidel und einer biographischen Einführung von Fritz Bamberger* (Berlin: Jüdische Verlagsanstalt, 2000); Gershon Greenberg, *Modern Jewish Thinkers: From Mendelssohn to Rosenzweig* (Brighton, MA: Academic Studies Press, 2011), 171–204.
39 For Hegel's attitude toward Judaism, see, e.g., Micha Brumlik, *Deutscher Geist und Judenhaß: Das Verhältnis des philosophischen Idealismus zum Judentum* (Munich: Luchterhand, 2000), 196–249; Gudrun Hentges, "Das Janusgesicht der Aufklärung: Antijudaismus und Antisemitismus in der Philosophie von Kant, Fichte und Hegel", in Samuel Salzborn, ed., *Antisemitismus – Geschichte und Gegenwart* (Gießen: Netzwerk für politische Bildung, Kultur und Kommunikation, 2004), 11–32.
40 "Der Glaube an etwas Göttliches, an etwas Großes, kann nicht im Kote wohnen. Der Löwe hat nicht Raum in einer Nuß; Der unendliche Geist hat keinen Raum im Kerker einer Judenseele." Georg W. F. Hegel, "Der Geist des Christentums und sein Schicksal", in Hermann Nohl, ed., *Hegels Theologische Jugendschriften. Nach den Handschriften der Kgl. Bibliothek in Berlin* (Tübingen: J.C.B. Mohr, 1907), 241–342, here 312. For Hirsch's attitude toward Hegel's philosophy, see Emil L. Fackenheim, "Samuel Hirsch and Hegel", in idem, *Jewish Philosophers and Jewish Philosophy*, ed. Michael L. Morgan (Bloomington, IN: Indiana University Press, 1996), 21–40; William Kluback, "The Jewish Response to Hegel: Samuel Hirsch and Hermann Cohen", The Owl of Minerva 18 (1986), 5–12.

At the center of this interpretation of the relationship between Judaism and Christianity within the context of Hirsch's refutation of Hegel is the problem of Original Sin and free will. He read Hegel's religious philosophy as a modern variant of the Pauline theology of Original Sin and incarnation that, in Hirsch's view, radically contradicts the Jewish worldview and conception of humankind and is a remnant of "heathenism" (*Heidenthum*). "The fundamental principle of Judaism" is not the notion of Original Sin, but the knowledge that evil "should remain a possibility and never become a reality".[41] In Hirsch's opinion, the truth of Judaism as an "absolute religion", as exemplified in the figure of Abraham, lay in its silent witnessing of the principle of moral freedom and in the protest against Christianity's anthropological pessimism.[42] It is Israel's providential duty to safeguard the prophetic concept of freedom and moral responsibility throughout history and to declare humanity Judaism's most precious legacy. In contrast, as a missionary world religion, Christianity diluted its Jewish legacy by incorporating pagan elements introduced by Paul. Nonetheless, Hirsch (as Moses Mendelssohn before him and as Abraham Geiger after him) conceded that Christianity did have a world-historical "Christian mission": the dissemination of Jewish concepts and values throughout the nations of the world.[43] However, Judaism too has a universal mission: for Jews to live their lives as an example of the belief in the one God and of the ethics of freedom in their role as the "light to the nations". In that way, they would contribute to the future kingdom of God in a world of peace and justice.[44]

In consequence, Hirsch's *Die Religionsphilosophie der Juden* culminates in reflections on the character of Judaism's messianic promises. They demonstrate that he – like the Reform movement in general – was challenged to account for the relationship between universalism and particularism in Judaism in order to counter anti-Jewish attacks against the integration of the Jewish minority into European societies. Hirsch made it very clear, in contrast to later versions of Reform theology, that Judaism was not a "confession" but a "nationality", and that Jews were Jews by virtue of their birth. He clarified, however, that his concept of "nationality" was a spiritual rather than a political one. Judaism's national character defines its historical existence, and, interestingly, even the "messianic age" (*Messiaszeit*) of the "absolute religion" – in which all peoples will realize peace on earth and will recognize God as the one God and all human beings as His free image – contains an enduring particularistic element. The na-

---

41 Samuel Hirsch, *Die Religionsphilosophie der Juden*, 41–42.
42 Ibid., 863–879.
43 Ibid., 832–839.
44 Ibid., 861–868.

tions will reconcile themselves with the people of Israel, will "become fond of them" (*es lieb gewinnen*) and bring them to Jerusalem. Not for the purpose of founding a state there, but rather to "establish the most exalted form of worship, the Jewish national religion" (*um dort den Cultus aller Culten, den jüdischen Nationalcultus zu errichten*). It would "be honored and loved by all humans who will indirectly participate in it while Israel will participate directly" (*der von allen Menschen geehrt und geliebt sein, an dem alle Menschen mittelbar, Israel aber unmittelbar Theil haben wird*).[45] This vision of the future reflects a theology of history inspired by the belief in chosenness, even in the messianic age, which aims to preserve Jewish identity by asserting the uniqueness and superiority of Judaism vis-à-vis Christianity.[46] In terms of the definition of the relationship between universalism and particularism, Hirsch's concept of the messianic future was initially markedly different than the one offered, for example, in Samuel Holdheim's book *Das Ceremonialgesetz im Messiasreich* (1845), according to which Israel's universal messianic role would cease at the end of days and give way to universal truth.[47] In his later writings, however, Holdheim came much closer to Hirsch's position, taking the historical and 'particular' aspects of Jewish tradition more seriously[48] and even speaking – in his work *Ha-emunah*

---

45 Ibid., 882.
46 For the concept of messianism in the early Reform movement, see the article by George Y. Kohler in this volume and his "Einleitung: Die Wiederentdeckung des Messianismus in der jüdischen Reformtheologie der ersten Hälfte des 19. Jahrhunderts", in idem, ed., *Der jüdische Messianismus im Zeitalter der Emanzipation: Reinterpretationen zwischen davidischem Königtum und endzeitlichem Sozialismus*, Mar'ot: Die jüdische Moderne in Quellen und Werken, vol. 2 (Berlin and Boston: De Gruyter and Oldenbourg, 2014), 1–91; for a critical analysis of Hirsch's interpretation of the relationship between Judaism and Christianity, see Judith Frishman, "Good Enough for the Goyim? Samuel Hirsch and Samuel Holdheim on Christianity", in Marcel Poorthuis, Joshua Schwartz, and Joseph Turner, eds., *Interaction between Judaism and Christianity in History, Religion, Art and Literature* (Leiden and Boston: Brill, 2009), 271–287.
47 See Samuel Holdheim, *Das Ceremonialgesetz im Messiasreich: Als Vorläufer einer größern Schrift über die religiöse Reform des Judenthums: Nebst einem kritischen Anhang über den Aufsatz: Reformbestrebungen und Emancipation in der Zeitschrift für die Interessen des Judenthums* (Schwerin: Kürschner, 1845). This very much corresponds with Abraham Geiger's attitude; see Michael A. Meyer, "Universalism and Jewish Unity in the Thought of Abraham Geiger", in Jacob Katz, ed., *The Role of Religion in Modern Jewish History* (Cambridge, MA: AJS, 1975), 91–107.
48 See, for instance, Samuel Holdheim, *Die Erhaltung des Judenthums im Kampfe mit der Zeit: Ein Bild aus der Vergangenheit belehrend für die Gegenwart. Predigt gehalten im Gotteshause der jüdischen Reformgemeinde zu Berlin (am 11. Mai 1851)* (Berlin: L. Lassar, 1851). For the transformation of Holdheim's thought, see Michael A. Meyer, "'Most of My Brethren Find Me Unacceptable': The Controversial Career of Rabbi Samuel Holdheim", in Wiese, *Redefining Judaism in an Age of Emancipation*, 3–22.

veha-deah (1857) – of Judaism's lasting ethnic dimension. In his chapter "Von dem Ceremonial- oder Ritualgesetz" (On the Ceremonial Law or Ritual Law), Holdheim now emphasized that cultural integration was not a matter of extinguishing the characteristic features of the Jewish people, of divesting Judaism of its historical shell and "merging it as a monotheistic people with other peoples". On the contrary: "Israel would never cease" – as Holdheim's imperative now put it – "to be a historical people, [nor] Judaism to be a historical religion."[49] Concerning the messianic age, this new emphasis on an "inextinguishable historical characteristic" replaced Holdheim's original concept of Israel's eventual merging with other nations with the conviction of the Jewish people's "eternal distinctiveness".[50] In this regard both Holdheim's and Hirsch's thoughts strongly differed from the Reform philosophy of their ally David Einhorn (1809–1879). The latter, despite its characteristic emphasis on the "priestly people's" essential distinctiveness during the course of history, firmly insisted that this role was, indeed, limited, outlining an image of the future according to which one day all "natural special characteristics" would vanish.[51]

---

49 Samuel Holdheim, *Ha-emunah veha-deah: Jüdische Glaubens- und Sittenlehre. Leitfaden beim Religionsunterricht der jüdischen Jugend. Zunächst für die Religionsschule der jüdischen Reformgemeinde zu Berlin* (Berlin: Julius Springer, 1857).
50 For a critical view of this shift, see David Einhorn, "Stein's Thora umizwah und Holdheim's Haemuna wehadea", Sinai 1, 4 (1856/57), 507–511; continuation under the title "Holdheim's Religionsbuch: Haemuna wehadea", Sinai 4 (1859/60), no. 2, 33–38; no. 3, 65–71; no. 4, 97–102; no. 5, 129–137; Holdheim's views are cited in no. 5, 136. Einhorn rightly saw Holdheim as taking a new direction and praised the latter's emphasis on Judaism's remaining historical distinctiveness, criticizing, however, that he went too far by insisting on the continuation of these "distinctive characteristics" in the messianic era. This, he argued, was a conspicuous return to particularistic thinking, against which one must protest determinedly (ibid.). Einhorn thus implicitly accused Holdheim of a covert return to rabbinical thinking, for in his view the idea of a continuation of the "eternally separate hereditary nobility" even in the kingdom of the Messiah was a characteristic feature of the Talmud. The fact that Holdheim embraced this Talmudic concept was, from Einhorn's point of view, a deviation from contemporary Reform Jewish interpretations of Jewish universalism. See David Einhorn, "Prinzipielle Differenzpunkte zwischen altem und neuem Judentum", Sinai 1 (1856/57), no. 6, 162–164; no. 7, 193–197; no. 10, 290–294; no. 11, 333–335; no. 12, 365–371; 2 (1857/58), no. 1, 399–404; no. 5, 540–544; no. 6, 572–576; 7 (1862/63), no. 12, 320–327, here 323–325.
51 See David Einhorn, "Holdheim's Religionsbuch: Haemuna wehadea", Sinai 4, 5 (1859/1860), 136–137: "The messianic kingdom shall no longer have need of it […], nor of the characteristic spiritual life of historical Judaism. Whatever retains any power of sanctification in this spiritual life, in the history of Israel, even amid a messianic humanity, shall and must penetrate the totality of peoples and wed itself closely to their peculiarities, just as our spiritual life as well as our history has become at least in part the innermost property of countless non-Israelites. It is impossible for this to be claimed exclusively for the Israelite tribe without at the same time grant-

In addition to presenting his system of thought and reform theory in his *Die Religionsphilosophie der Juden*, Hirsch also undertook to make his ideas accessible for a lay audience, particularly by publishing a collection entitled *Die Messiaslehre der Juden in Kanzelvorträgen* (1843). He based this book on sermons he had delivered or drafted in Dessau between 1839 and 1841/42 while working on his academic book.[52] These texts offer a glimpse of his thinking during this period as well as the way he tried to win over the Israelite Congregation in Dessau for his interpretation of Judaism. The sermons were devoted to the messianic period (*Messiaszeit*), the history of the Jews, the "essence of Judaism", a comprehensive reflection upon the specifically Jewish rituals and festivals, and questions regarding Israel's national character and messianic mission. They were to convey to his congregation what he had characterized in his introduction to the *Religionsphilosophie* as the task "to bring to mind the distinctiveness, the positive worldview of the Jewish religion and of the forms it has taken, i. e. to understand its ceremonies and customs in their absolute necessity and to elevate them in the hearts, making them a vital deed, to build up rather than pull down, to preserve rather than abandon [...]".[53]

One of the leitmotifs of Hirsch's sermons is the urgent warning not to sacrifice the Jewish faith and its distinctiveness for equality and integration. Even if the price to be paid was continuing deprivation of rights, the Jewish minority should hold on to precisely those messianic hopes which prompted non-Jews to argue that Jews were incapable of "loving their present Fatherland and to be loyal to it with their entire soul".[54] At the same time, Hirsch tried to dissipate potential religious doubts caused by the people of Israel's suffering in history, the contempt with which the nations confronted them, and Judaism's contempo-

---

ing it eternal holiness. By contrast, whatever no longer possesses any power of sanctification whatsoever, or at least not in the messianic stage in Jewish spiritual life, shall and must perish along with the distinctive features of the tribe in the world-encompassing divine covenant. This despite its appeal to the Jewish nature as charming and delightful, and to the national egoism as worthy of continued preservation. Judaism, as a historical religion, shall become the common property of the nations, but then the priestly people shall exit the scene just as once the Aaronic priesthood did with the destruction of the temple, [...] then shall Israel merge entirely with the nations amongst whom it lives in dispersion."

52 Samuel Hirsch, *Die Messiaslehre der Juden in Kanzelvorträgen. Zur Erbauung denkender Leser* (Leipzig: Heinrich Hunger, 1843), vi-vii.
53 Hirsch, *Die Religionsphilosophie der Juden*, ix.
54 Hirsch, *Die Messiaslehre der Juden in Kanzelvorträgen*, 2–3. In his further argument Hirsch rejects the image of Judaism as a nation that would wait throughout history for a cruel revenge, hoping for the annihilation of the nations in the Messianic period (ibid., 9–10). Cf. the article of George Y. Kohler in this volume.

rary inner crises. He reminded his congregation of God's covenantal loyalty: "It is He who allowed us to be despised, persecuted and oppressed, and who, even today, according to his wise, fatherly decision, tolerates our being powerless among the nations."[55] Hirsch held a firm belief in Israel's divine education and purification, which was designed to make God's chosen people an instrument of the fight against sin, to make it a people, "in whose spirit the Lord's teaching sits enthroned, in whose heart it has been inscribed for eternity".[56] Therefore the Jews should continue to trust in God's covenantal love, instead of allowing themselves to be deterred from their divine mission by the resistance of their non-Jewish environment against their providential role. The wish "to be acknowledged within the German Fatherland as Germany's sons and to be permitted [...] not only to love God and the King, God and his anointed one, but also to worship them", had to be borne by the awareness "that the people of Israel serves the Fatherland to a much greater extent if they hold fast to their religion".[57] Hirsch combined this plea for a patient loyalty to Jewish identity, despite potential disillusionment in view of the delayed process of emancipation, with a peculiar religious legitimization of the king: the latter, as he put it, fulfilled the divine will – in his capacity as God's "anointed one" – by provisionally continuing to exclude the German Jews from full political participation.[58]

Hirsch's sermons on the "Essence of Judaism" particularly emphasized Israel's role as a divine instrument for humankind's gradual liberation from heathenism.[59] They were devoted to the central themes of his years in Dessau: the rejection of a misguided turn to Enlightenment and *Bildung* for the sake of mundane indulgence whose price was the abandonment of true religiosity,[60] and the lament about an increasing alienation from tradition as well as the inclination to "divest [the Bible] of its holiness".[61] Hirsch coupled this to an urgent reminder that the Jews embrace their universal mission and remain – against all odds – visible in modern society as "Israelites".[62] In this period Hirsch still clearly de-

---

55 Ibid., 17.
56 Ibid., 22.
57 Ibid., 38.
58 Ibid., 41. Should the performance of the Jewish ceremonies inhibit "the divine goal of the state", it would even be forbidden by God; however, he believed, the overwhelming majority of these ceremonies served the same task "for which the state has been established by Him" (ibid., 45). See the article of Judith Frishman in this volume.
59 Ibid., 82–84.
60 Ibid., 89.
61 Ibid., 107.
62 See ibid., 125: "Get up, shine brightly in the darkness that reigns over the world; shine as an Israelite son and an Israelite daughter. Thank God for being an Israelite and for having a share in

fined the "essence" of Judaism as rooted in the holiness and authority of God's revelation in the Torah. This essence would not persist without a lived religiosity, a metaphorical language as well as specific forms, and should not be reduced to an allegedly purely religious faith, liberated from the burden of tradition.

The period of rationalistic reform projects, which were based on the assumption that "pure Judaism had been found as soon as one had removed everything that – alone – is capable of expressing and giving testimony to the pure Judaism in our lives", had definitely come to an end.[63] This is why Hirsch's sermons focus largely on providing a detailed account of the spiritual meaning of the Jewish "forms", the rites and festivals, hoping thereby to stop their abandonment. For many wished to escape the dictatorship of the ritual tradition and a traditionalism that slavishly worshipped the literal meaning of the Torah, "until the letter grows into entire books and the spirit is overwhelmed by the fine and overly subtle distinctions, circumventions and artifices".[64] It seems obvious that Hirsch, like so many of the contemporary reformers, regarded rabbinical literature as an "obscure product of dark centuries"[65] – an assessment evocative of contemporary Protestant stereotypes concerning Judaism's "legalism". Yet he was equally aware of the fact that many of those Jews who dissociated themselves from their tradition did so mainly for shame of the Jewish rituals and a desire to avert social discrimination.[66] In order to counter such feelings as well as the widespread opinion among contemporary scholars that Judaism was "a specter,

---

the lofty Israelite mission. Dismiss the misguided shame that prevents you from making the Israelites' light shine. Don't be ashamed to be called baneful (*Finsterling*) by those who are baneful, nor to be considered less enlightened by the obscurantists (*Dunkelmänner*), who are floundering about in the mist of finitude and temporality."

63 Ibid., 147.
64 Ibid., 170.
65 Ibid., 247. "Read the multi-volume works of the commentaries on the commentaries to the commentaries, of the commentaries on the commentaries to the Talmud, which itself intended to be only the – albeit transmitted – commentary on the observance of the Law. Read it, and you will ask yourselves with astonishment and wonder, where you have gotten. You will be appalled by this aberration of the human spirit! [...] This and that is discussed there, everything imaginable is being treated, the most pedantic issues are given inordinate importance – but you will hear nothing about religion; in the name of religion, religion is obliviated; the name of religion is intended to sanctify a wit and subtlety that otherwise – as can be sensed – would be considered pathetic" (ibid., 246).
66 Ibid., 178–179. For Hirsch's and the Reform movement's dilemma regarding the rabbinic tradition, see Judith Frishman, "The Pitfalls of Counterhistory: Abraham Geiger and Samuel Hirsch on Rabbinic Judaism", in Wiese, Homolka, and Brechenmacher, *Jüdische Existenz in der Moderne*, 341–358.

an inanimate body",[67] Hirsch attempted to convince both Jews and non-Jews of the deeper meaning of the Sabbath, circumcision, dietary laws as well as the traditional Jewish festivals. It was only by respecting and actively living their own religion, he insisted, that Jews in post-Enlightenment Europe would be able to "reconcile the world with Judaism",[68] whereas the idea that denying it would help eradicate hatred against Jews was an illusion. The task of bearing witness to Judaism in the world, however, necessarily included the observance of the Jewish religion's external customs, which Hirsch, as we shall see, interpreted in terms of a symbolic expression of Judaism's essential teachings.

Like Hirsch's *Religionsphilosophie der Juden*, his sermons on Israel's "mission" eventually led to thoughts on the character and relevance of Judaism's messianic hopes. They are particularly important for an understanding of his philosophy since they demonstrate the extent to which he, too, as in the case of other reformers, was struggling with the difficult matter of finding an adequate interpretation of the relationship between universalism and particularism in Judaism (including the question concerning the nature of Israel's messianic future). At the same time, he was being forced to fend off attacks from non-Jewish intellectuals who claimed that the Jewish minority, due to its particularistic tradition, was unable to integrate into the European societies. In a sermon entitled "Israel's Nationality and Return to Palestine", Hirsch attempted to give his congregation an understanding of the philosophical and political balancing act involved. He implored them, on the one hand, not to abandon the hope for the actual fulfillment of the prophets' messianic promises, and, on the other hand, encouraged them to brace themselves for the accusation of harboring particularistic-national aspirations:

> How many accusations [...] did we have to face because of this hope! How much does the reigning egoism that stubbornly opposes our endeavor to gain acknowledgement and legiti-

---

67 Hirsch, *Die Messiaslehre der Juden in Kanzelvorträgen*, 198. Hirsch accused contemporary Christianity of having appropriated Judaism's religious convictions and values without, however, being willing to attribute this "glorious truth" to Judaism itself: "To us Jews God is supposed to be alien and have been alien [...]; Judaism [according to Christian views] has allegedly never been capable of worshipping God as a loving father, of considering man as His precious, dignified child, of being aware of God's presence rather than believing in his absence. [They claim that] a new religion was needed in view of which Judaism, like paganism, was destined to disappear. Solely this religion was suited to redeem man from his sense of nothingness and ignobleness, make him aware of the nobility of his spirit and teach him that man is of divine origin and should imitate God on earth. God in heaven, we thank you that you have given us the Sabbath! The Sabbath will rescue us from this lie and honor the Truth!" (ibid., 199).
68 Ibid., 205.

macy for our heartfelt thoughts among contemporary humankind wish to use exactly this hope as a pretext to deprive us of everything of which we are so direly in need! [...] Don't you constantly hear that because we hope for the future restoration of Israel, we cannot have a Fatherland here; that we are at best entitled to ask for toleration; and that the happiest state is the one that does not even need to tolerate us and our way of worshipping God? And how many reproaches [...] do we, indeed, deserve because of that hope! Not because we are harboring it, but because we are starting not to harbor it; because we allow ourselves to be misled by the loud demands of our ill-wishers that we give up the firm belief in the holy and eternal word of God, just to please them. Our present aspirations are so near and dear to us that, for their sake, we have lost sight of the aspirations we had from the very beginning and should pursue until the very end. We have been foolish enough to believe that we might reach the goal of our present aspirations after having relinquished the goal of our existence on earth. Our hope for Israel's future restoration is the keystone of our entire teaching, and we are foolish enough to think that, after having renounced the keystone, we would nevertheless be more than a ruin![69]

Israel's unforsaken hope for the promised national restoration and return to Zion, was, however, as Hirsch hastened to emphasize, "of a religious rather than of political nature" and had absolutely nothing to do "with any questions concerning our civic aspirations in the present".[70] The history of the people of Israel in the Jewish state in antiquity as well as throughout their centuries-long exile was proof of the fact that they had never sought political power. It was thus also the case that Jewish messianism was not an expression of the desire of sovereignty and dominion, let alone for particularistic-national ambitions or an inner dissociation from Europe; it was rather the articulation of a yearning for the time when the goal of history and the hopes of all humankind would be fulfilled.[71] Hirsch's Dessau sermon on the Jewish people's messianic role consis-

---

69 Hirsch, *Die Messiaslehre der Juden in Kanzelvorträgen*, 375–376.
70 Ibid., 382.
71 Ibid., 382. Addressing non-Jewish society, Hirsch added: "Ask all times [...] whether we have ever betrayed you, whether we ever sought to leave you and conquer Palestine for ourselves; whether we haven't always patiently awaited the fulfillment of the time in which the land of our fathers would bear spiritual – and not just material – fruit; in which God Himself will move into Yerushalayim und will make His teaching pour forth from Zion, until you will rush there, too, in order to find the Lord there, explore His teaching and to walk in His ways!" The European Jews had never attempted to take the messianic future "by storm", nor had they declared Jerusalem their earthly Fatherland – instead they had gratefully embraced the new home in Europe. "We are aware that we are not to go to Yerushalayim on our own; rather you are meant to bring us there. Now, have we ever asked you to bring us there? Have we ever requested that you should conquer Palestine on our behalf and surrender it to us? Would we be grateful if you would develop such an idea, so as to eliminate us from your midst? [...] We have been sent

tently concludes with a confessional summary of his interpretation of history.[72] It reads like a passionate admonition to embrace the people of Israel's chosenness, to accept the suffering imposed by God as a price for their world-historical mission, and to resist the temptation, at the dawn of the new age of emancipation, to give up what distinguished Judaism from other religions and cultures. At the end of times, all of humankind would recognize the truth of Judaism regarding both its religious essence and its symbolical forms:

> Our Sabbath will point them to the day that will be the full Sabbath. Our festivals will show them, too, quite plainly the divine education of humankind. Our dietary laws will inform their hearts as well and show them how evil in the world will be overcome and how solely the good will persist in eternity. Our circumcision will educate them, too, about the goal of human existence on earth. That is why they, too, will lead us to Zion with singing and to Yerushalayim with tears of joy, so that we can celebrate the Sabbath there appropriately, observe the holy days with the most radiant splendor, and implant God's guidance into each and every heart, without exception. Evil will have disappeared, but not the potential for evil. Hoping that it will never again materialize, that one and all will resist any temptation, the nations will desire that we make them cognizant of our history, this holy history that has become their history as well, in which they have recognized the model of their own [history], from which they have received the same blessing.[73]

The insistence on the obligation to realize Judaism's truth by leading a conscious religious life is thus a *leitmotif* of Hirsch's sermons and his overall activities in Dessau. It is, unfortunately, difficult to tell whether it was his *Religionsphilosophie* that led to a severe conflict with his congregation in 1841/42,[74] or the severity with which he constantly criticized his listeners of religious indifference, or the mistrust some of the members of the congregation felt regarding potential reforms.[75] In general, Hirsch's activities in Dessau and his relationship to the congregation as well as its board can only be recounted in general terms since the archive of the community was destroyed in 1938 and the relevant documents and minutes seem to be lost. Traces of the conflict can, however, be found in the contemporary Jewish press indicating that – after several attempts of his oppo-

---

by God to live amongst you, and thus we can never depart from your midst. You are meant to bring us to Yerushalayim, but then you, too, should live amongst us there" (ibid., 386–387).
72 Ibid., 389–392.
73 Ibid., 392.
74 According to Charles und Graziella Lehrmann, *La Communauté juive du Luxembourg dans le passé et dans le présent* (Esch sur Alzette: Impr. Coopérative Luxembourgeoise, 1953), 56, it was the introduction to his *Religionsphilosophie der Juden* that triggered the conflict.
75 Michael A. Meyer, *Response to Modernity: A History of the Reform Movement in Germany* (Detroit: Wayne State University Press, 1995), 72.

nents in the congregation to get rid of him – he was deposed from office on March 30, 1841. An ironical report in the *Allgemeine Zeitung des Judenthums* in February 1842, probably phrased or at least inspired by Hirsch, noted that the rabbi had been fired after two years of serving the congregation for being "daring enough" to ask the members of the board to abide by their promise, make his position permanent and raise his salary by 200 Thaler.[76] In a reply published on March 7, 1842 the board of the Israelite Congregation of Dessau emphasized that Hirsch had by no means been removed from his office; rather his contract had not been renewed. Hirsch's employment as a rabbi in 1838 had been that "of a completely foreign candidate who was just passing through and whom nobody in the community knew", and thus deliberately "temporary" from the very beginning. The overwhelming majority of the community had, therefore, not been in favor of prolonging his rabbinate. This was, they added, completely natural and not, as depicted by Hirsch, an "act of cruelty or injustice", particularly since he was still living in Dessau and had received a generous monetary compensation. Furthermore, Hirsch shouldn't complain: he had come to Dessau with neither a rabbinical certificate nor a doctoral degree and was now leaving with both – a "crowning" which he owed to the congregation. "We wish him, the *Herr Dr.*, that he will – as a rabbi and doctor – find an educated community that would practice the teachings which he so eloquently preaches as Judaism's task, namely tolerance, leniency, and reconciliation, so that he might learn them while teaching them and recognize that erudition alone does not yet entitle you to claim *Bildung* for yourself."[77] This statement remains – as Hirsch himself – silent about the specific reasons for the discord, but in view of the tone, it seems obvious that what provoked it was most probably a blend of theological dissensus, mutual personal disappointment, and a specific conflict about the conditions of the extension of the contract.[78] In retrospect, Hirsch admitted

---

76 Allgemeine Zeitung des Judenthums 6, 9 (1842), 122–123; and see Samuel Hirsch, "Offenes Sendschreiben an die Herren Aeltesten zu Dessau", Allgemeine Zeitung des Judenthums 6, 15 (1842) (supplement). In a letter to the government from January 28, 1841 Hirsch indicated several factors motivating his opponents' resistance against him: "One part of them does not want any clergyman here [...] others feel hurt because of the confirmation quarrels. I did not flatter the third group enough [...] the fourth wants the job for themselves."; cited in Ulrich, "Samuel Hirsch als Rabbiner in Dessau", 124.
77 Allgemeine Zeitung des Judenthums 6, 12 (1842), 169.
78 This is corroborated by the archival documentation in the *Biographisches Handbuch der Rabbiner*, 446: apparently there was already a complaint lodged on September 15, 1840, claiming that: Hirsch had only presented one of the three obligatory ordination certificates; that he rarely visited the synagogue, being "rather one of the most frequent visitors of public houses"; his critique of Jewish customs caused "conflict and factions"; and he was too expensive (LA Oranien-

his own part in the conflict, emphasizing his lack of patience with the congregation: "It pains me to concede that all my goodwill and eagerness came close to being the vanity of a self-satisfied piety. This self-reproach shall serve me as a warning not to repeat such mistakes."[79]

Luxembourg 1843–1866. On Judaism's Relevance in the Modern Era: Polemics and Controversies

Despite the inglorious end of his first rabbinical position, Hirsch's Dessau writings did more than just lay down the intellectual foundation for his entire religious philosophy of the subsequent years and decades: They also earned him the prestige of an innovative scholar, which quickly opened some new possibilities. In its issue of August 1843, the Jewish journal *Der Orient*, edited by Julius Fürst (1805–1873) in Leipzig, informed its readers that Hirsch, "rabbi in Dessau, a meritorious man in all respects", had been named Chief Rabbi of the Duchy by William II, King of the Netherlands and Grand-Duke of Luxembourg, and that he had been ceremoniously inducted into office by the Israelite community in Luxembourg on June 23 of that same year. The new rabbi would now devote his energy to the task of advancing the education of the youth and to contributing to the preservation of Jewish religion – "not merely according to the outward form, but according to its true spirit [...]".[80] Conflicts overshadowed his more than two decades of service in Luxembourg as they had his tenure as a rabbi in Dessau. This time the cause was not mainly due to internal disagreements within the congregation but the anti-Jewish propaganda of the Catholic press. The *Luxemburger Wort für Wahrheit und Recht* continuously polemicized against him from 1848 onward, claiming, for instance, that "the impudent and roguish expressions of disrespect (*freche und bübische Sprache*) for the Christian religion by Jewish boys (*Judenjungen*) and Jewish rabbis (*Judenrabbiner*)" provoked "hatred of the people against the entire Jewish population".[81] Apart from this, however, Hirsch's

---

baum, Abt. Dessau, Rep. C15 [Judenschaft], No. 57). A vote on December 13, 1840 led to an extension of Hirsch's office, another vote on March 29, 1841, however, led to his dismissal.
79 Cited in Ulrich, "Samuel Hirsch als Rabbiner in Dessau", 127.
80 Der Orient 4, 31 (1843), 244–245, here 245. Hirsch had been recommended to the Luxembourg congregation by the reform-oriented Chief Rabbi of Trier, Joseph Kahn (1809–1875); see Ittenbach, "Samuel Hirsch", 23.
81 Cited in ibid., 31. This – apart from constant disagreements about his salary – may be one of the reasons why Hirsch tried, without success, to be appointed rabbi of Krefeld, Schwerin, and

period in Luxembourg was replete with active educational initiatives within the congregation and involvement in the public discourse on crucial issues relevant to the Reform movement. Relentlessly, he confronted the anti-Jewish tendencies in non-Jewish philosophy in the context of a series of significant intellectual controversies, took a position in the reform disputes of the 1840s and defended his interpretation of Judaism against other Jewish thinkers.[82] Also characteristic of his time in Luxembourg was his role as a member of the local Masonic lodge, in the context of which he made his mark by publishing a series of writings addressing Judaism's relationship to both Christianity and Masonry.

In terms of debates with non-Jewish intellectuals, Hirsch was particularly involved in the one that erupted in 1843 concerning the anti-Jewish attacks of the Young Hegelian Bruno Bauer (1809–1882). Already divested of his academic chair in theology and denounced as the "Robespierre of theology", Bauer published his theological and political views on the history, essence, and current position of Judaism in his sarcastic and polemic essay "The Jewish Question". In this pamphlet he rejected any emancipation of the Jewish minority, as in his view Judaism had no rational universal law, but rather – due to its "oriental nature" and the "stubbornness of the Jewish national spirit (*Volksgeist*)" – was caught up in an unalterable, a-historical system of particularistic, spiritless, and exclusive religious ceremonies. According to Bauer, the Jews lived outside of history in the imaginary, indeed "chimerical" world of the Talmud, dominated by "law", the manifestation of the Jewish dogma, trapped in the inability to regard non-Jews as people with the same rights, and separated forever from general society due to the conceit of chosenness and tribalism. Bauer claimed that Judaism had contributed nothing to the transformation of the modern world and that not even a radical religious and cultural redefinition of Jewish identity – as proposed by the Jewish Reform movement – would remove the boundary between Jews and the non-Jewish society. His only remedy for the Jewish minority, therefore, was for Jews to abandon all national characteristics and to orient

---

Berlin at an early stage of his Luxembourg rabbinate; see the article by Thorsten Fuchshuber in this volume and Ittenbach, ibid., 27.

[82] In 1842, Hirsch engaged in a fierce controversy with the Offenbach Reform rabbi and religious philosopher Salomon Formstecher (1808–1889), after having published a polemical review of the latter's main work, *Religion des Geistes: Eine wissenschaftliche Darstellung des Judenthums nach seinem Charakter, Entwicklungsgange und Berufe in der Menschheit* (Frankfurt am Main: Hermann, 1841); see Hirsch's review in Literaturblatt des Orients 3, 28 (1842), 433–444 and 3, 36 (1842), 561–565 as well as in the supplement to 3, 38 (1842), 1–8. For an interpretation of the debate, which revolved around the question regarding an adequate philosophical understanding of God and the danger of the dissolution of the Divine into anthropology, see Gershon Greenberg, "Zur Verteidigung Formstechers", Judaica 29 (1978), 24–35.

themselves toward freedom and humanity: in other words, modernization through the dissolution of Judaism.[83]

Hirsch, who shared with Bauer the affinity to Hegelian thought, felt that crucial aspects of his own understanding of Judaism and his program of Jewish cultural integration were profoundly challenged by the latter's vicious anti-Jewish polemics. He therefore responded in his work *Das Judenthum, der christliche Staat und die moderne Kritik* ("Judaism, the Christian State, and Modern Criticism") with powerful apologetics aimed primarily at specifying his understanding of the relationship between Judaism, Christianity, and the Christian state. Within that context, Hirsch, even though he advocated monarchy, contested the exclusive link between the State and the Christian religion. Furthermore, he emphasized that he did not actually "ask for" emancipation but endeavored to "force" the Christian state, by means of historical criticism, to acknowledge the fact that the Jews constituted "a necessary element within its vital organism (*Lebensorganismus*)". It needed to respond to the crucial question "how it [the Christian state] could possibly deny us emancipation without contradicting itself and the principle reigning its inner life".[84] Since Bauer's attack against the idea of Jewish emancipation was based mainly on the contestation of Judaism's historicity as well as the accusation regarding the "stubborness of the Jewish *Volksgeist*", the most effective counter-argument consisted in emphasizing the historical character of the Jewish religion and its compatibility with historical progress. That was of crucial importance for Hirsch: After all, the Reform movement had propagated the idea of a deep, intrinsic connection between reform as the true historical gateway to Judaism and political emancipation – and that was now at stake. To hold Judaism's "stability" throughout the centuries against Judaism, he argued, would be as absurd as to accuse Christianity of having ad-

---

83 Bruno Bauer, *Die Judenfrage* (Braunschweig: Otto, 1843); and see idem, *Das Judenthum in der Fremde* (Berlin: F. Heinicke, 1863); for Bauer's views, see David Leopold, "The Hegelian Antisemitism of Bruno Bauer", History of European Ideas 25 (1999), 179–206; for the controversy with Jewish reformers, see Nathan Rotenstreich, "For and Against Emancipation: The Bruno Bauer Controversy", Leo Baeck Institute Yearbook 4 (1959), 3–36; for Jewish responses to Bauer, see, for instance, Gustav Philippson, *Die Judenfrage von Bruno Bauer näher beleuchtet* (Dessau: Fritsche, 1843); Gotthold Salomon, *Bruno Bauer und seine gehaltlose Kritik über die Judenfrage* (Hamburg: Perthes-Besser & Mauke, 1843); Abraham Geiger, "Bruno Bauer und die Juden. Mit Bezug auf dessen Aufsatz: Die Judenfrage", Wissenschaftliche Zeitschrift für jüdische Theologie 5, 2 (1844), 199–234 and 325–371. In addition see the articles of Judith Frishman and Laurent Mignon in this volume.
84 Hirsch, *Das Judenthum, der christliche Staat und die moderne Kritik*, 9–10.

hered to its religion over a period of two thousand years.[85] According to Hirsch, Jewish history was rather defined by the interplay between the preservation of its fundamental religious doctrine and historical change: "The Jewish *Volksgeist* is stubborn only as far as its principles are concerned, precisely as every other principle is stubborn. Within that principle, however, the richest and most diverse development takes place."[86] For Hirsch, in fact the "oppressive spirit", the European Occident's spirit of intolerance, had restricted the development of Jewish doctrine on occasion, but the "oppressed Jewish spirit was certainly in no way less free than the oppressing Christian spirit. In fact, the Jewish spirit must have been even freer, for it had never thought to oppress anyone".[87]

Hirsch also emphatically rejected the accusation that Judaism, being fundamentally unmodernizable, had contributed nothing to *Bildung* and the transition into the modern era. He conceded that this contribution had been less significant in times of oppression, but as long as the Jews had been locked away in the ghettos, there had been no cultural or intellectual development in Europe in general. Instead, there had been "witch trials, invocations of the Devil, and relic worship". When the European nations finally reawakened "to a new spiritual life", the Jews, too, paid their contribution "with full mint".[88] Using similar historical argumentation, he also rejected the criticism of the supposedly immutable "legalism" of the Jewish tradition and the Talmud's casuistry, which, according to Bauer, appeared as a characteristic expression of the – equally unalterable – essence of Judaism, in contrast to Christianity's advanced spirituality. Hirsch and the entire Reform movement found themselves in a difficult position here, as Bauer's argument partially corresponded with the reformers' criticism of Orthodoxy in the internal Jewish discourse. Moreover, Hirsch's own criticism of the rabbinic tradition, formulated in his Dessau years, could have been understood in a similar vein. According to Hirsch however, a just historical interpretation must first consider the historical circumstances under which the Jews, at times, had lost their freedom and rationality and had become slaves of an abstract system. Moreover, a comparison with developments within Christianity was also indispensable. The Talmud and rabbinic casuistry were "merely the worthy counterpart of Christian dogmatism and scholasticism [...] and it was worth considering that precisely this deprecated production of the Jewish spirit

---

[85] Ibid., 17; and see ibid., 19: "True, in our relationship to the Christians we have always been stable, for we remained Jews. But hasn't the Christian been stable vis-à-vis us since he remained a Christian? We, however, have never reproached him for this."
[86] Ibid., 19–20.
[87] Ibid., 19–20.
[88] Ibid., 26.

prevented the latter from the aberrations from which the Christian world is recovering only with difficulty".[89] The pre-Enlightenment era's orthodox Protestantism had just as little to do with scientific, historical-critical analysis as "Polish rabbinism"; however, "justice would demand, with regard to the progress of the modern period, acknowledgement of Judaism's continuing advancement as well".[90] Furthermore, Hirsch emphasized, the Jews' alleged conceit of chosenness, which figured so prominently in Bauer's accusations, appeared in a very different light when compared historically with Christianity. Judaism had always – even during the period when the rabbinical tradition predominated – been so sure of its purpose that it "trusted the calm course of history in lieu of a zealous war of extermination" and had at no time understood its sense of being chosen for a world-historical mission in terms of an exclusivist attitude toward other religions.[91]

Perhaps the most interesting aspect of Hirsch's reaction to Bauer's attack, however, is his specification of the relationship between Judaism, Christianity, and the state. Bauer's critique was not only aimed against Judaism; it also viewed Christianity as a phenomenon that had not yet reached the level of free consciousness, not least because it ultimately represented a continuation of Judaism and had adopted parts of the latter's flaws. However, this did not prevent Bauer from insisting on the traditional construction (now accentuated by Hegelian concepts), according to which Christianity inevitably had to be built on the ruins of Judaism. Bauer argued that the idea of the Christian state from which it was necessary to emancipate oneself arose directly out of Judaism. He declared that the existing state was still not based on the fundamental principle of a free and critical human consciousness and thus urgently needed to be liberated from the shackles of Christian privilege. Nevertheless, the state would still have the right to exclude Jews – not only because they persistently remained at an even lower level than those within Christianity, but above all because it was they who were responsible for the deficiencies of the Christian state.[92]

Hirsch refuted that interpretation with a complicated argument, which, to a certain extent, anticipates later attempts of the *Wissenschaft des Judentums* to create a counter-history against anti-Jewish constructions of Jewish history by reflecting upon the Jewishness of Jesus and thus postulating Judaism's religious

---

89 Ibid., 31.
90 Ibid., 55.
91 Ibid., 62.
92 See Rotenstreich, "For and Against Emancipation", 10–11.

and cultural equality or even superiority.[93] The fact that Jesus was Jewish played a decisive role in the philosopher's line of argument. Even though Judaism rejected the Christological understanding of Jesus, it had no qualms about valuing the "historical Jesus", who had been "a true Israelite" and a "Jew in every sense of the word", i.e., to acknowledge him as the "classical character of monotheism" and thus as the "classical character of humankind".[94] While Jesus's teaching had embodied the inner tendency of the Jewish religion, Judaism had been forced to reject the heathen-inspired development of otherworldly Pauline Christianity. Both religions, each in its own way, had fulfilled their own mission in world history, with Christianity paying the price of ignoring the world's earthly significance. Judaism's role was to resist this tendency: It had not only given Jesus to the world, but had insisted that the life of Jesus belonged "in this terrestrial world". His life had been "that which God had stipulated from the very beginning, that which was possible for all people, and was thus actual, real, and not miraculous".[95] Hirsch thus claimed Jesus for Judaism and at the same time interpreted him as the embodiment of a moral, worldly individual who had already achieved the higher religious consciousness demanded by Bauer. He also made it known, however, that unlike Christianity, Judaism accorded *every* person the power and ability to reach Jesus's level. The logical consequence was that Jews did not have to become Christians in order to attain equal rights in European societies, for they were already aspiring to the ideal exemplified by the life of Jesus and stood at least as close to him as those within Protestantism.

Based on this argument, Hirsch suggested quite an ironic and indeed subversive twist concerning the meaning of the term "Christian state". Conservative representatives of the concept of a "Christian state" such as Friedrich Julius Stahl (1802–1861) refused Jews equal status by pointing to the Christian character of the state and its institutions, while radicals such as Bauer dismissed the "Christian state" as an outgrowth of Judaism and – for precisely that reason – wanted to exclude Jews from society. In reaction, Hirsch reinterpreted the "Christian state", which he supported, in Jewish terms: if understood correctly, this

---

[93] See Susannah Heschel, *Abraham Geiger and the Jewish Jesus* (Chicago, IL: University of Chicago Press, 1998); Christian Wiese, "Struggling for Normality: The Apologetics of *Wissenschaft des Judentums* in Wilhelmine Germany as an Anti-Colonial Intellectual Revolt against the Protestant Construction of Judaism", in Rainer Liedke and David Rechter, eds., *Towards Normality: Patterns of Assimilation and Acculturation in German Speaking Jewry* (Tübingen: Mohr-Siebeck, 2003), 77–101.
[94] Hirsch, *Das Judenthum, der christliche Staat und die moderne Kritik*, 88.
[95] Ibid., 92.

"Christian state" should not be construed as an exclusively Christian entity, but rather as the fulfillment of the history of Jewish resistance against the Christian misinterpretation of Jesus, as the realization of the fundamentals of Judaism. Hirsch thus explicitly conceded to Bauer that the "Christian state" had its roots in Judaism, but he radically reframed the concept of this state into one of a temporally oriented, open, tolerant state that incorporated Judaism as a positive force, conscious of the fact that in the end it owed the latter its understanding of religion and the world. With this argumentation, Hirsch wanted to compel the state to recognize the religio-cultural contributions of modern Judaism and then draw the necessary political conclusions. He challenged the very core of Christianity by pointing to its Jewish origins and suggesting that, if it wanted to engage in a modernizing process of historical criticism, de-dogmatization, and overcoming its otherworldliness, it must not define itself in contrast to Judaism but, instead, find its way back to its original – Jewish – essence. Jews are thus ultimately the true Christians, true Christianity bears a Jewish emblem, and a true "Christian state" that emancipates the Jews on its own initiative is the fulfillment of the messianic future. In contrast, a Christianity estranged from its intrinsic Jewish core held no relevance for the modern era. Bauer's verdict on Judaism thus provoked Hirsch into a polemical interpretation, according to which the truth or untruth, or rather the historical power or powerlessness of Christianity would be measured fully in terms of its relationship to its Jewish heritage and to Judaism's 'nay' to the traditional Christian theology and worldview:

> And if, indeed, the Christian state has a truly appropriate understanding of itself, how could it wish to exclude [...] Judaism, the true Judaism, the Judaism that has become self-conscious, from its realm? Didn't Judaism suffer and shed its blood for the sake of precisely that idea of a Christian state in need to be accomplished? What else led us to the stakes, if not the fact that we did not agree that this world is utterly corrupt, that it was too evil to allow for the kingdom of heaven to be realized? What else is the Messiah for us than the reality of the Christian state, the reality of the kingdom of truth and virtue on earth? Why else were we unable to concede that the Messiah had already come if not because we saw evil and darkness reign on earth instead of the good and light? [...] Consider Jewish history as what it really is – the positive and not solely the negative preparation for Jesus Christ! Acknowledge that God guided the history of this people in order to make it the archetype of all history for the world! Accept, indeed, that God created man, each and every human being, so that everybody would be Christ, so that everybody would make himself a Christ, so that everybody would follow the spirit of Christ, imitate the life of Christ, and so that nothing could prevent man from living here on earth according to this divine will! Acknowledge that, when humankind refused to be Christian, God chose a people and appointed it to be His firstborn son (which means that, for the Jews, all other people are also God's children). He did not abandon it to its evil ways but castigated and punished it until it recognized the Lord and until it accomplished a life in which it loved God with its entire heart, its entire soul and its entire might, until it was capable to

bring Jesus forth! [...] We are supposed to become Christians before being allowed to be part of the Christian state! But what does it mean to be a Christian? Does it mean to act and to live the way Jesus acted and lived? In that case we are Christians, and we aspire with all our might to be Christians. However, does this mean that we must admit that everything mundane is still in a state of corruption, unworthy and unable to serve the Spirit's self-expression? Must we first be symbolically cleansed from this earthly impurity in order to receive the new, sublime spirit that is homeless on this earth and only feels itself at home in a new world? Then refrain from talking about a Christian state and talk rather about Christianity, but then please surrender the state to its fate! Well then, you will also have declared Christianity a lie. And even two thousand years will not have sufficed to make Christianity a world-transcending power; and so too Christianity, being powerless, is irrelevant for this world and all mundane circumstances![96]

In the controversy with Bauer, Hirsch emphasized the difference between Judaism and Christianity above all, as he had already done in his *Religionsphilosophie*. Ten years later he highlighted it in a different way in his book *Die Humanität als Religion* ("Humanity as Religion", 1854) – a book that resulted from speeches he had delivered as a member of the Luxembourg Masonic lodge "Les Enfants de la Concorde fortifiée". He had joined the lodge on June 9, 1843, apparently attracted by the benefits this would yield for his position within the local bourgeois society and by the Masonic principles of freedom of conscience, tolerance, and humanity, which were very much in accord with his own religious convictions. In *Die Humanität als Religion*, in connection with his defense of Jewish participation in the Masonic movement, he went so far as to speak of a common universal Jewish-Christian religion from which Christianity and Judaism were differentiated solely by their symbolic forms of expression of the one and the same truth. With that, he made the unique attempt in nineteenth-century Jewish religious philosophy to construct a joint Jewish-Christian Masonic religion, a religion of tolerance for the new era: "not out of indifference but based on religion, a religion of humanity, of humaneness, of the true, practical, active and faith-appropriate love. In other words, the religion of anthropology, a religion in which the truly educated people agree with one another, even if they are committed to different churches, or to different forms, different symbolic expressions of religious life."[97] The apologetic dimension of his

---

96 Hirsch, *Das Judenthum, der christliche Staat und die moderne Kritik*, 100–101. For Hirsch's interpretation of Christianity, see Jacob Fleischmann, *The Problem of Christianity in Jewish Thought from Mendelssohn to Rosenzweig, 1770–1929* [Hebrew] (Jerusalem: Magnes Press, 1964), 78–92.
97 See Samuel Hirsch, *Die Humanität als Religion in Vorträgen gehalten in der Loge zu Luxemburg* (Trier: C. Troschel, 1854), ii.

work is conspicuous: Hirsch challenged the exclusion of Jews by the Prussian lodges and wanted to demonstrate that "humanity, perfected humanity, transfigured humanity touches on what is common to both Judaism and Christianity" and that "Christianity does not contain a single humane thought of which Judaism cannot also boast".[98] Interestingly enough, his identification of Masonic ideals, Christian values and the Jewish religion also led to criticism among his Masonic brethren, some of whom considered his thoughts "too Jewish" – one of the reasons why Hirsch left the lodge on October 15, 1855.[99]

However, Hirsch's philosophy also had an important intrinsically Jewish dimension. The public discussion around Bauer's radical views strengthened the necessity within the Reform movement to define the character and the limits of the modernization of Judaism, and to reach an agreement on the authority of religious sources in order to draw conclusions regarding the shaping of religious practice. What price was one ready to pay to prove the universality of Judaism and its worthiness of emancipation? Hirsch first addressed these questions systematically in his 1844 work entitled *Die Reform im Judenthum und dessen Beruf in der gegenwärtigen Welt* ("The Reform in Judaism and Its Mission in the Contemporary World"). As he had already emphasized in his Dessau writings, he was strongly opposed to reforming Jewish religious practices for the sake of equality and recognition, or to mimicking the aesthetics of the Church, "so that, also in this respect, nothing would appear foreign to Christians, who would thus be more inclined to grant us our emancipation".[100]

In critical response to Bauer's accusation regarding Judaism being antiquated, particularistic, and resistant to modernization, Hirsch asserted that to the contrary, it had an "intimate friendship" with modernity's worldview. Judaism, being neither a confession nor a nation, he argued, fulfilled the role of a "born witness of history",[101] endowed with the messianic task to "realize here on earth the kingdom of truth and reason, of the true rational legality (*Gesetzlichkeit*), inspired by the spirit". This, however, required "removing everything from our lives that exacerbates the fulfillment of this task or, in fact, makes it

---

[98] Ibid., vii. For Hirsch's relationship to Freemasonry, see Jacob Katz, "Samuel Hirsch – Rabbi, Philosopher and Freemason", Revue des études juives 125 (1965), 113–126; in his article, Katz furnishes proof of Hirsch's membership in the Luxembourg lodge since 1843 and the fact that he frequently gave speeches there.
[99] Ittenbach, "Samuel Hirsch", 30–31.
[100] Samuel Hirsch, *Die Reform im Judenthum und dessen Beruf in der gegenwärtigen Welt* (Leipzig: Heinrich Hunger, 1844), 5.
[101] Ibid., 60.

impossible".[102] Specifically modern Judaism was challenged, in the face of the *Zeitgeist*, "to overcome the external, slavish adherence to and imitation of a past ceremoniousness".[103] However, he gave strong warnings against what he called "fraudulent reform", referring to the heated public controversy about the manifesto of the Frankfurter "Society of the Friends of Reform", a small, short-lived movement composed of intellectual laity who had written a declaration of principle for a radical reform of Judaism in 1843. Conforming to a general trend in the Reform movement, they rejected the hope for a "Messiah, who would lead the Israelites back to Palestine", disputed any dogmatic or practical authority held by the Talmud, and postulated the possibility of "unlimited development" of the "Mosaic religion". It was obvious, of course, that the consequences of such a view were far-reaching and represented an implicit challenge to the revelatory character and validity of the Bible.[104] The concept of the "Mosaic religion" or "Mosaism" originated in contemporary Protestant biblical scholarship's popular distinction between an early, prophetic – Mosaic-Israelite – and a later, priestly-rabbinical religion. Hidden behind its use was a deliberate or unwitting internalization of a negative non-Jewish perception of the rabbinical tradition as well as the attempt to demonstrate that Judaism could return to a universalism that was profoundly rooted in its history. Among the reformers, only Mendel Hess (1807–1871) from Saxony-Weimar embraced the position of the "Reformfreunde" "with joyful exaltation" as the foundation of a "vital, humane, modern Judaism" in contrast to "rigid rabbinism".[105] The overwhelming majority of the rabbis rejected the idea of abandoning a major part of tradition together with the rabbinical literature and was anxious that the principle of "unlimited

---

102 Ibid., 39.
103 Ibid., 18.
104 Cited in Meyer, *Response to Modernity*, 122; for the phenomenon of the radical lay groups that emerged also in cities such as Breslau and Berlin, see ibid., 119–132; for the Frankfurt "Reformfreunde", see idem, "Alienated Intellectuals in the Camp of Religious Reform: The Frankfurt Reformfreunde, 1842–1845", AJS Review 6 (1984), 61–86; David Philipson, *The Reform Movement in Judaism* (New York: Macmillan, 1931), 107–139. For Hirsch on Mosaism see Judith Frishman, "True Mosaic Religion. Samuel Hirsch, Samuel Holdheim and the Reform of Judaism", in Judith Frishman, Willemien Otten, and Gerard Rouwhorst, eds., *Religious Identity and the Problem of Historical Foundation. The Foundational Character of Authoritative Sources in the History of Christianity and Judaism*, Jewish and Christian Perspectives Series 8 (Boston and Leiden: Brill, 2004), 195–222.
105 Mendel Hess, "Der Frankfurter Reformverein", Der Israelit des neunzehnten Jahrhunderts 4 (1843), no. 46, 183–185 (here 183); no. 47, 187–188; no. 48, 191–192. In contrast, see David Einhorn, "Gutachtliche Äußerung eines jüdischen Theologen über den Reformverein an einen sich dafür interessierenden Christen", Allgemeine Zeitung des Judenthums 8, 7 (1844), 87–89, here 87.

development" might result in a Judaism with no revelatory foundation. This Judaism, according to Ludwig Philippson (1811–1889), would no longer be a positive religion but, at best, "a mere non-Christianity".[106] Moreover, the "Reformfreunde" demanded the abandonment of dietary laws and circumcision, which they saw as pre-mosaic, exclusive elements of an outmoded Jewish particularism that would prevent integration into non-Jewish society. For many this seemed to constitute an overly sectarian radicalism – a radicalism that had to be restricted as it did not leave any of the core religious traditions untouched in the end.[107]

Hirsch, too, accused the "Reformfreunde" of "divesting [Judaism] of all characteristics", thereby threatening the Jewish religion's right to exist. To be sure, Hirsch shared the "friend's" critique of the authority of the Talmud: Originating in a time of decline and doubt, it stood for the traditions of the past. Rabbinical Judaism, he held, had overlooked that Moses and the Prophets had already understood the ceremonies as symbolical representation of the "inner religious thought" (*innerlichen Religionsgedanken*) rather than as unalterable laws.[108] Nevertheless, Hirsch saw Judaism's main religious laws and ceremonies (Sabbath, circumcision, dietary laws) – when understood correctly – as necessary means toward the realization of Israel's messianic role, as symbols that made abstract ideas and ideals sensible. The Jews – as the "martyrs" of divine-human history – must retain a "special Jewish symbolism", "that would always be capable of making their testimony concerning the holiness of history clearly and precisely perceptible to themselves and to the world".[109] While the "Reformfreunde" were right in suggesting that everything should be removed from religious practice "that prevents us from contributing with our spiritual and material forces to the preservation and prosperity of bourgeois society",[110] Hirsch argued, "true re-

---

106 Ludwig Philippson, "Wohin?", Allgemeine Zeitung des Judenthums 7, 34 (1843), 502–503, here 502. For a conservative voice, see Michael Sachs, "Gutachten über den Reformverein", Zeitschrift für die religiösen Interessen des Judentums 1, 2 (1844), 49–60 as well as the "postscript" published by Zacharias Frankel (ibid., 60–73).
107 For the background of the controversy on circumcision triggered by the Frankfurt "Reformfreunde", see Robert Liberles, *Religious Conflict in Social Context: The Resurgence of Orthodox Judaism in Frankfurt am Main, 1838–1877* (Westport, CT.: Greenwood Press, 1985), 23–65; Andreas Gotzmann, *Jüdisches Recht im kulturellen Prozeß: Die Wahrnehmung der Halacha im Deutschland des 19. Jahrhunderts* (Tübingen: Mohr-Siebeck, 1997), 251–302.
108 Hirsch, *Die Reform im Judenthum*, 17.
109 Ibid., 64; and see Hirsch, *Das Judenthum, der christliche Staat und die moderne Kritik*, 73–74. For Hirsch's symbolism, see Ken Koltun-Fromm, "Public Religion in Samson Raphael Hirsch and in Samuel Hirsch's Interpretation of Religious Symbolism", Journal of Jewish Thought and Philosophy 9 (1999), 69–105.
110 Hirsch, *Die Reform im Judenthum*, 67.

form" had to hold on to the crucial biblical symbols such as the Sabbath, the circumcision, and the dietary laws. The "Reformfreunde" offered no acceptable reform principle as they did not assume any incontrovertible essence of Judaism beyond the controvertible forms; Bauer decried Judaism due to its supposedly insurmountable particularism.

In response to the "Reformfreunde" and Bauer, Hirsch characterized Judaism, as opposed to Christianity, as the superior embodiment of human freedom and of the universal; however, he insisted that the Jews must remain recognizable as Jews precisely because they were a people with a universal mission. That remained Hirsch's basic line of thought during the discussions at the rabbinical conferences in Braunschweig, Frankfurt, and Breslau in the mid-1840s, where he took part prominently in the discussions. On the one hand, he advocated the retention of circumcision[111] and of Hebrew as the language used in worship; on the other hand, like Samuel Holdheim, he critically opposed a fundamentally strict adherence to the dietary laws[112] and argued for the precedence of civil service in cases where religious laws collided with state duties (as in the army, for example). Furthermore, he pushed resolutely for a "complete alignment of doctrine and life in respect to the Sabbath" and spoke out decidedly for celebration on Sunday – despite the widespread fears that doing so might be construed as converging with Christianity.[113] Interestingly enough, however, Hirsch's practical reforms in Luxembourg were far less radical; apparently, they did not go beyond moderate liturgical changes to the service.[114] Nevertheless, he acquired the rep-

---

[111] See Hirsch's expert opinion on circumcision in Salomon Abraham Trier, ed., *Rabbinische Gutachten über die Beschneidung. Gesammelt und herausgegeben von Salomon Abraham Trier, Rabbiner. Als Manuskript gedruckt* (Frankfurt am Main: Bach, 1844), 48–57. For Hirsch's position during the controversy on the circumcision, see Judith Frishman, "True Mosaic Religion: Samuel Hirsch, Samuel Holdheim and the Reform of Judaism", in Frishman, Otten, and Rouwhorst, *Religious Identity and the Problem of Historical Foundation*, 195–222, esp. 204–208.

[112] For a symbolic interpretation of the – predominantly outmoded – dietary laws (for instance as symbol of the priestly role of every Israelite or of the sanctity of the natural laws), see Samuel Hirsch, "Die Speisegesetze (Aus einem demnächst erscheinenden Handbuch für israelitische Religionslehrer)", Der Israelit des neunzehnten Jahrhunderts 7, 18 (1846), 137–140; no. 19, 145–148; no. 20, 154–159.

[113] See "Des Dr. Hirsch Votum über die Sabbathfrage", Der Israelit des neunzehnten Jahrhunderts 7, 34 (1846), 266–268, here 266; and Samuel Hirsch, *Die Sabbathfrage vor der dritten Rabbinerversammlung. Ein Votum* (Berlin: self-published, 1846).

[114] Greenberg, "The Historical Origins of God and Man", 131–132. However, Hirsch dissociated himself from the use of the Hebrew language and emphasized that the Jewish liturgy had developed historically and was, therefore, at all times, subject to the spirit of the respective times: "Whatever edifies the community should be introduced, and whatever does not edify, should be removed." See Samuel Hirsch, *Systematischer Katechismus der israelitischen Religion, auf Be-*

utation of a consistent, if prudent, reformer during his years in Luxembourg – a reputation that would soon go beyond Europe's borders.

Hirsch as a Radical Reform Rabbi in Philadelphia (1866–1889)

In August 1866, Samuel Hirsch accepted the invitation from the reform community Keneseth Israel in Philadelphia, where he would become David Einhorn's successor and one of the leading intellectual figures of radical Reform Judaism in the United States. On November 8, 1866 he and his family took the steamer "Ville des Paris" to New York, leaving Europe behind and embarking on a new chapter of his life. The fact that he was offered a life-long contract[115] indicates that the congregation in Philadelphia wished to engage a rabbi who – in his capacity as an acknowledged religious philosopher and as a pioneer of German Judaism – promised to continue Einhorn's work and to become an intellectual leader of the American Reform movement.[116] Apart from financial reasons,[117] it was apparently Hirsch's hope of eluding the Luxembourg Jesuits' constant hostility toward him[118] and of being able to realize his reform concepts in America under very different and freer conditions that played a crucial role in his decision to start a new life beyond the Atlantic. In a sermon held in 1867, Hirsch presented the main aspects of his thoughts to his new congregation. He indicated that the abolishment of slavery after the Civil War had made this decision easier, for the enslavement of people definitely contradicted the ideal of Judaism: "All humans

---

schluß des Vorstandes der israelitischen Gemeinde zu Luxemburg (Luxembourg: Bück, 1856), 129–130. For the catechism, see Bernd Schröder, "Jüdische Katechismen in Deutschland am Beispiel eines Katechismus aus der Feder von Samuel Hirsch (1815–1889)", in Klaus Herrmann, Margarete Schlüter, and Giuseppe Veltri, eds., *Jewish Studies Between the Disciplines – Judaistik zwischen den Disziplinen: Papers in Honor of Peter Schäfer on the Occasion of His 60th Birthday* (Leiden and Boston: Brill, 2003), 456–477 and the article by Ken Koltun-Fromm in this volume.
115 *Reform Congregation Keneseth Israel: Its First 100 Years 1847–1947* (Philadelphia: Elkins Park, 1950), 15–16.
116 Hirsch was apparently offered the position at the suggestion of David Einhorn; see Greenberg, "Samuel Hirsch's American Judaism", 362. For the development of the American Reform movement in nineteenth-century America, see Meyer, *Response to Modernity*, 225–295.
117 According to his own words, Hirsch came to Philadelphia as a "poor man" after having run up debts in Luxembourg; see Samuel Hirsch, *Dr. Jastrow und sein Gebaren in Philadelphia: Ein ehrliches, leider abgenoethigtes Wort* (Philadelphia: n.p., terminus post quem 17 February 1868), 1–2.
118 Greenberg, "Samuel Hirsch's American Judaism", 362.

are created equal; all people are the children of God; nobody may be his brother's slave."[119] Above all however, he hoped that there would be less pressure in the United States than in Europe for individuals to conceal their Jewishness and that his own message that Jews should be proud of their tradition would fall on more fertile ground: "Judaism can, must and should be our pride. Whatever has transpired in the course of two thousand years in this world in terms of greatness, nobility, and beauty, is Judaism and nothing but Judaism. [...] Judaism alone is the religion of progress and thus it alone is the religion of the present, and even more so of the future."[120] The only threat to Israel's priestly mission, Hirsch emphasized, was the kind of religious indifference toward Judaism that characterized many Jewish congregations in Europe and undermined Judaism's messianic mission in the modern world. He implored his new congregation to spare him experiencing a prevalent secularizing tendency in America:

> But there is one enemy whom I anticipate, and I wish to caution you against him. What prompted me to follow your invitation a year ago with enthusiasm was the following: In Europe, too, beautiful temples and synagogues are being built [...]. There, too, the organ and choral singing enhance religious services. There, too, prayers in the language of the heart, the mother tongue, have been introduced. There, too, the prayer: "May God lead us back to Palestine", is no longer heard, as the Jew and Judaism feel at home everywhere on God's earth, everywhere called upon to act and live for the sake of the honor of God. However, there is one aspect that made me recognize the call to leave that land as a call by God. The European Jews in the larger cities suffer from thoughtless obsession for imitation. The Christian churches in Europe are empty, are perceived by all those who claim superiority through true *Bildung* and independent thinking, with indifference, if not repugnance. [...] And because the Christians do not visit their churches and have reasons to refrain from doing so, the European Jews do not visit their synagogues either, even though they are without reason. Beware of this mistake; pay homage to Judaism, as it deserves this

---

119 Samuel Hirsch, *Predigt gehalten am Schemini Azereth 5628, in der Synagoge der Gem. Keneseth Israel in Philadelphia* (Philadelphia: Stein und Jones, 1867), 6. Hirsch used the example of slavery in order to make the point that the Jewish law, too, bore the imprint of antiquity and thus contradicted the true "teaching of God", which first had to gradually become prevalent in the life of the Jewish people: "True, Judaism has, indeed, created a Law; however, it is not limited to the Law. Judaism is more, is profounder, offers more truth than the Law. The Law [...] bears the marks and is afflicted with the infirmities of its time, whereas the teaching is valid for all times. [...] Each period must represent it in a more truthful and profound way than the preceding period" (ibid., 8). In his European writings he had drawn the attention to the disgrace of slavery in America on a number of occasions; see, e. g., Hirsch, *Die Messiaslehre in Kanzelvorträgen*, 410; for the debates about slavery among American rabbis during the Civil War, see Bertram W. Korn, *American Jewry and the Civil War* (Philadelphia: Jewish Publication Society of America, 1957), 15–55.
120 Hirsch, *Predigt gehalten am Schemini Azeret 5628*, 14.

honor! I would mourn the day I arrived in this country should I discover that it is left to others to visit the house of God instead of going there oneself.[121]

Although Hirsch held to the most important elements of his philosophy in the United States, it is impossible to overlook the fact that the difference in conditions there contributed to a significant shift in his thinking. Gershon Greenberg has demonstrated that this was not just about Hirsch conforming to the reigning pragmatism popular in America at the time; nor did it have to do with the focus on contemporary rationality in the Reform movement there. Rather, he diagnosed a "fundamental religious transformation" in Hirsch's thought with respect to his time in Dessau – albeit one that had already been anticipated in part in writings composed in Luxembourg.[122] One conspicuous aspect of Hirsch's time in America is that, despite 22 productive years in Philadelphia, he stopped publishing systematic philosophical works, limiting himself to predominantly journalistic articles, e.g. in Isaac Mayer Wise's journal *Die Deborah* (1819–1900), David Einhorn's *Jewish Times*, or in the Chicago Reform journal *Der Zeitgeist*.[123] This may be explained by the less philosophical character of the American Reform movement, probably also by a certain disillusionment regarding philosophy's impact on practical life.[124] The main reason, however, seems to be that he felt that a much stronger focus on social commitment, societal issues, and the practical concretization of the philosophical ideal formulated in Europe rather than on theological reflections was needed. This conviction is confirmed by his greater involvement in social activities, for instance by his role in establishing a benevolent society for orphans (1868) as well as of the American branch of the *Alliance Israélite Universelle*, and a contribution to the designing of the curriculum of the Hebrew Union College in Cincinnati in 1878.

As much as Hirsch's writings in America continued to provide succinct conclusions from his earlier philosophy, the shifts in his thinking are remarkable: In Europe he still had rejected French-style republicanism and supported the monarchy because he had expected that only this political system would guarantee fair, impartial recognition and equal status to the Jewish people.[125] Having been

---

121 Ibid., 16.
122 Greenberg, "The Historical Origins of God and Man", 129.
123 See Adolph S. Oko, *Bibliography of Dr. Samuel Hirsch (b. June 8, 1815; d. May 14, 1889)* (Cincinnati, OH: n.p., 1916).
124 Greenberg, "Samuel Hirsch's American Judaism", 381.
125 See Hirsch, *Die Messiaslehre in Kanzelvorträgen*, 43–44; his series of sermons from Dessau culminates in the emphatic confession that "merely under the rule of a monarch who has received his grandeur and office from God, true liberty can flourish in perpetuity and be secured

disillusioned by his political experiences in the 1840s and 50s,[126] however, he would now pin all of his hopes on the constitutional foundations of American democracy, according to which religion – including Judaism – would be liberated from persecution and discrimination and allowed to participate in politics and society. In contrast to Europe, he argued, in America the state was the true embodiment of human freedom and the true instrument of the divine spirit. Secular reality and religious ideas, he maintained, were finally reconciled, with the result that the traditional Orthodox fixation on an ideal of the past could finally give way to an orientation toward the present and the future.

Along with this optimistic political reorientation came a clear shift in the ideological and religious controversies in which Hirsch was involved. His main opponent was no longer contemporary philosophy, or the exclusive truth claims of an anti-Jewish Christian theology, but rather Jewish Orthodoxy. For Hirsch, America, the "land of freedom", was also the land of reform, in which the individual and the community could freely adapt their religious consciousness to their environment without fear of abandoning Jewish identity and distinctiveness. In Europe, despite insisting on the aspect of freedom, Hirsch had advocated a rather cautious reinterpretation of the essence of Judaism and emphasized an autonomous, rational interpretation of the Halachah. Now, in America, he was even more determined to reject the Orthodox concept of the – eternally valid – inherent authority of halachic tradition and called for a deliberate detachment from any ritual forms that had lost their meaning in modern American

---

forever in its unrestrained development. All other forms of government, as much as they may boast about their freedom, warrant and secure only the latter's illusion, since only under the rule of the Lord's Anointed can the Divine gain strength. Behold the state that so strongly boasts about its freedom, behold North America – not even the holiest human rights are respected there. As much as those who are well-meaning aspire to return to the poor slaves their inborn human rights, they fail to succeed, since those who profit from that deplorable situation, which God abhors, are sitting on the benches of power and do not wish, of course, to relinquish their might. No – solely under a king's rule can liberty flourish and gain power, since only a king is a fair-minded judge, who provides an impartial judgment on all those aspirations. Only a king can implement justice, as he has no part in the proliferation of injustice" (ibid., 409–410).

126 This is not to say that Hirsch did now reject Germany and everything German. On the contrary: in a speech delivered on the occasion of the German peace celebrations after the Franco-German War of 1870/71 he emphasized the affinity between Germans and Jews; see Samuel Hirsch, "Sermon, Delivered on Sunday, May 14th, the Opening Day of the German Peace Festival", The Jewish Times 3 (1871/72), 196–198. For the significance of Germany and German culture for the Reform rabbis who emigrated to America, see Christian Wiese, "Inventing a New Language of Jewish Scholarship: The Transition from German 'Wissenschaft des Judentums' to American-Jewish Scholarship in the 19th and 20th Centuries", Studia Rosenthaliana 36 (2003), 273–304.

society. "Talmudism", he argued, which understood Judaism as "law, external law",[127] contradicted the Jewish principle of freedom according to which God had given the human mind the true "inner law" that enabled him to find the path toward truth and justice as much as Christianity did. This "law of reason", he wrote, demanding only what was demanded by the human mind, was "the religion of modernity, because freedom is the true expression of our times".[128]

Orthodoxy had been overcome by the progress of the human mind. Based on Judaism's eternal principle of freedom, Jews had to find new forms: "An eternal principle, such as the Jewish principle, is eternal merely in that it renews itself with the progress of time. The principle remains the same, however the form is alterable."[129] According to Hirsch, the rabbinic tradition, although it was an important part of Jewish history, was outdated and embodied "the Judaism of oppression, of the *golus* [i.e., Diaspora mentality]". At this point in history, with the hopes engendered by American democracy, it was crucial to create the "Judaism of freedom".[130] As far as the practical religious traditions were concerned, Hirsch now rethought his earlier interpretation of the ceremonies and customs as Judaism's symbolic "sign language" and made their retention dependent on the cultural and aesthetic norms of contemporary society. Customs originally stemming from the Orient, such as wearing a head covering, he argued, should not be maintained in America: "I do not reject oriental customs and mores in the synagogue; however, they should only be practiced by those who also appear in public in oriental clothes and who live according to the oriental dietary laws, in short, by those who wish to appear as Orientals everywhere."[131]

The basis for the transformation of Hirsch's interpretation of the relationship between Reform and tradition was formed by a newly accentuated concept of revelation, which affected his understanding of the Talmud and – above all – the Bible. Following earlier ideas developed in Luxembourg, Hirsch now radically emphasized both the irrelevance of supernatural sources of divine knowledge

---

[127] Samuel Hirsch, "Freiheit und Judenthum", The Jewish Times 1, 3 (1869/70), 11–12; no. 4, 12; no. 5, 12–13; no. 6, 11–12; no. 7, 11–12; no. 8, 12–13; quotation no. 5, 12.
[128] Ibid., no. 4, 12.
[129] Ibid., no. 8, 13.
[130] Samuel Hirsch, "Die talmudische Auffassung des Judenthums nicht falsch sondern nur ein überwundener Standpunkt", The Jewish Times 1, 14 (1869/70), 10–11. For Hirsch's critique of Orthodoxy, see, e.g., idem, "Die amerikanische Orthodoxie", Die Deborah 13 (1867), 100, 114, 118, 122 and 126; idem, "Rechte und falsche Orthodoxie", Die Deborah 13 (1867), 130; idem, "Die amerikanische Orthodoxie und das mosaische Erbrecht", Die Deborah 13 (1867), 146–147; 150–151.
[131] Samuel Hirsch, "The Reform Worship", The Jewish Times 1, 18 (1869/70), 3–4; no. 19, 3–4; no. 20, 4; no. 21, 5–6; no. 22, 3–4; no. 23, 4; here no. 19, 4.

and natural, autonomous inborn knowledge of God to the extent that one wondered if Hirsch still actually believed in a divinity differentiated from human understanding or whether he had now embarked on a complete anthropologization of religion.[132] While his *Religionsphilosophie* (1842) was still permeated with quotations from rabbinical literature despite his critique of medieval Talmudic mentality, he now consistently radicalized the historicization of the Talmud that had characterized his polemics against Bruno Bauer. In America he came to understand the rabbinical tradition as an unfree form of piety, estranged from society, that had been overcome by modernity.[133] He explicitly questioned its authority, thus embracing views similar to those of the Frankfurt "Reformfreunde". This historicizing approach also extended to the Bible itself. In his *Religionsphilosophie*, Hirsch had still held to the heteronomy of biblical revelation; he understood the scripture (including its mythical elements) as a precise representation of the history between God and Israel that stood above academic critique. His *Die Humanität als Religion*, which – printed in English translation in parts in *The Jewish Times* (1869/70) and the *Reform Advocate* (1915) – became one of his most important publications in America, had already indicated a shift in his views. There he interpreted the Bible as a decidedly historical expression – subject to critique – of a specific period of Jewish history whose language and time-bound myths were aimed at people of every era. According to him, therefore, people in the present time must search for the eternal meaning behind those myths.[134] In America, Hirsch further radicalized this idea, suggesting a form of biblical criticism that would consistently interpret the Bible as a product of ancient culture subject to progressive human knowledge. Since the biblical truths were ultimately of human nature, they had to be understood from the perspective of the intellectual development of contemporary society. Nonetheless, Hirsch did not want to fully renounce the category of the divine: the Bible's human origin is simultaneously of a divine nature, as God infused human beings with the divine spirit that asserts itself in the Bible – as it was asserting itself in the contemporary Reform movement.[135]

---

132 See Greenberg, "The Historical Origins of God and Man", 132.
133 See, e.g., Samuel Hirsch, "Das Judenthum der Freiheit und die Offenbarung", Die Deborah 13 (1870), 130–131, 134, 138, 143.
134 See Hirsch, *Die Humanität als Religion*, 33–35; idem, *Systematischer Katechismus der israelitischen Religion*, 131–133.
135 See Samuel Hirsch, "Die Bibel und das moderne Judenthum", Die Deborah 13 (1867), 158–159; idem, "Die Bibel und die freie Forschung", Die Deborah 13 (1867), 162–163; idem, "Bibelkritik und Reformjudenthum", Der Zeitgeist 2 (1881), 143; idem, "Was ist Frömmigkeit im Sinne des Judenthums?", Der Zeitgeist 2 (1881), 244, 258, 273.

Hirsch's election as President of the Philadelphia Conference (November 3 to 6, 1869), where the basic principles of radical Reform were first systematically defined, confirms the importance of the position he and his radicalized philosophy occupied in the American Reform movement. Despite Hirsch's leading role the conference was dominated by David Einhorn, the then towering figure of American Reform. Nevertheless, we may assume that, in general, Hirsch agreed with the majority of Einhorn's suggestions. Those attending the conference were America's most prominent Reform rabbis, who had embraced "the uncompromising religious progress".[136] Their focus was the attempt to promote the universal mission of a modern Judaism – a Judaism divested of all purely historically determined particularistic elements – as the standard measure for Jewish identity, in order to dissociate themselves from Orthodoxy and to refute anti-Jewish prejudice. As the American reformers stated, Israel's messianic aim was not the restoration of the Jewish state, the "repeated separation from the peoples", but "the unification of all people as God's children" in recognition of the uniqueness of God as well as "the unity of all rational beings and their calling to moral observance". The destruction of the Second Temple and Israel's Exile, the *galut*, were not to be understood as a "punishment for the sinfulness of Israel." They were rather the expression of the divine intention "to disperse the members of the Jewish lineage to all corners of the earth, to fulfill their high priestly task of leading the nations to the true acknowledgement and glorification of God". "Israel's status as the people chosen for the religion" and as the bearer of the highest idea of humanity was to be emphasized, but only in the same breath as the universal mission of Judaism and the idea of the "equal love that God has for all his children".[137]

Central themes from the nineteenth-century European and American Reform movement emerged in the Declaration of Principles from Philadelphia. These had developed since the Enlightenment as part of continuous debates with non-Jewish theologians and philosophers about the character of Judaism, often in the context of political-social debates on the Jews' alleged "particular identity" and the conditions for their integration into the European societies. At the same time, it was also about a modernizing, universalist reinterpretation of the fundamental themes of Jewish tradition: Israel's chosenness; the meaning of exile and suffering in Judaism's diasporic existence; the relationship of Juda-

---

136 "Aufruf zu einer Rabbiner-Conferenz", The Jewish Times 1, 14 (1869/70), 8.
137 *Protokolle der Rabbiner-Conferenz abgehalten zu Philadelphia, vom 3. bis zum 6. November 1869* (New York: S. Hecht, 1870), 86; on the practical resolutions in Philadelphia, see Meyer, *Response to Modernity*, 255–258.

ism to humanity and to other religions; as well as the relevance of ceremonial laws for modern Judaism.

The internal Jewish discourse about the relationship between universalism and particularism, indissolubly connected as it was with the question regarding the Jewish minority's eligibility for emancipation and Judaism's capability for modernization, was not simply a harmonious one,[138] as the heated public controversy between Samuel Hirsch and David Einhorn in the wake of the Philadelphia conference attests. The issue at stake was the consequences of Judaism's universalism for mixed marriages and conversion to the Jewish faith. Hirsch's series of articles under the title "Darf ein Reformrabbiner Ehen zwischen Juden und Nichtjuden einsegnen?" ("May a Reform Rabbi Consecrate Marriages between Jews and Non-Jews?") deplored the rigorous rabbinical rejection of mixed marriages and suggested, very much along the lines of Abraham Geiger's and Samuel Holdheim's views, that Reform Judaism should respect the state law regarding marriage and permit non-Jews to marry a Jewish partner without urging the former to convert to Judaism and – in the case of men – to undergo circumcision. Hirsch assumed that committed Christians would not marry Jewish partners in any event because of the deep religious contradiction. Therefore, the case at hand involved non-Jews who rejected the Christian dogmas, accepted the teachings of Judaism in principle, and would allow their children a Jewish upbringing, but "would not wish to take on the priestly vocation of Israel" and therefore were not obligated to its symbol, circumcision.[139] Hirsch's arguments consistently followed the view held by Holdheim. In his book *Gemischte Ehen zwischen Juden und Christen* (1850), Holdheim had justified his practice of blessing mixed marriages "in the name of the religion of the purest human love, in the name of Judaism", by invoking the Reform movement's universal vision. This included emphasizing God as the father of all humankind, and the will "to replace the holy people with the holy race of humankind, to replace the covenant between God and Israel with a covenant between God and humankind".[140] In the rabbinical

---

138 See Christian Wiese, "The Philadelphia Conference (1869) and German Reform: A Historical Moment in a Transnational Story of Proximity and Alienation", in Christian Wiese and Cornelia Wilhelm, eds., *American Jewry: Transcending the European Experience?* (London and New York: Bloomsbury, 2017), 136–158.
139 Samuel Hirsch, "Darf ein Reformrabbiner Ehen zwischen Juden und Nichtjuden einsegnen?", The Jewish Times 1, 27 (1969/70), 9–10; no. 28, 10–11; no. 30, 9–10; no. 31, 10; no. 32, 10; no. 33, 10; no. 34, 10; no. 35, 11; no. 36, 13; here no. 27, 10. And see Hirsch's controversy with Markus Jastrow: "Herrn Dr. Jastrow", The Jewish Times 5 (1874/75), 542–543, 559, 574–575.
140 Samuel Holdheim, *Gemischte Ehen zwischen Juden und Christen. Die Gutachten der Berliner Rabbinatsverwaltung und des Königsberger Konsistoriums beleuchtet* (Berlin: L. Lassar, 1850), 64–65.

literature, he argued, the prohibition of mixed marriages had nothing to do with the religious differences between the partners, but resulted from the desire to preserve the purity of the ethnic character of the Jews. This was valid as long as they represented a separate, autonomous people living in a theocracy, in accordance with the plan of history under God's saving grace, a time long past.

In contrast to Holdheim and Hirsch, David Einhorn strictly rejected the consecration of mixed marriages. Not – as he never tired of emphasizing – for the reason of Talmudic "belief in the higher sanctity of the blood of the Jewish line", but because it was his firm conviction that this meant "hammering a nail into the coffin of the tiny Jewish race with its high calling". The polemical sharpness with which Einhorn rejected a more liberal practice had quite evidently to do with his concern about a potential dissolution of Jewish identity. Mixed marriages, in his eyes, were not a sign of the overcoming of particularism, but a threat to Israel's universal mission to spread and deepen the eternal truths and moral laws. Einhorn's estimation that "the tiny Jewish line, a grain of sand among the peoples", would have perished long ago had the barriers of separation in its history of exile been lifted, echoes the predominantly German anti-Jewish calls for a gradual dissolution of the "distinctive Jewish character" through assimilation and mixed marriage. Einhorn countered that with the duty of Israel to hold fast to its distinctiveness, and asked: "May [Judaism], through mixed marriage, lead its nationality, the actual fulcrum of its missionary activity, gradually toward destruction or even just allow it to be weakened?" Therefore, from his point of view, a precondition for marriage between Jews and non-Jews was formal conversion, including ritual bath or circumcision.[141] Hirsch thereupon accused Einhorn of thinking in the racist categories of Ernest Renan (1823–1892) and of proselytizing. "The hope [of Reform Judaism] is surely not", he objected, "that one day all people shall become Jews, but that without being Jews, they shall live in truth, morality and holiness."[142]

This was, however, a misunderstanding of Einhorn's thinking, who held that the particular covenantal relationship between the Jewish people and God would end in the messianic future. He did however put even more emphasis on the particular role of the *am ha-kohanim*, the "priestly people", in human history than did Hirsch, insisting strictly on the preservation of Judaism's distinctiveness and separateness. We are thus confronted with the paradox that Einhorn's radical messianic universalism was, regarding the present, dependent on a strong par-

---

141 David Einhorn, "Noch ein Wort über gemischte Ehen", The Jewish Times 1, 48 (1869/70), 10–13, here 11.
142 Samuel Hirsch, "Der Nagel zum Sarge der winzigen jüdischen Race", The Jewish Times 1, 47 (1869/70), 10–11, here 11.

ticularistic element,[143] whereas Hirsch, who strongly accentuated Judaism's distinctive identity also for the messianic age, was able to allow for a more liberal practice regarding the relationship to non-Jews in the present.

A late echo of this controversy on mixed marriage can be heard in 1880, after Einhorn's death,[144] when Kaufmann Kohler (1843–1926), Einhorn's son-in-law and successor as rabbi of the New York congregation Beth-El, publicly denounced Hirsch's readiness to give mixed marriages his blessing, accusing him of encouraging indifferentism.[145] Hirsch responded polemically by maintaining that Kohler, seduced by his anxiety regarding American Jewry's lack of identity, resorted to the inefficient means of "excommunication" rather than trusting in Reform Judaism's persuasive power. In his Dessau period, Hirsch had given priority to the fight against indifferentism and apostasy. In America, where the general atmosphere of secularization and materialism rather than the pressure resulting from the struggle for emancipation was responsible for religious indifference, he emphasized the need to recapture the hearts of those alienated from Judaism cautiously by integrating them into the community and presenting them with the model of a convincing religious life. Instead of forcing a non-Jewish partner to formally convert by threatening to deny him or her the consecration of the mixed marriage, rabbis should believe in the "power of conviction" and hope that at some point they would join the Jewish congregation voluntarily and without pressure.[146] The idea that Jews had to truly fulfill their mission as God's priestly people in order to be acknowledged as a valuable element of modern culture remained a central element of Hirsch's thinking throughout his life. The American experience apparently caused a certain shift from the moral demand to practice a Jewish life to the belief in the irresistible power of this mission and the miracle of Judaism's survival in history – a miracle that neither indifferentism nor the increasing number of mixed marriages could ever jeopardize:

---

143 For Einhorn's theology of history, see Wiese, "Samuel Holdheim's 'Most Powerful Comrade in Conviction'", 344–373.
144 See Hirsch's conciliatory eulogy at the funeral of Einhorn, who was the father-in-law of his son Emil G. Hirsch: Samuel Hirsch, *Rev. Dr. David Einhorn, Rabbiner der Beth-El Gemeinde, New York. Gedächtniss-Rede, gehalten vor seinem Sarge in der Synagoge obiger Gemeinde, den 6ten November 1879, und dem Inhalte nach wiederholt, den 8. November, 1879 in der Keneseth Israel Synagoge in Philadelphia* (Philadelphia: Congregation Keneseth Israel, 1879).
145 Kaufmann Kohler, "Über Mischehen. Ein Gutachten", Der Zeitgeist 1 (1880), 76–78, 180–182. As an immediate response, see Samuel Hirsch, "Offenes Sendschreiben an Herrn Dr. K. Kohler", Der Zeitgeist 1 (1880), 202–203.
146 Samuel Hirsch, *"Unerhörte Pilpulistik". Offenes Sendschreiben an Rev. Dr. K. Kohler, Rabbiner der Beth-El Gemeinde in New York* (Philadelphia: s.n., 1880), 6–7.

It is this miracle that we could neither be annihilated nor spiritually oppressed; that all the nations with their indomitable hatred and their boundless fanaticism were against us; that also – and this is not due to our strength, but to God's power – God has entrusted us with a great mission. Now, who is more faithful, Herr Dr. [Kohler]? I who, inspired by this strong faith in Israel's mission, does not fear anything that could compromise this mission? I, who, like the ancients, considers the children of Jewish mothers as Jews and thus am prepared to open the doors of our religious schools and our synagogues to them? Or you, who would like to excommunicate them – since this is what denying the consecration of such marriages amounts to – because you are shivering in fear of this mission?[147]

Conclusions: On the Significance and Relevance of Hirsch's Religious Philosophy

The intellectual representatives of the European and American radical Reform movement went to great lengths in attempting to refute anti-Jewish prejudice and the denigration of Judaism amongst contemporary non-Jewish theologians, historians, and philosophers. The strength of their efforts lies in what historian Shulamit Volkov has described as the "invention of a tradition", i.e. the philosophical-ethical reinterpretation of crucial elements of Jewish tradition in support of demands for recognition as a legitimate religious and cultural force of the modern era.[148] Samuel Hirsch's work was part of a rebellious attempt to undermine those Christian-inspired verdicts on Judaism shaped by the biased concept of "Jewish particularism" versus "Christian universalism" as well as the traditional Christian cultural sense of superiority, including its antisemitic implications, i.e. those referring to Judaism's alleged "distinctive identity" and "conceit of chosenness" (*Erwählungsdünkel*). By way of contrast, the Jewish philosopher presented a self-conscious interpretation of Judaism as an equal if not superior universalistic religion with a human messianic mission, thereby justifying claims to a position of equal status in a pluralistic culture. This strategy was, in general, characteristic of liberal Judaism in Germany and found its impressive continuation in the history of *Wissenschaft des Judentums* well into the twentieth century.

As Amos Funkenstein has suggested in his reflections on Jewish apologetics, there is a risk to this kind of "counterhistory" for the construction of identity. For it tends to be highly dependent on the (negative) premises held by the intellec-

---

147 Ibid., 8–9.
148 Shulamit Volkov, "Inventing Jewish Tradition: On the Formation of Modern Jewish Culture", Jewish Studies at the Central European University 3 (2002–2003), 211–227.

tual, religious or cultural opponent.[149] It was exceptionally difficult, particularly in nineteenth-century Germany, to bluntly assert the right to religious and cultural particularity in a pluralistic society given the extreme cultural reservations expressed about Judaism's continued right to existence in modern European culture and society. Hirsch's interpretation of Judaism frequently reveals an internalization of the dominating negative conceptualization of "particularism". Moreover, the ensuing compulsion to strongly emphasize Judaism's universalism threatened to push the specific character of the experience of Jewish religiosity along with its identifiable forms into the background, resulting in an (at least theoretical) dissolution of Judaism into a universal, ethical, human religion.[150]

The Jewish contemporary intellectual who most polemically pointed to this dilemma was the socialist and proto-Zionist thinker Moses Hess (1812–1875), with whom Hirsch had maintained cordial relations since their time together as students in Bonn. It was Hirsch's book *Die Humanität als Religion* that prompted Hess in *Rome and Jerusalem* (1862) to present his "friend Hirsch from Luxembourg" – although he considered him to be the best representative of contemporary Reform Judaism – as a paradigmatic case of what he perceived as the latter's complete ideological failure. Hirsch's attempt to "make use of Freemasonry in order to fuse the various historical traditions", was, from Hess's point of view, just an extreme expression of the inner tendency of the Reform movement in general to downplay historical particularity and difference for the sake of emancipation. They thereby reduced Judaism to a rationalistic construct, and extinguished all traces of national identity, ignoring the Germans' refusal to allow the Jews to forget their Jewishness.[151] The reformers, he maintained, including Hirsch, were "spiritual dwarfs" – whose concept of Judaism's religious mission in the Diaspora along with the abandonment of the notion of a Jewish people and a Jewish national rebirth – were inevitably bringing about the loss of Jewish distinctiveness, sucking out "the last reminders of Judaism" and leaving "only the shadow of a neo-Christian and neo-Jewish skeleton".[152] Especially their understanding of Judaism's role as the custodian of "ethical monotheism" was a

---

149 Amos Funkenstein, *Perceptions of Jewish History* (Berkeley, CA: University of California Press, 1993), 48.
150 The extreme consequences of this tendency can be seen in the *Society for Ethical Culture* that was initiated by Felix Adler (1851–1933); see Benny Kraut, *From Reform Judaism to Ethical Culture: The Religious Evolution of Felix Adler* (Cincinnati, OH: Hebrew Union College Press, 1979); for the response of the radical reformers, see Meyer, *Response to Modernity*, 265–266.
151 Moses Hess, *Rom und Jerusalem, die letzte Nationalitätenfrage: Briefe und Noten* (Leipzig: Eduard Wengler, 1862), 64.
152 Ibid., 47–48.

pathetic and vulgar, even "nihilistic" imitation of a rationalistic version of Christianity with no future whatsoever.[153]

Hirsch, in an unpublished review of *Rome and Jerusalem*, responded in kind, comparing Hess's rejection of assimilation to Bruno Bauer's antisemitic attack against Jewish integration into European society, ridiculing the primary role Hess gave to the concept of race, and asserting the superiority of his own – spiritual – nationalism.[154] Hess's critique, he argued, was based on sheer ignorance regarding the Reform movement. Otherwise, he would have understood that, rather than implying a lack of Jewish identity, his – Hirsch's – Masonic inclinations were not at all a call for Jews to join Masonic lodges and Freemasonry, but to appeal to the lodges, and to Christianity itself to embrace their essentially Jewish character. In a later article published in the *Archives israélites* in 1864, Hirsch emphasized that Hess was utterly wrong in suggesting that German Reform rabbis wanted to imitate the Church as a means of integration.[155] Hess responded by clarifying that his real argument was actually a different one: By converting the ancient, national, humanitarian forces of Judaism into a "second, rational Christianity", he argued, the Reform movement was bound to become a passing phenomenon that would suffer the same fate as post-Enlightenment Christianity – disintegration and irrelevance. Judaism's real mission, he claimed in 1865 in his "Letters on Israel's Mission in the History of Humankind", would have to be the rejuvenation of the national-humanitarian nature of Jewish historical religion, which would then also facilitate a renewal of Christianity as well as a universal socialist redemption.[156]

The skirmish between Hess and Hirsch reveals both thinkers as representatives of rather different concepts of a Jewish universalistic mission in the modern period as well as of the relationship between Judaism and Christianity. To a much greater extent than Hirsch, Hess seems to have had a strongly ambivalent and inconsistent relationship toward religion in general. In his diaries of 1837 the young Spinozist expressed his aspiration to become the "Napoleon of religion",

---

153 Ibid., 51–52.
154 See Gershon Greenberg, "The Reformers' First Attack upon Hess' Rome and Jerusalem: An Unpublished Manuscript of Samuel Hirsch", Jewish Social Studies 35 (1973), 175–197.
155 Samuel Hirsch, "La Verité du Dieu-Un et la Mission d'Israel", Archives israélites 26 (1864), 194–200.
156 Moses Hess, "Briefe über Israels Mission in der Geschichte der Menschheit", in idem, *Jüdische Schriften*, ed. and intr. Theodor Zlocisti (Berlin: Lamm, 1905), 16–49; see idem, "Noch ein Wort über meine Missionsauffassung", ibid., 68–69.

implying that he wished to play a revolutionary role in regenerating religion.[157] He appears to have oscillated between agnosticism and secularizing appropriations of religious concepts in what Shulamit Volkov has identified as a lifelong personal struggle with the meaning of his faith and religious identity.[158] The alienation from religious faith did not prevent him, however, from embracing – in his *Die heilige Geschichte der Menschheit* (1837) – an eschatological view of history strongly influenced by Christian chiliastic concepts. In later works he argues for the liberation of humankind not only from material but also from spiritual servitude – an attitude that implied a scathing critique of both Judaism and Christianity – before recapturing some of his earlier religious inclinations.

Characteristically, the early Hess's attitude toward Judaism fluctuated greatly. Influenced by the images and symbols drawn from the Hebrew Bible and the history of the Jews, Hess presented a narrative in which the Jews were given a prominent role, "only to be dismissed as embodying a preliminary stage superseded by Christianity", as Isaiah Berlin notes. It is the narrative of a chosen people rendered obsolete by Christianity, which, paradoxically, has not yet played out its role because the new Jerusalem will, after all, retain some specific Jewish traits.[159] Shlomo Avineri characterizes Hess's *Die Heilige Geschichte der Menschheit* as "an ambitious attempt to propose a socialist synthesis of Judaism and Christianity mediated through Spinoza's philosophy". Avineri convincingly interprets the book as the expression of the "inner *Zerrissenheit* of a first-generation emancipated Jewish intellectual who was looking for room for himself in the new, European order, yet who was highly reluctant to adopt even the secularized Christian verdict over Judaism".[160] Hess's *Die europäische Triarchie* (1841) displays an even greater ambivalence. He distinguishes between the purely tribal God of the Jews and the universal God of Christianity and then adopts the language of contemporary Christian verdicts when ascribing to Judaism a mere

---

157 "Wenn ich meine Berufe glücklich erfüllen werde, wird man mich den Napoleon der Religion nennen." Moses Hess, "Notiz- und Tagebücher 1837", in Wolfgang Mönke, *Neue Quellen zur Heß-Forschung. Mit Auszügen aus einem Tagebuch, aus Manuskripten und Briefen aus der Korrespondenz mit Marx, Engels, Weitling, Ewerbeck, u.a* (Berlin: Akademie-Verlag, 1964), 41.
158 Shulamit Volkov, "Moses Hess: Problems of Religion and Faith", Zionism 3 (1981), 1–15. Cf. Philipp Lenhard, "Ein lebendiger Organismus: Der jüdische Hegelianismus", in idem, *Volk oder Religion? Die Entstehung moderner jüdischer Ethnizität in Frankreich und Deutschland 1782–1848*, Religiöse Kulturen im Europa der Neuzeit, vol. 4 (Göttingen: Vandenhoeck & Ruprecht, 2016), 283–316, for Hess 289–303.
159 Isaiah Berlin, "The Life and Origins of Moses Hess", in Philipp Rief, ed., *On Intellectuals: Theoretical Studies, Cases Studies* (Garden City, NY: Doubleday, 1966), 125–166.
160 Shlomo Avineri, *Moses Hess: Prophet of Communism and Zionism* (New York: NYU Press, 1985), 22, 26.

ghostly presence, "unable either to die or to come to life", a mere skeleton or fossil, doomed to disappear by assimilation.[161]

Hess's views on Christianity, however, were no less blunt. Jesus and Christianity signify the universalistic stage of human history and are superior to Judaism. However, in his pamphlet *Über das Geldwesen* (1845), the socialist thinker emphasized that the Christian religion had experienced a dramatic decline in the modern period, mainly due to its focus on the individual soul, its divorce from politics and the profane, as well as its narrow contemplation of an otherworldly salvation.[162] Christianity tends to abandon real life and thus is to be blamed, to a much higher degree than Judaism, for its conservative role in modern capitalist society and for legitimizing social exploitation and alienation.[163] In *Rome and Jerusalem* (1862), finally, Hess claimed that Judaism, with its non-transcendental outlook, its fundamentally social democratic Mosaic Code and its political messianism, had, in contrast to Christianity, the true potential to build the foundation for a socialist society.[164] Striking is Hess's indication that Judaism rather than Christianity could, indeed, turn out to be the religion of the future. Being a national culture instead of a mere religion of personal salvation, it may play a creative role, while Christianity might be doomed to disappear in a secular, socialist society. This is an intriguing polemical inversion of the typical Protestant insistence on Christian universalism versus Jewish particularism: It may well be, Hess argues, that Judaism, with its particularistic traits, is better equipped to survive and become the instrument of a universal transformation of humankind than is Christianity with its universalistic claim, which could well be rendered irrelevant.[165]

Despite the mutual polemics between Hirsch and Hess, they shared at least one characteristic element when it came to defining the future relationship between Judaism and Christianity, namely a strong determination to refute Christianity's claim to superiority over Judaism. This was coupled with a vision of a future reconciliation between the two religions based on a Jewish acknowledgement of

---

161 Moses Hess, "Die europäische Triarchie", in Wolfgang Mönke, ed., *Moses Hess. Philosophische und sozialistische Schriften, 1837–1850. Eine Auswahl* (Vaduz: Topos Verlag, 1980, 2nd edition), 75–168, here 98.
162 Moses Hess, "Über das Geldwesen", in Mönke, *Moses Hess*, 329–347, here 331, 342–343.
163 Ibid., 345.
164 Hess, *Rom und Jerusalem*, 48–56.
165 Ibid., 48. For a perceptive discussion of Hess's views on Judaism, Christianity, and materialism and how these relate to the philosophies of Spinoza, Hegel and the Young Hegelians, see Sven-Erik Rose, "Moses Hess: Beyond the Politics of Self-Possession", in idem, *Jewish Philosophical Politics in German, 1789–1848* (Waltham, Mass.: Brandeis University Press, 2014), 241–271.

Christianity's historical achievements as well as on a Christian rediscovery of its originally Jewish essence, and finally the hope that this process would have creative universal consequences for humankind's future. We have seen that Hirsch attributed Christianity an important world-historical mission, insisting, however, that Jesus, if understood correctly, i.e., on Jewish terms, should remind contemporary Christianity of the need to assume responsibility for this world, instead of subscribing to an otherworldly ideal of personal salvation. This is, of course, parallel to Hess's critique of Christianity's spiritualistic individualism and his insistence on the universal political dimension of messianism. Historian Heinrich Graetz (1817–1891) offered Hess a new rationale for minimizing the dichotomy between Judaism and Christianity: "By depicting the origins of Christianity as part of the history of Israel", Hess wrote in *Rome and Jerusalem*, "Graetz has proven that a Jew devoted to the religion of his fathers can acknowledge the truth found in Christianity",[166] without reducing Judaism to a vulgar cosmopolitanism or denying its distinctive character. Hess emphasized his conviction that "Christianity was a step further on the road toward humanity, termed by the Jewish Prophets as the messianic age", but also added that he had never believed "that Christianity is more than a mere episode in the sacred history of humanity".[167] Humankind strives for a form of redemption, which Christianity is ultimately incapable of supplying, and it is the Amsterdam Jew Spinoza who marked a new epoch in which Christian spiritualistic mysticism would be overcome.[168]

Like Hirsch, Hess maintained that Christianity had a future in modernity only if it learned to embrace its inherent Jewish origins, and it could only do so if the Jewish people fulfilled their mission. In Hirsch's case, this is the universalistic, exilic mission of a priestly people embodying the truth of ethical monotheism. For Hess, as he wrote in his *Letters on Israel's Mission in the History of Humankind*, the mission depends on the "national rebirth of the Hebrew people" (*nationale Wiedergeburt des Hebräervolkes*).[169] Hess calls for a "new Christianity", a Christianity that re-discovers its rootedness in its original soil. If Christianity wanted to meet the moral and religious needs of the future, it had to go back to its Jewish sources. Any other possible reform of Christianity would clearly fail:

> You may reform Christianity as much as you like. You may cleanse it from superstition; transform it into Protestantism, rationalism, or philosophy. You may write critical or apologetic accounts of the Life of Jesus; you may reduce Jesus' divinity to his human nature. You

---

166 Ibid., 134–135.
167 Ibid., 159.
168 Ibid., 28.
169 Hess, "Briefe über Israels Mission in der Geschichte der Menschheit", 37.

may even, if you so dare, proceed with [Ludwig] Feuerbach and transform Christianity into anthropology, religion into ethics. You will thus uncover the essence of Christianity, you will render it profane, but despite all efforts you will not have turned it into a religion that would be capable of meeting the needs of modern society.[170]

"Old Christianity", Hess continued, being the very opposite of the social religion needed by the modern nations, would never be capable of leading man back into the solidarity of family, fatherland, and human society, "unless it regains its roots in Judaism, in the soil from which it originated". Without turning back to Judaism, Hess claims, Christianity was not qualified to become a "religion of modern humankind".[171] The parallel to Hirsch is obvious: Christianity's future and its potential to become a modern, humane, and socially progressive religion are indissolubly linked to its inherent Jewishness. However, Judaism, too, must be modernized and rejuvenated, and here lies the crucial difference between the two thinkers: From Hess's point of view, Judaism can achieve this rejuvenation only by recovering its historical and national resources, not from an imitation of dogmatic or philosophical reforms of Christianity. Judaism, Hess was convinced, could help humankind regain its lost faith, since it possessed "the mystery, given by Providence, of that human era, that messianic era which has begun with the French Revolution, whose seeds, however, must be traced back to the Hebrew people. But how can the modern nations get access to this mystery if the nation that is supposed to provide that access, is not involved as a nation in the process of history?"[172]

Whether or not Hess did justice to Hirsch, is probably a matter of perspective. Hess's intellectual path led him to embrace a national interpretation of the Jewish mission. Therefore, he was certainly not inclined to appreciate the dilemma confronting reformers such as Hirsch within the context of contemporary voices that identified "Jewish particularism" as an obstacle to emancipation. Nor would he have conceded that their approach was one of several legitimate responses to that dilemma. Rather, he bluntly and unsparingly uncovered its essential weakness, maintaining that Hirsch's vision of a universalist mission of a modern Jewish religion – divested of its national elements – as the crucial criterion of Jewish identity was disastrous. It was a futile attempt to turn Judaism into a Protestant-inspired rationalistic construct, developed for the sake of an illusory integration into European culture and society and doomed to vanish in the same abyss of irrelevance and disintegration as contemporary Christianity.

---

170 Ibid., 38.
171 Ibid.
172 Ibid., 40.

With this diagnosis, Hess indeed identified one of the crucial dilemmas encountered by many Reform thinkers, and his critique certainly helps to develop a better sense of the problems inherent in Hirsch's approach. However, it appears that Hess tends to overlook the great intellectual strength and dignity inherent in Reform philosophies such as those presented by Samuel Hirsch. Perhaps this is due to a familiarity solely with Hirsch's *Die Humanität als Religion.* In any event the sources make no mention of either Hirsch's *Religionsphilosophie* with its critical re-reading of Hegel or his response to Bruno Bauer.

Hess's polemical characterization of Hirsch's theory of a Jewish messianic mission in terms of an adoption of modern liberal Protestant values and concepts is apt: "Protestantization" is clearly one aspect of the liberal-Jewish response to the contemporary intellectual atmosphere, at least in Germany. On the other hand, there are elements in Hirsch's thinking demonstrating that he was determined to resist the pressure to abandon elements of Jewish identity that were sources of separation. This included his strong emphasis on the chosenness of the Jewish people as well as on the polarity of universal and particular elements within the Jewish religion, including Judaism's continuing distinctiveness even in the messianic future. With this, Hirsch's Reform philosophy offered an instrument both for the refutation of Christian claims of superiority and for limiting its own inner tendency to over-emphasize the element of universalism. What Hess's scathing critique of the Reform underestimated, one could argue, is the intellectual fortitude involved in the appropriation of certain elements of the dominant Protestant culture while lending them a distinctively Jewish accent by making them the basis of the concept of Judaism's universal prophetic and messianic mission in exile. This may very well be a legitimate alternative to his own nationalist-inspired approach – at least within the specific historical time and context.

Overall, the influence of Hirsch's philosophy was, despite a variety of interesting parallels in Franz Rosenzweig's concept of history, broadly limited to the nineteenth century. He quickly faded from memory in Germany, mainly because of radical Reform's loss of relevance and the comparatively conservative character of the German Reform movement.[173] However, well past his death on May 14,

---

[173] See Heymann Steinthal, "Ein jüdischer Religionsphilosoph unseres Jahrhunderts", Allgemeine Zeitung des Judenthums 59, 10 (1895), 126–128; 59, 11 (1895), 138–140. According to Steinthal, none of the Jewish religious philosophers of the nineteenth century had exerted a significant influence: "The philosopher reaches the people only with great difficulty, and the scholars, including the rabbis, have been [...] historians [...]. And this is the case today even more than in the previous generation, since in the second half of our century philosophy in Germany is in

1889, he was considered one of the pioneers of the radical Reform movement in the United States, whose ideological profile, as expressed in the Pittsburgh Platform (1885), he had strongly influenced. The German-born American Rabbi Kaufmann Kohler acclaimed him in a eulogy as a "prince" and "pioneer in the realm of the spirit", and one of the "most unbending and principled standard-bearers of Reform". Hirsch had contributed to "lifting Judaism up out of the confines of the Jewish ghetto (*Judengasse*), out of its oriental shroud and ritual overgrowth, up into the heights of modern culture, into one of the great world religions striving to advance the ideal of humanity".[174] On a par with major reformers such as Holdheim, Einhorn and Geiger, Hirsch had fostered the reconciliation of Judaism and Christianity, proved that "Judaism, scorned by Master Hegel himself", was a superior religion of humanity and thus become "Judaism's most radical herald of progress on American soil. [...] He did not seek popular favor; he knew no fear of man. As with the great prophets he scorned popularity". Kohler's eulogy culminated with the words: "light of Israel, firm pillar of progress, sparkling hammer of God."[175] Hirsch, however, was a figure of transition from German to American Judaism and a member of a very distinctive generation of émigré intellectuals. So too the "classical period" of this variant of Radical Reform, dominated in subsequent decades by Kaufmann Kohler and Hirsch's son, the Chicago Rabbi Emil G. Hirsch (1851–1923), turned out to be a phenomenon of transition even in America. On the occasion of the centenary of Hirsch's birth in 1915, when the influence of Radical Reform was drawing to a close and new tendencies, including Zionist thinking, started to gain ground among American Jews, Samuel Hirsch was praised once again in a special issue of the journal *Reform Advocate*. However, he was clearly no longer praised as a relevant voice within contemporary debates but rather as a historical figure, a representative of an influential, albeit past form of religious philosophy that had its legitimate place in the nineteenth century but no longer sufficed for the intellectual challenges of the present.[176]

---

such decline in general." However, he personally had been strongly shaped by Hirsch's thinking, as the latter had provided him the intellectual armor for his fight against Hegel; see ibid., 127.

174 Kaufmann Kohler, "Leichenrede für Dr. Samuel Hirsch gehalten von Dr. K. Kohler, Rabbiner der Beth El Gemeinde, New York. Chicago, 17. Mai 1889", in *In Memory of Dr. Samuel Hirsch*, 18–22, here 18–19.

175 Ibid., 20–22; and see the other eulogies in that same commemorative book, e.g. the "Gedächtnisrede" written by Bernhard Felsenthal (1822–1908); ibid., 23–25.

176 See the special issue of the Reform Advocate, May 29, 1915 (with contributions, for instance, by Emil G. Hirsch, Kaufmann Kohler, Joseph Krauskopf und Max Landsberg); and see Maurice Lefkovits, *Samuel Hirsch* (New York: Central Conference of American Rabbis, 1915); Gerson B. Levi, *Samuel Hirsch: Address at Tempel Keneseth Israel, Philadelphia, at the Celebration of the Centenary of the Rev. Dr. Samuel Hirsch, November 7, 1915* (Cincinnati, OH: n.p., 1916/17).

In Germany two classical presentations of Jewish thought published in 1933, Max Wiener's *Jüdische Religion im Zeitalter der Emanzipation* and Julius Guttmann's *Die Philosophie des Judentums*, devoted a brief chapter to Hirsch, tellingly focusing completely on the thoughts he had expressed in his *Religionsphilosophie* in Germany in 1842.[177] Ignoring his subsequent intellectual development, they overlooked important elements of the transnational dimensions and influence of Hirsch's philosophy. Yet they were probably right in emphasizing that his interpretation of Judaism developed in the 1840s had seminal importance both for his ensuing work and for the emergence of Radical Reform in Europe and the United States. During the few years of his rabbinate in Dessau, Hirsch had formulated the central lines of thought, which, despite the later metamorphoses of his philosophy in Luxembourg and Philadelphia, embody the inner continuity and coherence of his philosophy and reform activities. The analysis of his intellectual path allows us to discern a decisive moment of the religious and intellectual development of a branch of the Jewish Reform Movement during the first half of the nineteenth century. Particularly the lesser-known sermons held in Dessau provide insight into his attempt to convince a specific congregation of his own theological, philosophical, and political interpretation of the challenges Judaism was exposed to during the period of emancipation. They represent a crucial chapter of the religious and intellectual development of the Jewish Reform movement during the first half of the nineteenth century that first remained limited to German Jewry but, at a later stage and under very different social and political circumstances, came into its own and left its imprint on American Jewish culture.

Today, Samuel Hirsch seems to be widely forgotten, even though there are at least two crucial dimensions to his intellectual work as a religious philosopher that justify continuing attention. Firstly, his path from Dessau to Philadelphia is a most interesting mirror of a crucial moment in the process of Jewish modernization, i.e. the transnational history of the radical Reform movement and its gradual shifting from Germany to the *goldene medine* across the Atlantic, where it encountered new and unprecedented challenges. Secondly, and even more importantly, at least in philosophical terms, there are several aspects of the themes negotiated by Hirsch that are still relevant today. These include questions concerning: the modernization of religious tradition during an era of increasing secularization; the social and cultural integration of minorities and

---

[177] A comprehensive intellectual biography of the philosopher within the context of the history of radical Reform and the emigration of German-Jewish intellectuals to America that would explore his thinking in more detail remains an important *desideratum* of German-Jewish historiography.

the concomitant preservation and reformulation of tradition; and interreligious encounter, conflict, and dialogue in a pluralistic society and culture.

Part II: Hegelian and Defender of the Faith: The Fundamentals of Samuel Hirsch's Philosophy

Gershon Greenberg
Samuel Hirsch in Dessau (June 1838 – June 1843). Freedom, Emancipation and the Christian State

The emancipation of Jews in western Europe opened uncharted territory for intellectual activity – bordered on one side by the previously boundaried autonomously-structured Jewish society and on the other by exclusively Christian society. The space provided room for the development of *Judentumswissenschaft* and historicism. It also created a stage for new and original departure points for systematic Jewish thought. One such departure point was the principle of freedom, as developed by Samuel Hirsch (1815–1889) in Dessau as grounding for his Jewish religious philosophical effort. The principle emerged out of the correlation between God as the absolute ground of freedom, and the unique (to the created world) "I" consciousness of man. It became activated within history's matrix through Abraham, and it was inherited by the people of Israel, where it stood as antithetical to the principles of religions of nature. Christianity served to extend Israel's trait of freedom to the rest of the world, and to actualize potential freedom until it became absolute in history.

The identification of freedom as the principle of Judaism remained throughout Hirsch's life. After he settled in America, he wrote in 1869 that Judaism could claim to be the only developing religion in the world because of its complete devotion to freedom. Judaism's very essence was freedom, its one-thousand-year struggle with paganism was a struggle against un-freedom. With a general reference to Jean-Jacques Rousseau, he said that this freedom was natural, internal, independent of outside influences. It was a divine law for the human spirit to find truth and justice within itself, to be its own master, to follow reason, i.e., to be free.[1]

---

[1] Samuel Hirsch, "Freiheit und Judenthum", Jewish Times 1, 3 (19 March 1869), ii-iv. See also Samuel Hirsch, *Rev. Dr. David Einhorn: Gedächtniss-Rede, gehalten vor seinem Sarge den 6ten November 1879* (Philadelphia: Emil Hirsch, 1879).

Psychological Freedom

Hirsch established freedom as the basis for Judaism during his Dessau years. He alluded to the principle in the foreword to his very first published address, a 17 June 1838 bar mitzvah sermon in Dessau arranged for him by his mentor Leopold Zunz (1794–1866). He complained that Jewish responses to the *Zeitgeist* and the actualizing of *Zeitbildung*, i.e., inner character in contemporary terms, were materialistic, rather than idealistic, in character. The most money that could be raised for the Jewish theological faculty in Germany proposed by Ludwig Philippson, for example, was a mere 7,000 *Reichsthaler* out of a needed 100,000.[2] To respond properly to the demands of the post-emancipation environment, a central principle was required. This did not mean creating a new Jewish religion, rather, providing an essential starting point for Judaism's self-understanding, addressing Jewish-Christian relations as well as suggesting a basis for reconciling old and new Judaism. As examples of unsatisfactory approaches then available, he referred to Samson Raphael Hirsch and Salomon Ludwig Steinheim. Samson Raphael Hirsch's reliance on rabbinical principles of unconditional belief and obedience was wanting when it came to the role of reason. Steinheim's shibboleth was that the knowledge communicated by God directly contradicted reason. But he arrived at it empirically, pointing out that no philosophical system had developed the central doctrines of monotheism, freedom and *creatio ex nihilo* out of itself, contradicting himself; and these doctrines were no different than those of Christian dogma. Authentic revelation, for Samuel Hirsch, meant God's providing truths to the unmediated consciousness of the collective people of Israel through an objective historical event. Towards this end, he said, he was preparing a scholarly work to establish a theological basis for the idea.[3] As he wrote to Zunz

---

[2] David Sorkin identifies *Bildung* as a process of innate self-development in terms of forms inherent to the individual. David Sorkin, *The Transformation of German Jewry, 1780–1840* (Detroit: Wayne State University Press, 1987), 15. For Hirsch, freedom and *Bildung* were intertwined. Thus, he praised Christian Leopold Friedrich Franz, Duke of Dessau, for enhancing both freedom and *Bildung* by instilling religion into the state. Samuel Hirsch, *Friede, Freiheit und Einheit. Sechs Predigten gehalten in der Synagoge zu Dessau* (Dessau: Hermann Neubürger, 1839), 3, 11, 12, 17.
[3] On the bar mitzvah sermon in Dessau see Michael A. Meyer and Michael Brenner, eds., *German-Jewish History in Modern Times*, vol. 2 (New York: Columbia University, 1996), 122. On Philippson's October 1837 proposal, see Alfred Jospe, Eva Jospe, and Raphael Jospe, eds., *To Leave Your Mark: Selections from the Writings of Alfred Jospe* (New York: KTAV, 2000), 186. On Zunz and Hirsch see Emil Hirsch, "My Father and Teacher", The Reform Advocate (29 May 1915), 497–503. Samuel Hirsch, "Vorwort", in *Was ist Judenthum und was dessen Verhältniss zu andern Religionen? Predigt zur Einsegnungsfeier seiner beiden Zöglinge Theodor und Oskar Heymann gehalten am 17 Juni 1838* (Berlin: Carl Heymann, 1838), 3–10.

in Berlin on 16 April 1841, this was his *Die Religionsphilosophie der Juden* – a "philosophical presentation of a system of Jewish theology".⁴ Its starting point was freedom.

Die Religionsphilosophie der Juden began with a probe into freedom as the distinctive characteristic of the human being. It emerged as the child stopped referring to itself in the third person and began to use the term "I". "I" separated the child out of world-consciousness, where it was part of the natural world, and initiated self-consciousness. The "I" declaration, the first moment of freedom, initially responded to outside conditions. It was abstract, empty of content and application, and determined by outside conditions. As such it was together free and unfree. This contradictory condition became transcended, as the abstract, formal expression of freedom began to apply itself to the content of nature surrounding it and the (Hegelian) "subject" found itself in the "object", drawing the object into consciousness. Innermost being integrated with what was outside; and the person's actions became its own. As the human being utilized nature, objectifying itself and impressing its innermost thoughts upon the surroundings, potential freedom became actualized, concrete and real. The self-objectification involved the internal spirit's confronting a choice between spiritualizing nature or naturalizing the spirit. As nature became spiritualized and the internal spirit advanced, freedom developed. When this did not take place, there was sin. In turn, the concretization of freedom, the actualizing of its potential in spiritual terms, the process of becoming, was only possible because actual freedom had absolute existence. There was an ever-present spiritual grounding, a Being of freedom – namely God. Through freedom, Hirsch moved from the existential, anthropological plane, to an essential, theological one.⁵

---

4 Hirsch sent the manuscript of his *Die Religionsphilosophie der Juden* to Zunz between November and December 1841 in parts. Hirsch's relationship to Zunz is a separate desideratum. His attacks against Bruno Bauer (infra) were in the form of letters to Zunz. Included in his correspondence were complaints about *Schutzjuden* status and about Jews who were suppressing their spiritual needs for the sake of employment. Jewish National University Library mss. division 40792-G14. I am grateful to my colleague Andrea Tschemplik for transcribing the Gothic texts of the Hirsch-Zunz correspondence. According to his son Emil, Hirsch was denied rabbinical appointment in Dessau because of his criticism of *Schutzjuden*. Emil Hirsch, "My Father and Teacher", 498. Samuel Hirsch, *Die Religionsphilosophie der Juden oder das Prinzip der jüdischen Religionsanschauung und sein Verhältniß zum Heidenthum, Christenthum und zur absoluten Philosophie dargestellt und mit den erläuterten Beweisstellen aus der heiligen Schrift, den Talmudim und Midraschim versehen* (Leipzig: Heinrich Hunger 1842; reprint Hildesheim, Zurich, and New York: Olms, 1986). Hereafter referred to as *Die Religionsphilosophie*.
5 Hirsch, *Die Religionsphilosophie*, 8–14, 25–30, 35–36, 38–42, 48–49. Bruno Bauer also identified God as a free, self-referential subjectivity; see Bruno Bauer, *Kritik der Geschichte der Offenbarung: Die Religion des alten Testaments*, vol. 1 (Berlin: Dümmler, 1838), 148. On theology and anthropology see further Samuel Hirsch, *Das Judenthum, der christliche Staat und die moderne*

Freedom in History

Abraham

As detailed in *Die Religionsphilosophie der Juden*, the driving force in Hirsch's historiosophy was the ongoing correlation between the divine ground of freedom and the human actualization of potential freedom. He used the framework of the Protestant theologian Karl Immanuel Nitzsch, his professor at the University of Bonn, which distinguished between passive (pagan or "false") religion and active ("true") religion. In the former, external nature was venerated and consciousness of God was imposed from without. Feelings for divinity were developed in a non-conscious manner and unfolded with necessity. In active religion, God, along with His revelation, were perceived as coming from outside and they were processed by human consciousness – with consciousness also revealing the pre-conscious presence of divinity in the perceiver. While in passive religions the adherents were too indolent to grasp themselves in truth, or to respond actively to the outside experience while mind/spirit remained unreconciled with nature, active religion involved self-consciousness, active response,[6] and reconciliation of mind/spirit with nature.

God the creator, as free, awaited the moment for man to become a free creator, to master the inclinations of nature and to appropriate nature for spirit in such a way as to impact historical development. That is, to turn from passive to active religiosity. This occurred with Abraham who, the rabbinic sages said, "transformed the evil desire within him into good" (yBer 9:24). As Hirsch articulated when he later returned from Luxembourg to deliver a sermon in Samuel Holdheim's synagogue in Schwerin, Abraham, by himself, proclaimed the freedom of the human being and that the human being was called upon to master the earth and have spirit freely administer the flesh. Abraham was the first to release himself from the control of nature's laws of necessity and from the assumption that the human being was a creature of nature.[7] In *Die Religionsphilosophie*

Kritik: Briefe zur Beleuchtung der Judenfrage von Bruno Bauer (Leipzig: Heinrich Hunger, 1843), 33; and idem, *Die Humanität als Religion in Vorträgen, gehalten in der Loge zu Luxemburg* (Trier: C. Troschel, 1854), 1.

6 Karl Immanuel Nitzsch, *System der christlichen Lehre* (Bonn: Adolph Marcus, 1851), 33–34. Hirsch, *Die Religionsphilosophie*, xxx.

7 Hirsch, *op. cit.*, 456. Samuel Hirsch, *Der rechte Kampf für die Wahrheit: Gast-Predigt in der Synagoge zu Schwerin in Mecklenburg gehalten den 31 October 1846* (Schwerin: Kürschner, 1847).

der Juden Hirsch described in detail how Abraham passed through three dialectical stages: Extensive religiosity (thesis), intensive religiosity (anti-thesis) and true, comprehensive religiosity (synthesis). The first took place when Abraham was selected by God to bring the world to Him and he abandoned the natural environment of his homeland (Gen 12:1). According to the rabbinic sages:

> 'And be thou a blessing (*berakhah*)' (Gen 12:2). This means be thou a *berekhah* (pool): Just as a pool purifies the unclean, so do they bring near to Me those who are far. R. Berekhiah said, Seeing that it is already written 'And I will bless thee' [Gen 12:2], why is 'And be thou a blessing' added? God said to him, 'Hitherto, I had to bless My world; henceforth the blessings are entrusted to thee: whom it pleases thee to bless, do thou bless.' (BerR 39:11)

The encounter was sealed when Abraham performed the "covenant of pieces" (Gen 15:10). The second stage came with Abraham's acts of circumcision (Gen 17:23–27) and his commitment to educate his family to consecrate actions to God (Gen 18:19). The third stage was the *Aqedah*, Abraham's binding Isaac for sacrifice. Responding to God purely out of love, indifferent to reward and punishment, Abraham was poised to sacrifice and to overcome everything that belonged to the realm of nature, in feelings, for an absolute, spiritual ideal. He was ready to do his duty to God unconditionally – indeed with such intensity that God had to call out twice in order to stop him from carrying out the sacrifice.[8]

The People of Israel

Abraham's freedom became instilled into the people of Israel, and they were to lead the world to absolute freedom, to the messianic era, where the divine spirit would be shared for man to be spiritually free.[9] According to the rabbinic sages, as Abraham bound Isaac below, God bound the princes of the heathens above – indicating that the nations of the world were to be subservient to the people of

---

Hirsch's naturalization enabled his appointment as rabbi in Luxembourg, 6 April 1943. Letter of Rabbi of Luxembourg Dr. Emanuel Bulz to the author, 18 February 1974.
8 Hirsch, *Die Religionsphilosophie*, 457–529, especially 514–520; 882. For a discussion of Hirsch's interpretation of Abraham's faith, see Aharon Shear-Jashuv, "Hadatiut shel avraham be-filosofiyat hadat shel shemuel hirsh", in Mosheh Halamish, Hannah Kasher, and Yohanan Silman, eds., *Avraham avi hama'aminim: Demuto birei hehagut ledoroteha* (Ramat Gan: Bar Ilan University, 2002), 281–294.
9 Samuel Hirsch, *Die Messiaslehre der Juden in Kanzelvorträgen: Zur Erbauung denkender Leser* (Leipzig: Heinrich Hunger, 1843).

Israel (BerR 56:5). And should the people of Israel become victim to persecution in the process, God would ultimately redeem them with the ram's horn, as He once redeemed Isaac (BerR 51:9).[10]

Under God's leadership, Israel's history – and Judaism was of history – was a process of overcoming sin and realizing freedom.[11] Hirsch's volume of sermons entitled *Die Messiaslehre der Juden* offered a synopsis of Israel's history, as distilled by Jewish festivals. Passover, which celebrated the liberation of the people out of Egypt, a land of darkness where the spirit submitted to vile, profane lust, represented Israel's extraction from the earthly environment into an arena with potential for spiritual life. The Feast of Weeks signified the beginning of Israel's historical mission and the explication of God's intentions for Israel in the Torah. Israel grasped its higher mission, but without comprehending it internally – which explains why the people complained about their plight. The Ninth of Av represented Israel's recognition of God's presence following exile, with its suffering, in the Torah, as well as Israel's progression from solely obeying God to freely choosing to follow His teachings. The New Year festival enacted Israel's return from exile, and internalized understanding and acceptance of Torah. The sounding of the *shofar* (ram's horn) in particular recalled Abraham's closeness to God – which by now was an experience for all of Israel. The Day of Atonement signified Israel's complete understanding of how the human being was inherently good, that sin was a matter of free choice – and that sin was devoid of lasting reality and existed solely to enable that choice. When the people recognized that sin was a function of Israel's responsibility alone, its nothingness (in and of itself) was exposed. God forgave Israel and Israel's pre-exilic intimacy with God became restored. Finally, the Feast of Tabernacles enacted Israel's reaching out to illumine the rest of the world, for it to become spiritual as well. Ultimately, the world would recognize that naturality and materiality yielded to absolute spirit and God.[12]

Israel's history included Christianity. Insofar as Israel was inherently free, it had no means of communicating with the passive, pagan universe. But, as demonstrated by Jesus, a Jew who overcame sin to become absolutely free and was completely spiritual, Christianity could mediate between the two realms. It was potentially the "extensive" expression of "intensive" Judaism, and was in fact assigned by providence to bridge Israel (selected by God) to the world (alienated from God). Through Christianity, it was possible for the void in the act of sin among the nations to be exposed and for all mankind to achieve absolute freedom.[13]

---

10 Hirsch, *Die Religionsphilosophie*, 519–523.
11 Hirsch, *Was ist Judenthum*, 12–13.
12 Hirsch, *Die Messiaslehre der Juden*.
13 Hirsch, *Die Religionsphilosophie*, 621–645, 832–833.

Hirsch's concept of history defined itself further in his response to Bruno Bauer's attack on Judaism. According to Bauer, the nation of Israel was a nonhistorical entity which, indeed, obstructed the historical development of the world. To the contrary, Hirsch countered: Israel's unique ability to progressively master nature spiritually and to pursue freedom was the very basis, source, and driving force of that historical development. In Bauer's view the Hebrew Bible, in which minute regulations and moral principles were equally valid because both were commanded by the same inscrutable higher being, was incompatible with historical experience. After Judaism entered history, for Bauer, it should have yielded to Christianity, which perfected it. But the people of Israel mistakenly and stubbornly refused. Then the Talmud's non-worldly imaginings deepened the existing separation between religion and real society. Along with the absence of national-political life, it intensified Israel's a-historical condition. On the one hand, Bauer continued, Jews were so obsessed with the past that they turned away from the arts and sciences and intellectual development. On the other, their messianism drew them into a trans-historical future reality. Over the generations, Jews separated themselves increasingly from the allegedly unclean world. If they touched historical development at all, it was as the oppressed, as history's martyrs. Hirsch rejected all of this. It was Christianity with its doctrine of inherited and permanent sin that was anti-historical, not Judaism. Christianity protested what was worldly and incorporated itself into a mystical, purely and exclusively spiritual world, a new heaven-earth diametrically opposed to the material world which was locked in sin. Judaism, with its freedom driven commitment to history, protested the Christian protest.[14]

State and Freedom

Hirsch's principle of freedom – whereby freedom was the core of human psychological and ethical development – and the positive impetus of Israel-centered linear historical progress, was also at the heart of the relationship between humanity and divinity in the political arena. Having established that freedom was at the core of man's relationship with God; that freedom entered the historical matrix with Abraham, and that Abraham instilled it into the nation of Israel; that Israel's own advance through and with history made freedom increasingly

---

14 Bruno Bauer, *Die Judenfrage* (Braunschweig: Friedrich Otto, 1843), 11–12, 35–36. Originally published in Deutsche Jahrbücher für Wissenschaft und Kunst, nos. 274–282 (1842), 1–115. Hirsch, *Das Judenthum, der christliche Staat und die moderne Kritik*, 17, 26–27, 44, 84, 91–92, 105.

real; and that with Christianity's mediation Israel led the world towards absolute freedom, Hirsch was ready to speak of freedom in the state. Having explained how the inner spirit (abstract freedom) was to objectify itself in nature and draw nature towards itself and thereby concretize freedom (the existential perspective); and how the active, spiritual religion of Israel was to draw the passive, natural religion of the rest of mankind into its light through the mediation of Christianity (the historical perspective), he was ready to project these dynamics onto the political scene. The ideal state, he held, should express the divine, while spiritual (divine) reality became instilled into the material (human) context as a corporate structure for freedom. Enabled by the presence of divine, absolute freedom, the subjects of a state could and should actualize their potential freedom. That this would happen under the name of Christianity, which indeed was there to mediate between Israel and the world, was completely acceptable to Hirsch. That is, the authentic Christianity of Jesus and Luther.[15]

In an address at the Dessau synagogue on the last day of Passover 1839, Hirsch explained that the people of Israel did not seek to build a divine, heavenly world which was apart from the earthly. They rather sought to integrate the one with the other, to have the divine and human coalesce. He pointed to the ancient Israelites, who sought a divinely human and humanly divine way of life ("ein wahrhaft göttlich-menschliches und menschlich-göttliches Leben führen ... diese innige Verschmelzung, alles menschlichen mit dem göttlichen ..."). Then, priest (representing divinity) and king (representing humanity) functioned jointly, and miraculous directives streamed into routine activities.[16] The rabbinic sages confirmed that the state was a religious institution (bSan 56b, bGit 10b).[17] Later in Luxembourg, Hirsch agreed with Samuel Holdheim's historical division: Ancient Mosaic legislation, where religion (the internal dimension) was absorbed into the political structure of the state (the external dimension) was in effect until the first exile. Following the second exile, the political structure and its laws were transmuted into an abstract, spiritual bond, as formulated by Talmudic discourse. Political ingredients such as land, Temple and Sanhedrin were retained, but without the actual state as instilled with the divine, without the spiritual organism. Indeed, the empirical reality became so absorbed into the religious universe as to be forgotten.[18]

---

[15] Hirsch, ibid., 99–103.
[16] Hirsch, "Schlusspredigt gehalten am letzten Pesachtage 5599 (1839)", in *Friede, Freiheit und Einheit*, 41–59.
[17] Hirsch, *Die Religionsphilosophie*, 837.
[18] See Samuel Hirsch's review: "Samuel Holdheim, *Ueber die Autonomie der Rabbinen und das Princip der jüdischen Ehe. Ein Beitrag zur Verständigung über einige das Judenthum betreffende*

Hirsch believed that the two realms were properly joined under Christian Leopold Friedrich Franz, Duke of Dessau, principality of Anhalt. Had it not been for the likes of the duke, he preached in 1840, Jews would still be persecuted and have to be as quiet as lambs led to slaughter ("Sonst blieb uns Nichts übrig als stilles Dulden; sonst müssten wir uns wie das sich schweigsame Lamm, zur Schlachtbank führen lassen").[19] Franz, Hirsch stated, was devoted to the idea that the human spirit was of divine light, and that he himself was responsible for bringing it forth. The government was to develop the moral and spiritual potential of each citizen (*Bildung*) and instill divine spirit into the state. That is, to advance freedom. Franz encouraged Jews to develop spiritually – instead of focusing on earthly powers – for this would bring them both internal (Jewish) and external (political) satisfaction.[20]

To Hirsch's mind, Germany stood in positive contrast to America in this regard. Over the last thirty years, since Jews were elected to city assemblies and councils in Prussia in 1809, the German state showed proper concern for religious *Bildung*. There was recognition that eternal values should permeate temporal ones; that the government was responsible for developing a life desirable to God; and that the state was to be a divine institution, a means for the spiritual

---

Zeitfragen (Schwerin: C. Kürschner, 1843)" (Kurze Anzeigen), Literaturblatt des Orients 44 (31 Oktober 1843), cols. 696–699.

19 Samuel Hirsch, *Predigt zur hundertjährigen Geburtsfeier Sr. Hochfürstl. Durchlaucht unseres hochseligen Herzogs Leopold Friedrich Franz* (Dessau: Hermann Neubürger, 1840), 4, 10.

20 Hirsch expressed his devotion to the king in his 28 March 1840 sermon: "Heiss durchglüht der Wunsch seit fünfzig Jahren Jisraels Herzen, im deutschen Vaterland als Deutschlands Söhne [anerkannt] zu werden, im deutschen Vaterlande Gott und den König, Gott und seinen Gesalbten nicht nur lieben, sondern auch verehren zu dürfen ... O Jisrael! ein schmerzliches Hochgefühl muss sich unserer Herzen bemächtigen, wenn wir bedenken, wie heiss sich unsere Liebe seit fünfzig Jahren zum König und zum Vaterlande bewährt hat (Hirsch, "Israels Gegenwart, oder das Verhältniss des jetzigen Jisraels zum Staate gehalten Shabbat parashat hahodesh 5700 am 28 März 1840", in *Die Messiaslehre der Juden*, 33). The Dessau *Jüdische Haupt- und Freischule*, which offered religious and secular subjects, was named after Franz (the *Franzschule*). Hirsch reported his mistreatment there, citing Dessau's rabbi David Fraenkel, to Zunz (JNUL mss. Division 40792-G14). Records of the 1839 controversy are held at the Staatsarchiv Magdeburg-Abt-Dessau, Rep 15 [Judenschaft] no. 2 B6 B1. 63. See Michael Graetz, "The New Schools", in Michael A. Meyer and Michael Brenner, eds., *German-Jewish History in Modern Times*, vol. 1 (New York: Columbia University Press, 1996), 367–368; Christian Wiese, "Von Dessau nach Philadelphia: Samuel Hirsch als Philosoph, Apologet und radikaler Reformer", in Giuseppe Veltri and Christian Wiese, eds., *Jüdische Bildung und Kultur in Sachsen-Anhalt von der Aufklärung bis zum Nationalsozialismus* (Berlin: Metropol, 2009), 363–410; David Sorkin, "Preacher, Teacher, Publicist: Joseph Wolf and the Ideology of Emancipation", in Frances Malino and David Sorkin, eds., *From East and West: Jews in a Changing Europe, 1750–1870* (Cambridge, MA: B. Blackwell, 1991), 107–128.

development of its subjects.[21] In America the people, not the state, dominated and they ruled by caprice. There was no incentive coming from above for Jews to advance spiritually (internally) before they would be allowed to do so politically (as was so in Germany). As a result, religiosity in America was disappearing or becoming increasingly secularized, and Jewish houses of worship were falling into a medieval-like darkness.[22] In *Die Religionsphilosophie der Juden*, Hirsch wrote that with a monarchy, if a king turned bad, it was traceable to God's response to subjects who turned bad. In a constitutional arrangement (i.e., America), the government was subject to the unbridled power of those who were able to control the constitution.[23] In one of the letters attacking Bauer, Hirsch included his observation that because the state in North America had no religion, materialism dominated to the point that even the emancipation of slaves became impossible.[24] Later in America, he differentiated Catholicism, which divided heaven and (sinful) earth, and erroneously divided state from religion, from Judaism, which regarded the state as the revelation of God, a means for religious development, its laws as binding as Sinai's. Indeed, when Judaism and state conflicted, Jews looked to the state for resolution.[25]

Freedom and Jewish Auto-Emancipation

In his preface to *Die Religionsphilosophie der Juden*, Hirsch wrote that he regarded the quest for emancipation as a lofty endeavor which was driven from on high ("Wahrlich, man verkennt uns ganz und gar, wenn man glaubt, die Anstrengun-

---

[21] Hirsch, "Schlusspredigt gehalten am letzten Pessachtage 5699 [1839]", in *Friede, Freiheit und Einheit*, 41–59.
[22] Hirsch, "Israel's Gegenwart oder das Verhältniss des jetzigen Jisraels zum Staate", in *Die Messiaslehre der Juden*, 26–46.
[23] Hirsch, *Die Religionsphilosophie*, 127–130, 870–871, 882–883.
[24] Hirsch, *Das Judenthum, der christliche Staat und die moderne Kritik*, 9. Once in America, Hirsch praised its integration of state and religion, the free role of religion in politics, and concluded that full participation in American life expressed full religious life simultaneously. In discussing Jewish emancipation, he added that the continued existence of Negro slavery in North America in 1842 had moved him to be a monarchist rather than a republican. Samuel Hirsch, "Staatrechtliches", Die Deborah 13 (1867), 190, 194–195. On the question of Hirsch's monarchism in America, see the article by Michael A. Meyer in this volume.
[25] Samuel Hirsch, "Die rabbinische Ehescheidung, der Get", Die Deborah 14 (1868), 6, 10–11, 14. "Die amerikanische Orthodoxie: Hut auf oder Hut ab", Die Deborah 13 (1867), 110, 114, 118, 122, 126, 158–159. "Die Humanitarier und das Reformjudenthum", Jewish Times 1, 15 (1869), 10–11; 1, 16 (1869), 10–11. "The Reform Worship", Jewish Times 1, 18 (1869), 3–4; 1, 19 (1869), 3–4; 1, 20 (1869), 4; 1, 21 (1869), 56; 1, 22 (1869), 3–4; 1, 23 (1869), 4.

gen, die wir machen, unsere Emanzipation zu bewirken, seihen nicht von einer höhern Nothwendigkeit geboten, sondern blos das willkührliche und daher auch zurückzuweisen mögliche Streben einiger nach Stellen und Aemtern geizenden Individuen"). For their part, Jews dedicated themselves to adapting to the *Bildung* of the times, when they were liberated from the ghetto fifty years earlier ("Aus den Gehetto's befreit, haben wir ungefähr funfzig Jahre damit zugebracht, die Bildung der Zeit uns anzueignen").[26] Yet the state, which was influenced by the Christian church, did not include Judaism as a recognized religion.[27] Nevertheless, even though he resented the state for not including Judaism in its own terms as an integral part, and instead merely tolerated Jews until they would be gone, Hirsch attributed the failure of emancipation primarily to Jews themselves and to Christians.

Jews interpreted emancipation as a means of advance in secular *Ausbildung* and material terms and hid their religion to do so. Instead, they should have made religion their way of life, until it permeated their relationship to God, their fellow man, the family, synagogue and state. Over the last thirty years, while this process continued, human and divine life were being split apart – leaving religion ice cold. Contrary to what Jews imagined, they were being rejected from service to the state, Hirsch asserted, because they remained uncommitted to the state as a vessel of divinely-human life of freedom. Until Jews proved that the purpose of their life was religious, and that this purpose was identical to that of the state, they would never achieve their goal of equal rights and duties. Their enchantment with some dazzling prospect of fulfilling the messianic dream in the Land of Israel ("Zion") only diverted them from the matter at hand.[28] In his 28 March 1840 sermon, Hirsch identified authentic Israelites as those who were filled with the divine and served as God's image in terms of freedom, such as to both relate to his/her surroundings freely and to fulfill the purpose of the state. Over the last fifty years Jews were sacrificing their religious convictions, even converting to Christianity, in the mistaken belief that this would facilitate equal citizenship and serving the king. They overlooked the fact that the king was God's representative on earth. Their offers of service

---

26 Hirsch, "Vorwort", in *Die Religionsphilosophie*, v-x, here v.
27 See further, Erhard Hirsch, "Das für ihre Nation wiedergefundene Land! Erziehung zur Toleranz: Erfolg der Aufklärung: 'Judenemanzipation' von Anhalt-Dessau aus", in Veltri and Wiese, eds., *Jüdische Bildung und Kultur in Sachsen-Anhalt*, 67–114.
28 See further, Gershon Greenberg, "The Reformers' First Attack on Hess' *Rome and Jerusalem*: An unpublished Manuscript of Samuel Hirsch", Jewish Social Studies 35, 3–4 (1973), 175–197. Hirsch, "Schlusspredigt gehalten am letzten Pessachtage 5599 (1839)", in *Friede, Freiheit und Einheit*, 41–59.

were inevitably rejected, because they separated divine from human goals, neglecting the fact that God led history and the state. Indeed, the rejection was a divine sign, delivered by the king as His instrument (Prov 21:1).[29] An anonymous reviewer of Hirsch's sermons spoke approvingly of his position that Israelites could not expect to be emancipated before they recognized that the goal of Jewish religion was to realize freedom, and became internally free. Having been tasked by God to surpass others in advancing freedom, it should not be important whether non-Jews, with less *Bildung* and commitment to freedom, were able to fully participate in state life.[30] In his attack on Bauer, Hirsch wrote that Jews had to emancipate and free themselves – and in this way they would force their emancipation upon the state and not have to beg for it. Once they emancipated themselves, they would de facto belong to the organism of state life.[31]

The Role of Pauline Christianity

Christianity also played a role in the failure of Jewish emancipation. Emancipation, Hirsch wrote in the foreword to *Die Religionsphilosophie der Juden*, was more than a matter of gaining political rights.[32] The demand for equal duties and rights in and of themselves, he said in his Bauer attack, was not the real issue ("Wenn blos vom staatsrechtlichen Gesichtspunkte ausgegangen wird, ist für die Emanzipation in Deutschland wenig zu gewinnen und sie ist nicht einmal wünschenswerth"). For example, there was nothing in itself desirable about being able to serve in the military.[33] Jews were rather looking for a sincere form of acceptance, while the state just waited until it could get rid of the Jewish religion – which it viewed as an ungodly and sick form of contemporary humanity that should be annihilated ("...[d]uldet der Staat blos unsere Religion, so fühlt er sich im innersten seines Wesens verpflichtet, die Zeit herbeizuführen, wo er sie gar nicht zu dulden braucht und also auf die Vernichtung des Judenthums hinzuarbeiten"). For its part, the Catholic church (with Protestant consent) proclaimed that there was no salvation outside the church (*extra ecclesiam nulla*

---

[29] Hirsch, "Israels Gegenwart, oder das Verhältniss des jetzigen Jisraels zum Staate", 26–46, esp. 44-45.
[30] A., "Die Messiaslehre der Juden in Kanzelvorträgen ...", Literaturblatt des Orients 18 (2 May 1843), cols. 273–279; no. 19 (9 May 1843), 291–296; no. 20 (16 May 1843), 309–313.
[31] Hirsch, *Das Judenthum, der christliche Staat und die moderne Kritik*, 9–10, 101. See also 28–30, 51–54, 73–75, 92–95, 98.
[32] Hirsch, "Vorwort", in *Die Religionsphilosophie*, v-x.
[33] Hirsch, *Das Judenthum, der christliche Staat und die moderne Kritik*, 9.

salus), when it should have said there was no salvation outside the church except in the Jewish religion (*nisi Judaeis in religione eorum*).³⁴ The church, Hirsch declared in his 17 June 1938 sermon, should have been using its influence to remove Judaism's isolated status in the state, in the name of the principle of freedom, which Christianity shared with Judaism. Moreover, Christianity and Judaism differed over the matter of the triumph over evil: Christianity spoke of the objective (external) realization of the triumph-idea upon the coming of Christ, and the subjective (internal) realization with His return. Judaism spoke of the idea's not yet being realized, its own role in the realization; Christianity was the blossom of Judaism's seed and its God-man could only have come about where monotheism belonged to popular consciousness. The church should have this in mind, and instead of helping to exclude Judaism, should act on its behalf. Jews and Christians shared much, and when it came to emancipation they should be joined. For their part, Jews would even identify with Christians in this respect ("Ich meine, die Wahrheit dieses Standpunkts vorausgesetzt, dass wir alsdann Juden-Christen sein müssten, und uns nicht in der christlichen Kirche verlieren dürften").³⁵

In *Die Religionsphilosophie der Juden*, Hirsch traced the exclusion to the Pauline tradition. Jesus, for his part, intended to mediate between Israel and a world alienated from God. As such, he actualized and perfected the principles of moral freedom; he showed the vanity of sin and thereby eliminated it. For Paul, however, human sin ran so deep as to make liberation impossible for man himself. Freedom depended upon the more-than-human, trans-individual Jesus. This left Judaism trapped in a sin-anchored system of law and had to be set aside. It was Paul who shattered the commonality between Judaism, defined by Abraham, and Christianity, defined by Jesus.³⁶

New Testament Roots

According to the Gospel of Matthew, Jesus was the exemplar of the spiritualized free life in the image of God. By overcoming Satan's temptation to misuse freedom and abandon holiness, Jesus exposed the vanity of evil. Then in the Sermon on the Mount, He called upon every Israelite to activate his/her inborn freedom. Jesus annulled sin through His suffering, and by emulating Him and enduring

---

34 Hirsch, "Vorwort", in *Die Religionsphilosophie*, v-x, here v and vi.
35 Hirsch, *Was ist Judenthum*, 8–10.
36 Hirsch, *Die Religionsphilosophie*, 722–767.

suffering generated by sin, Israel would also show sin's impotence ("I will be to him for a father, and he shall be to Me for a son, if he commit inequity, I will chasten him with the rod of men, and with the stripes of the children of men." 2 Sam 7:14). Jesus' resurrection, which brought life out of death and evoked eternity, enacted the truth of His message, and signaled that history would culminate in an eternal kingdom of God where evil turned into nothing and absolute freedom reigned. For Matthew, God created man in His image, and the world in goodness. Sin and evil were but disposable instruments for men to use in developing their inner freedom; and they had no inherent reality.[37] John's gospel, which described God's creation of the world and God's eternal thought of man as His image in the world who was to be educated towards authentic freedom, extended Matthew's themes. God's thought became flesh with Jesus, and Jesus created conditions for every individual to incarnate the thought along with Him.[38] Their differences had to do with the fact that Matthew was a realist, and John was an idealist. To Matthew, Jesus was the perfect Israelite, grounded in history. For John, Jesus was the ideal of humanity, the Logos-become-flesh who suffered in anticipation of messianic redemption and who inspired suffering mankind to persist on the path to freedom.[39]

Paul radicalized John's thought, by removing Jesus from His historical, earthly, and thereby Jewish, grounding. His heavenly Jesus suffered to atone for, and remove, inherited sin. Meanwhile, for their part, Jews held to the belief that sin was not part of human nature and that man need never sin. When an individual sinned, it was that individual's responsibility, but God would ultimately restore the sinless world He originally created.[40] In his letters attacking Bauer, Hirsch asserted that Paul projected his personal, traumatic experience into a universal theory. Namely, that mankind had been abandoned to sinfulness, and that only God's grace through His son could bring about life no longer infected by sin.[41]

The Church

Paul's extraction of spirituality from its material, earthly and Jewish-historical context, and his universalizing of atonement through Jesus to the exclusion of the individual quest for freedom in history, became embedded in the church.

---

[37] Ibid., 648, 668, 689, 875–879.
[38] Ibid., 706–707.
[39] Ibid., 721–722.
[40] Ibid., 706–707, 737–740.
[41] Hirsch, *Das Judenthum, der christliche Staat und die moderne Kritik*, 90.

Reconciliation with God now required mediation by Jesus on the trans-human, miraculous level. In time, it progressed to require mediation by the church between Christians and Jesus. The state, of the earthly sphere, had no importance other than to adhere to the church – where the lowest priests were imbued with loftier status than the highest king. Jews, who were outside the church, were left with no mediator at all.[42]

Hirsch believed that Luther's Reformation signaled a return to the Jesus of Matthew. Now, each Christian, as an individual, could be reconciled with God. Instead of being infected by sin, nature became grounding for spirit. Sin could be overcome by the heart of man, and his own activities could serve as mediators for realizing the free image of God. Further, the state was instilled with divinity, instead of being an entity separate from the church.[43] In his letters attacking Bauer, Hirsch wrote that Luther removed the infection of sin from the state for it to become an arena which was potentially pleasing to God. His was a Christian state, a divine institution, a spiritual and sacred polity.[44] Hirsch implied that when the Christianity of Germany allowed the state to compromise emancipation of the Jews, it undermined its own Lutheran environment.

Hegel

Jewish emancipation, understood in terms of the principle of freedom, was thus undermined by the failures of Jews and Christians to foster the coalescence between the divine (spiritual) and human (material) realms requisite for the state to be a vessel of religion. Freedom, as a process of drawing external nature into consciousness, as the choice of good over (an ultimately non-substantive) evil, manifested itself politically when the state instilled spirituality into the individual, thereby enhancing *Bildung* (enacting a collective spiritual-subject and concrete-object dialectic). By separating church (heavenly) and state (earthly) or yielding to the state, Christianity undermined the process. By failing to spiritualize their own lives and integrating into state life in spiritual terms, Jews obstructed it. Hirsch was encouraged by the leadership of Leopold Friedrich Franz in Dessau; and thought Lutheran Christianity was on the right track. But freedom's actualization in the German polity overall was now at a standstill.

---

42 Hirsch, *Die Religionsphilosophie*, 783. Hirsch, *Das Judenthum, der christliche Staat und die moderne Kritik*, 90–91.
43 Hirsch, *Die Religionsphilosophie*, 786–787.
44 Hirsch, *Das Judenthum, der christliche Staat und die moderne Kritik*, 96–99.

Hegel and his disciples did not help. Hegel excluded Jews from his state program and his disciples were antagonistic towards Jews. He proposed a dialectical relationship between religion and state, whereby free subjectivity (religion) actualized its freedom by objectifying itself in the state. He wanted neither to infuse the non-worldly into the worldly, such that religion dominated the state, nor for Christianity to release the world to profane secularism. In his kingdom of God, spirit was realized by men and in men, but without ceasing to be divine. The essence of God, and the essence of man with nature, correlated dialectically, such as to negate opposition between sacred and profane. God (subjectively) stood over-against itself as an "other" – an other that included self-consciousness; while man was the object of God's infinite love and of infinite value.[45]

In these respects, Hirsch would agree with Hegel. But Hegel's state was Christian, and one that excluded Jews. He rebuked Judaism categorically and found it unworthy of trust. Jews, Hirsch wrote, would support a "Christian state" as a divine institution as long as Judaism was respected and occupied an integral place along with other religions. In such a situation, whatever rights the state deemed just for Jews would, in fact, be so. Such a state would be one which represented belief in revelation, a state that was not pagan ("Der Staat ist ein christlicher, das ist ein wahres Wort. ... Der Staat ist ein christlicher heißt, er ist kein heidnischer, sondern auf die Offenbarung des lebendigen, freien, geistigen Gottes gegründet").[46] When it came to Judaism and freedom, Hegel misinterpreted Jesus' distinction between present freedom and earlier servitude to sin in the Gospel of John, as a reference to Jews as not fully free (John 8:32, 34; John 15:15). Moreover, he wrongly claimed that Judaism's freedom was less intensive than Christianity's, because Christianity made itself free internally, while Judaism, without inherited sin, unfolded only externally. In fact, while for Christianity

---

45 This synopsis is based upon Walter Jaeschke, "Staat aus christlichem Prinzip und christlicher Staat: Zur Ambivalenz der Berufung auf das Christentum in der Rechtsphilosophie Hegels und der Restauration", Der Staat 18 (1979), 349–374. See Georg Wilhelm Friedrich Hegel, "The Relationship of Religion to the State According to the Lectures of 1831", in G.W.F. Hegel, *Lectures on the Philosophy of Religion*, vol. 1. *Introduction to the Concept of Religion*, ed. Peter C. Hodgson (Oxford: Oxford University, 2007), 451–460. On freedom, religion and world history for Hegel, see "Die Absicht und das Wohl", para. 124; and "Die Weltgeschichte", paras. 341–360, in G.W.F. Hegel, *Grundlinien der Philosophie des Rechts*, ed. Georg Lasson (Leipzig: F. Meiner, 1911), 105–106, 271–279; and Georg Wilhelm Friedrich Hegel, *Introduction to the Philosophy of History*, trans. Leo Rauch (Indianapolis: Hackett Publishing, 1988), 22, 92–98. See also Paul Franco, *Hegel's Philosophy of Freedom* (New Haven: Yale University Press, 1999), 337–341.
46 Hirsch, *Die Religionsphilosophie*, 836–837, footnote.

one was enslaved internally to unfreedom (sin), in Judaism un-freedom was imposed from without, allowing the spirit greater freedom.[47]

As to the Young Hegelians: On the one hand, Arnold Ruge and Ernst Theodor Echtermeyer attacked Friedrich Julius Stahl for allegedly calling for a religious inquisition where the police would deal with any "heresy" against Christianity. On the other, there were Hegelians who supported the Christian Prussian state as long as it blocked Jewish emancipation – and this, while Jews sacrificed their lives to help liberate the fatherland. But they attacked the Christian state-idea when alleging that David Strauss' *Das Leben Jesu* was a source of disbelief. The common element was Jew-hatred: "Nun kitzelte bekanntlich der alte Adam aller Christen, nämlich der Judenhass, die Hegelianer am meisten."[48] For his part, Bauer held that Judaism, having failed to yield to Christianity, alienated itself from historical progress. For Pauline Christianity Jews were outside the reach of salvation, and for Bauer they were outside the reach of the healthy advance of (Christian) history.

Hirsch countered with his theme that Jews sought freedom in the political arena and a spiritualized state – a "Christian" state in the sense of Jesus or Luther. In his letters against Bauer, he wrote that Jews had been burned to death precisely because of their refusal to surrender to the Pauline doctrine of an irretrievably damned earth, and they were committed to the principle of redemption on earth. That is, they bled for the sake of the true "Christian" state. If being a Christian meant living for the freedom of spirit on earth (as Jesus wanted) Jews were "Christian" and wished to belong to a "Christian state" ("Was ist Christ sein? Heisst das so handeln, so leben, wie Jesus Christus gehandelt hat? Dann sind wir Christen und streben es mit aller Kraft zu sein").[49]

Conclusions

During his five Dessau years, Hirsch established freedom as the principle of Judaism. He began with the psychological development of the child, and its advance

---

47 Hirsch, ibid., 465, 528, 584, 623, 817, 829, 835–837. Hirsch, *Das Judenthum, der christliche Staat und die moderne Kritik*, 20, 103.
48 See Friedrich Julius Stahl, Augsburger Allgemeine Zeitung: Beilage (12 March 1841). Friedrich Julius Stahl, *Die Philosophie des Rechts nach geschichtlicher Ansicht*, vol. 2: *Christliche Rechts- und Staatslehre*, Abth. 2 (Heidelberg: Mohr, 1837); David Friedrich Strauss, *Das Leben Jesu* (Tübingen: C. F. Osiander, 1838); Arnold Ruge and Ernst Theodor Echtermeyer, *Der Protestantismus und die Romantik: Zur Verständigung über die Zeit und ihre Gegensätze: Ein Manifest* (Hildesheim: H. A. Gerstenberg, 1972); Hirsch, *Die Religionsphilosophie*, 835–836.
49 Hirsch, *Das Judenthum, der christliche Staat und die moderne Kritik*, 100–101.

to self-consciousness whereby nature became spiritualized. The individual becoming-of-freedom through time was enabled by the divine being of freedom in eternity. Freedom entered history with Abraham, who instilled it into the people of Israel. Then, through the potential mediation of Christianity, it was to lead world history towards a messianic culmination of absolute freedom. The spiritual reality of freedom, Hirsch believed, was to seep down into the human community through the monarch's transmission of divinely spiritual values into the state. Hirsch rejoiced in the situation in Dessau, under Franz, in this regard. But he despaired over Germany as a whole. He did not focus on the governmental forces but instead blamed the Jews for not freeing themselves, that is, for not being fully religious and viewing the state in religious terms. If they emancipated (freed) themselves, they surely would find themselves free politically. He also criticized the church for not influencing the state. He attributed this to Christianity's turn from Jesus. Jesus was a perfect example of what Abraham had in mind and served to mediate the freedom he had instilled in the people of Israel. But Paul separated Jesus from the historical context: he left individual responsibility for sin and Jewish life to a darkened earth and concentrated sinlessness on the heavenly life of a universalized Christ. The Catholic Church followed suit. Hegel and the Young Hegelians compromised the heritage of Luther, who sought to return Christianity to earth and to the individual, with their arbitrary exclusion of Jews and Judaism from history and from the state.

Irene Kajon
Back to Mediaeval Jewish Philosophy. Hirsch's Criticism of Modern Times

Introduction

In mid-19th century Samuel Hirsch recognized a crisis in modern thought and sought to find a philosophical solution to this crisis. Modern society and thought, according to him, were unable to offer a connection between life and spirit, between the individual human being and the social whole, between history and time on the one hand and the universal and eternal on the other. This assessment anticipated the criticism that 20th century philosophers like Franz Rosenzweig, Karl Löwith, Theodor W. Adorno and Max Horkheimer would express of European culture after the dissolution of Hegelianism.[1] Nihilism, for all these philosophers, means maintaining both the infinite variety in time and history as the only reality for human beings (an attitude which could be defined as a nihilism of weakness), and considering only the abstract One, be it a theory, a social organization, God or the State, as the real and true (an attitude which could be defined as a nihilism of power). In both cases meaning, which requires a deep relation between existence and sense, disappears and only nonsense and absurdity remain. Hirsch, like those philosophers after him, was aware that this crisis had deep roots in European culture. As I hope to demonstrate in what follows, post-Hegelianism according to Hirsch was the final result of a history of ideas grounded in the concept of an *ego cogito*, which was only the correlate, or the mask, of the *ego* determined by its own *conatus essendi*. To this result Hirsch simply opposed Jewish life – at least in its highest expressions – because in this life he could find soul and spirit: Ethical ideas and affections flourish in the Jewish people when they reach their highest level, and philosophy has the task to clarify these ideas and affections, to reflect

---

[1] Cf. Franz Rosenzweig, *Der Stern der Erlösung* (Frankfurt a. M.: Kauffmann, 1921); Karl Löwith, *Von Hegel zu Nietzsche. Der revolutionäre Bruch im Denken des neunzehnten Jahrhunderts* (Zürich: Europa Verlag, 1941); Theodor W. Adorno and Max Horkheimer, *Dialektik der Aufklärung* (Amsterdam: Querido, 1947). The leitmotif of these books – beyond the differences in their contents and perspectives – is the description of the end of the civilization founded on the Logos because of the incapacity of the Logos to embrace reality in its fullness and articulations, and the consequent uprising of myth, faith, instinct, and human irrational impulses. The books analyze the genesis of such a catastrophic end.

on them, and to make their content explicit. Thus, a philosophy grounded in Judaism, as a model or example, could give European culture and human beings a way out of their unhappy condition of oscillation between being circumscribed within their own mortality and dissipating in the All. Violence and dream as well could, in this manner, be superseded and substituted with a peaceful and righteous life and with a sober and realistic (although still ideal-loving) mind. But this requires a turn from a metaphysics grounded in the problem of being – be it either the being of nature and history or the being of a divine substance or essence – to a metaphysics grounded in human ethical actions and divine ethical attributes.

Jewish Thought in Mediaeval Spain in the *Religionsphilosophie*

In his book *Die Religionsphilosophie der Juden* published in Leipzig in 1842, Hirsch wrote a long note on the situation of European Judaism in the context of mediaeval Christian and Muslim culture.[2] He observes that this culture's ascetic tendencies were such as to uphold a rupture between man and the world, between thinking and reality. Thought was subsequently dominated by false speculation and vain problems, and life untouched by reflection, and so constrained by dogma, custom, and conformity to external rules. The Jews who lived in this culture were certainly influenced by their milieu: in different fashion both western and eastern Judaism developed an intellectual attitude out of touch with living human reality. Hirsch writes:

> All the questions that scholasticism took so seriously seem empty niceties to us, as we have more important things to concern ourselves with than such trifles. Only to a world like the mediaeval one, which envisions life solely in the organization of the community and where only dogma and the Church offer salvation, would such consequences seem serious concerns, vital questions. Things went no better for the Jews when they were driven by the persecutions of the crusades back to the Talmud. Here too an analogous scholasticism arose. One takes the premises of the Talmud as the starting points of the *Halachah*, is infinitely sharp-witted in thinking up new cases, and what is most trivial becomes supremely important. But even ignoring this dark period of Polish-Jewish scholasticism, which has nothing

---

2 Cf. Samuel Hitsch, *Die Religionsphilosophie der Juden oder das Prinzip der jüdischen Religionsanschauung und sein Verhältniß zum Heidenthum, Christenthum und zur absoluten Philosophie dargestellt und mit den erläuterten Beweisstellen aus der Heiligen Schrift, den Talmudim und Midrashim versehen* (Leipzig: Heinrich Hunger, 1842); reprint (Hildesheim: Olms, 1986), 784–786. (All the following quotations are taken from this reprint).

in the least in common with philosophy, one would have to concede that not even the Spanish Jews, who were familiar with Greek philosophy from the Arabs, were able to construe a true philosophy. The God of revelation was bound to the world only extrinsically; life was not in accordance with this God. And so not even the Spanish Jews were creative enough to produce a true philosophy, but had to merely assimilate what Aristotle and Holy Scripture had created before them.[3]

For Hirsch, then, the Jews in the Middle Ages lacked an authentic philosophical spirit: the Polish Jews had "schools" (*Schulen*) in which the Torah was interpreted with the aim of drawing from it external prescriptions regarding daily life down to the last detail, with no inner contact with the God revealed to the Patriarchs, to Moses and to the Prophets. And though the Spanish Jews were familiar with the Greek philosophers, whom they had read in Arab translation, the connections they made between Jewish and Greek philosophical sources were not intimate. Jewish life itself within a Europe oppressed by Christian and Muslim religious traditions – regarded as beyond criticism and discussion, formed only by dogmas or reduced to mere praxis – was unfamiliar with any human freedom, or any relationship of man with a God whose word is present in the soul and heart.

And yet, Hirsch says, there is still something significant in the thought that the Spanish Jews expressed, a seed that might become a tree bearing much fruit. The passage quoted above continues:

> They [the Spanish Jews], however, enjoyed an advantage over both the Neo-Platonists and the Scholastics. Even though the Jewish principle could not be realized in the State, yet Judaism did not share the fragmentation of the Catholic world. In the family and in the community the Jewish principle had been made real in a way that was both beautiful and holy,

---

[3] Ibid., 785: "Für uns scheinen alle die Fragen, die die Scholastik so ernsthaft beschäftigten, leere Spitzfindigkeiten, denn wir haben Wichtigeres zu thun, als uns mit solchem Minutiosen zu beschäftigen. Allein einer Welt, die, wie die mittelalterliche, im Leben nur die Gemeinheit sieht und nur ins Dogma und in die Kirche sich zu retten vermag, mussten solche Konsequenzen ernsthafte Beschäftigungen, Lebensfragen sein. Es erging den Juden daher nicht besser, als sie durch die Verfolgungen der Kreuzzüge auf den Talmud zurückgedrängt wurden. Auch hier tritt die Scholastik fast mit demselben Namen auf. Man geht von den Voraussetzungen des Talmud in Beziehung auf die Halacha aus, ist endlos scharfsinnig in der Erfindung neuer Fälle, und das Minutioseste wird zur höchsten Wichtigkeit. Sehen wir aber auch von dieser trüben Periode der polnisch-jüdischen Scholastik, die mit der Philosophie nicht mehr das Geringste gemein hat, ab, so konnte es auch bei den durch die Araber mit den griechischen Philosophen vertrauten spanischen Juden zu keiner eigentlichen Philosophie kommen. Der Gott der Offenbarung war mit der Welt nur äußerlich verbunden, das Leben war nicht diesem Gotte gemäß. Deswegen konnten auch sie nicht schöpferisch eine eigentliche Philosophie hervorbringen, sondern mussten sich darauf beschränken, das aus Aristoteles und aus der h. Schr. Geschöpfte zu assimiliren."

a reality that exalted every Jew in the whole of his being. Hence also the fact that for this philosophy, the logical and metaphysical writings of the Greeks were much less interesting than their ethical writings.⁴

The important point of the philosophy that Spanish Judaism affirmed during the centuries of the expansion and then the domination of Christianity in Europe, with the Church of Rome as its guide, was – according to Hirsch – conceiving the reality of human relations marked by justice and loving-kindness as the premise of philosophy itself. The ideas of justice and loving-kindness were able, first, to get to the core of human reality – a center that Scripture and Jewish tradition, with their concern for the relations between man and man, and man and God, had brought so clearly to the fore – and then, to point out the necessity of meditating on them. These ideas were realized in Jewish family and Jewish community – Jewish family and Jewish community as models of a society whose members certainly live in the world, but are able to reach the divine through their ethical intentions and actions. For this reason, the representatives of Spanish Judaism, when they philosophize on the ground of their true Jewish life, provided an ethical reading of the works of the Greeks, from Plato's *Republic* to Aristotle's *Metaphysics*. In this way, Hirsch concludes, the Spanish Jewish philosophers, despite their affinity with the Christian Scholastics, maintained a deep awareness of the unity between finite and infinite, life and spirit, that was typical of Judaism but was absent elsewhere in their days. They were guided to this awareness by remaining within the Jewish family and Jewish community and conceiving philosophy as a reflection on them. Through a shared, universal perspective they extended the meaning of their experience, both as men and philosophers, to others as well and so defended the sense of Judaism for human culture.

In the second passage quoted above Hirsch presumably alludes to Maimonides, the greatest of the Spanish Jewish philosophers of the Middle Ages, when he dwells on the positive core of the Jewish philosophy that flourished in the past – a philosophy, exactly because of this core, deeply meaningful not only for the Jews, but for all humanity. Assuming this to be the case, it is in-

---

4 Ibid., 785–786: "Nur unterscheiden sie sich vortheilhaft sowohl von den Neuplatonikern als von den Scholastikern. Wenn auch das jüdische Prinzip seine Wirklichkeit nicht im Staate erkennen konnte, so theilte doch auch das Judenthum die Zerrissenheit der katholischen Welt nicht. In der Familie und in der Gemeinde hatte sich das jüdische Prinzip eine schöne und heilige Wirklichkeit zu geben gewußt, eine Wirklichkeit, in der das ganze Sein eines jeden Juden aufging. Daher denn auch für diese Philosophie die logischen und metaphysischen Schriften der Griechen viel weniger Interesse hatten, als ihre ethischen."

teresting to note that Hirsch's interpretation of Maimonides' *Guide for the Perplexed* anticipates the interpretation expressed in the twentieth century by Hermann Cohen, Leo Strauss and Emmanuel Levinas: They regard ethical problems – the attributes of divine actions as examples for human actions, the relation between God and human beings, communities, states, history and redemption – as the aim of this work rather than metaphysical problems – God's being, God's relation with the world, the creation, or Providence.

Cohen, in his *Charakteristik der Ethik Maimunis* (The Characteristic of Maimonides' Ethics), points out how the true key of understanding the *Guide for the Perplexed* may be found in chapters 51–54 of the third and final part of the book.[5] It is in these last chapters that Maimonides explains that the aim of his explanations and arguments is to indicate to his pupil the right way of life, which is nothing other than an imitation of God's ethical attributes, i.e., the capacities of judging (*mishpat*), of loving (*chesed*), of exercising justice (*zedaqah*). Between these virtues there is a tension and at the same time a profound unity. It is absolutely necessary that the individual has these three virtues in order to act righteously among other human beings, giving them their just deserves and helping them when they are poor, downtrodden, or strangers. Individuals acquire these virtues only through the light of the intellect and passionate love for God. According to Cohen's exegesis of the *Guide for the Perplexed*, when interpreting the ontological attributes of God – self-sufficiency, creativity, omnipotence – one should keep the ethical attributes in mind: self-sufficiency as God's uniqueness, i.e., God as the Other with regard to nature and history; creativity as the divine capacity of making the world dependent on spirit, i.e., of giving revelation and redemption to the world; omnipotence as the ethical energy that acts in history and temporality. Maimonides' preference for the problem of the good beyond the being would indicate that he is a follower of Plato rather than Aristotle and his idea of the being as the highest object of metaphysical thinking.

Leo Strauss, when writing about Maimonides in the thirties,[6] points out that the theological-political question is central to Maimonides' thinking. The law, given by God to the Jewish people at Sinai, is the basis and starting point of Mai-

---

5 Hermann Cohen, "Charakteristik der Ethik Maimunis", in Wilhelm Bacher et al., eds., *Moses ben Maimon. Sein Leben, seine Werke und sein Einfluß*, vol. 1 (Leipzig: Buchhandlung Gustav Fock, 1908), 63–134, reprinted in Hermann Cohen, *Jüdische Schriften*, vol. 3 (Berlin: Schwetschke & Sohn, 1924), 221–289. Cohen returns to the interpretation of Maimonides developed in this essay in his *Religion der Venunft aus den Quellen des Judentums* (Frankfurt a.M.: Kauffmann, 1929, 2nd revised edition), especially in chapter 6.
6 Leo Strauss, *Philosophie und Gesetz. Beiträge zum Verständnis Maimunis und seiner Vorläufer* (Berlin: Schocken, 1935).

monides' philosophizing; only the law ensures the right social and political order. Therefore, the prophets are the true founders of the City: if the founders were human beings without any relationship with God, the laws of society and State, which they intend to build, would be relative, weak, and unstable. There is, according to Strauss, a drama in Maimonides' *Guide for the Perplexed* because law and philosophy, religious tradition formed by rules and prescriptions and intellectual criticism, *vita activa* and *vita contemplativa* in Jewish spiritual life, never identify with each other. Yet exactly this complexity of Maimonides' philosophical perspective is what makes his book extremely rich, written with subtlety because directed to different readers, full of metaphors as well as of strict reasoning. Strauss thinks that for Maimonides ethics – an ethics necessarily connected with politics – is the *philosophia prima*: ethics that allude to a divine revelation. Strauss, like Cohen – whom he considers his mentor in his historical-philosophical studies – underlines Plato's influence on Maimonides: Especially the *Republic*, which Strauss assumes that Maimonides read in an Arabic translation, yielded the latter fundamental insights.

For Levinas, writing in the thirties,[7] Maimonides is the thinker who victoriously stands in contrast to philosophy that analyzes the human being only in relationship to time, nature, and death. Naturalism, historicism, the existential approach to human reality can not envision human freedom, i.e., the capacity to live in a world which is radically different from the world of the *ego* involved in interests, impulses, needs. When the *Guide for the Perplexed* describes how the world depends on God's intellect and will, the intention is not to express the meaning of creation – the order of the world, Providence, science as research on the firm laws of phenomena – but rather to affirm ethics, i.e., the field of human actions, choices, free perspectives regarding existence and experience. Maimonides declares his discomfort and his doubts about, and his independence from a world that is fixed and permanent. The most profound teaching of Maimonides – Levinas, Cohen, and Strauss would agree – is not his reflection on the *kosmos* and on God as the fundament of the *kosmos*, but his emphasis on human spirit beyond the world.

Hirsch, pointing out how Jewish philosophy of the Middle Ages had an ethical ground and orientation, then projects Maimonides as the most prominent figure within this philosophy. This innovation resulted in the repeated defense of an ethical interpretation of the *Guide for the Perplexed*. Hirsch denoted Spanish mediaeval Jewish philosophy as his own precursor in constructing a univer-

---

[7] Emmanuel Levinas, "L'actualité de Maïmonide", Paix et Droit 15, 4 (April 1935), 6–7, reprinted in Traces 5 (Automne 1982), 142–144.

sal philosophy with its roots in Jewish experience, insofar as this experience is ethical in content. But how exactly did he envision the link between philosophical thinking and human reality? What exactly was the shape of what Hirsch defined as the "Jewish principle"? How would a philosophy, founded on this "principle", acquire the character of truth and authenticity relevant not only for Jews, but for man in general? And how might this philosophy offer solutions to a human situation that, both in the mediaeval and the modern age, seems difficult, not at peace with itself, and entailing the permanent risk of a divide between concrete, lived existence and the Logos?

"Philosophy of Religion" as Philosophical Foundation and as Philosophical System

At the beginning of Hirsch's note on mediaeval Judaism considered above, there are a few lines that explain what we should understand by the term "philosophy":

> Philosophy need not produce truth, but only find it and welcome it. It is only the consciousness of the consciousness of man, the thought of thought. It need only conceive the necessity of what others know too. And so philosophy can exist only where a principle is not only present as a principle, but has taken form in the world, and has subordinated the world to itself.[8]

Hirsch – unlike Descartes or Fichte – does not believe that thinking is the beginning of philosophizing. Thinking rests on another kind of thinking, one that is not produced by theoretical reason, which questions the being of things, but by practical reason, which expresses the ethical ideas underlying human action: philosophical consciousness takes ethical consciousness as its object and subjects it to clarification. For Hirsch there is a difference between the ethical plane, which is inherent to human life, and the ontological plane, which is where philosophical thought takes place, and which aims to determine the essence of beings or determine the supreme being in which they are grounded or from which they originate. Life is not opposed to the spirit when this spirit

---

[8] Samuel Hirsch, *op. cit.*, 784: "Philosophie hat nicht die Wahrheit zu erzeugen, sondern nur sie zu finden und aufzunehmen. Sie ist nur das Bewußtsein über das Bewußtsein der Menschen, das Denken des Denkens. Das, was die Andern auch wissen, hat sie nur in seiner Nothwendigkeit zu begreifen. Daher kann es nur da eine Philosophie geben, wo ein Prinzip nicht nur als Prinzip vorhanden ist, sondern in der Welt sich Gestalt gegeben, sich die Welt unterworfen hat."

is thought of ethically; but when the spirit, as an organ of philosophy, takes the form of theoretical reason, it radically distances itself from life. Yet the primary aim of philosophy is to indicate just what human reason is, and therefore to look at those actions that display ethical characteristics. Theory starts from practice, and its end and aim are practice. Theory arrives at truth, but it begins with life – a spiritual life.

In the Introduction to his *Religionsphilosophie* Hirsch describes *Bewußtsein* (consciousness) – which coincides with that awareness of the ethical that arises in human familial and social relations, i.e., the *Bewußtsein* that should be studied by philosophers – as *religiöses Bewußtsein* because it implies the reference of these relations to God. Thus, the *Religionsphilosophie* or *Philosophie der Religion* coincides with philosophy when philosophy is understood as the analysis of human reason.

"Philosophy of religion", for Hirsch, can be understood both in a stricter and broader sense. In the former it studies religious consciousness in its form and content, i.e., how it is active in human experience. In the second sense it studies religious consciousness in all its different productions, all of which are based on a specific experience, such as cognitive activity, artistic creativity, or linguistic capacity. In the first case "philosophy of religion" is the foundation, the premise and the aim of philosophical enquiry concerning the human spirit in the variety of its manifestations; more broadly "philosophy of religion" coincides with the *System der Philosophie* – philosophy that describes the totality of the life of the spirit. Living, saturated in the spirit, is always richer than philosophizing; but philosophizing shows us the highest point of consciousness – its link with God through its link with other consciousnesses – as the core and origin of human culture, and as the ultimate end of this culture. Philosophy can thus be identified with an *Offenbarungsphilosophie* or "philosophy of revelation", in regard to the former sense of fundamental enquiry into human reality, and with a *Philosophie des Geistes*, or "philosophy of the spirit", if understood in terms of the latter, i.e., an enquiry into an all-embracing human reality. In both cases philosophy rests on the familial and social relations that form the basis of human culture.

In the volume published in 1842 the author offers his "philosophy of religion" as the basis of his "philosophical system". However, he never wrote the latter and so provided us only with his "philosophy of religion" in the strict sense of the term. He discovers in Jewish religious literature – from the Bible to the Talmud to the Midrash – the original, eloquent expressions of that religious consciousness that are attested in the history of the Jews from the very earliest times. The concept of "revelation", which coincides with that of "religion", can be illustrated bearing in mind what Genesis recounts about Adam, the first man. Philosophy's underlying theme for anthropological analysis is a narrative that shows us in poetic form the essential life of man, his being raised to freedom by hearing the divine commandments and his permanent ability to accept or to transgress these commandments. For Hirsch it is the first of these freedoms, the hearing, which is the substantial one; the second, i.e., free will, is the formal one. Yet both are necessary to man, so that what transpires may be considered the result of choice rather than fate, and repentance is always possible: returning to the high road after we have lost ourselves in twisting paths.

Paganism as a Perversion of Religion: From Idolatry to Modernity

For Hirsch *religiöses Bewußtsein* is essential to humanity, but it comes into being only when man chooses it. Philosophical thought cannot demonstrate the truth of "religious consciousness", but can only recognize it as a fact that shows both man's belonging to nature and history and his difference from it: man as a finite-infinite being, part of natural and historical being, but able to have an ethical relation with other men in the world. It is within this ethical relation that divine transcendence takes shape. Anyone who is convinced of the truth of "religious consciousness" already has within himself a sense of elevation from the *mundus sensibilis* to another, purely intellectual, reality: thinking starts from this immediate sense.

Although "religious consciousness" can never be wholly negated or destroyed in man, it may be suffocated by a choice that subordinates it to that which binds man to his natural being – instincts, passions, egoism, economic gain, social conformity, or impersonal political systems. Religion then is substituted by paganism. Like Kant, Hirsch identifies moral evil as a perversion of the will that voluntarily gives supremacy to what should be regarded as inferior.[9] In place of the moral commandments human beings prioritize their belonging to nature, the world and history in their daily actions, and so they relinquish making contact with the divine or the eternal, remaining enclosed in time.

Hirsch opposes "religion" or "revelation" – in which man becomes aware of, and chooses his ethical nature, or, in biblical terms, holiness – to paganism in which man understands only obscurely and confusedly what in himself is higher

---

[9] See Immanuel Kant, *Die Religion innerhalb der Grenzen der bloßen Vernunft* (1793) (Berlin: Akademie Ausgabe, 1914, VI), especially Part 1.

than his mere existence, and chooses to be enclosed in himself or to obey irrational forces. So too Hirsch writes in his *Religionsphilosophie:*

> There are only two philosophies, the pagan one [...] and the philosophy of revelation, or true philosophy. Paganism did not contain the thought that God is absolute freedom, eternally real and eternally made real, and that God's freedom is man's destiny and essence.[10]

Hirsch sees the religion that manifested itself in Judaism as opposed in the course of history to the oriental religions, the ancient cults of the stars and of nature, and Greek religious feeling. These are all included under paganism, which is also characterized as *passive Religiosität:* in them man is either subjected to his natural inclinations or dominated by a reality that is absolutely beyond him, and takes the form of fate, chance, fortune, or enigmatic divine power. The lowest level of paganism is represented by the idolatry of the early Asian peoples – the Phoenicians, the Assyrians, the Babylonians and the Canaanites – in which natural phenomena were worshipped. But the Chinese and Persians too, according to Hirsch, seem to have been subjected to natural necessity in their religions, either through ancestor worship or by adoring natural elements like the sun or light. Hinduism, Buddhism and the Egyptian religion also refuse to recognize human freedom: but they subject it not so much to nature as to abstractions, without any real relation to human existence. In these religions dark forces loom over human beings, who are unable to flee from divinities that are ambiguous and changing, or indeterminate and mysterious. Greek religious feeling, by contrast, has a dual aspect: on the one hand man's natural or spiritual qualities are made divine; on the other man subordinates himself to fate. Paganism originated in an act of freedom: instead of choosing freedom as holiness or even piety (*Frömmigkeit*), man has chosen to make himself independent of a God who emerges as a source of ethical commandments, and so also independent of other human beings united each with the other in spirit. Thus man abandons himself to things, natural events or occult divinities. In this way Hirsch outlines the history of oriental and ancient religions as the history of paganism. All this ends in Roman civilization, which becomes aware, at first obscurely and then clearly, of the "nothingness" (*Nichts*) that is inherent to it.[11]

---

10 Samuel Hirsch, *op. cit.*, 794. "Es giebt nur zwei Philosophien, die heidnische [...] und die Philosophie der Offenbarung, oder die wahre Philosophie. Das Heidenthum ahnte den Gedanken kaum, daß Gott die absolute, ewig wirkliche und ewig sich verwirklichende Freiheit sei, und daß die Freiheit Gottes die Bestimmung des Menschen wäre."
11 Hirsch certainly takes inspiration for his phenomenology of the different religions in the history of ancient East and West from Hegel, *Vorlesungen über die Philosophie der Religion*, first edit-

Christianity too, although deriving from the Jewish religion – we shall return in the next paragraph to the link Hirsch finds between Judaism and Christianity – contains a pagan orientation, like the religions mentioned earlier. It was Paul of Tarsus, Hirsch claims, who transformed a religious feeling that was still close to Judaism in the Gospels into one that was split between a sense of man's infinite intrinsic guilt and a salvific faith in God who redeemed man through the sacrifice of His son. Absent in Pauline Christianity is the idea of freedom as an ethical category, as the capacity of obeying ethical commandments, conceded to man as a finite being by a transcendent God, granting the human possibility of self-redemption. As for paganism, for Paul of Tarsus too man is either subject to his nature or obeys an inscrutable God. Thus, for Hirsch, Christianity was not able to oppose the pagan world victoriously, but – he conceded – it had in its own particular way helped spread that religion that had been expressed in the Hebrew Bible.

Christian religious feelings also introduced aspects typical of paganism into the culture that originated from it in Europe and the West. Hirsch saw signs of a profound crisis in this culture in his day: confinement to one's own finiteness and subordination to an All whose rules one does not understand, so characteristic of paganism, was emerging forcefully in European culture once again. The disintegration of patriarchal social relations and the creation of economic systems and sovereign states beyond the control of those who belong to them, caused modern man to be torn between self-exaltation and conforming to powers whose meaning is no longer even questioned. What is required, then, is a philosophical perspective that arouses man's need to recover his essence – i.e. his "religious consciousness" – alive (though often suffocated by passions) in all human beings who continue to maintain their differences as individuals.

Jewish Tradition as Memory of the Human

The conclusion Hirsch deduces from his analyses and arguments about philosophy of religion and the history of religion – which is the narrative of a complicated, progressive-regressive movement – is that Judaism is indispensable to the modern world. Precisely because religion – what characterizes the human, i.e., the capacity to unite time and the eternal in the spirit of holiness, in freedom or

---

ed in 1832 (new critical edition by Walter Jaeschke, Hamburg: Meiner, 1983–85, 3 vol.). Yet unlike Hegel, Hirsch does not think that the reconciliation between rational and real, God and man, affirmed by Christianity, is the last point of the development of this phenomenology. He maintains the kind of relationship between God and man that is specific to Judaism.

in justice and mercy – finds its expression in Jewish sources, he sees Judaism as a religion of the present. Jews are present in the modern world not as people who continue to follow the precepts of an antiquated religion now superseded by Christianity, but as bearers of a universal outlook on humanity that enables men to recognize their dignity. Through its sources, its history and its experience, Judaism in the past has defended a humanism centered on the idea of a God who gives ethical rules to man deflecting the naturalistic, pessimistic, skeptical concepts of human nature. Still today it can perform the role of reminding humanity of what it means to be human, and of the heights man must reach if he wants to achieve his true essence, which is beyond yet connected with his existence. Thus for Hirsch, the participation of the Jews in the modern world following their emancipation does not obviate their need to maintain their tradition. Hirsch entrusted the Jews with the memory of the true sense of the biblical texts, convinced that they above all had the task of averting paganism by preserving the revelation of that dimension of human existence that coincides with independence from being and dependence on God.

For Hirsch, Abraham, the progenitor of the Jews, was the individual who, unlike the pagan, chose justice and mercy, and in this way became a "model" (*Vorbild*) for humanity. His religious attitude is an *aktive Religiosität*, which has an "intensive" side – as it is performed inside the family and community circle –, and an "extensive" side as it is directed outwards towards other human beings through action, word and prayer. Judaism subsequently delegated "extensive religious feeling" to Christianity, reserving "intensive religious feeling" for itself, despite knowing that the daughter religion would modify its teachings and stray from its roots.[12] Abraham remains the archetype of *homo religiosus*, not because, as Paul of Tarsus thought, he had faith against all rational evidence and beyond the law, but because he was animated by a rebellious spirit that opposed whatever might subjugate him to the weightiness of the earth, the cycle of nature, and the will of the powerful, and directed himself solely to God, whom the Patriarch intuited and felt close to, despite His infiniteness. Abraham understood the sense of commandments whose aim was the creation of justice and peace on earth.

Hirsch was convinced that the religious feeling that had been realized in Abraham and his small group of descendants should be implemented in the world and so become universal. Opposing Hegel – who pointed to contemporary

---

12 In this view of the roles of Judaism and Christianity in the world – the first concentrated in itself, the second directed to conversion of the pagans – Hirsch is inspired by Maimonides (*Mishneh Torah*, *Hilkhot Melakhim*) and Jehuda Ha-Levi (*Kuzari*, Part 3). Rosenzweig (*Stern der Erlösung*, Part 3), like Hirsch, had recourse to this view.

Christianity as inspired particularly by John's Gospel – Hirsch refused to identify any extant religion with "absolute religion". This was to be a messianic religion of the future, when war, violence and injustice would end. Thereby Hirsch's "philosophy of religion" – aimed at clarifying "religious consciousness" as the center and fulcrum of the history of human culture and inspired by the religious literature of the Jews as an expression of that consciousness – assumes the features of a messianic philosophy. Hirsch hopes that this "philosophy of religion" will equip men to continue the journey towards their redemption. However, this philosophical teaching proves true only if one first accepts the *Faktum* of practical reason – a reason that, as Kant already knew, cannot be founded on any argument concerning the being of the cosmos or of God. Only adhering to an indemonstrable ethical certainty can provide a foundation for philosophy as recognition of the human.

Conclusions

In Hirsch's *Religionsphilosophie der Juden*, mediaeval Jewish philosophy, especially in the renowned person of Maimonides, anticipates a philosophical anthropology aimed mainly at analyzing what is ethical in human actions. That is why Hirsch turns to this philosophy when formulating ideas endeavoring to solve the crisis of his day. Like the representatives of this mediaeval Jewish philosophy, he believed that thinking should start from a given reality – that of familial and social relations marked by justice and loving-kindness.

In the light of this interpretation of mediaeval Jewish philosophy Hirsch freed the *Guide for the Perplexed* from its scholastic casing, grasped its deeper substance, and anticipated some remarkable interpretations of the 20th century. Having divulged the deeper meaning of medieval Jewish thought, he delineated the continuity between the rationalism of mediaeval Judaism flourishing in Spain and that of modern German and European Judaism. Jewish rationalism may thus be understood as an ethical rationalism of great significance for the present age and for the future. This kind of rationalism recognizes firstly that the origin and beginnings of philosophizing lie in the firm conviction that God is the true reality: we cannot embrace Him as a subject, but we can understand His attributes of action.

Judith Frishman
Judaism Transformed and the Divine on Earth. Samuel Hirsch's Appropriation of the Hegelian Ideal State

The Welfare of Humanity or the State as the Divine Image on Earth

On March 28, 1840, Samuel Hirsch addressed a sermon to his Dessau congregation entitled "Israel's Present, or the Relationship between Present-Day Israel and the State".[1] March 28th was a Sabbath just prior to Passover, a holiday commemorating the Exodus from Egypt, and therefore an opportue moment for Hirsch to reiterate his philosophy in which freedom from slavery is central. Freedom, Hirsch says, is not just escape from tyranny but love of God. Traditionally Passover marks the beginning of the formation of the people of Israel. However, rather than devoting attention to the history of the community of the people, Hirsch chooses to emphasize the importance of contributing to the welfare of society at large. "One should not devote one's efforts to a specific group", he says, "but to the community that encompasses all communities", i.e. the state that forms the divine image on earth, in which humanity is swept up as a whole.[2] "The life of the state, love of the fatherland, working so that it flourish, is living in God, working for the welfare of humanity, the unfettered love (*die freitäthige Liebe*) that makes free (*frei*) and endows freedom (*Freiheit*)."[3]

Hirsch is aware that he preaches these unexpected words at a time when Jews in Germany have not been emancipated and are not able to take part in public life and serve their country, while in other countries they have already attained equality. Those countries, Hirsch opines, entertain a destructive theory that teaches that people originally lived without societal ties; individuals did as they pleased until they arbitrarily joined up and arbitrarily decided on the rights and duties of man. They then chose one from among themselves to serve them and care for the rights and duties; the king was to do that which

---

[1] Samuel Hirsch, "Israels Gegenwart, oder das Verhältniß des jetzigen Jisraels zum Staate", in idem, *Die Messiaslehre der Juden in Kanzelvorträgen. Zur Erbauung denkender Leser* (Leipzig: Heinrich Hunger, 1843), 26–46.
[2] Ibid., 29.
[3] Ibid., 30.

was relegated to him and no more than that. The people are the fatherland, the king but their representative. Religious upbringing remained outside his field of authority, and it was left to the individual to deal with in arbitrary fashion. In those countries the Jews were admitted to public service and subsequently felt no desire to fulfill Israel's mission. The synagogues became cold and empty, the gloom of the Middle Ages hung over them.[4]

While critical of the paths of emancipation elsewhere, Hirsch thanks God repeatedly for Germany's demand that the Jews first free themselves inwardly before being admitted to outward freedom. The king's heart is in God's hands, he avers, and when the king rejects Israel's service, it is in fact God's doing.[5] How did Hirsch come to such an assessment; why did he reject social contract theories and seemingly acknowledge society's critique of the Jews and their condition? The answer to these questions brings us to the heart of Hirsch's philosophy, a philosophy whose central ideas remained fairly constant – yet not without development – during his Dessau and Luxembourg periods. As a Hegelian philosopher, Hirsch was directly influenced by Hegel's concept of the state as expressed in his *Elements of the Philosophy of Right* (1821) and elsewhere. According to Hegel, autonomy, the subjective, the development of self-consciousness and freedom are that for which individuals should strive through a dialectical process leading them to reason and the absolute. Central in Hegel's philosophy is the idea of alienation: at the first level the individual, as an atomized being, is alienated. He becomes self-conscious and free when recognized by another conscious being whereupon mutual recognition ensues. The next level concerns the relationship between the believer and the divine: In the course of history the divine was first identified with nature, and subsequently understood as separate from nature, yet in the divine's transcendence God became alien to the believer. This alienation is finally overcome when God is recognized as spirit, comes in contact with other self-conscious subjects, and thereby becomes self-conscious. The final level of alienation is societal: Unlike the proponents of social contract theories, Hegel does not view the state as an artificial construction. Human beings have a need for interaction, he asserts, and it is only through relationships that self-consciousness becomes possible. On the societal level it is within a larger social structure, specifically in the generality of the state, that empirical particularity is transcended through the manifestation of the universal in the consciousness and will of individuals. In the ideal state the denizens recognize their will in that of the state and therefore voluntarily sacrifice their lives for

---

4 Ibid., 39–40.
5 Ibid., 30, 39, 45–46.

the greater good. It is in this ideal state that true freedom is realized, the state that is described by Hegel as the divine Idea as it exists on earth.

In practice Hegel envisioned the realization of the state through the estates that were to meet in a general body to express the general will. However, it was the constitutional monarch who had to add the form of a royal decree to the content of the legislation. By saying "I will", the king makes the general will willed. His proclamation is not simply an expression of his own will nor is it an automatic form of approval. It is an action acknowledging that the legislation is neither arbitrary nor the result of a compromise but actively willed by the citizens. For Hegel, the monarch's approval of Jewish emancipation would be an expression of society's will; for Hirsch it is the expression of God's will. The king is no egoist, Hirsch claims; he seeks neither titles nor status for his own sake. He is an unprejudiced judge whose well-being is tied to the whole; he executes God's work.[6]

Clearly for Hirsch the ideal state is the religious state, a divine institution whose purpose it is to realize everything divine on earth. The state desires to perfect what religion promulgates. If the state remains unconcerned with religion, ceases to be religious, it relinquishes its own health and even its life. Why then has the king – or God – refused to emancipate the Jews? Jews have not yet been admitted to the state because they do not make the connection between the Israelite religion and the purpose of the state. Interesting here is that Hirsch admonishes his congregants and readers for fearing the king alone rather than serving both God and the king. The reality, he explains, is that Jews are eager to join society and to do so, cast off their religion. Hirsch is not very concerned about those who simply drop the name Israelite for convenience's sake because these people are of little value. There are, however, intellectual, gifted Jews, who have abandoned Judaism after a long struggle in order to serve the state; they represent a loss for the Jewish community.[7] Thus, while at the beginning of his sermon Hirsch points to the Jews' parochial interests as problematic, he ends by admonishing those who leave the fold for the sake of public service for misunderstanding the Israelite mission.

In Hirsch's ideal state, religion and state service are not contradictory but complementary. This holds equally true for Judaism as for Christianity: neither Jews nor Christians need to renounce or abandon their religion to serve the state. Nothing in Judaism conflicts with the state, he says, not even the ceremo-

---

6 Ibid., 41.
7 Ibid., 43.

nial rites that are the Jewish expression of the covenant.[8] The Jews are to remain separate – and the king reiterates and reinforces this by refusing them citizenship – in order to fulfill their mission, i.e., the recognition and worship of God in freedom throughout the earth. Only by devoting themselves to their task can Jews serve the state with whose interests theirs coincide. By adhering to their faith Jews will become even more faithful servants of God *and* the king and be recognized as such. The Jews' duty is to demonstrate the blessedness of a holy life by bringing their actions to the attention of the public, demonstrating what it means to embrace God in one's heart. The true Israelite is not meant to become like all others, serving stone and wood, earthly and transient things, but rather serve as the image of divine freedom in all his doings and thought. God motivates the king to demand that the Israelite free his own heart and fulfill his task, after which he will be granted outward freedom.[9] Humanity too needs to be refined and freed, recognizing evil as worthless and adhering to the good and the Godly. The freedom that is central to Hirsch's philosophy is more specifically the freedom to love God and to labor, i.e., to carry out spiritual work for work's sake rather than for any selfish benefit or derivable pleasure. This freedom is granted by God and was revealed to the Jews. It opposes the slavery of paganism, the service of stone and wood, evil and sin.

As is obvious from the above, Hirsch's vision of the role of the Jews in the state as expressed in this sermon only partially meets Hegel's description of the ideal state and its citizens. This is hardly surprising because the latter's assessment of the Jewish contribution to his teleological philosophy of religion is limited, and the role Jews and Judaism play in his dialectics is outright negative.[10] Hegel groups the Greeks with the Jews – representing the religions of

---

8 Ibid., 45.
9 Ibid., 46.
10 For Hegel on Judaism see: *Hegel's Phenomenology of Spirit*, trans. Arnold Vincent Miller (Oxford: Clarendon Press, 1977), 466–470; Georg Wilhelm Friedrich Hegel, *Lectures on the Philosophy of Religion*, vol. 2, ed. Peter C. Hodgson, trans. Robert F. Brown et al. (Berkeley: University of California Press, 1984–1987), 152–160, 423–454, 669–687, 738–742; Georg Wilhelm Friedrich Hegel, *Lectures on the Philosophy of Religion*, vol. 2, trans. E.B. Speirs and J. Burdon Sanderson (London: Routledge and Kegan Paul; New York: The Humanities Press, 1968), 170–219. For the secondary literature, see a.o.: Martin Arndt, "Hegel und das Judentum", Hegel Jahrbuch 19, 1 (2013), 28–35; Bernard Bourgeois, "Judaïsme", in idem, *Hegel à Francfort ou Judaïsme, Christianisme, Hegelianisme* (Paris: Vrin, 1970), 35–55; Micha Brumlik, *Deutscher Geist und Judenhass* (Munich: Luchterhand Literaturverlag, 2000); Joseph Cohen, *Le Spectre juif de Hegel* (Paris: Galilée, 2005); Hans Liebeschütz, *Das Judentum im deutschen Geschichtsbild von Hegel bis Max Weber* (Tübingen: Mohr Siebeck, 1967); Michael Mak, "The Metaphysics of Eating. Jewish Dietary Law and Hegel's Social Theory", Philosophy and Social Criticism 27, 5 (2001), 59–88; Yirmiyahu

beauty and sublimity respectively – in an intermediary stage of the three-stage history of the advancement of the Spirit.[11] This stage surpasses the initial stage of immediate religion of the primitive and oriental peoples who are at one with nature and unaware of Spirit and therefore not free. True freedom is only realized in the final phase, in Christianity, the absolute religion, in which spirit and nature come together through revelation, i.e., the incarnation. The Divine is then in the human and the human recognizes that humans comprise elements of divinity.

Humans, who are not nature but spirit, need to self-extricate themselves from nature to become spirit, whose essence is self-elevated above nature. This takes place over a long period of development. Judaism recognizes the autonomy of God and thus his subjectivity, but the Jewish God is transcendental, eternal, and infinite. In contrast to this God, the believer sees himself as changeable, finite, and sinful. In short, the God of the Jews is alien and the relationship between God and the Jews is one of alienation.[12] The giving of the law remediates the situation somewhat, yet Hegel's Jews, like Kant's, are not autonomous because they obey the heteronomous law of a remote, transcendent, and therefore unknowable God. The Jews do not consciously consent to this law by acknowledging it to be rational and as a universal to which they adhere for the sake of the common good.[13] They offer slavish obedience to their God who demands obedience. He is the master, and the Jews are in turn unfree or slaves.[14] The happiness promised to the Jews is immediate, material, and in the empirical world. The Jews are not able to transform the material because, as the Bible indicates (Gen 2:15, Ps 24:1), their God owns the earth and as such the Jews are at best its stewards and therefore remain dependent, non-autonomous beings. They possess the earth but never own it (it is *Besitz* rather than *Eigentum*) and hence may never interfere with it. They are thus concerned with the material and their

---

Yovel, *Dark Riddle: Hegel, Nietzsche, and the Jews* (University Park, PA: The Pennsylvania State University Press, 1998), 21–59.
11 See for example Hegel, *Lectures on the Philosophy of Religion*, vol. 2, trans. E.B. Speirs and J. Burdon Sanderson, 170, 172, 179, 184, 187.
12 On the Jewish God as abstract see, for example *Hegel's Philosophy of Mind*, trans. William Wallace and Arnold Vincent Miller (Oxford: Clarendon Press, 1971), §384.
13 The understanding of adherence to the law as a common good, as the universal that takes priority over selfish individual desires or capriciousness reflects Hegel's idea of the ideal state. If Jews are not free but slaves, their potential participation in the ideal state would seem to be questionable.
14 Hegel applies his famous master-slave dialectic (Miller, *Hegel's Phenomenology of Spirit*, 111–119) to the relationship between God and the Jews. See Hegel, *Lectures on the Philosophy of Religion*, 153–157, 449–450.

possible control or loss of control over it, and they see the absolute in the immediate.[15]

For Hegel, developing self-consciousness and subjectivity involves seeing the natural as objective; man must possess the natural,[16] show his superiority over nature and transform it, thereby raising himself above his drives and natural instincts. One of these instincts is that of self-preservation; surmounting this instinct entails the willingness to sacrifice oneself. Through self-consciousness the human mind will participate in self-knowledge of the Absolute, just as infinite Reason or Spirit knows itself in and through the finite spirit and mind of individual human beings. Here the particular and the universal meet. The self-sacrifice requisite in the first stages of self-consciousness is paralleled by the self-sacrifice expected from members of the ideal state. The foregoing of particular, selfish interests is indispensable for the universal as embodied by the state, in which the particular and the universal are unified.

The natural is in the end finite and illusory and in this sense, Jews do not take part in reality. They remain outside of Hegel's dialectic where the real entails the processes of change, of becoming, of transformation. The Jews are thus not free in the Hegelian sense of freedom and therefore not able to participate in Hegel's ideal state.[17] While Christianity does not form the absolute or consummate religion of Hegel's philosophical history,[18] it does come close, offering through its *Vorstellungen*, a figurative (and thus lesser) analogy to Hegel's philosophical concept (*Begriff*) of the modern state. The "eating of oneself" that serves as a metaphor for the annihilation of the empirical, necessary both for the process of self-actualization, as well as for the suffering and self-sacrifice

---

15 *Besitz* characterizes the Jews' stewardship of the earth rather than ownership (*Eigentum*), precluding the vanquishing and transformation of nature. See Mack, "The Metaphysics of Eating", 78 and the following two notes in this article.

16 Miller, *Hegel's Phenomenology of Spirit*, §109.

17 Michael Mak provides a good summary of Hegelian freedom: "The autonomous transformation of empirical objects and the consequent self-consciousness of one's own participation within this material existence (which finally issues in the internalization of a politics of sacrifice, in which man, having realized his own empirical limit, transcends it by willingly risking his life for a greater general good) adequately describes Hegel's notion of freedom as he makes clear in his differentiation between *Eigentum* and *Besitz*." See Mack, "The Metaphysics of Eating", 78.

18 According to Hegel, philosophical insight is best. "But if this insight is lacking, the religious disposition may lead to the same result. Consequently, the State may have need of religion and faith. But the State remains essentially different from religion." Georg Wilhelm Friedrich Hegel, *Elements of the Philosophy of Right*, ed. Allen W. Wood, trans. Hugh Barr Nisbet (Cambridge: Cambridge University Press, 1991), §270 quoted by Sven-Erik Rose, *Jewish Philosophical Politics in Germany, 1789–1948* (Waltham, Mass.: Brandeis University Press, 2014), 77.

of the citizen for the sake of the state, is symbolized by Jesus's self-sacrifice unto death and the eating and drinking of wine and bread.[19]

The juxtaposition of Christianity with absolute religion is problematic even if it is qualified as a *Vorstellung*. While transforming its meaning, Hegel maintains traditional Christian typology and the concomitant stereotypical portrayal of Jews and Judaism. The Christianity upon which his philosophy hinges is as unreal as the Judaism he describes; it is an *ideal* Christianity (referred to by some as a secularized Protestantism),[20] a Christianity that has yet to be realized and, in fact, stands in stark contrast to the reality of the Church of Hegel's own time.

Despite his description of both the Jewish religion and the Jewish people as reprobate, Hegel did support the emancipation of the Jews, a fact that has puzzled many a Hegel scholar. It would seem, however, that the clue lies in Hegel's discussion of the universal and the particular. While the universal can only exist in and through particulars, Hegel says, no particular can fully express the universal. The universal does not consist of the sum of the particulars, but of the infinite that is within the finite of the particulars. Hegel describes the times in which he lives as tumultuous, and the modern state as still far from the ideal state. On the contrary: the universal has still not reached its highest stage. The process towards the universal continues while the particularities of the various religions persist and will continue to persist in the unforeseeable future. Sven-Erik Rose notes that Hegel opposes the Christian state as a "fusion of state and religion" where difference and particularity would not be tolerated. Hegel, he says, "underscores the danger of substituting religious piety, authority and conviction for the rule of rational law. He argues vigorously that the ethical totality of the state must protect diversity and determinate particularity from the threat of religious fanaticism that would destroy them".[21]

---

19 Mak, "The Metaphysics of Eating", 67–76 offers a fascinating explanation of the role of eating in Hegel's works. For dietary law and the metaphor of eating in Feuerbach, see Jay Geller, *The Other Jewish Question. Identifying the Jew and Making Sense of Modernity* (New York: Fordham University Press, 2011), 150–168. For Marx on Jews and defecation see Sven-Erik Rose, *Jewish Philosophical Politics in Germany*, 189–197.
20 Scholars debate whether Hegel's absolute religion is commensurate with Christianity. As will become evident in what follows, Hirsch does understand Hegel to be equating the two, only to counter this equation with a combination of Judaism and Christianity in order to arrive at the universal, i.e., a combination of the two religions.
21 Rose, ibid., 77. Mack, "The Metaphysics of Eating", 66, offers a different solution to this seeming contradiction by pointing out that for Hegel particular difference is only "real" for those who perceive immediate being as real "... whereas it actually exists only as an illusion. As such, difference needs to be ignored, and must not be discriminated against in a 'modern', that is, 'enlightened' state". Mak offers his solution as a more adequate understanding than

Hirsch's sermon needs to be read as an attempt to not only cede Jews and Judaism a place in history in the past, as had Hegel (albeit in the form of a failed progress), but also in the present and the future. Accomplishing this was contingent upon the allocation of a lasting and indispensable role for religion in the ideal state, based on an interpretation of the principles of Judaism and Christianity in their ideal forms. Hirsch formulates his defense by remaining within the Hegelian system yet redefining key concepts. However, he would soon be confronted with new political and material turns in the (theological) philosophies of Hegel's heirs regarding the ideal form of the state and the related question of the emancipation of the Jews. We will turn to these as well as Hirsch's replies to the same in the sections that follow.

Religion as the Source of Hate. Bruno Bauer's Political Theology, the "Jewish Question", and the Ideal State

In 1843, the same year that Hirsch's sermon was published, Bruno Bauer's *Die Judenfrage* appeared.[22] In this booklet the question of the emancipation of the Jews serves as a point of departure for a much broader discussion of society and the ideal state in which Bauer stood at odds with Hegel. "The problem of emancipation", Bauer claims, "is the problem of our age",[23] for not only the Jew needs to be emancipated: it is only because no one is free and privilege is the ruling power that the Jews were not granted freedom. Bauer thus criticizes the contemporary Christian state in Germany and the privileges granted to Christian institutions and individuals as well as Hegel's depiction of the ideal state, which although ostensibly no longer Christian, retained not only a Christian character but preserved the privileges of the nobles, estate owners and a new bureaucratic class that was to serve the state. Central to his criticism is the idea that

---

Yirmiyahu Yovel's in the latter's *Dark Riddle: Hegel, Nietzsche and the Jews* (University Park, PA: Pennsylvania State University Press, 1998). See Mak, ibid., 66–67. It is also more plausible than the analysis of Micha Brumlik in his recent book *Hegels Juden. Reformer, Sozialisten, Zionisten* (Berlin: Neofelis Verlag, 2019), 16–28. Brumlik (28) portrays Hegel as precursring the French Revolution's proclamation of human rights.

22 Bruno Bauer, *Die Judenfrage*, Deutsches Jahrbuch für Wissenschaft und Kunst V, 1842, reprinted as a brochure *Die Judenfrage* (Braunschweig: Friederich Otto, 1843). All references are to the 1843 edition.

23 Ibid., 19. See further ibid., 60, 92.

all religions are intrinsically exclusive, and that emancipation cannot be realized if the possibility of exclusion persists.[24]

The focus of Bauer's assessment of Jews and Judaism is on their place in history and their law.[25] His criticism is intermingled with traditional accusations of a lack of morality and lack of love for others i.e., misanthropy,[26] combined with the themes of egoism and personal advantage with which the reader will be familiar from both Christian and philosophical literature such as Kant's *Religion within the Limits of Reason Alone* (1793). Bauer, like Hegel, repeats a well-known Christian trope when accusing the Jews of being a-historical, of voluntarily and stubbornly living outside of history, and thus incapable of evolution.[27] Not only had they failed to recognize that the progression of Christianity from Judaism had made the latter redundant,[28] but as egoists they also had altogether lost interest in the progress of men and concentrated on personal advantage. Lacking historical consciousness, they could contribute neither leaders nor thinkers to society. While the Christian world was fighting for truth, for men and for freedom, the Jews were chimerical.[29] The supplemental theme of egoism is typical of the idealist philosophers and is developed at length in the materialist critique of Feuerbach[30] and Marx. Bauer points to Jewish suffering and rebuffs those who would defend the Jews by attributing this suffering to Christian oppression. In Hegelian fashion, Bauer equates this suffering with the unhappiness that is inherent in a religion whose adherents remain in the immediate and seek their happiness in the empirical. They developed no moral principle from

---

24 For an examination of Bauer's understanding of exclusiveness and universalism, see Massimiliano Tomba, "Exclusiveness and Political Universalism in Bruno Bauer", in Douglas Moggach, ed., *The New Hegelians. Politics and Philosophy in the Hegelian School* (Cambridge: Cambridge University Press, 2006), 91–113.
25 For discussions of Bauer's criticism of Judaism and Hirsch's reaction, see the articles by Gershon Greenberg and especially Laurent Mignon in this volume.
26 Bauer, *Die Judenfrage*, 30–31. For the Hegelian turn in Bauer's antisemitism see David Leopold, "The Hegelian Antisemitism of Bruno Bauer", History of European Ideas 25 (1999), 179–206.
27 Ibid., 10–11, 81–82.
28 Ibid., 34. For Bauer "Judaism was the preparation for Christianity and Christianity the completion and perfection of Judaism". Judaism is "an uncompleted, unfinished Christianity", and Christianity "a Judaism which has elected its own completion". Ibid., 45.
29 Ibid., 24, 27.
30 Ludwig Feuerbach's *The Essence of Christianity*, in which the Jews were accused of egoism, was published in 1841, prior to Bauer's *Die Judenfrage*, and was known to both Bauer and Marx. See the discussion of Feuerbach below.

their suffering[31] and failed to recognize the development of their own consciousness. However, their survival does serve an important purpose:[32] to remind Christians that their own essence is one of privilege rather than perfection.

Like Kant and Hegel before him, Bauer criticizes Jewish character as reflected in Jewish law: it was petty, arbitrary and had to be served unconditionally.[33] It could not be fulfilled but only made one aware of the gap between the finite human and the absolute God, a God who in Hegelian terms could not be known. Jews feared nature, lacked inner moral strength, and couldn't form a relationship with the environment or the world of man. The true function of their law was the preservation of the Jews as a separate people, restraining them from participating in European culture. Surely no state law could grant Jews equality when they continued to adhere to laws that pronounced their own privileged position.[34]

Bauer follows Hegel's philosophy of history when accusing the Jews' natural spirit of being opposed to the arts and sciences (*Wissenschaften*) that raise man beyond his immediate needs.[35] The achievement of monotheism, Hegel says, was its separation of God from nature. But because they considered nature as God's possession, the Jews were not able to transform it, were not free, and by extension could not create art. The Greeks, as autonomous beings, were able to conquer and transform nature and create things of beauty. Yet they granted nature autonomy, and therefore the Greeks, like the Jews, remained in the intermediate stage of Hegel's historical account of religion.[36] Unlike Hegel, for whom Christianity most closely represented the stage of the development of absolute spirit and absolute religion, Bauer deemed not only the privileged status of the Christian state but Christianity itself to be problematic.[37] While the link between Christianity and the absolute of Hegel's ideal state is still a topic of debate (i.e., does Hegel equate Christianity and the absolute religion), for Bauer Chris-

---

31 Bauer, *Die Judenfrage*, 9–10. In the Hegelian system, Jewish suffering is said to be due to the failure to find happiness in empirical existence (unhappy consciousness) whereas in Christianity, as exemplified in the life of Christ, suffering gives meaning to the general unhappiness of the world and reconciles it to a notion of happiness. See Mak, "The Metaphysics of Eating", 83.
32 Bauer gives a modern theological-political twist to Augustine's apologetic interpretation of the enigmatic persistence of Jewish existence after the coming of Christ.
33 Bauer, *Die Judenfrage*, 12, 24, 27, 36–37, 42.
34 Bauer, *Die Judenfrage*, 29–30.
35 Ibid., 49.
36 In the Hegelian system, humans were to be autonomous and subjugate nature. See the discussion of the metaphor of eating above as well as Mak's summary of the Hegelian notions of beauty and sublimity in Mak, ibid., 76–83, especially 79–81.
37 Bauer, *Die Judenfrage*, 20, 95–96.

tianity, conceived in a weak moment when "the manly spirit of Greek philosophy and classic culture embraced lustful Judaism", was nowhere near the ideal. Christianity, like all religions, was exclusive and Christian faith and love excluded those who were not Christian and who did not believe in the correct way. It was not love but hate that Christianity sowed. Employing Hegelian dialectics, Bauer claims that precisely because the Christian had grasped the meaning of consciousness, he should be able to struggle against Christianity; his all-pervasive lack of freedom must lead to freedom.

The Jews' desire for emancipation turns out to be a demand for privilege. For Bauer this desire functions as a proxy for the notion of privilege in general, its inherent problems and the inequities of society in his days, the roots of which are religion. Bauer's solution: The Jews needed to free themselves from Judaism, make the transition to the (surely imperfect) freedom of Christianity and progress onwards to the ultimate freedom of critical, scientific man. But Christians too must be self-critical and recognize that they too are not free – albeit to a lesser degree than the Jews – and abandon subordination and faith. Until that time, Jews were neither capable of being emancipated nor had they the right to demand emancipation, least of all in a Christian state where privileges must be respected and protected precisely because the state is organized upon them.[38] In the *juste milieu* the Jew should not be emancipated as a Jew but as a human being in a society that consists of human beings, one that is not based on religious privilege but had made the transition to (secular) real freedom.[39]

Religion as Anthropology. Feuerbach's Materialist Hegelianism and the Critique of Judaism

Bauer was not alone in instrumentalizing the Jews when moving in new directions of societal critique. In 1841 Ludwig Feuerbach (1804–1872) had published his *Essence of Christianity*[40] in which he described religion as a projection.[41] Hirsch had admittedly not yet taken cognizance of Feuerbach's *Essence of Chris-*

---

38 Bauer, *Die Judenfrage*, 53, 58, 68.
39 Ibid., 106–107.
40 Ludwig Feuerbach, *Das Wesen des Christentums* (Leipzig: Otto Wigand, 1841). The English translation is taken from Ludwig Feuerbach, *The Essence of Christianity*, trans. George Elliot [Marian Evans] (London: John Chapman, 1854).
41 Feuerbach, *The Essence of Christianity*, 224.

tianity when writing his *Religionsphilosophie der Juden*[42] but he was certainly familiar with it when working on his retort to Bauer, *Das Judenthum, der christliche Staat und die moderne Kritik*.[43] Feuerbach had already criticized Hegel in 1839:[44] Hegel, he said, viewed everything from the standpoint of development, so that the last stage of development is regarded as the totality that includes all previous stages. The result is a misrepresentation of nature as well as culture and religion, because it ignores their varieties and particularities. Moreover, the conjunction of nature and spirit foreseen in the Hegelian system of presupposition and consequence led to an antipathy toward nature and the sensible. Feuerbach disagreed with Hegel's claim that Christian theology had expressed in the form of imaginative symbolism (*Vorstellung*) that which philosophy had brought to clarity about the relationship between individuals and the world in the form of concepts (*Begriffe*). This relationship could not be explained by abstract philosophical concepts but through emotion, which lay at the heart of religion; the essence of Christianity was not the Absolute but human feeling. Whereas for Hegel Christianity was the consummate religion, for Feuerbach, Christianity, if consummate, was so only in the sense that it was a religion of pure selfhood.

Feuerbach's criticism of Hegel was an initial step in the development of his material anthropology that in time would come to include a critique of religion. Feuerbach, like Bauer, drew what he saw as the logical conclusions from Hegel's depiction of the incarnation as the sign of the divine in the human and of the infinite value of the finite individual. These Young Hegelians characterized religion as entailing man's worship of that which he is himself, hence in Feuerbach's words, religion is anthropology.[45] For Feuerbach this self-worship resulted in the disuniting of man from himself. Man sets God before him as the antithesis of himself: God is not what man is, and man is not what God is. Negative characteristics pertained to man and positive ones to God: God, for example, is infinite, man finite; God perfect; man imperfect; God eternal; man temporal; God

---

[42] Samuel Hirsch, *Die Religionsphilosophie der Juden oder das Prinzip der jüdischen Religionsanschauung und sein Verhältniß zum Heidenthum, Christenthum und zur absoluten Philosophie dargestellt und mit den erläuterten Beweisstellen aus der heiligen Schrift, den Talmudim und Midraschim versehen* (Leipzig: Heinrich Hunger 1842).

[43] Samuel Hirsch, *Das Judenthum, der christliche Staat und die moderne Kritik. Briefe zur Beleuchtung der Judenfrage von Bruno Bauer* (Leipzig: Heinrich Hunger, 1843). See Hirsch's remarks on p. 33 regarding his earlier lack of familiarity with the works of Bauer and Feuerbach.

[44] Ludwig Feuerbach, "Zur Kritik der Hegel'schen Philosophie", in Arnold Ruge and Theodor Echtermeyer, Hallische Jahrbücher für Deutsche Wissenschaft und Kunst 208 (1839), 1157–1160; no. 209, 1165–1168; no. 210, 1673–1677; no. 211, 1681–1684; no. 212, 1689–1693; no. 213, 1697–1702; no. 214, 1705–1709; no. 215, 1713–1718; no. 216, 1721–1725.

[45] Feuerbach, *The Essence of Christianity*, 228–229 and elsewhere.

holy, man sinful. God is absolute, positive, the sum of all realities; man is absolutely negative, comprising all negations. God is man's alter ego, his other lost, better half; God is the complement of man and in God he is first a perfect man.[46] The "essential standpoint of religion", Feuerbach writes, "is the practical or subjective". The goal of religion is the welfare, the salvation, the ultimate felicity of man; the relation of man to God is nothing else than his relation to his own spiritual good.[47] God is the realized salvation of the soul, or the unlimited power of effecting the salvation, the bliss of man. The Christian religion is especially distinguished from other religions in that no other religion has given equal prominence to the salvation of man.[48] Feuerbach regards the anthropologization of God that followed the divinization of man (i.e., Jesus as Son of God and the subsequent incarnation) as a positive development in the reuniting of man with himself through this divinization. However, at the same time he notes that religion – and Christianity in particular – has no idea of the universe, no consciousness of the truly infinite, no consciousness of the species.[49] Contrary to Hegel, Feuerbach claims that nature and spirit do not conjoin in religion (not even or especially not in Christianity) but rather that religion divorces itself from the world, from nature and from the appreciation of beauty. He refers here to those Christians who, regarding the this-worldly as one full of suffering, fail to find enjoyment in the here and now and seek compensation for this loss in God and the otherworldly.[50] God is a substitute for the true life of rational contemplation.[51]

Where Christianity fails despite the central role of the senses so essential for Feuerbach, love succeeds, and it is love that Feuerbach locates at the heart of virtue and as the essence of Christianity.[52] The opposite of love is egoism, and it is the practical or subjective view – whereby an individual has a relation to a thing only for his/her own sake – that is *tainted* with egoism.[53] We have already encountered the term egoism applied to the Jews in our discussion of Bauer. Whereas for Bauer the Jewish desire for emancipation stood for the Jews' egoistic

---

46 Feuerbach, ibid., 32.
47 Ibid., 184.
48 Ibid.
49 Ibid., 195.
50 Ibid., 184–185.
51 Ibid., 195.
52 For Feuerbach on love, see below. In *Die Judenfrage* Bauer pointed to Christian love as universal (ibid., 30) and says of the Christian God that he "does not discriminate among the nations but accepts into his kingdom everyone who accepts the true faith" (ibid., 17). However, Bauer also states that Christianity is exclusive (ibid., 17). See note 60 below.
53 Feuerbach's use of the subjective is other than Hegel's where subjectivity is an essential step in the development of religion. See the discussion above.

desire for the privilege of rights while refusing to join mankind, Feuerbach identifies *pure* egoism (and not simply subjectivity tainted by egoism) as the principle that is at the foundation of Judaism,[54] a description that would later be enrolled by Marx in an economic context.

As noted earlier, for Hegel, God's transcendence and the heteronomous law destine the Jews to remain in the immediate, unable to subjugate and transform nature, and unhappy in the limited happiness of the empirical over which they have little control. Their egoism lies in their attempt to secure control of the empirical, an impossibility because the empirical is under the control of a demanding and transcendent God. Judaism is thus a religion of unhappy consciousness. Feuerbach, for whom nature is not something to be subdued, reinterprets the Jews' egoism, recognizing it as the source of the doctrine of creation. If man looks at the world solely from a practical standpoint, he is at odds with nature and makes it an abject vessel of his selfish interest, his practical egoism.[55] This is theoretically expressed as: nature is created, the product of a command (as in the story of creation in Genesis, for example Genesis 1:3: "God said: 'Let there be light'") rather than something in itself. Nature is degraded to the level of a servant, a product or object of man's will and needs. When man separates himself from nature, he asks why it is there (thus the spirit/nature divide and the question as to their relationship). For he who experiences nature as beautiful, however, the question as to why it exists doesn't arise. Thus, the Jews, having separated themselves and their God from nature – for which they were positively evaluated by Hegel – have now become the selfish exploiters of nature.

Hegel and Feuerbach's assessment of paganism match in so far as both consider pagans to be closer to nature. However, while for Hegel this identification with nature is located at the lowest level of the development of the spirit, for Feuerbach the heathen evaluation of the world is far superior to that of monotheism: heathens did not utilize but contemplated nature and made it the object of their admiration. They did worship objects, so to say, but this was only because worship is the childish or primitive form of contemplation.[56] Religion, Feuerbach concludes, is nothing other than man's primitive, unemancipated consciousness of himself and of nature. The identification of nature and God

---

54 For Feuerbach on Judaism as egoism, see Feuerbach, "The Significance of the Creation in Judaism", in idem, *The Essence of Christianity*, 111–118.
55 Ibid., 111–112.
56 Ibid., 115.

in man's consciousness denotes humanity at one with the world; the idea of the world is the idea of the cosmos, of majesty, of deity itself.[57]

Feuerbach is reminiscent of Bauer when positing that the utilitarianism at the heart of Judaism is also expressed in the notion of a special divine providence, including chosenness and a belief in miracles. Applying his understanding of religion as a reflection of man's longings to Judaism, Feuerbach describes Yahweh, the God of Israel as troubling himself only for this people. Yahweh is nothing other than the personified selfishness of Israel to the exclusion of all other nations.[58] This absolute intolerance is the secret essence of monotheism, the religion that has only one – the individual – as its end. Feuerbach concludes that in worshipping the power of its God, Israel does none other than take power over the world.[59] Thus Feuerbach, like Bauer, has transformed key concepts in Christian anti-Judaism, particularly stubbornness and exclusiveness, into secular philosophical, political, and material arguments and has compounded these with an accusation that will reappear in 20th century antisemitic conspiracy theories.

Yet Feuerbach insists that not only Judaism, but also all religions are intolerant. Feuerbach, concurring with Bauer,[60] deems the entire concept of faith as intolerant from the start: the cause of faith and the cause of God are identified and ultimately faith will have no opposite. Love, as opposed to faith, is tolerant. It recognizes virtue even in sin and truth in error. Love, Feuerbach says, is reconcilable with reason alone; … for as reason, love is free, universal in its nature whereas faith is narrow-hearted, limited. Only where reason rules, does universal love rule; reason is itself nothing else than universal love.[61] It was faith, not love,

---

57 Although spirit and nature do coincide in absolute religion in the third stage of Hegel's philosophy of history, nature has been transformed by the human spirit, a transformation that Feuerbach would deem undesirable. See Mack, "The Metaphysics of Eating", 77.
58 Feuerbach, *The Essence of Christianity*, 117–118.
59 Ibid., 118.
60 Tomba explains that according to Bauer, "Christianity, which presents itself as the religion of universal love, offering to all the gift of faith, is also the religion of universal hatred, because it would exclude all that contradicts faith." Tomba, "Exclusiveness and Political Universalism in Bruno Bauer", 97–98, referring to Bauer, *Die Judenfrage*, 17.
61 Feuerbach explains that "Faith makes belief in its God law: Love is Freedom". See Feuerbach, "The Contradiction of Faith and Love", in idem, *The Essence of Christianity*, 245–266, here 245. Yet he also distinguishes between Christian love and true love. Like Bauer he claims that Christian love is exclusive: "God, it is true, loves all men; but only when and because they are Christians, or at least may be and desire to be such. To be a Christian is to be beloved by God; not to be a Christian is to be hated by God, an object of the divine anger. The Christian must therefore love only Christians – others only as possible Christians …", ibid., 251. True love,

not reason, which invented hell. To love, hell is a horror; to reason, an absurdity. It would be a pitiable mistake to regard hell as a mere aberration of faith, a false faith. Hell is already present in the Bible. Faith is everywhere like itself; at least positive religious faith, faith in the sense in which it is here taken – and must be taken – unless, Feuerbach writes, we would mix with it the elements of reason, of culture, – a mixture which indeed renders the character of faith unrecognizable.[62]

In Feuerbach's definition of true religion (i.e., emancipated consciousness) love and morality are supreme. Thus, reason and love rather than reason and the Hegelian qualities of knowledge, intellect and absolute Spirit lead to the general, the universal. True religion consists of the relations between human beings, relations based on the affections, on the heart. Whereas this relation has been sought in a mirror image of reality that attributed superhuman qualities to the Gods, it may be found directly without mediation in the love between two people. Rational self-restraint regarding oneself and love in relations with others are the basic laws of Feuerbach's morality; from them, all others are derived.[63]

The Ideal State is a Christian State. Samuel Hirsch on Jews, Judaism, the State and Society

Upon the request of his friend Leopold Zunz, Hirsch reluctantly replied to Bauer in a series of letters bearing the title *Das Judenthum, der christliche Staat und die moderne Kritik* (1843).[64] In his three-part review of this work in *Literaturblatt des Orients*,[65] Hermann Jellinek praises Hirsch for having done a service by replying to Bauer's *Die Judenfrage* and its accusations against the Jews. However, he criticizes Hirsch for making use of theological arguments to answer Bauer's antitheological approach to a human problem; Hirsch never really deals with Bauer's central thesis concerning emancipation. The reviewer's remarks are astute; however, he ignores the fact that Bauer's critique of Jews and Judaism is complicat-

---

unlike Christian love, is reconcilable with reason alone for like reason, it is free and universal, ibid., 255.
62 Ibid., 255.
63 Ibid., 154–155.
64 Hirsch, *Das Judenthum, der christliche Staat und die moderne Kritik*. Hirsch addresses Zunz directly on pages 2, 4, 5, 8.
65 Hermann Jellinek, "Die Judenfrage. Teil 1", Literaturblatt des Orients 25 (20 Juni 1843), 385–390; "Die Judenfrage. Teil 2", Literaturblatt des Orients 26 (27 Juni 1843), 401–408; "Die Judenfrage. Teil 3", Literaturblatt des Orients 27 (4 Juli 1843), 423–430.

ed, thereby complicating the formulation of any possible reply. Bauer's arguments are initially theological but are transformed philosophically in the line of the Hegelian critique of Judaism, only to take an anti-religious political turn. In view of Hirsch's sermon on the relationship between Israel and the state, it might be unfair to expect anything different from Hirsch's pen. However, it must of course be noted that it is one thing to address one's own congregants and yet another to enter a public debate; hence the arguments Hirsch delivered in the synagogue would not necessarily be convincing to a non-Jewish audience. Moreover, Hirsch and Bauer were both Hegelians, and in the past had held similar positions on many points, even though Hirsch, unlike Bauer, could never accept Hegel's identification of Christianity as the consummate or absolute religion. We would therefore expect Hirsch to use Hegelian weapons to beat Bauer at his own game. However, by 1843 the rules of play had changed drastically. Whereas in his earlier works of 1839 Bauer employed a historical-critical approach to both the Old and New Testaments,[66] by 1842, in his third volume on the Synoptic Gospels,[67] Bauer's view of religion had changed drastically. His criticism was no longer limited to the Jews for having outlived themselves, in Hegelian terms a presupposition (*Voraussetzung*) sublated by its consequence (*Konsequenz*). He now aimed his arrows at religion in general and at Christianity more specifically in his most rabid and anonymously published work *Das entdeckte Christentum* (1843).[68] Surprisingly, this did not prevent Bauer from engaging earlier Hegelian arguments in *Die Judenfrage*, including the advantaged position granted Christianity – arguments that he no longer accepted. In this work he also stooped to employ age-old Christian anti-Jewish polemics as well as more modern stereotypes, one of the reasons why it was so hard to counter his massive accusations.

Throughout the letters Hirsch attempts to answer the following accusations: 1) the Jews are relics of the past, living outside of history; 2) they have produced nothing of value; 3) they abhor nature and exploit it only for their own benefit.

---

66 Bruno Bauer, *Kritik der Geschichte der Offenbarung. Die Religion des Alten Testaments in der geschichtlichen Entwicklung ihrer Prinzipien dargestellt*, 2 vol. (Berlin: F. Dümmler, 1838); Idem, *Kritik der evangelischen Geschichte der Synoptiker*, 2 vol. (Leipzig: Otto Wigand, 1841).
67 Bruno Bauer, *Kritik der evangelischen Geschichte der Synoptiker und des Johannes* (Berlin: Friedrich Otto, 1842).
68 Bruno Bauer, *Das entdeckte Christentum* (Zürich: Verlag des Literarischen Comptoirs, 1843). The title is of course reminiscent of Johann Andreas Eisenmenger, *Entdecktes Judenthum* (Frankfurt, 1700). Much to Hirsch's surprise, Bauer refers to Eisenmenger in *Die Judenfrage*, whose work Hirsch considered unworthy of scholarly attention. On Bauer, Eisenmenger and Hirsch, see Hirsch, *Das Judenthum, der christliche Staat und die moderne Kritik*, 116 and the article by Laurent Mignon in this volume.

His discussion includes an alternative to Hegel, Bauer and Feuerbach's understanding of sin and freedom and ends with a vision of the ideal state and ideal religion.

Hirsch notes that Bauer, when treating the course of history, makes use of the Christian terms preparation and fulfillment as parallels to the Hegelian dialectical terms *Voraussetzung* and *Konsequenz*. By reverting to arguments of the Orthodox Church and using the terms preparation and fulfillment, Bauer apparently views Christianity as a necessary product of Judaism. A product is something quite other than a consequence, Hirsch claims; a product allows its producer to continue to exist while in the consequence, the premise is without rights.[69] Bauer, however, posits an indirect, negative preparation: Jewish law – an eternal, unrealizable "Must" – can't possibly be fulfilled because of sin. Judaism or the Jewish presence, choosing to remain under the curse of the law, serves a negative purpose by making people aware of the Jews' infelicity. Hirsch concludes that the Church is thus not even the consequence of Judaism but its opposite. Through faith and grace the contamination of nature through Adam's sin is broken for believers but not removed. Therefore, as it is impossible to remove sin on earth, a whole new earth and a whole new heaven, a new creation are needed.

Despite the difference between the Hegelian approach (which is somewhat more positive) and that of the traditional church, sin also plays a central role in Hegel's philosophy. According to Hegel, man's nature is evil because he is part of nature and not free. Choosing to remain in this natural state left man in a state of enslavement and suffering. The Jews, who are constantly aware of their finite state and sinfulness,[70] remain enslaved; for them there is no reconciliation. The philosophical negation of this situation meant freedom or virtue. The parallels here to the Christian doctrine of Original Sin overcome by the Incarnation are obvious. Indeed, for Hegel, Christ's willing acceptance of suffering and death represent the negation of this situation (the negation of the negation caused by the Fall), reconciliation and the beginning of the final phase of the ultimate triumph of the Spirit.

---

69 Hirsch, *Das Judenthum, der christliche Staat und die moderne Kritik*, 27–28. The Hegelian term *Aufhebung* can mean to abolish, preserve, or transcend and is most often translated as to sublate. Hirsch understands Bauer's use of *Voraussetzung* and *Konsequenz* to mean that Judaism should have surceased existence, but the Jews refused to move on.

70 Hegel's attribution of this perpetual sense of sinfulness to Jews, based on passages in the Psalms, would infer that the concept of Original Sin is more applicable to Judaism than to Christianity.

Hirsch contrasts Judaism's positive evaluation of the role of nature and of this world to the Christian and Hegelian notions of the necessity to sin and the Christian turn to otherworldliness. Through his critique of Bauer, Hirsch is also able to respond to Feuerbach's evaluation of Judaism as egoism, the exploitation of nature and the lust for power. Hirsch defines monotheism as the honoring of one, imageless God who is neither opposed to nature nor for whom nature need disappear; to the contrary: He created nature and saw it was good.[71]

While admitting that it is possible to define monotheism without referring to its opposite – paganism – Hirsch doesn't let the opportunity pass to compare Judaism and paganism. He is thus able to return to a prominent theme in his major philosophical work,[72] claiming that the comparison makes things much clearer.[73] This also offers Hirsch the opportunity to introduce his alternative to the Hegelian teleological account of the history of religions once more. According to the author, worship of nature takes on one of two forms: either one surrenders to nature and seeks to implement its laws, or regards nature as the enemy, something to escape by way of self-infliction. Bauer's description of the law as heteronomous and a form of enslavement pertains to paganism rather than to Judaism, where nature is recognized in its own right. Nature is neither absolute, something to flee, nor sinful because it is of God and created well according to its own qualities despite its finitude.[74] As for God's omnipotence – both Feuerbach and Bauer pass negative judgment on this quality. Bauer, like Hegel, concluded that nothing can be independent before the transcendent God of the Jews, and nothing can resist him; autonomy and subjectivity are therefore impossible. For Hirsch, if God is all-powerful, everything is of necessity good because everything comes from him. So too, the creation story in the first chapter of Genesis emphasizes that all individual parts of nature are good, something Feuerbach ignores. If, as Feuerbach claims, theology is anthropology, once man knows God as the creator and as omnipotent, he knows his own essence, that it is not foreign to God's. He will understand that God's will is attainable and can be fulfilled because he will gain his true essence as God wished it. Therefore, if man fulfills God's will, he fulfills his own true will. Thus, man does not surrender

---

[71] Ibid., 33.
[72] Hirsch, *Die Religionsphilosophie der Juden*. For a discussion of the difference between Hegel's and Hirsch's understanding of monotheism see Robert Erlewine, "Samuel Hirsch, Hegel, and the Legacy of Ethical Monotheism", Harvard Theological Review 113, 1 (2019), 89–110.
[73] Hirsch, *Das Judenthum, der christliche Staat und die moderne Kritik*, 34.
[74] Ibid.

himself to something foreign to himself: God's will is not foreign to man, but truly human and the law is therefore moral law.[75]

In what appears to be a critique of Kant, Hegel and Bauer,[76] Hirsch emphasizes that moral will is of value only if it performs deeds, labors voluntarily without compensation and is pleased, just as God was pleased with his own work. The second chapter of Genesis relays this very message: it is the story of God's voluntary labor, labor for its own sake rather than a result of the sinfulness of nature, or a necessary evil for the derivation of pleasure. Sin is in fact not entrenched in man's nature – as pagans would have it – but in unauthorized enjoyment, desiring to reap where one hasn't sown. The biblical text encourages man to look sin directly in the eye and see it for the lie that it is, escape unhappiness by reaching for the tree of life and for free labor. In sum, the Bible protests the idea that the finite must be sinful.[77]

Having countered the Christian and Hegelian interpretations of sin and rejection of nature as well as Feuerbach's claim that Jews exploit nature, Hirsch next reviews the course of Jewish history and Jewish creativity. He is willing to concede that a lot went wrong, that Jews did not always develop the important principle of freedom and labor throughout history. However, he says, as far as this is

---

[75] Ibid., 38–39. This is Hirsch's initial understanding and application of Feuerbach's slogan "theology/ religion is anthropology". This catchphrase is recurrent in *Das Judenthum, der christliche Staat und die moderne Kritik* and developed more fully by Hirsch in *Die Reform im Judenthum und dessen Beruf in der gegenwärtigen Welt* (Leipzig: Heinrich Hunger, 1844). There (26–28) Hirsch says that God is nothing other than a higher state of human consciousness and that Judaism is a revealed religion, yet not in the sense of its being a supernatural mystery. It proclaims only that which is clear and available to all men through reason from the start and declares its truths to be common to humanity, encouraging acceptance even without a Mt. Sinai or the miraculous appearance of God. What is revealed is not a teaching but a secret of history (*Geschichtsgeheimniss*). On these developments in Hirsch's philosophy see Judith Frishman, "True Mosaic Religion. Samuel Hirsch, Samuel Holdheim and the Reform of Judaism", in Judith Frishman, Willemien Otten, and Gerard Rouwhorst, eds., *Religious Identity and the Problem of Historical Foundation. The Foundational Character of Authoritative Sources in the History of Judaism and Christianity* (Leiden: Brill, 2004), 195–222.

[76] Hirsch, *Das Judenthum, der christliche Staat und die moderne Kritik*, 27, quotes Bauer as saying that by adhering to Judaism, Jews refuse to move on and are therefore unethical. He uses the term *sittlich*, a term that goes beyond morals in the sense of adhering to societal mores, and entails striving for the progress of the universal, public affairs and the life of the state. Kant's moral imperative was understood to be internal, in thought rather than leading to deeds. Hirsch's interpretation of the creation story most directly opposes Hegel's. See Erlewine, "Samuel Hirsch, Hegel, and the Legacy of Ethical Monotheism", and idem, "Resolving Contradictions: Samuel Hirsch and the Stakes of Modern Jewish Thought", AJS Review 44, 2 (2020), 317–344.

[77] Hirsch, *Das Judenthum, der christliche Staat und die moderne Kritik*, 35–38.

concerned, the Jews are no worse than the Christians. Their histories are parallel: having lived as an oppressed minority under the Christians, Jews followed Christian trends. When the Christian cultivated his otherworldly faith (*bildete seinen jenseitigen Glauben aus*), the Jew followed suit with his law that too had become otherworldly (*jenseitig gewordenes Gesetz*). That is the mystery of the Talmud. When Greeks infiltrated the Arab world, Jews took part in academic work, and wrote philosophical treatises in Arabic. If in the Middle Ages Christians were scholastic and casuistic – Jews had their counterpart in the Talmud study of France. Christian mysticism was paralleled by *Kabbalah*; Reformation by Levita and Lutheran dogmatics by pilpul. If the Jews had no world, they could hardly create art and therefore Bauer's lambasting would seem unfair. On the positive side, Jews refused the spiritual, otherworldly life. The alternative of turning to the past did have adverse consequences because the turn was not to the past's spirit but to its outward forms and symbols. Nonetheless, despite this negative history, when passing judgment, Christians should consider the Jews of the 19th century and their use of text and tradition, rather than solely those Jews who followed their law without meaning. Would Christians consider only Orthodox Christians to be representative of Christianity, as Bauer had done? In short, Hirsch concludes, a simple essentialist approach would not do.[78]

Having criticized Christians, their history, and accomplishments by way of Jewish self-criticism, Hirsch affirms that the Jews now demand equality while claiming no privilege. They have proven that they can live their lives according to their essence, and have removed all deceit, shame and half-heartedness from their lives. How then could the state imbued with religion, the Christian state, deny Jews emancipation without contradicting itself and its principle? The Jews, Hirsch claims – here employing Hegelian terms – indeed consider the state law to be nothing less than the expression of universal legal consciousness and ethics (*Ausdruck des allgemeinen Rechtsbewusstseins und ... Sitte*), recognized and validated as the truth by the general will. Nevertheless, Christians will always remain prejudiced and appalled by what they view as unabashed demands made by Jews. Before all else, Christians will expect the Jews to concede that they need improvement – although in fact, Hirsch notes in an aside, the Jews need no more improvement than do Christians! – and acknowledge Christian superiority prior to broaching the topic of their (i.e., the Jews') adverse societal position.[79]

---

78 Ibid., 19.
79 Ibid., 10–11.

In the final sections of his refutation, Hirsch returns to his preferred Hegelian philosophical system (and that of Bauer as well) of *Voraussetzung* and *Konsequenz* to present his version of the ideal state. In doing so he takes a radical step. Whereas in his *Religionsphilosophie* he had called Judaism an intensive and Christianity an extensive religion,[80] in *Das Judenthum, der christliche Staat und die moderne Kritik* Hirsch describes Judaism as a *Voraussetzung*. However, this time it is not the Church that is the *Konsequenz* of Judaism but Jesus, for the Church is nothing but Christianity gone wrong. In the *Religionsphilosophie*, Hirsch posits that Jesus provided no reason for the Jews to form a new religion. He had fulfilled his task, as every Israelite must do; he was perfect only in the sense that others were and can be. Jesus is the classical character of monotheism and thus the classical character of humanity and truth. Jesus knew his mission as a man and as an Israelite and fulfilled it. He knew that man's purpose was to labor and by free, voluntary labor preserve his freedom. He understood that Israel was to set an example and by serving as such he was a true Israelite. He invited others to join the community, not by becoming Jewish but by recognizing that God is the creator of all, that everything on earth is good and not in opposition to the Creator. Through labor, the fulfillment of the mission on earth, and in free love for God salvation could be obtained on earth in the here and now. This work of Jesus was the consequence of Judaism in the strictest sense.[81]

Rushing through an overview of Christian history, Hirsch arrives at his own times that he sees, following Hegel, as having come to self-realization, as having become conscious of what it wants to be: the Christian state. Unlike the Christian state of the Middle Ages, this Christian state represents true progress. The old church recognized only itself; the state had no rights; the emperor had to obey the Pope or was removed. This Church had created neither privilege nor bureaucracy (*Beamtenstaat*) because the state was simply not important. Now that the Protestant church appointed the sovereign ruler (*Landesherr*) as its highest bishop, the first step towards the birth of the Christian State has been taken. The Christian State is recognizable by its Godly demeanor; that life in and for the state is holy. When the State – which will be worldly Christianity – is not pervaded by Original Sin, then the new heaven and earth will have arrived.[82]

Reversing Bauer's claim that emancipation in a Christian state is pointless as it simply comes down to privilege, Hirsch opines that it is precisely in the constitutional state that there is not much to win by emancipation. In a constitutional

---

80 See the article by Gershon Greenberg in this volume.
81 Hirsch, *Das Judenthum, der christliche Staat und die moderne Kritik*, 88–89.
82 Ibid., 98–99.

state equal rights must mean equal duties, but Jews do not have equal duties – as they are excluded from military service. Moreover, the constitutional state has no religion, as is the case in North America where material welfare is so important that even slavery is perpetuated. Germany has rightly rejected this model. While it is true that it is dangerous for the state to give too much preference to one confession, the other extreme is equally dangerous. In the constitutional states the masses have obtained what they wish; they have little interest in religion. In France Jews are emancipated and the state bears all costs of the cultus; there is even a Jewish faculty. Yet the French Jews are far behind the German Jews in academic pursuits.[83]

What then is the place of Judaism in this State? If the Christian State truly understands itself, how can it exclude Judaism, *true Judaism* that has come to self-consciousness? Jews and Judaism suffered for the realization of the Christian State, and the Messiah is nothing other than the realization of the Christian State, the reality of the kingdom of truth and virtue on earth![84] Jewish history is the positive, and not the negative, preparation of Christ; God guided the history of this people, so that it serve as the paradigm (*Urbild*) of all history.[85] Hirsch urges Christians to insight with the following words:

> Acknowledge that God created man that they all become Christ and walk in the way of his spirit, live his life ... the life of God's will. Acknowledge that when humanity didn't want to be Christian, God chose a people as his first-born son ... and punished it so that it knew the Lord and spent its life loving God with all its heart, its soul and might until it brought forth Jesus. Admit God left the peoples to their fate so that they reap the wages of their self-chosen ways. Yet He didn't lose sight of them: ... when they perceived that their ways had been evil, He gave them the ripe fruit of the first-born. Admit this new fruit took root among the peoples and healed depravity and confess your readiness to become Christians. Or do you need a creed other than Holy Scripture? And is this something other than the sacred history of humanity? ... We must become Christians before we are allowed to par-

---

83 Ibid., 8.
84 For an account of Hirsch's ideas concerning the Messiah and the messianic age, see the article of George Y. Kohler in this volume.
85 On the back side of the title page/ facing the dedicatory page of *Das Judenthum, der christliche Staat und die moderne Kritik*, Hirsch includes the following quote by Johann Caspar Lavater on the paradigmatic nature of Jewish history, thereby opening and closing his work in the same vein: "Ich möchte diese dramatische Geschichte der jüdischen Nation die grossgezeichnete, poetisirte Geschichte jeder Nation, jeder Familie, jedes Menschen, ich möchte Sie das teleskopische Medium nennen, wodurch das Dramatische in allen Geschichten gemeiner Völkerschaften, Familien, Personen angesehen werden könnte." (I would like to consider the dramatic history of the Jewish nation as the grandly portrayed, poetic history of every nation, every family, every person, and recognize it as the telescopic medium by means of which the drama in the histories of all peoples, families, and persons may be viewed.)

ticipate in the Christian state. What does it mean to be Christian if not to act, to live in the manner that Jesus did? If this is so, then we are Christians and strive with all our might to be so. [...] But if we must consider the world corrupt, think that we must first be symbolically cleansed from this impurity in order to receive the sublime spirit that is homeless on earth and only feels at home in the other-worldly, a new world – then don't talk of a Christian State. Speak of Christianity and leave the State to its fate. Well then you have reckoned Christianity a lie. ... As such Christianity is powerless and thus irrelevant for this world and all worldly matters![86]

The Christian State can and shall live according to the spirit of Christ; and that spirit of Christ will rule on this earth that is created by God and is not unworthy of serving as a homeland for the human spirit, spirit of Christ. The Christian State will recognize the true Jews as Jews, – those who live God-pleasing lives and are a blessing for the peoples, who bring the reign of truth on earth, and recall their double duties to their mission and the State by way of their symbols and ceremonies. The Christian State will love them and say: "God bless you, you dwelling of true piety (*Frömmigkeit*), unmovable holy mountain" (Jer 31:23).[87]

Conclusions

One of the (if not the main) driving force(s) behind Hirsch's writings is to secure a place for Judaism in modern society. He does so in *Die Religionsphilosophie der Juden* by pointing out that the Hegelian concept of freedom is *the* principle of Judaism and is in fact expressed most fully in Judaism. Hirsch must challenge the order of Hegel's stages of the historical development of religion where Judaism, along with the Greeks, is relegated to the intermediate stage. He does not stop at locating Judaism in the final stage of development closest to the ideal – and for Hirsch messianic – State, but instead adopts alternative categories of the pagan, the passive versus Judaism, the active religion. Christianity, a conjoining of both, is accorded a place in the development toward the absolute because it transformed the Jewish message, making it suitable for the pagans, thereby guaranteeing its acceptance and dissemination.

In his refutation of Bauer, Hirsch is eager to explain why Jews are worthy of emancipation and beyond that, of total acceptance as equals in a state to which they are committed and will serve loyally. He goes a step further when identifying the Christian State with the ideal state. Nevertheless, this ideal state corresponds

---

86 Ibid., 100–101.
87 Ibid., 103.

more closely with the ideal, unrealized state envisioned by Hegel rather than with the present-day Christian State. Going one – for a Jewish thinker – logical step further, Hirsch, in *Die Messiaslehre*, relates this ideal state to the messianic world, a world that has spiritually progressed to such a degree that the Messiah would come. As George Kohler explains, Hirsch's Messiah would not come to bring about change but would come only after society had transformed itself; his task would be to keep people on the path of justice and goodness.[88] Hirsch's rejection of a miracle making Messiah[89] is most likely a reaction to Hegel's description of miracles as something that God brings about in nature but that does not relate to his ultimate goal. Miracles represent only partial and ad hoc divine appearances; God will appear fully in the form of spirit, that is, in the form of Jesus. Hegel's (and the Young Hegelians') emphasis on the development and meeting of human and divine consciousness as reflected in God's human manifestation would account for Hirsch's emphasis on a personal Messiah[90] rather than a messianic era, as opposed to the concepts of many of his reform contemporaries. Moreover, Hirsch's unusual claim that the Messiah would be subordinate to *Keneseth Israel*[91] parallels Hegel's description of the monarch in the ideal state whose task it would be to enact that which the *totality* of the citizens willed as a group. The union of the will of the people and the will of the monarch would only transpire in the state representing "real freedom", the ultimate purpose of history. That this Messiah/King[92] would arise from the Jewish people is surely a logical identification for Hirsch to draw because it is in Judaism that the principle of ultimate freedom is best expressed – an assertion that Hirsch defends throughout his works.

The Christianity Hirsch describes is not just the ideal Protestant (secularized) Christianity of Hegel; it is none other than the *true* consequence of Judaism, i.e., religion as practiced by Jesus. Hirsch's embrace of the Hegelian ideal state is tied to his desire to include Judaism, and the Jewish understanding of freedom within that state, apparently leaving him with no other option than to acknowledge the Christian State. It is difficult to imagine that Christians, Hegel, or the Young Hegelians such as Bauer and Feuerbach would accept Hirsch's description of the absolute religion or ideal state. Indeed, Bauer would later ridicule what he regarded as Hirsch's unsupported declarations, e.g.: Judaism remains the driving force of all

---

88 See the article of George Y. Kohler in this volume, esp. 171, 176, and 179.
89 *Die Messiaslehre*, 399.
90 Ibid., 397.
91 Kohler, ibid., 176.
92 The Hebrew designation *melech ha'mashiach* (messianic or Messiah-King) represents a widespread concept in Judaism and accords with Hirsch's identification of the Messiah with the monarch, albeit in a form adapted to Hegelian concepts.

history and will continue to be so in the future; Judaism's protest against the abstract, otherworldly spirituality of the Middle Ages led society back to the concrete grounds of knowledge (*Wissenschaft*). Instead of making all sorts of unfounded claims, Bauer retorts, it would have been wiser had Hirsch seriously engaged with Bauer's arguments particularly concerning the logical unwillingness of a Christian State to grant anything more than tolerance to other religions. Bauer is also unconvinced that the different religious groups will ever be able to agree about overarching values and general principles, as they will present arguments arising from their own backgrounds and specific history. This holds true even for the current state of indeterminacy because each party will conceive its own ideas about the directions, expanse, and intensity of future development.[93]

In his later works Hirsch would shift the emphasis from freedom to work/labor and more especially love when outlining Israel's principle.[94] This turn is due to several factors, most prominent among them: the centrality of love in Feuerbach's dissection of religion and rejection of Hegelian philosophical concepts; Marx's materialist theory; and Hirsch's involvement in the Masonic lodge in Luxembourg. He also became more critical of Church intervention in state law. The future religion of the ideal state envisioned by Hirsch continued to resemble the transformed version of Judaism in Hegelian terms as attested in *Das Judenthum, der christliche Staat und die moderne Kritik*. Yet this "religion of tolerance", as Hirsch called it, not only encompassed Judaism, Christianity, and Freemasonry, but was to be a melding, a new form embodying the divine-human truth present in all three.[95]

---

[93] "Über die Judenfrage", Allgemeine Literatur-Zeitung 1 (December 1843), 1–17, here 8–10. This journal was edited by Bruno Bauer and the article, although published anonymously, is without doubt written by Bauer himself as an answer to various reviews of his *Die Judenfrage*.

[94] Samuel Hirsch, *Die Humanität als Religion, in Vorträgen gehalten in der Loge zu Luxemburg* (Trier: C. Troschel, 1854).

[95] For my discussion of these developments see Judith Frishman, "On Religion, Humanity and Tolerance. Samuel Hirsch's Addresses to the Freemasons Lodge in Luxemburg", in Norbert Franz and Jean-Paul Lehners, eds., *Nationenbildung und Demokratie. Europäische Entwicklungen gesellschaftlicher Partizipation*, Luxemburg-Studien/Études luxembourgeoises, vol. 2 (Frankfurt am Main: Peter Lang Edition, 2013), 157–170. Hirsch's synthesis of Judaism and Christianity paralleled the efforts made by his predecessors in the *Verein für Cultur und Wissenschaft der Juden*. For the attempt made by the members of the *Verein* to identify the essence of Judaism with *Wissenschaft* in order to define their relationship to Judaism and the state, see Rose, *Jewish Philosophical Politics in Germany*, 44–89. For Salomon Formstecher's alternative Hegelian solution to the place of Judaism in the progressive development of spirit and his understanding of the relationship between the universal and the particular, see, for example, Rose's compact and sharp analysis. Rose, ibid., 283–289.

Part III: **Edifying the Congregation: Jewish Answers to Pressing Societal Questions**

Laurent Mignon
The Challenges of Alterity: Notes on Samuel Hirsch's Contemporaneity

Orientalism

A couple of footnotes in the early pages of Rabbi Samuel Hirsch's *Das Judenthum, der christliche Staat und die moderne Kritik* (Judaism, the Christian State and Modern Criticism, 1843), paint a serene picture of a peaceful and mutually beneficial Judeo-Christian coexistence in Hirsch's native Thalfang, a small town in the Rhineland Palatinate, where "since the French era, Jews have been the equals of the Christians in civic relations".[1] Hirsch stresses that Jews and Christians lived in perfect harmony in his hometown:

> The priest has even preached in the synagogue and in the Jewish cemetery and no one found this objectionable. Whenever a somewhat exciting sermon is to take place, all the Jews go to Church and nobody finds this objectionable. At Christian funerals, Jews are also invited. When the corpse is carried through the streets to the grave, everyone follows, singing hymns, bareheaded. Only the Jews constitute an exception, they follow with their heads covered and no one finds this objectionable either.[2]

That Hirsch chose to put such an emphasis on his own witnessing of a multi-religious society at the beginning of a work countering *Die Judenfrage* (The Jewish Question, 1843), the anti-Jewish treatise of the Young Hegelian philosopher Bruno Bauer (1809–1882),[3] was indicative of his desire to undermine Bauer's othering of Jews and Judaism with arguments based on a rereading of history and on occasional empirical observations. The extent to which Hirsch himself believed in the accuracy of his representation of life in Thalfang in the first half of the 19th century is open to debate. Indeed, in the same work he also noted that even the most unprejudiced and humane Christians nurtured some

---

[1] Samuel Hirsch, *Das Judenthum, der christliche Staat und die moderne Kritik: Briefe zur Beleuchtung der Judenfrage von Bruno Bauer* (Leipzig: Heinrich Hunger, 1843), 13. A French-language version of this chapter was published bearing the title "Le défi de l'altérité religieuse: Samuel Hirsch, le judaïsme et l'islam", in Alberto Ambrosio and Laurent Mignon, eds., *Penser l'islam en Europe: Perspectives du Luxembourg et d'ailleurs* (Paris: Hermann, 2021), 247–267; ©Hermann, www.editions-hermann.fr.
[2] Hirsch, *Das Judenthum, der christliche Staat und die moderne Kritik*, 14.
[3] Bruno Bauer, *Die Judenfrage* (Brunswick: Druck und Verlag von Friedrich Otto, 1843).

hate for the Jews.[4] Nevertheless, he enjoined his readers to go and inform themselves in his hometown.[5] It is meaningful that Rabbi Hirsch sketched the possibility of an inclusive society where religious difference was not an obstacle for inter-communitarian relations in his response to the Prussian philosopher's claims, because Bruno Bauer stipulated in his own work the absolute otherness of the Jew. In *Die Judenfrage*, published while the debate on the political emancipation of Jews in Prussia was raging, the philosopher rejected Jewish emancipationist demands by arguing that nobody could be free in a Christian state. The abolition of all religions and the establishment of a secular state were *sine qua non* conditions for political emancipation. Particularistic religious demands, including Christian ones, were incompatible with the principles of the universal "Rights of Man". However, there were limits to Bauer's universalism. The Young-Hegelian principle that Christianity was the ultimate religion that led the way out of religion was the ideological subtext of his essay. This had consequences in the political field: As long as Jews remained faithful to their a-historical and chimerical religion they did not deserve political emancipation, a product of a modernity which they had not helped shape. Jews were outside of modernity, outside of history, of their own choice.[6] Bauer deplored the "oriental essence" (*orientalisches Wesen*) of Judaism that was at the basis of what he considered to be the stagnancy of rabbinic Judaism,[7] a claim that amounted, as maintained by Judith Frishman, to the orientalization of Judaism.[8]

A number of scholars have indicated that 19th century anti-Jewish argumentation shares similarities with current day anti-Islamic and anti-immigration discourses. In the introduction to his groundbreaking, yet controversial, *Oriental-*

---

4 Hirsch, *Das Judenthum, der christliche Staat und die moderne Kritik*, 11.
5 Ibid., 14.
6 In this essay Bauer did not yet profess his racist post-Hegelian antisemitism. Nonetheless there is little doubt that his contempt for Judaism and his views on its immutable alterity contributed to the modern antisemitic discourse that denounced Jews as a foreign minority whose doubtful allegiance represented a danger for the national state. For a discussion of the evolution and nature of Bauer's antisemitism see David Leopold, "The Hegelian anti-Semitism of Bruno Bauer", History of European Ideas 25 (1999), 179–206.
7 Discussions of Bauer's main arguments can be found in Nathan Rotenstreich, "For and Against Emancipation: The Bruno Bauer Controversy", Leo Baeck Institute Yearbook 4 (1959), 3–36, here 3–11; Judith Frishman, "True Mosaic Religion: Samuel Hirsch, Samuel Holdheim and the Reform of Judaism", in Judith Frishman, Willemien Otten, and Gerard Rouwhorst, eds., *Religious Identity and the Problem of Historical Foundation* (Leiden and Boston: Brill, 2004), 195–222, here 195–200.
8 Frishman, "True Mosaic Religion: Samuel Hirsch, Samuel Holdheim and the Reform of Judaism", 196.

ism, Edward Said pointed to the common roots of orientalism and Western antisemitism.⁹ He went as far as calling orientalism the "anti-Islamic" branch of antisemitism, a remark that led scholars to the comparative study of anti-Islamic and anti-Jewish discourses and the relation between Jews and orientalism. Authors such as Bryan S. Turner and James Pasto – though not necessarily agreeing with Said's premise that antisemitism and orientalism were comparable discourses – argued that orientalism produced two related discourses on Semites: "the Islamic discourse of gaps and the Judaic discourse of contradictions".¹⁰ Pasto, discussing German orientalist scholarship by focusing in particular on biblical scholarship, studied its impact on the debates on Jewish emancipation in Germany in the 19th century.¹¹ Commonalities between the debates on Jews, two hundred years ago, and on the place of Muslims in contemporary European societies have also been underlined by scholars working on the Jewish Enlightenment, the *Haskalah*. Referring in particular to on-going arguments about the Turkish minority in Germany and the complex and controversial concept of the *Leitkultur* (the dominant culture), Christoph Schulte noted in his introduction to *Die jüdische Aufklärung* (The Jewish Enlightenment) that the calls for assimilation directed at "an ethnic, national and religious minority that has no political rights" were only different in "proportion and severity" from those that had been addressed at German Jews in the early 19th century.¹² Indeed Bauer's condemnation of Judaism as an archaic, inferior, primitive, monolithic and un-reformable system of belief, essentially different because of its alleged oriental nature, rings a bell in contemporary debates on the place of Muslims in western societies and the rise of Islamophobia.¹³

---

9 Edward Said, *Orientalism* (New York: Vintage Books, 2004 [1979]), 27–28.
10 Bryan S. Turner, *Religion and Social Theory* (London: SAGE Publications, 1983), 29.
11 James Pasto, "Islam's 'Strange Secret Sharer': Orientalism, Judaism and the Jewish Question", Comparative Studies in Society and History 40, 3 (July 1998), 437–474.
12 Christoph Schulte, *Die jüdische Aufklärung* (München: Beck, 2002), 15–16.
13 See, for instance, the "closed views" of Islam listed in the 1997 report of the Runnymede Trust Commission on Islamophobia in the United Kingdom: *Islamophobia: A Challenge for Us All* (London: Runnymede Trust, 1997), 4–12. The Commission was established upon a recommendation of the report published by the Antisemitism Commission. See *A Very Light Sleeper: The Persistence and Dangers of Antisemitism* (London: Runnymede Trust, 1994), 9 and 55 and *Islamophobia a Challenge for Us All*, 70. However "Islamophobia" is a controversial concept that needs clarification. The definition proposed by Chris Allen in *Islamophobia* (Farnham: Ashgate, 2010) – an enlightening study of the phenomenon – is a meaningful conceptual framework, displaying the necessary safeguards against the denunciation of legitimate criticism of religion and cultural practices as "Islamophobic". Allen delimits Islamophobia as an ideology which constructs Muslims and Islam as Other, leading to exclusionary practices against Muslims and Islam in social, economic and political areas (Allen, *Islamophobia*, 190).

That the condemnation of Judaism and Islam has occasionally been made in the name of secular and progressive values and is not always the product of bigoted and chauvinistic approaches to societal questions is an important dimension of the debate that should not be overlooked. Indeed the 2015 Muhammad cartoons controversy in Denmark offered interesting parallels in secular demands for Jews and Muslims to assimilate. Flemming Rose, the former culture editor of the Danish daily *Jyllands Posten*, defended his decision to commission and publish caricatures of the prophet Muhammad by arguing that "the cartoonists treated Islam the same way they treat Christianity, Buddhism, Hinduism and other religions. And by treating Muslims in Denmark as equals they made a point: We are integrating you into the Danish tradition of satire because you are part of our society, not strangers. The cartoons are including, rather than excluding, Muslims".[14] Rose's expectation that in order to become part of contemporary Danish society, the Muslims of Denmark had to agree that their culture and beliefs be criticized, satirized perhaps even demonized, did not take into consideration that the largely immigrant, working-class and undereducated Muslim communities of Denmark had little active access to the media and thus could not put forward alternative views on their culture and religion. His argument exhibited noteworthy resemblances to Bruno Bauer's call to nineteenth century German Jews, deprived of political rights, to submit to what Karl Marx (1818–1883) ironically called "Critical Criticism" in order to be granted entrance into modern German society as citizens with equal rights. In *Die Judenfrage*, the Prussian thinker articulated this idea in the following terms:

> At a time when Criticism has dared to question everything that hitherto dominated the world, it let the Jews and Judaism be what they were or rather nobody even asks what they are. And without studying whether [the Jews'] essence is compatible with freedom, some people want to grant them freedom. Some even cry out as if it were a betrayal of humanity when Criticism prepares to study the essence that makes a Jew a Jew. Those who experience satisfaction when Christianity is subjected to Criticism or who believe this Criticism to be necessary and call for it, are capable of condemning those who also subject Judaism to it. Should Judaism therefore be privileged, now that privileges are being felled by the blows of Criticism, and even later when they have all fallen?[15]

Despite different contexts of production and notable differences in the goals advocated by their respective authors, their discourses are remarkably similar. In both cases, largely disempowered and marginalized minorities are asked to sub-

---

14 Flemming Rose, "Why I Published Those Cartoons", *The Washington Post* (February 19, 2006).
15 Bauer, *Die Judenfrage*, 2.

mit to principles of the Enlightenment, without having been given the opportunity to contribute to the debate on, and perhaps the reformulation of, those principles.

Though it would be wrong to postulate an equivalence between antisemitism with its various avatars and Islamophobia – a much more recent phenomenon fueled by geopolitical concerns and fears regarding immigration – these two exclusionary ideologies that developed in different contexts do share common features, among other discursive similarities that can be decrypted jointly.[16] There is no doubt that the comparative study of these two exclusionist discourses is a rich field of investigation. In that context, the response strategies developed by victims of this discourse are a fertile area of research that could stimulate debates on the development of policies promoting multicultural and interreligious exchange and countering exclusionist ideologies.[17] The discursive similarity in anti-Jewish and contemporary anti-Islamic attacks makes such a study even more relevant as it can contribute to the reinvention of the Thalfang that Rabbi Hirsch described in the footnotes in his book.

---

[16] For a comparative discussion of antisemitism and Islamophobia, see Matti Bunzl, *Anti-Semitism and Islamophobia: Hatreds Old and New in Europe* (Chicago: Prickly Paradigm Press, 2007). Though his distinctions between antisemitism – as a late nineteenth century ideology serving the ideal of an ethnically pure nation-state –, and Islamophobia – as a contemporary and supra-national phenomenon expressing mainly pan-European civilizational concerns – as well as between religiously motivated anti-Judaism and racist antisemitism are too clear cut, Bunzl's essay and the responses it produced (also reprinted in the pamphlet) are a stimulating invitation to explore the differences, parallels and intersections between those discriminatory ideologies and practices. However, Bruno Bauer's essay on the Jewish question, which is not mentioned by Bunzl, is a good example of a text which does not fit these parameters and combines, albeit implicitly, religious prejudices with supra-national, civilizational, rather than identity concerns. For a different approach, see more recently Esther Romeyn, "Anti-Semitism and Islamophobia: Spectropolitics and Immigration", Theory, Culture & Society 31, 6 (2014), 77–101.

[17] For a comparative study of Samuel Hirsch's response to Bruno Bauer and Namık Kemal's response to Ernest Renan's 1883 lecture "Islam and Science" (*L'islamisme et la science*) at the Sorbonne, see Laurent Mignon, "Of Moors, Jews and Gentiles", Journal of Turkish Studies 35, 1 (2011), 65–83. Kemal (1840–1888), a leading Ottoman intellectual, challenged Renan's argument that Islam and "Arabness of the mind" (*être arabe d'esprit*) had impeded intellectual and scientific developments in the Islamic world. See also Laurent Mignon, *Uncoupling Language and Religion: An Exploration into the Margins of Turkish Literature* (Boston: Academic Studies Press, 2021), 115–141.

Responding to Bauer

Samuel Hirsch was not the only German Jewish thinker who responded to Bruno Bauer's *Judenfrage*. Several leading intellectuals and rabbis, favorable to the ideals of political and religious reform, such as Gotthold Salomon (1784–1862), Wilhelm Freund (1806–1894), Samuel Holdheim (1806–1860), Gabriel Riesser (1806–1863), Gustav Philippson (1814–1880), and Abraham Geiger (1810–1874) produced responses to Bauer's essay.[18] Leaving Bruno Bauer's views unanswered was not an option for progressive Jews. On the one hand Bruno Bauer was a notorious philosopher and theologian whose controversial views on sacred history had provoked a storm of protest and whose teaching license at the faculty of theology of Bonn University had been revoked on grounds of his openly professed atheism in 1842. Although his views did not gain much foothold, he was the topic of much conversation. His radical political stance could have made him an objective ally in the struggle for the democratization of the Prussian state. More importantly, perhaps, his essay was not only a passionate tirade against religion – Judaism and Christianity – and a critique of society; it also dealt with themes at the heart of Jewish reformist thinking. Bauer highlighted issues such as the petrification of religious law and segregation, which had also been criticized by the leaders of the emerging Reform movement in their analysis of Rabbinic Judaism. However, they could not agree with Bauer's assessment that Talmudic Judaism was a "chimerical, illusory, soulless development" of Mosaism[19] which had "no capability to evolve historically" because of its "oriental essence".[20] The advocates of Reform argued that Judaism was a flexible and progressive religion that adapted to historical circumstances and this interpretation gave legitimacy to their calls for doctrinal renewal. Aside from the wish to counter Bauer's instrumentalization of reformist arguments in his attack on Judaism, Rabbi Samuel Hirsch had other motives for responding to the radical thinker's book: Bauer's analysis of Judaism was based on Hegelian premises and Hirsch himself worked within the Hegelian tradition. In *Die Religionsphilosophie der Juden* (The Religious Philosophy of the Jews, 1842), arguably his major work, the rabbi had problematized Hegel's interpretation of Judaism

---

18 Kaufmann Kohler and Isidore Singer, "Bauer, Bruno", *https://www.jewishencyclopedia.com/articles/2668-bauer-bruno* [accessed: 08.05.2022]. The main arguments of the debate are summarized and analyzed by Nathan Rotenstreich, "For and Against Emancipation: The Bruno Bauer Controversy", Leo Baeck Institute Yearbook 4 (1959), 3–36.
19 Bauer, *Die Judenfrage*, 26.
20 Ibid., 11.

and developed a rival Hegelian analysis of Judaism, conceived as a rational religion, incarnating freedom and moral values. According to Hirsch, its historical role had not been superseded by the emergence of Christianity, whose historical aim was the dissemination of monotheism throughout the world. In *Das Judenthum, der christliche Staat und die moderne Kritik,* Hirsch went further in his discussion of the historically progressive nature of Judaism. Combining religious and political issues, he maintained that the aims of Jewish religious development and the principles of the Christian state were convergent – an idea that he would continue to develop further in *Die Reform im Judenthum* (*Reform in Judaism,* 1843).[21]

Another fundamental point of disagreement between the two Hegelian thinkers was Bauer's stipulation that religion had outlived its historical function and had no place in the modern state. This was anathema for Hirsch. Condemning indifference towards religion, he used Jewish religiosity as an asset to argue the case for Jewish political emancipation within the boundaries of a democratic Christian state. Hirsch was opposed to the idea of a secular state and maintained that Jews, as Jews, ought to be granted political rights in a Christian state. Had Jews not always lived according to the very principles and ideals which had underpinned Jesus' quest? Jesus, according to Hirsch, had achieved the full potential a human being could reach.[22] Furthermore, the rabbi argued that the Jewish messianic expectations coincided with "the reality of the Christian state, the reality of the reign of truth and virtue on earth".[23] Hence a state, "permeated by religion", had to emancipate "truly religious Jews" unless it contradicted its own founding principles.[24] Jews were not Christians, but every Jew, every human being had the potential to be "a Christ": "Accept that God has created Man, every man so that he can be Christ, that he can make himself a Christ,

---

[21] On the development of Hirsch's ideas while in Luxembourg, see Gershon Greenberg, "The Historical Origins of God and Man: Samuel Hirsch's Luxembourg Writings", Leo Baeck Institute Yearbook 20, 1 (1975), 129–148; Judith Frishman, "Good Enough for the Goyim: Samuel Hirsch and Samuel Holdheim on the Relationship between Judaism and Christianity", in Marcel Poorthuis, Joshua Schwartz, and Joseph Turner (eds.), *Interactions Between Judaism and Christianity in History, Religion, Art, and Literature* (Leiden: Brill, 2008), 271–287; and idem, "True Mosaic Religion: Samuel Hirsch, Samuel Holdheim and the Reform of Judaism". See also Mignon, "Of Jews, Moors and Gentiles", 67–69, 71.
[22] Samuel Hirsch, *Das Judenthum, der christliche Staat und die moderne Kritik,* 92.
[23] Ibid., 100.
[24] Ibid., 9–10. See also Greenberg, "The Historical Origins of God and Man: Samuel Hirsch's Luxembourg Writings", 143.

that he can evolve in the spirit of Christ, imitate the life of Christ and that nothing on earth can prevent Man from living according to the will of God."²⁵

At a time when Jews were still barely tolerated within the walls of German universities, the significance of Hirsch's response should not be underestimated: A religious leader of an oppressed minority questioned the authority of a biblical scholar and radical philosopher who, until his dismissal from the university, had been a major figure in the academic establishment. Hirsch not only defied the Young Hegelian philosopher; he challenged the academic institution and its hierarchy as well. Politically it was a sign that the minority would no longer submit silently to the condemnation by the majority. That the rabbi was aware of this particular dimension of his project transpires in the fact that he reminds his interlocutor that in the past too, after the Protestant revolution, "the Jews had become the teachers of the Christians" in the latter's endeavor to study Hebrew, "the language of the Ancient Covenant".²⁶ Moreover, Hirsch was of the opinion that Christians still had a great deal to learn. This is apparent in his remarks on Bauer's arguably cavalier treatment and overly simplified translations of Hebrew religious terminology. Hirsch maintained that Bruno Bauer and Christian scholars in general, ought to stop referring to Jewish "laws", since that term did not adequately reflect the meaning of the various Hebrew terms it was used to signify:

> The law is called in Hebrew *ḥoq* (חק); the ceremonial law is a *miṣwah* (מצוה) and also *'edot* (עדות). However if one mentions the Pentateuch as a whole, then it is called *torah* (תורה), "the teaching". The "Ten Commandments" (*Zehn Gebote*) are unknown in the Pentateuch, there are only "Ten Words", *'Aśeret ha-Debarîm* (עשרת הדברים).²⁷

With these remarks Hirsch was also problematizing the suitability of the German language for the study and analysis of Jewish canonical law and Hebrew terminology, a stance which could also be interpreted in the context of his subversion of academic hierarchies. Though Reform rabbis advocated the use of German during religious services, Hirsch emphasized the need to maintain terminological distinctions and respect the particularities of the Hebrew language. These were preconditions in order to achieve a proper understanding of Judaism.²⁸ Throughout the pages of his book, Hirsch did not only question Bauer's claim that there had been no Jewish intellectual contributions to the shaping of mo-

---

25 Hirsch, *Das Judenthum, der christliche Staat und die moderne Kritik*, 100.
26 Ibid., 96.
27 Ibid., 30.
28 Mignon, "Of Jews, Moors and Gentiles", 74–75.

dernity, he also challenged the mainstream Christian narrative of the Enlightenment. Indeed, in the final paragraphs of his book he emphatically noted that Jews too "went on an exploratory journey" when it came to "uncovering the essence of Christianity" and this they did out of "pure love of science".[29]

In order to undermine Bauer's authority, the Chief Rabbi of Luxembourg focused on his opponent's status as an author studying Jewish history and on the cultural context in which he worked. He discussed the evolution of Bauer's thought, from his early Hegelian interpretation of Christian dogmas in which Jewish doctrinal differences were largely interpreted as deficiencies, to his later Young Hegelian rupture with Christianity,[30] without questioning the Hegelian tenets that he and the Prussian thinker shared. Hirsch was not exclusively concerned with Bauer's writings; he took the opportunity to develop arguments that questioned the authority of all academics and thinkers who pontificated on Judaism. This applies to Hirsch's fundamental critique that Christians could not objectively assess Judaism because of their belief in the superiority of Christianity, censorship, Jew-hatred, and proselytism. Taking his argument one step further, he maintained that Jews were more methodical in their analysis of the Christian faith because Jews did not proselytize among Christians and were thus "unbiased and truth-loving" in their studies of Christian doctrine and history.[31]

Focusing on Bauer, Hirsch wondered about the motivations of some of the philosopher's most outrageous claims. The rabbi, who knew and respected Bauer's earlier scholarly work, suspected that the philosopher willingly misrepresented aspects of Judaism, such as the significance of *kashrut* (Jewish dietary laws): "If someone, though he knows better, fosters hatred, then one is entitled to call this shameful."[32] Hirsch was referring to Bauer's transposition of Jewish beliefs regarding impure foods and animals to segregative Jewish attitudes towards *goyim*.[33] Still, rather than questioning Bauer's personal motives, the rabbi chose to unveil the scholarly and methodological deficiencies underlying Bauer's biased representation of Judaism and Jewish life. Needless to say Hirsch's criticism of Bauer's methodology was an issue of great importance at a time when the presence of Jews in the university was still a matter of contention. Here too the Jew was teaching the Christian. Hirsch denounced Bauer's references to works on Judaism that had no scholarly value such as Johann Andreas

---

29 Hirsch, *Das Judenthum, der christliche Staat und die moderne Kritik*, 117.
30 Ibid., 54.
31 Ibid., 117.
32 Ibid., 56.
33 Ibid., 48 and 57. See also Mignon, "Of Jews, Moors and Gentiles", 74.

Eisenmenger's (1654–1704) virulently anti-Jewish *Entdecktes Judenthum* (Judaism Unmasked, 1700).[34] He had little time for Eisenmenger's book:

> During his nitpicky labor, [Eisenmenger] was not guided by any scientific considerations, but only by practical interest – that one should at least expulse the Jews from the land. Whenever, by chance, he got hold of a Jewish book, he quoted the apparently most meaningless parts or the passages that were most hateful against those who thought differently, categorized them according to arbitrary schemes and thus Judaism was readily exposed.[35]

That *Entdecktes Judenthum* provoked such strong feelings in Hirsch was not a surprise: the book was so vitriolic that upon its publication in Frankfurt in 1700, the Jewish community – worried about the possibility of anti-Jewish riots – had successfully applied to the authorities for its confiscation and ban. The surprise was that a serious scholar should pay it some attention. Hirsch showed that Bauer's argumentation had much in common with Eisenmenger's. In his essay, Bauer, like Eisenmenger, tended to stereotype Jews, a methodological error that did not escape Hirsch's attention. The rabbi denounced Bauer's showcasing the Sabbath as a symbol of failed Jewish integration into mainstream society[36] and he deconstructed Bauer's caricatured description of scholarly disputation (*pilpul*) by reminding his antagonist that similar disputations also existed among Lutherans, the branch of Christianity to which Bauer formerly belonged.[37] But Hirsch was particularly sensitive to Bauer's denunciation of the supposed Jewish "selfish" and "hypochondriac"[38] obsession with self-interest and economic activities such as "money-lending", "pawn broking" and "small retail".[39] He attempted to contextualize Jewish social and economic life, something that Bauer refused to do, and stressed that the aforementioned activities were not restricted to Jews. Furthermore he enjoined his readers not to underestimate the importance of such activities in socio-economic life while simultaneously maintaining that Jews, if given the opportunity, would engage in a greater variety of economic activities such as agriculture.[40]

---

[34] Johann Andreas Eisenmenger, *Entdecktes Judenthum* (Frankfurt, 1700). Echoing Eisenmenger, Bauer anonymously published his critique of Christianity entitled *Das entdeckte Christentum* (Zürich: Verlag des Literarischen Comptoirs, 1843).
[35] Hirsch, ibid., 116.
[36] Ibid., 13–14.
[37] Ibid., 19.
[38] Ibid., 49.
[39] Bauer, *Die Judenfrage*, 9 and Hirsch, ibid., 12–13.
[40] Hirsch, ibid., 13.

The rabbi advocated an empirical approach to the study of Jewish social life and, by referring to his own childhood experiences in the footnotes of his essay, suggested the possibility of a peaceful, tolerant and mutually beneficial Judeo-Christian coexistence.[41] He could not but reject Bauer's description of Jewish life in Poland and Galicia, "whose only source was a text written by an enemy of the Jews". Neither Bauer, nor Hirsch for that matter could make any meaningful judgments about the life of Jews in Eastern Europe since "they did not know the facts from observation".[42] Perhaps society there was far more congenial than the life sketched by Bauer, Hirsch implied, in juxtaposing the latter's writings on life in Eastern Europe to his own remarks on his hometown.[43]

"De-Orientalizing" the Jews

Hirsch also addressed theoretical issues regarding the Young Hegelian philosopher's dehistoricization and essentialization of Judaism, at least for the Christian era. Indeed one could argue that the Luxembourgish rabbi was aware that Bauer's orientalization of Jews and the East – West dichotomy could not stand up to closer scrutiny. With a healthy dose of irony, he ridiculed Bauer's distinction between a dynamic Judaism in Palestine before the advent of Jesus Christ and the oriental passivity of exilic Judaism during the Christian era:

> As long as we really lived in the East, [oriental] disposition (*Naturbestimmtheit*) could not make us passive. We were working hard in order to develop our principles. But, once we ceased living in the Orient and were dispersed throughout the world, the oriental character affected us, making us inert and we knew nothing more delightful than to sit under a fig tree – which we had never seen – and vines in order to protect ourselves from the oriental sun, which, however, no longer warmed us.[44]

Bauer's refusal to contextualize Jewish experiences throughout Europe was fundamental to his approach. The Young Hegelian philosopher argued that the essence of Judaism determined the behavior and the actions of the Jews. Hence the oppression suffered by Jews was legitimate. It was the consequence of their religion, not of a repressive political system or of institutionalized discrimination: "They were responsible for the pressure they were submitted to because they deserved it for sticking to their law, their language and their whole being", he wrote

---

41 Hirsch, ibid., 13.
42 Hirsch, ibid., 21.
43 For a discussion of the above points, see Mignon, "Of Jews, Moors and Gentiles", 81–82.
44 Hirsch, ibid., 18.

in his essay.⁴⁵ Bauer thereby inverted the arguments of Reform rabbis for whom doctrinal sclerosis and segregationist tendencies had developed partly as a consequence of Christian anti-Judaism, fanaticism and the discriminatory laws of Christian states and also countered the theses of emancipatory Christian thinkers such as Christian Wilhelm von Dohm (1751–1820).⁴⁶

Hirsch pinpointed some of Bauer's interpretative errors that were the consequence of his dehistoricization of Judaism. The Young Hegelian philosopher's disregard for chronology caused him to misinterpret the acts of biblical figures. Hirsch, among others, responded to Bauer who had characterized the exhortations of the Prophets as "attempts to destroy prevailing conditions among the people",⁴⁷ by arguing that "[the exhortations of the Prophets] might well have been fighting against circumstances of which we are no longer aware, but they cannot have been attempts to destroy the *status quo* which is being referred to here, since it did not yet exist at the time of the Prophets".⁴⁸ Humor was central in Hirsch's rebuttal strategy.⁴⁹ In what is perhaps the most famous passage in the Bauer-Hirsch exchange, the rabbi noted that if Jews were, as Bauer stated, an a-historical people that had only exerted a "counter-pressure" against history, they had definitely been part of and had shaped history: "True we were pressurized, and one cannot pressurize a nothing."⁵⁰ This exchange attracted Karl Marx and Friedrich Engels' attention in *Die heilige Familie oder Kritik der kritischen Kritik: Gegen Bruno Bauer & Consorten* (*The Holy Family or Critique of Critical Criticism*, 1845), their refutation of the Young Hegelians. Referring to Bauer's comparison of Jewish presence in history to an eyesore (*Dorn im Auge*), they ran to the rescue of the rabbi: "Something which has been an eyesore to me from birth, as the Jews have been to the Christian world, and which persists and develops with the eye is not an ordinary sore, but a wonderful one, one that really belongs to my eye and must even contribute to a highly original development of my eyesight."⁵¹ In their views "the Critical 'eyesore' had not hurt the 'rhetorician' *Hirsch*". Indeed, for Hirsch, Judaism and Jews were very much part of history

---

45 Bauer, *Die Judenfrage*, 4.
46 On Dohm's engagement for Jewish political emancipation, see Christian Wilhelm Dohm, *Über die bürgerliche Verbesserung der Juden: Kritische und kommentierte Studienausgabe*, ed. Christoph Seifert (Göttingen: Wallstein Verlag, 2015).
47 Bauer, *Die Judenfrage*, 32.
48 Hirsch, *Das Judenthum, der christliche Staat und die moderne Kritik*, 108.
49 Mignon, "Of Jews, Moors and Gentiles", 76.
50 Hirsch, ibid., 24.
51 Karl Marx and Friedrich Engels, *Die heilige Familie oder Kritik der kritischen Kritik: Gegen Bruno Bauer & Consorten* (Frankfurt a. M.: Literarische Anstalt, 1845), 131–132.

and had contributed to the emergence of modernity. The latter point was a particularly sensitive issue. In his essay Bauer had asserted, commensurate with his views on the a-historical nature of Judaism, that no Jew had made any meaningful contribution to philosophy. According to Bauer, Moses Maimonides' (1135– 1204) and Moses Mendelssohn's (1729–1786) works were not of universal value; they were only meaningful in the context of Jewish theology. In the case of Mendelssohn he went even further and stated that the father of the *Haskalah* had not even had any impact on his Jewish contemporaries.[52] Bauer suggested furthermore that Baruch Spinoza (1632–1677), whose importance he could not deny, had ceased being a Jew when he started to develop his philosophy.[53] Hirsch considered Bauer's arguments as yet more evidence for his careless appraisal of historical facts. He maintained that Spinoza had not willfully abandoned Judaism but had been excommunicated by a rabbinic court advocating an ultraconservative interpretation of Judaism.[54] The discussion of Spinoza's Jewishness was not only about the correct interpretation of historical evidence. The issue was central in Hirsch's vision of Judaism: Judaism, he claimed, was broad enough to incorporate Spinoza's philosophy. Bauer, on the other hand, stuck to a caricatured and misunderstood traditionalist form of rabbinic Judaism. Unsurprisingly perhaps, Bauer sided with those who adhered to an orthodox interpretation of the Jewish tradition.

Hirsch also disagreed with Bauer's evaluation of Maimonides and Mendelssohn. Though he broadly agreed that Mendelssohn's philosophical works had had little impact on his co-religionists at the time of their publication, he explained that this was to be expected, since Jews had not been the philosopher's intended audience. Published in the German language, they dealt with the general philosophical debates of the time and were addressed at the general German-reading public. However, Mendelssohn provoked Jews into embracing German culture, while remaining faithful to their religious roots. His philosophical works too signified a turning point in Jewish thought and history and had shaped contemporary Judaism.[55] The rabbi also dismissed Bauer's comments on Maimonides as unoriginal. He not only questioned Bauer's discourse, but he considered his attitude to be symptomatic of a reigning attitude within the broader academic community: the lack of academic interest for Jewish thought and its exclusion from the historiography of philosophy. Hirsch conceded that most his-

---

52 Bauer, *Die Judenfrage*, 82–83.
53 Bauer, ibid., 9.
54 Hirsch, *Das Judenthum, der christliche Staat und die moderne Kritik*, 26.
55 Hirsch, ibid., 112–3.

tories of philosophy mentioned Maimonides, but only "out of curiosity". In truth, he wrote, "nobody ever bothered to read a Jewish philosopher".[56] The subtext to Hirsch's argumentation was that it was less the absence of Jewish philosophy than the refusal of the academic establishment to acknowledge its existence, which explained the silence of major works on the topic. It was nothing less than an invitation to question and decrypt the historiography of western thought.[57]

In hindsight it seems obvious that Bauer's approach had much in common with the orientalization of 19th century colonial populations in North Africa and Muslims. In an article that aimed to respond to the criticism unleashed on him upon the publication of *Die Judenfrage,* he commented that "those who want to emancipate the Jews as Jews are putting themselves to needless trouble, like attempting to clean a Moor in order to whiten him",[58] a statement disclosing the similarity between colonialist and anti-Jewish ideologies. Hirsch was conscious that Bauer not only denied the existence of evolution and diversity within Judaism, but that he also made categorical generalizations about all non-Western peoples of antiquity, into which pre-Talmudic Judaism had to fit: "[According to Bauer] the life of the Jewish people must have evolved, *nolens volens*, in line with the categories which shaped the life of the other peoples of Antiquity",[59] Hirsch complained. His discomfort with Bauer's interpretative framework was caused by the Young Hegelian philosopher's inattention to the antagonism between Jewish monotheism and pagan polytheism, which was fundamental in Hirsch's thought. Moreover, Bauer's refusal to acknowledge any difference and variety in his presentation of Jewish history and thought was unacceptable for Hirsch. Maintaining that Bauer's Judaism was a fantasy (*Phantasiegebilde*) with no link to reality,[60] Hirsch also made the point that Jews were not responsible for Bauer's misunderstandings and misrepresentations of their religion.[61] Ironically it is as if Hirsch reversed Bauer's call to Jews to give up their religion by summoning Bauer to abandon the "unhistorical" and "chimerical" construction of Judaism that he had envisioned.[62]

---

56 Hirsch, ibid., 116.
57 Mignon, "Of Jews, Moors and Gentiles", 77.
58 Bruno Bauer, "Die Fähigkeit der heutigen Juden und Christen frei zu sein", in Georg Herwegh, ed., *Einundzwanzig Bogen aus der Schweiz* (Zürich and Winterthur: Verlag des Literarischen Comptoirs, 1843), 56–71, here 57.
59 Hirsch, ibid., 45
60 Ibid., 111.
61 Ibid., 30.
62 Mignon, "Of Jews, Moors and Gentiles", 78.

Hirsch's denunciation of Bauer's monolithic approach to Judaism allowed him to make a case for the recognition of the plurality of Judaisms which had existed throughout history; a point which was meaningful not only in his controversy with Bauer, but also in his ongoing dispute with the upholders of rabbinical orthodoxy. *Das Judenthum, der christliche Staat und die moderne Kritik* can thus be read as a celebration of diversity in Judaism, as it enumerates a variety of writers and thinkers who imprinted their mark on the intellectual history of their times such as the philosopher Isaac Abrabanel (1437–1508), the grammarian Elias Levita (1469–1549), the mystics Isaac Luria (1534–1572) and Hayyim ben Joseph Vital (1543–1620), Baruch Spinoza, Moses Mendelssohn (1729–1786) – the father of the Jewish Enlightenment – and his followers and the scholar Joseph Salvador (1779–1873). By illustrating the contribution of Jews to intellectual culture and history, Hirsch highlighted the variety of Jewish experiences.[63] A proper understanding of Judaism and Jewish history required a recognition and analysis of this multiplicity: "Now down to business! What is Judaism? Is it pure Mosaism or is it the Talmud? In truth it is neither of the two. Judaism has produced Mosaism and the Talmud and more besides these. All these products, identified and understood together, not individually, are Judaism."[64]

Hirsch also emphasized that the evolution of Judaism, Jewish thought and culture had been affected by historical and geographical circumstances. A myriad of forms of Jewishness existed. He stressed that scholarship among Jews was more common in times when there was less oppression,[65] a reference to the context of production of knowledge and the need to contextualize it:

> During times when Jews were less oppressed, scholarship among them was much more common than in darker times. [...] Jews did not willingly allow themselves to be excluded from general education, nor did they exclude themselves. As long as they were confined to ghettos there was no general education, but there were witch-hunts, exorcisms and relic worship. Once the peoples of Europe awoke to a new intellectual life, we too contributed wholeheartedly.[66]

The geographical and cultural contexts were other important dimensions that shaped Jewish life, Jews being "civilized in civilized lands" and "rough" elsewhere.[67] This point was political as Hirsch had already argued in his magnum

---

63 Hirsch, *Das Judenthum, der christliche Staat und die moderne Kritik*, 19.
64 Ibid., 28–29.
65 Ibid., 26.
66 Ibid., 26.
67 Ibid., 16.

opus, *Die Religionsphilosophie der Juden*, that Judaism was a "purely spiritual [nationality], and is unconcerned by worldly, stately and political conditions".[68] Indeed, if Judaism represented a spiritual identity, it did not constitute an obstacle to citizenship, a central emancipationist argument: Jews were "a people in matters of religion",[69] not a foreign nation in exile.[70]

Thinking about Islam

By emphasizing the need for a scrupulous and careful approach to religion and culture as objects of study, Hirsch seems to invite us today to question the representations of Islam as an essentially different, morally and intellectually inferior, monolithic and static religion. Then again Hirsch would most probably have subscribed to such a description of Islam, a religion that, despite his interest in comparative religious studies, he knew very little about. Having failed to mention Islam in the *Religionsphilosophie der Juden*, he devoted one and a half pages to Islam and its civilization in his response to Bauer. The picture he painted was bleak. As Hirsch's main concern was to establish the kinship between Christianity and Judaism and enable a fruitful dialogue between them, "othering" Islam was a way of drawing together Jews and Christians. Hirsch's essentialized binary opposition between the abstract spirituality of the Church and Islam's sensuousness (*Sinnlichkeit*) and focus on earthly achievement was one way of accomplishing this. Reiterating a scholarly truism, he argued that Islamic civilization had been incapable of contributing to the development of science, having adopted only select aspects of the Greek heritage. The latter was nothing more than a "toy" in the eyes of Muslims who only desired to "beautify their lives". Judaism too, like Christianity, had to counter Islamic worldliness. However, Jewish intellectual life under Islam was restricted by too great a dependency on Greek philosophy and the Talmud in a climate that was not conducive to scientific and intellectual investigation. Nonetheless Hirsch was too honest not to recognize that his discourse on Judeo-Christian intellectual and religious kinship, which he opposed to the Muslim "other", was called into question by historical facts which he could not ignore. He noted that the conflict between Christians and Muslims reached its peak with the church's desire to liberate the tomb of Christ in Jerusalem, a doomed enterprise that yielded Jews and Muslims a

---

68 Samuel Hirsch, *Die Religionsphilosophie der Juden* (Leipzig: Heinrich Hunger, 1842), viii.
69 Hirsch, *Das Judenthum, der christliche Staat und die moderne Kritik*, 23.
70 Mignon, "Of Jews, Moors and Gentiles", 76–77.

common death by Christian swords: "Crowds roamed, without order and discipline. Even a band of youths joined with the aim to conquer the Holy Grave. How could one now tolerate the infidels in one's own midst? Butchering the Jews in the cities of the Rhine were the first heroic deeds of the holy crusaders."[71]

Despite his awareness of the Christian rejection of both Jews and Muslims, the rabbi did not question contemporary representations of Islam. Others, however, did. Indeed, less than two centuries ago, some of the leading scholars of Islam of the nineteenth century, among them Jews, made major contributions to the understanding of Islam in their own time. So too Abraham Geiger, at least in his *Was hat Mohammed aus dem Judenthume aufgenommen? (What has Mohammed Derived From Judaism?*, 1833) where he put much emphasis on the sincerity of the prophet Muhammad and the latter's belief in the need to combine "various religious views to secure the salvation of humankind".[72] Ignác Goldziher (1850–1921) was more sincere in his approach than Geiger, for in Goldziher's work Islam as an object of study served as more than a foil against Christianity. Despite these differences, they romanticized and idealized Islam and Islamic civilization in their scholarly works, which comes as no surprise: In a century when anti-Judaism was transforming into an increasingly racist discourse, reminding the Gentiles of the major cultural, scientific and intellectual contributions of Arabic-speaking Semitic cousins could only have a beneficial impact on the debates on civic equality and emancipation of the Jews. But, more importantly perhaps, as noted by Bernard Lewis, those Jewish scholars of Islam contributed not only to "the advancement of scholarship but also [to] the enrichment of the Western view of Oriental religion, literature, and history, by the substitution of knowledge and understanding for prejudice and ignorance",[73] partly because they were "less affected by nostalgia for the

---

[71] Hirsch, ibid., 93–94.
[72] Abraham Geiger, *Was hat Mohammed aus dem Judenthume aufgenommen?* (Bonn: F. Baden, 1833), 35. On Geiger and Islam, see Jacob Lassner, "Abraham Geiger: A Nineteenth Century Jewish Reformer on the Origins of Islam", in Michael Kramer, ed., *The Jewish Discovery of Islam* (Tel Aviv: The Moshe Dayan Center for Middle Eastern and African Studies, 1999), 103–136; Susannah Heschel, "German Jewish Scholarship on Islam as a Tool for De-Orientalizing Judaism", New German Critique 117 (2012), 91–207; idem, *Jüdischer Islam. Islam und jüdisch-deutsche Selbstbestimmung* (Berlin: Matthes & Seitz, 2018); and Ottfried Fraisse, ed., *Modern Jewish Scholarship on Islam in Context: Rationality, European Borders, and the Search for Belonging* (Berlin/Boston: De Gruyter, 2018).
[73] Bernard Lewis, "Pro-Islamic Jews", in idem, *Islam in History: Ideas, People, and Events in the Middle East* (Chicago: Open Court, 1993), 144.

Crusades, preoccupation with imperial policy, or the desire to convert the 'heathen'".[74]

Indeed, in the twenty-first century, where the need for Samuel Hirsch's utopic Judeo-Christian Thalfang to expand and encompass ethno-religious communities reaching beyond the people of the Bible is sorely felt, the endeavor of those scholars has a particular significance. Among the new communities, Muslims have had to struggle with conditions not unlike those experienced by Jews in the nineteenth century. Could perhaps the study of the history of Judaism in Europe by Muslims – like the study of Islam by Jews in the nineteenth century – play a constructive role in the development of strategies promoting the full acceptance of migrants and European Muslims? In this context Rabbi Samuel Hirsch's response to Bruno Bauer, challenging academic hierarchies and celebrating diversity, draws the outline of a methodology which could help us decrypt contemporary discriminatory discourses on religious alterity, including his own views on Islam.

---

[74] Quoted by Michael Kramer in idem, *The Jewish Discovery of Islam*, 2.

Ken Koltun-Fromm
Religious Borders of Reason and Sentiment: Samuel Hirsch and Abraham Geiger on Jewish Education

For both Samuel Hirsch (1815–1889) and Abraham Geiger (1810–1874), two of the foremost liberal Jewish theologians of nineteenth-century Europe, Jewish education could both ground Jewish identity and enable a broader participation in European culture and knowledge. Yet their pedagogical ideals were under siege as educational opportunities opened for Jewish children who could abandon their traditional learning for success elsewhere. Hirsch and Geiger approached this modern educational scene quite differently: Hirsch produced a liberal religious catechism that offered progressive Jewish answers to pressing spiritual questions, while Geiger appealed to foundational experiences and sensibilities to inform Jewish obligations. In these ways, their educational programs fit within their larger philosophical tendencies: Hirsch promoted a Judaism that was at once universal and primary, whereas Geiger grounded modern Judaism in personal sentiment and history. Hirsch's Judaism as both universal and tolerant nonetheless secured boundaries against those ignorant of or apathetic to religious truths, and Geiger defended personal meaning against incursions from rational authorities. This boundary maintenance arose as Hirsch and Geiger situated Jewish education within the marketplace of competing alternatives, and justified Jewish learning as a necessary foundation for human flourishing. In what follows, I will analyze both pedagogical approaches in order to assess how each constructs and maintains religious borders.

Abraham Geiger and Religious Sentiment

Abraham Geiger opened his first educational school in Breslau on May 7th, 1843. There were six classes altogether, three for girls and three for boys. The girls studied translations of Hebrew prayers, analyzed biblical history and texts, and were instructed in the basic teachings about God, religion, and ethics. The boys also learned translations of Hebrew prayers, and studied the Pentateuch and its history (together with more general Jewish history). But the young men also moved beyond this curriculum to become proficient in the Hebrew language alongside their religious education.¹ In general, only young men would become familiar with biblical Hebrew.²

This focus on biblical studies, history, ethics (for the girls), and language (at least for the boys) marks Geiger's school as a modern Reform institution.³ The Bible replaced the traditional emphasis on the Talmud, compilations and catalogues yielded to history, law ceded to ethics, and Hebrew (and not, for example, Aramaic) became the most significant religious language of study. This new curriculum, Geiger argued, offered an appropriate and necessary response to the times. It was moderate, contemporary, and grounded in the sources, but for all that practical and worldly. Earlier generations could simply educate their young men in Hebrew Bible and Talmud, and then quickly launch them into a world with die *bestimmende Richtung* (a decisive line of thought). Jewish women, in turn, could easily learn the practical features of homemaking (*auf die Umgebung des Hauses*) most suited to their *Beruf* (profession). But if these earlier generations appeared somewhat deficient and had, in Geiger's words, "weniger ein klares Begreifen der religiösen Wahrheiten" (a less clear understanding of religious truths), they nonetheless followed the impulses of their time.⁴ Yet such impulses would no longer prove compelling now, when women advanced beyond the home and enjoyed new freedoms,⁵ and men entered professional trades where their Talmudic studies offered little help and, it appeared to many, even stunted their professional advancement. Geiger's educational program sought to bolster Jewish identity even as it prepared Jews for economic and cultural success in Europe. Emancipation for both sexes, Geiger believed, required a revolution in Jewish education.

Yet Geiger recognized that social emancipation brought with it another kind of revolution: a profound indifference to Jewish educational studies. He had to fight for his school, in part because of the apathy to all things Jewish among his laity.

---

1 Abraham Geiger, "Abhandlungen aus den Programmen der jüdischen Religionsunterrichts-Anstalt in Breslau 1844–1863", in Ludwig Geiger, ed., *Abraham Geiger's Nachgelassene Schriften*, vol. 1 (Berlin: Louis Gerschel, 1875), 311–351; also see Ludwig Geiger, *Abraham Geiger: Leben und Lebenswerk* (Berlin: Georg Reimer, 1910), 132.
2 Geiger, "Abhandlungen aus den Programmen der jüdischen Religionsunterrichts-Anstalt", 319.
3 See Mordechai Eliav, *Jewish Education in Germany in the Period of Haskalah and Emancipation* [Hebrew] (Jerusalem: Jewish Agency, 1960), 3, 162–173.
4 Geiger, "Abhandlungen aus den Programmen der jüdischen Religionsunterrichts-Anstalt", 311.
5 Eliav argues that the *maskilim* first raised the issue of female education as a significant problem for Jewish enlightenment. Yet only upper-class German Jewish women took advantage of this new learning, and many of them went to Christian schools. See Eliav, *Jewish Education in Germany*, 169, 173, 271–279.

Enlightened parents insisted that learning respond to broader, cultural concerns. So the parents of young Jewish children proved both indifferent and dissatisfied, for with new access to the professional goods of European society, these parents wanted more for their children than they had won for themselves. Geiger admits that "verlangen oft die Eltern selbst, dass die Religion dem Unterrichte in der Musik, dem Tanze, der französischen Sprache und dergleich weiche" (the parents themselves demanded that religion give way to instruction in music, dance, French language and the like). These parents desired "Virtuosen und Salonmenschen" (virtuosos and salonnières),[6] educated in European culture, philosophy, the arts and high society. Though he harbored only disdain for this view, Geiger nonetheless was forced to contend with it. Here we see an initial glimpse of how Geiger's educational philosophy mirrors his more general approach to Jewish tradition. That tradition has a history, one embedded in personal meaning and authority.[7] So too, then, does Jewish educational practice: one does not simply abandon the Jewish community for the goods of Western society. Instead, Jewish education should help cultivate a deep-seated commitment to historical traditions. Yet Geiger must contend with modern sensibilities and cultural formations, rather than dismiss them as illegitimate yearnings that undermine Jewish sentiment. For modern Jews to thrive both within a Jewish framework and among Europeans, they must recognize Jewish education as both meaningful and productive. Geiger's approach to Jewish education sought to appease these parental concerns and desires, even as he attempted to undermine them.

Jewish studies, once the only educational game in town, now competed with other cultural sport. Geiger knew this, and so he forcefully defended (if not apologized for) his Breslau Jewish educational program. One should not teach a few religious truths, Geiger responded, and send Jewish children into a world of new professional and social demands. Teachers must impress these truths in memory. But even more, these truths "aus dem Geiste und dem Gemüthe des Zöglings entwickelt" (must develop out of the spirit and disposition of the pupil):[8]

> Die Religion ist nicht bloss ein Zweig des Wissens, der Unterricht in ihr muss eine Erweckung des tiefsten Gefühls, die Anregung des Innersten sein, er ist zugleich die Predigt für das jugendliche Alter.

---

6 Geiger, "Abhandlungen aus den Programmen der jüdischen Religionsunterrichts-Anstalt", 318. See also Eliav, *Jewish Education in Germany*, 3, 168.

7 See Ken Koltun-Fromm, *Abraham Geiger's Liberal Judaism: Personal Meaning and Religious Authority* (Bloomington: Indiana University Press, 2006).

8 Geiger, "Abhandlungen aus den Programmen der jüdischen Religionsunterrichts-Anstalt", 312.

> Religion is not merely a branch of knowledge, and so the instruction of it must arouse the deepest feelings and stimulate the most inner part of our being. Religious instruction is, at the same time, the sermon for the younger generation.[9]

The modern rabbi both instructs and edifies.[10] Such education, left to the professional, well-trained rabbi (*wissenschaftlich gebildete Rabbiner*), stimulates the innermost part of our being.

I emphasize this appeal to personal sentiment and authenticity, because so much of this contrasts with Samuel Hirsch's approach to religious education. For Hirsch, as we will see, Jewish education inculcates truths that resonate as universal principles. This can only make sense for Geiger if those truths "arouse the deepest feelings" and so stimulate inner worlds of passion and affection. Geiger doubts such knowledge can produce such emotion, and so his pedagogical approach moves away from imparting knowledge and truth claims and turns instead to personal sentiment. Without that emotional trigger, Geiger warns, religion as a branch of knowledge is but a dead letter. This was less a call for religious truth, and far more an appeal to religious passion and experience. Jewish education must be meaningful; otherwise, Geiger fears, it could never compete with other schooling that offers far more worldly goods to their pupils.

For Geiger, Jewish education can no longer afford to simply impart information through texts, dogmas, and laws. Instead, Jewish education must be personal and arouse heartfelt longings that stimulate and motivate inner dispositions. It must stir passionate convictions that confer upon religious studies the necessary authority to command allegiance. Mordechai Eliav calls this period in Jewish education "the century of pedagogy" and "pedagogical innovations".[11] Geiger's liberal Jewish education edifies by substituting passionate commitment for rote learning, a longing of the soul for the rational conditions of the mind. Only in this way could Geiger's educational programs command allegiance within the marketplace of values. But it also suggests how Geiger imagines the religious borders of his own time: religion speaks to the heart, and arouses spiritual delights in modes quite foreign to other human endeavors. In tones that often echo Schleiermacher's defense of religion, and his own strategy to protect it from science and reason, Geiger too cordons off a protected zone of religious edification that accesses and satisfies spiritual needs unmet in other cultural pursuits.

---

9 Ibid., 350; also see Ludwig Geiger, *Abraham Geiger: Leben und Lebenswerk*, 136.
10 See Ismar Schorsch, "Emancipation and the Crisis of Religious Authority: The Emergence of the Modern Rabbinate", in Werner Mosse, Arnold Paucker and Reinhard Rürup, eds., *Revolution and Evolution: 1848 in German-Jewish History* (Tübingen: J.C.B. Mohr, 1981), 205–247.
11 Eliav, *Jewish Education in Germany*, 3, 162.

Geiger claims that his educational program moves beyond "die Grundsätze des Judenthums" (the foundational principles of Judaism) to train young children as full members of the community (*Mitglieder der Gemeinde*).[12] For Geiger and others within the German Enlightenment tradition represented by Humboldt,[13] "Die wesentlichste Aufgabe der Erziehung ist die *Charakterbildung*" (the essential business of education is the *formation of character*). Liberal Jewish education prepares Jewish children for universal ends, and instills the virtues and dispositions necessary to succeed in the larger community.[14] Access to this broader, cosmopolitan society requires, according to Geiger, a firm footing in one's own, more limited community:

> Auf einem bestimmten Punkte muss der Mensch feststehen, mit diesem ganz einig und innig verbunden sein, von diesem festen Standpunkte aus wirken. Der Begriff der "Weltbürgerlichkeit" muss eine sehr nothwendige Begränzung haben. Man gehört der Menschheit dadurch an, dass man einem bestimmten Kreise angehört, in demselben und für denselben und *vermittelst dessen* für die Gesammtheit wirkt.
> One must be grounded upon a fixed point ... and work out of this solid standpoint. The concept of 'world citizenship' must necessarily be restricted. One belongs to humanity through belonging to a particular circle, in which and for which and *by means* of which one acts for the whole.[15]

The road to European salons and professional advancement goes through the Jewish community, and not at its expense. And it must do this, Geiger believes, because only there, within more intimate communities, will persons cultivate strong, affective ties. Only within intimate communities will personal authority resonate and, Geiger hopes, command Jews to remain within a particular circle. This is in keeping with Geiger's overall philosophical approach to Judaism in

---

12 Geiger, "Abhandlungen aus den Programmen der jüdischen Religionsunterrichts-Anstalt", 318.
13 See Bill Readings, *The University in Ruins* (Cambridge, MA: Harvard University Press, 1996), 62–69: "As Humboldt puts it, the principle of culture embodied in the University fuses the advancement of objective science (cultural knowledge) with subjective spiritual and moral training (cultivation)" (66).
14 Geiger, "Abhandlungen aus den Programmen der jüdischen Religionsunterrichts-Anstalt", 342–343.
15 Ibid., 345. Note Michael A. Meyer's point regarding the Berlin Jewish community of the 1820s and 1830s: "One either chose *Bildung* or one chose Judaism. The Jewish schools attempted to overcome this dichotomy, relating general culture to Judaism, so that the quest for *Bildung* would not seem to necessitate the abandonment of Judaism, that, on the contrary, the child would gain general culture within a Jewish framework." See Michael A. Meyer, *Judaism Within Modernity: Essays on Jewish History and Religion* (Detroit: Wayne State University Press, 2001), 175.

general: Judaism is less a world religion than an historical, affective one within which Jews flourish as reflective, emotional, and productive citizens. A worldly Jew, or the Jew with *Charakterbildung*, becomes so by acting for and in the Jewish circle. Geiger's Jewish education appeals less to the character of a "Salonmensch", and leans far more to the comforts and safety of local communities. One cannot simply abandon the religious frontiers to engage in the boundless space of world citizenry. Only through the particular (and so constricted) instruction of religious education can Jews hope to engage productively in broader communities of value. For Geiger, human character is rooted in more narrow settlements.

Geiger's view of communal education, while drawing upon the German Enlightenment tradition, nonetheless remains at odds with it. Humboldt and Fichte described the German university as the guardian of German culture and national character (*Bildung*). The university, especially for Fichte, inscribed a national ethnic identity upon its students. Even for Humboldt, the university served the ends of the state in cultivating a unified citizenry.[16] But Geiger understood that this social world, despite the enlightened rhetoric, marked a distant one still closed to Jewish elites.[17] Aware that "world citizenship" enthralls more as propaganda than real possibility, Geiger argues for a socially contingent and local space of Jewish learning. He could not endorse pedagogical reforms to cultivate a world citizenry, as some liberal educators do in more recent times.[18] Instead, he believed it necessary to police religious boundaries so that persons could cultivate strong local ties before joining more expansive national communities. Yet even after joining those wider communities, persons still must develop strong religious bonds to those closer to home. In this sense, religious boundaries serve general, more comprehensive ends: to flourish as a world citizen, one must continually develop character as a particular human being.

---

[16] Readings, *The University in Ruins*, 65–69.
[17] Note Schorsch's claim that the "persistent exclusion of young Jewish scholars from university careers in Judaica further enhanced the scholarly character of the German rabbinate. *Wissenschaft des Judentums* soon became the preserve of practicing rabbis because the rabbinate provided one of the few professional careers in which it could be pursued". See Schorsch, "Emancipation and the Crisis of Religious Authority: The Emergence of the Modern Rabbinate", 244.
[18] See, for example, Martha Nussbaum, *Cultivating Humanity: A Classical Defense of Reform in Liberal Education* (Cambridge, MA: Harvard University Press, 1997).

Samuel Hirsch and Religious Truths

Despite Geiger's appeal to personal meaning and authority, parents in Breslau did see in their children new world citizens, cultured in middle-class manners and dance, all the while moving beyond national and religious borders. Now parents could choose how to educate their children, and some, at least in Breslau, were opting to educate their boys and girls at home.[19] Jewish education should enable this kind of social advancement, they believed, and teach less religious home truths and more practical and worldly ones. In this sense, Samuel Hirsch's approach to Jewish education in the form of the Jewish catechism spoke more directly to their concerns, and contrasts sharply with Geiger's own. Jewish learning through doctrine became a leading pedagogical tool in early nineteenth-century liberal Judaism. The local, flexible, and creative approaches that Geiger favored in education were often abandoned for general and dogmatic views that offered students broad strokes and religious knowledge. Jewish catechisms in the first half of the nineteenth century dominated the educational scene in many liberal Jewish circles (but not only there), especially as these works prepared young students for confirmation.[20] Many historical-school Jewish educators employed catechisms in their teaching (and many liberals chose other methods). Scholars of nineteenth-century Judaism such as Petuchowski and Eliav highlight the Christian foundations for Jewish catechisms, and their focus on dogma and universal principles of faith.[21] Even Geiger employed a catechism

---

[19] Geiger, "Abhandlungen aus den Programmen der jüdischen Religionsunterrichts-Anstalt", 348–350. Eliav adds that many parents sent their children to private teachers as well. See Eliav, *Jewish Education in Germany*, 278.

[20] See Eliav, ibid., 257–270; Jakob Petuchowski, "Manuals and Catechisms of the Jewish Religion in the Early Period of Emancipation", in Alexander Altmann, ed., *Studies in Nineteenth-Century Jewish Intellectual History* (Cambridge, MA: Harvard University Press, 1964), 47–64; Andreas Gotzmann, "The Dissociations of Religion and Law in Nineteenth-Century German-Jewish Education", Leo Baeck Institute Yearbook 43 (1998), 103–126; Simone Lässig, "Bildung als kulturelles Kapital? Jüdische Schulprojekte in der Frühphase der Emanzipation", in Andreas Gotzmann, Reiner Liedtke and Till van Rahden, eds., *Juden, Bürger, Deutsche: Zur Geschichte von Vielfalt und Grenzen in Deutschland* (Tübingen: Mohr Siebeck, 2001), 263–298 and Beate Reupke, *Jüdisches Schulwesen zwischen Tradition und Moderne* (Berlin/Boston: De Gruyter, 2017).

[21] Petuchowski, "Manuals and Catechisms of the Jewish Religion in the Early Period of Emancipation", 47–48: "It is relatively easy to show that the institution of confirmation, its very name, and the terminology used in connection with it are borrowings from the Christian environment. ... Some arch-Conservatives, like Salomon Plessner, wrote catechisms, while religious radicals,

in his confirmation classes. His son and biographer, Ludwig Geiger, ruefully defends its limited use. He appears embarrassed that his father would use such a tool to instill religious piety. But the catechism could be a highly effective pedagogical approach to instill respect, religious competence, and a sense that one's own religious beliefs faired well against critical inquiry.

An illustrative example of the liberal catechism is Samuel Hirsch's *Systematischer Katechismus der israelitischen Religion*, published in Luxembourg in 1856.[22] The liberal Samuel Hirsch, though unrelated to the orthodox Samson Raphael Hirsch, still shares with him a dogmatic view of Jewish theology and practice. I do not employ the term "dogma" here pejoratively, but rather heuristically to highlight the principled character of religious knowledge. Unlike Geiger, who shied away from overarching religious principles that could undermine local variance, Hirsch actively defended those principles as conducive for Jewish practice. Where Geiger appealed to sentiment, Hirsch focused on rational truth; if Geiger sought to convince through personal testimony and experience, then Hirsch believed universal principles carry their own authoritative weight. These sharp philosophical differences carried over to their educational philosophies. These fundamental distinctions in educational approach is important to keep in mind, for if one only considered Hirsch's catechism as a Christian inheritance, then one would miss this deeply philosophical argument within modern Jewish thought. My point is that Hirsch traveled a different road than Geiger, but it is a difference within modern Jewish categories rather than a subversion of them. Geiger secured Jewish identity from within, as it were, by appealing to personal sentiment. Hirsch, in contrast, sought to establish Jewish citizens as full members of a broader national community, and he would do that not through Geiger's sentimental education, but through the rational principles of a catechism.

Hirsch's catechism results from some twenty years of communal reflection upon what he calls "daß Wesentliche der jüdischen Religion" (the essence of the Jewish religion) and the "Grundsätze, Begriffe, und Lebensanschauungen" (foundations, concepts, and views) that sustain the spiritual life.[23] Already this language distances Hirsch's educational approach from Geiger's. Recall Geiger's claim that religion "is not merely a branch of knowledge, and so the instruction of it must arouse the deepest feelings, and stimulate the most inner part of our being". Appeals to foundations, essences, and concepts, as Hirsch does here, do

---

like Isaac Ascher Francolm, preferred other styles of presentation." Petuchowski footnotes Eliav, *Jewish Education in Germany*, 257–259.
22 Samuel Hirsch, *Systematischer Katechismus der israelitischen Religion, auf Beschluß des Vorstandes der israelitischen Gemeinde zu Luxemburg* (Luxemburg: V. Bück, 1856).
23 Ibid., i.

not elicit this inner self, so Geiger believes. But in the very first page of Hirsch's catechism a reader encounters these rational appeals as rhythmic structures governing the text: 1) this is a "systematic" treatment of the Jewish religion, and one that articulates in language the essence of that religion; 2) that essence can be accessed, revealed, and translated into the German language; 3) Hirsch establishes his authority (after some twenty years of personal reflection) to articulate religious truths that 4) become known as philosophical concepts and worldviews. Hirsch can expose a Judaism rooted in essential concepts and views because it is a particular manifestation of the more universal category of religion (even the title of the catechism hints at this as a catechism of *israelitischen Religion*). Not the essence of Judaism, but rather "daß Wesentliche der jüdischen Religion" is the subject of Hirsch's systematic catechism.[24] Judaism, as it were, is a particular exposure of the broader human religious character. Here we recognize Hirsch's project to translate Judaism into a fundamentally human, religious expression. A Jewish (or *israelitischen*) catechism, in this sense, tears down the borders between Jews and others, and re-establishes the Jewish community within the broader human, national community of religious persons. And it does so, contrary to Geiger's approach, by appealing to universal truths and categories.

The catechism solidifies and distills two central tenets of Hirsch's Reform Judaism: 1) religion (what Hirsch calls "die Religion des Menschen") responds to "ein Bedürfniß des menschlichen Herzens" (a need of the human heart), "so daß wir nur die Sprache des eigenen Herzens lesen zu lernen nöthig haben, um eben die ganze Religionslehre auch gefunden zu haben" (such that one must only learn to read the language of one's own heart in order to discover all the teachings of religion); and 2) Judaism really is "diese Religion des Herzens", (this religion of the heart), and even more, "auch nur diese, und diese ganze enthält" (indeed, it is only this, and this entirely).[25] If religion is a language of the heart, then Hirsch presents his catechism less as a linguistic translation and more as a mimetic representation. His catechism reveals rather than translates; it captures rather than interprets a primordial language of the heart. A *Religionslehre* – like Hirsch's catechism – is rooted in that foundational language. And Judaism adequately transcribes that original language into religious dogma. Like many other religious works of this period, Hirsch's text begins with a discourse on religion, and only then moves to a particular form of it (Judaism)

---

24 The distinction made by the alternating use of *israelitischen Religion* and *jüdischen Religion* is unclear.
25 Hirsch, *Systematischer Katechismus der israelitischen Religion*, ii.

as the most fitting example of a universal human need. As Amos Funkenstein once argued, Judaism's universality lies in its particularity: it expresses for all the religious needs of the human heart. For Hirsch, and even for Geiger, Judaism represented the most vibrant and expressive religion in the modern period.

But note how different Geiger's expressive religion is from Hirsch's religion of the heart. Hirsch's Judaism does not expose inner sentiment but religious dogma – a *Religionslehre* that responds to yearnings for truth. This is why the catechism is the most appropriate form and style for translating that yearning into language. Desire for truth yields its written expression. Religious dogma, in this sense, is the scriptural materialization of an inner need for truth. Once again, Hirsch's educational approach mirrors his philosophical account of Judaism. In both cases, Hirsch appeals to and provides rational principles for universal laws. These truths compel in and of themselves, without recourse to sentiment, personal experience, or history – domains belonging to Geiger's educational theory and understanding of Judaism. In these and other ways, Hirsch and Geiger offer two competing approaches to Jewish education because they maintain two opposing views of Judaism.

Geiger attempted in vain to protect the inner, affective life from religion as "a branch of knowledge". Hirsch fixated on that branch and made it the root of his educational pedagogy. And though he warned that his catechism should not displace the rational yearnings of the heart, the very nature and form of Hirsch's work effectively do so. Hirsch divided his catechism into five books: *Geschichte*, *Offenbarung*, *die Lehre*, *die Anbetung*, and *Leben* (history, revelation, teaching, worship, and life). Each book contained numerous chapters with subtitles. The book *Geschichte*, for example, includes chapters on "Der Mensch" (the human being), "Der Garten der Wonne" (the garden of bliss), and "Die Speisegesetze" (the laws of *kashrut*), among others. The formulaic style established in the very first chapter of *Geschichte* runs throughout the catechism. Hirsch opens with the question, "Wozu brauchen wir Religionsunterricht" (why do we need religious instruction)? The answer immediately follows, but in much larger typeset: "Um zu erfahren, wie wir leben sollen, damit wir den Zweck erfüllen, den wir auf Erden zu erfüllen haben" (In order to discover how we should live so that we fulfill the goal set for us here on earth). Hirsch cites two biblical sources (Deut 30:20 and Deut 32:46–47) as proof texts, indented beneath his answer. He then moves on to a second question that builds upon the first: "Wie nennt die Schrift den Zweck, den der Mensch auf Erden zu erfüllen hat" (How does the Bible describe the goal that human beings must fulfill on earth)? Hirsch's response again follows in larger script, but here he interweaves biblical texts into his reply.[26] This pattern continues right through: first a question printed in reduced font, then Hirsch's answer in larger typeset that may include biblical texts or indented proof texts below his more prominent response. Often, but certainly not in every case, Hirsch cites biblical sources only after he responds thoroughly to the more general religious question. This formal layout mirrors Hirsch's theory of religion: Judaism responds to the religious needs and questions of the human heart. But the typeset reveals that the questions merely prompt the more evident, because more discernable, Jewish concepts. Hirsch foregrounds Jewish views (*Lebensanschauungen*) in ways that tend to displace the original question. If the catechism does its work, then a reader recalls only Hirsch's dogmatic response, even less the biblical texts, and barely the provocative questions.

The textual form, then, reveals much about Hirsch's catechism. This text retains its own agency, as it were, through its deployment of typeset and script. Though we know very little about how Jewish readers actually read this text, the catechism certainly positions the reader as one who approaches the biblical text through Hirsch's interpretation. The systematic nature of Hirsch's catechism moves from the general to the specific: from an overarching question, to Hirsch's Jewish-inflected answer, to biblical proof texts. But the textual format moves a reader to reverse this process, and to highlight the Jewish answer to what have become merely subsidiary questions that expose Judaism as a religion of the heart. Hirsch invites neither critical scrutiny nor interpretive probing, but only basic knowledge of the biblical texts that justifies the liberal Jewish concepts articulated in his catechism. The formal effect is cumulative: each question builds upon the previous answer, and the student assembles a base of knowledge and the relevant biblical texts to discover a Jewish *Religionslehre*.

To be sure, Hirsch must bend the biblical texts to conform to his liberal views of Jewish religion. At one point, Hirsch adds a rare footnote[27] to one biblical citation to clarify its meaning (only a handful of footnotes appear in this catechism). If the texts themselves cannot stand alone and perform as proof texts, then Hirsch must add some interpretive gloss to prod them along. In still other places, Hirsch explicitly challenges a more literal reading of the Bible. Responding to a question concerning God's creation of the world in six days, Hirsch asserts: "Vor Gott giebt es keinen irdischen Tag und keine irdische Nacht" (for God there is no earthly day and no earthly night), and so Genesis cannot be understood reasonably as an historical record of God's acts.[28]

---

26 Ibid., 3.
27 Ibid., 95.
28 Ibid., 115.

As a pedagogical tool, the catechism instills Hirsch's liberal Judaism through the repetitive and formal patterns of question, answer, and (sometimes) proof text in ways that highlight Judaism as a rational response to an inner yearning for truth. But for the student who after some one hundred and eighty pages still fails to capture the essence of Jewish faith, Hirsch gratefully appends a *Bekenntniß* (confession).[29] Rather than listening to the "language of the heart" to find both God and Judaism, Jewish students, in the end, learn to read Hirsch's catechism and speak the language of religion as a branch of knowledge. But this merely transposes on paper the desire inscribed upon the human heart for truth. What once remained concealed within has now been revealed to and recounted by the lips of Hirsch's disciples. This is indeed a confession of the *Religionslehre*.

As a confession, Hirsch's catechism discloses a strategy for religious border control.[30] Recall the systematic feature of presentation: Hirsch opens with a question posed not to Judaism but to an audience already sensitive to "ein Bedürfniß des menschlichen Herzens". Hirsch answers that question boldly with a typeset that promotes a Jewish answer to a universal question. But as I have suggested, the text motivates a formulaic reversal, such that the Jewish answer actually displaces the originating question. Hirsch endorses this pedagogical reversal in the *Bekenntniß* (confession) attached to the end of his catechism. What is happening here seems to me to be quite brilliant: Hirsch moves from the universal borders of human needs to the particular concerns of Judaism, only to show how Jewish particularity *informs* and *advances* those universal aspirations. He collapses the borders between Jews and others only to establish Jewish borders as universal ends. And this, as I have noted above, is exactly what Hirsch's philosophy of Judaism dictates: Judaism is a universal religion that grounds all religious truths, for only Jewish concepts and worldviews (*Begriffe* und *Lebensanschauungen*) cultivate a religion of the heart. To flourish in our religious lives, Hirsch argues here, is to live a Jewish life. The foundational principles that outline a liberal Judaism, and so establish boundaries of Jewish religious expression, turn out to be less Jewish than an essentially human language of the heart; or (and this is the brilliance of Hirsch's reversal) the more Jewish, the more human religion becomes.

---

29 Ibid., 186–188.
30 I do not mean to invoke a Foucaultian reading of surveillance here, but merely want to think through how a text like this constructs religious boundaries.

Conclusion

I have argued that the educational pedagogy and practice of both Hirsch and Geiger have been structured by their philosophies of Judaism. Geiger believed in a local, contained Judaism that still reached beyond its limited borders to wider, national circles. But one could not become a universal citizen without being grounded in the sentimental and personal attachments to a Jewish community. His educational program sought to harness those attachments in order to make Jewish practice both compelling and real. For Hirsch, Judaism is a deeply humanitarian religion because it speaks to universal human desires. Those desires for universal truths come from within, but end in a confession of dogma as the most appropriate language of the heart.

Geiger never authored a catechism for young Jewish adults, though he did institute a confirmation class for his religious schools in Breslau, whereby the final exam consisted of an oral question and answer session for the young men and (more often) young women.[31] When Ludwig Geiger describes these exams in the synagogue, he recalls the "Erguß der Rede" (flood of words) and the "Unmittelbares, Persönliches" (immediate, personal) tone of the event that, so Ludwig states, left an unforgettable impression (*der Eindruck ein unvergeßlicher*) on those present.[32] Written as apologetic, Ludwig's account regards this more expressive confirmation as working "trotz des Konventionellen" (despite their conventional form), and one that offers something "immer neuer und mächtiger" (new and more powerful) for child and parent alike. Despite protocol and precedent, Geiger "war ein geborener Lehrer" (was a born teacher) who infused his confirmation classes with "seine lebendige Frische" (his living freshness).[33] This account fits nicely with Geiger's approach to Jewish education, even within a pedagogical setting in which the question/answer format remains central. Geiger's son emphasizes religious immediacy and experience, an elevation of the spiritual register, and an emotional sensitivity in his father's religious education. Geiger believes he must tap into this "language of the heart" to instill an enduring commitment to Jewish values and community. With such a strong, ex-

---

31 See Ludwig Geiger, *Abraham Geiger: Leben und Lebenswerk*, 132. The first confirmation class in 1845 graduated three boys and thirteen girls, and this pattern of greater female participation continued throughout Geiger's tenure in Breslau, culminating in 1863 with six male and fifteen female graduates.
32 Ibid., 132–133.
33 Ibid., 133–134.

periential foundation, these young Jewish adults might contribute to a national community as *Jewish* citizens.

Hirsch's educational approach diverged from Geiger's because he did not fear, as Geiger surely did, that the notion of *Weltbürgerlichkeit* (world citizenship) would only separate Jewish children from their historical and local environment. Instead, Hirsch sought to define the world citizen in Jewish terms. In the confessional appended to the end of the catechism, Hirsch describes the modern Jew as model exemplar and witness to universal brotherhood.[34] The Jew as *Beispiel* inculcates Hirsch's view that Jews are, by religious temperament and trade, already world citizens because Judaism is already a universal, world religion. Indeed, Jews reveal how a religion of the heart is universal in scope and dimension. For Hirsch, Jews display a mode of citizenship that advances world citizenry. If Geiger worried that such fellowship would weaken local bonds, Hirsch responded that Jewish identity could flourish only within a broader, national community. Geiger circumscribes Jewish religious borders in order to strengthen local, sentimental ties; Hirsch expands those boundaries to enable Jewish universal truths to become the inheritance for all.

I conclude by reflecting upon how these two divergent trajectories in modern Jewish thought – the one more insular, sentimental, and communal, the other more universal, rational, and worldly – still resonate within contemporary educational theory. The suggestion here is that Geiger and Hirsch hold down two contrasting poles in Jewish philosophy, and so also provide two competing, but still complementary, approaches to Jewish education. In his *Commandments and Concerns* (1987), scholar Michael Rosenak distinguishes between two "orientations" in Jewish educational theory and practice. The "explicit" paradigm focuses upon the text as "constituting the spiritual reality being encountered", and understands Judaism as a peculiar language game that teachers master and students learn. The "implicit" view, however, concentrates upon student concerns and the environment of educational learning. This implicit model emphasizes "environments and significance-perceived-by-pupils", whereas the explicit paradigm stresses "subject matter and teacher competence".[35] One might assume that Geiger falls somewhere in the implicit camp of Jewish theologians and educators, for he recognizes the "significance-perceived-by-students" as the crucial starting point for engaged learning. And Hirsch might very well slide to the explicit view that focuses on texts, knowledge, and a language

---

34 Hirsch, *Systematischer Katechismus der israelitischen Religion*, 187.
35 Michael Rosenak, *Commandments and Concerns: Jewish Religious Education in Secular Society* (Philadelphia: The Jewish Publication Society, 1987), 129–133.

game of fitting answers to spiritual questions of the heart. If Hirsch's catechism reflects the explicit model by providing the language and structure of Jewish discourse, Geiger's pedagogical concerns focus on individuals and their local environments.

However, Jewish education (and this is Rosenak's point) often travels in both implicit and explicit directions, and we can see this in Geiger's and Hirsch's pedagogical approaches. Once within local areas of concern, Geiger distances his educational program from dominant cultural trends to better instill experiential knowledge and commitment (the implicit model). Yet he secures religious borders (the Jewish "environment") so that Jews are better equipped to engage broader areas of knowledge – a move to the more explicit paradigm. Hirsch promotes his catechism as a pedagogical tool that educates through responsible knowledge of religious history and ideas (the explicit model), but he does so in order to align Jewish values of the heart (the implicit paradigm) with universal goods. Yet even as Geiger and Hirsch embody both the implicit and explicit models of Jewish education, their differences should not be minimized. If Geiger's education seeks personal commitment, Hirsch's catechism instills core knowledge; if Geiger's student engages the sources to reveal the developments and tensions within Jewish history, students of Hirsch's catechism turn to those sources as proof texts; if Geiger situates Jewish education within local communal needs and resources, Hirsch's catechism responds to the desire for world citizenry. For Hirsch, knowledge confers power to engage the world at large. For Geiger, knowledge engenders responsibility to rebuild and energize particular Jewish communities. In the end, Geiger's educational philosophy resonates most fully with Rosenak's implicit model, while Hirsch's appeals broadly to the explicit paradigm.

I have attempted to frame this pedagogical debate in the terms of Geiger and Hirsch's philosophy of Judaism, and especially in the language of religious boundary maintenance. Both Hirsch and Geiger desire to secure Jewish identity in the modern world, and both develop progressive educational approaches to do so. Yet Hirsch saw that world as essentially Jewish, whereas Geiger retreated from a world that appeared hostile to Jewish aspirations. The boundaries that each Jewish thinker sought to protect and expand traverse these hopes and fears, and map out the place of Jewish religious practice within a national, political community. Rarely do we discover pure implicit or explicit views of Jewish practice and commitment. Most educational philosophies tend to slide to one side or the other in the very attempt to balance competing demands. In the heated climate of nineteenth-century Jewish educational politics, neither Geiger nor Hirsch found that equilibrium. But in their failures and triumphs, they offered us something more: they chart the various boundaries Jews cross to become honorable citizens, even as they rely on those borders to strengthen their commitment to Jewish distinctiveness. In the United States, but not only there, striking that balance between access and security has been a thorny political issue. But it is also a pedagogical one for both Abraham Geiger and Samuel Hirsch, who labor to secure Jewish education for a citizenry desirous of worldly goods. To be sure, their nineteenth-century politics is no longer ours, but that boundary too must be crossed, if only to secure access to foundational debates that still resonate within contemporary educational philosophy and practice.

George Y. Kohler
"Humankind is Advancing". Samuel Hirsch's Rediscovery of Messianism and its Consequences for Modern Jewish Religious Philosophy

"I for my part have no concept of the education of the human race", wrote Moses Mendelssohn in *Jerusalem* in 1783 – and the Berlin philosopher could not conceive of how his "esteemed late friend Lessing" had come up with such peculiar ideas. Mendelssohn thought that human progress was only possible for the individual over the course of earthly life, and that "the purpose of Providence does not appear to me to have been for humankind as a whole to perpetually advance itself here on earth, perfecting itself over the course of time".[1] This very clear critique of Lessing also has a theological dimension perhaps not completely obvious at first glance. The long rationalist tradition in Jewish Talmudic and medieval thought had always understood the biblical-prophetic ideas of messianism as just that: as an education of the (whole of) humankind on morality and the fear of God, as an improvement of worldly conditions and the attainment of eternal peace through universal wisdom and awareness. In the 12th century, Maimonides wrote the following about the coming of the Messiah: "The entire world will concern themselves with nothing other than the knowledge of God. For that reason, all will be superbly wise and they will fathom that which is hidden and comprehend the thoughts of their Creator as far as that is possible within the realm of human potential – as written in Isaiah: 'For the earth shall be full of the knowledge of the Lord, as the waters cover the sea (Isa 11:9)'."[2] However, Mendelssohn's religiously motivated rejection of the concept of humankind's ethical development also barred his path to such an eschatology of wisdom. He cites the same verse from Isaiah in his *Counter-reflections to Bonnet's Palingenesis*, but derides it: "The human spirit is so delighted by this concept that it lingers on it lust-

---
[1] Moses Mendelssohn, *Jerusalem oder über religiöse Macht und Judentum*, ed. David Martyn (Bielefeld: Aisthesis, 2001), 92. On Mendelssohn and Lessing, see the classical essay by Ernst Cassirer "Die Idee der Religion bei Lessing und Mendelssohn", in *Festgabe zum zehnjährigen Bestehen der Akademie für die Wissenschaft des Judentums* (Berlin: Akademie-Verlag, 1929), 22–41.
[2] Maimonides, *Mishneh Torah*, "Kings and Wars", ch. 12 (end of the entire treatise) https://www.sefaria.org/Mishneh_Torah%2C_Kings_and_Wars.12.1?ven=Laws_of_Kings_and_Wars._trans._Reuven_Brauner,_2012&vhe=Torat_Emet_363&lang=bi.

ily, and in the delusion enjoys the happiness coming to the human race after such a curative revolution."[3] In the same text, he writes that an individual's bliss must be rooted in the recognition of the universal laws of reason, not in the recognition of the mandate of a divine envoy.[4] Mendelssohn's skeptical view of messianism was probably not only shaped by the emergence of numerous pseudo-messiahs, but also by attempts to "calculate" the coming of the Redeemer using traditional kabbalistic numerology.[5]

Important dimensions of the Jewish Messiah concept remained foreign to the Maskilim of the generation following Mendelssohn: in 1823, Lazarus Bendavid declared in an essay *On the Jews' Belief in a Future Messiah* that today Jews would find their Messiah in "good leaders who accord them rights equal to that of their fellow citizens, and who have granted them the hope of obtaining all civic rights with the complete fulfillment of all civic duties".[6] The good leader as the Redeemer of the Jews – here, Judaism's belief in the Messiah was fully secularized and messianism as a theological-eschatological debate about the future gave way to a striking imminent eschatological expectation. The fact that the rediscovery of messianism as a central theme of Jewish theology was reserved to 19th century Reform thinkers is just further evidence that the religious reform of Judaism in modern times did not originate directly out of the *Haskalah*, as is often assumed. Its roots were rather in traditional rabbinic circles that were coming into conflict with their Talmudic Judaism due to both university studies and a lack of civic emancipation. One of the most interesting examples of how these tradition and reform conflicts were managed – in a manner that was ambivalent on the one hand, but creative and future-oriented on the other – is the first Reform rabbis' intensive examination of the Jewish concept of messianism.

At the beginning of the 1840s, a debate broke out across Germany about a Reform prayerbook published by the Hamburg Temple congregation – a main point of conflict being the issue of the Messiah. Could Jews in the modern world still hope and pray for miraculous redemption and return to the Holy Land? Did this form of belief in the Messiah not contradict their own patriotic duties, and wasn't the exile actually God's eternal plan for the universal dissemination of strict monotheism? These complicated questions were the focus of the

---

[3] Moses Mendelssohn, *Schriften zur Philosophie, Aesthetik und Apologetik*, ed. Moritz Brasch, (repr. Hildesheim: Olms, 1968), 594.
[4] Ibid., 586.
[5] In *Jerusalem*, 58 Mendelssohn refers to the year 2240, year 6000 according to Jewish calculations. According to bSan 97a, the world will only last a total of 6000 years.
[6] Lazarus Bendavid, *Über den Glauben der Juden an einen künftigen Messias* (Berlin: Trowitzsch, 1823), 225.

discussion around concepts of the Messiah at the 1845 Frankfurt rabbinic conference that included the most important Reform theologians. Something astonishing quickly became apparent: despite all the opposition to the messianic restorationist formulations of the Jewish liturgy, none of the participants wanted to renounce the actual messianic ideas in Judaism. There was a variety of reasons for that: alongside the increasing urgency to differentiate Jewish Reform theology from Christianity, which had for its part appropriated and transformed the concept of the Messiah, there was a return to the biblical prophets whose texts were understood as the principal message of a *modern* Judaism and who had also shaped Jewish messianism. However, the desire to preserve messianic ideas in a modern Judaism required new, or at least transformed content of the traditional Talmudic concept of the Davidic Redeemer King, who would first lead Israel to Zion, followed by the remaining peoples who would either come to Zion or be vanquished by the sword.[7] As a result of this necessity of reinterpretation, extensive literature on messianic themes soon emerged – from sermons to philosophical and theological pamphlets.[8] The Jewish thinkers of the 1840s were assisted by the fact that the entire literary tradition of Judaism – from the prophets to the Talmud to the greatest rabbinical thinkers of the Middle Ages – recognized (at least) two different messianic approaches: the apocalyptic, eschatological and above all supernatural process of redemption, alongside the worldly kingdom of wisdom and peace (theologically formulated primarily by Maimonides), which did not depict the *end of time* but the precise historical point at which a socially equitable and spiritually pure society would

---

[7] On traditional Jewish Messiah literature, see: Raphael Patai, *The Messiah Texts* (Detroit: Wayne State University Press, 1988).

[8] This literature has barely been noted by scholars; in general, a transformation of Jewish messianic thinking is first recognized in Hermann Cohen's work (1842–1918). For Cohen's "modern rediscovery of messianism" see Pierre Bouretz, "Messianism and Modern Jewish Philosophy", in Michael L. Morgan and Peter Eli Gordon, eds., *The Cambridge Companion to Modern Jewish Philosophy* (Cambridge: Cambridge University Press, 2007), 170–91, here 178. In contrast, see the messianic texts by: Salomon Formstecher, *Die Religion des Geistes* (Frankfurt: Hermann, 1841), 175–194, 325–329, 348–350; Levi Herzfeld, *Zwei Predigten über die Lehre vom Messias* (Braunschweig: Friedrich Bieweg, 1844); Samuel Holdheim, *Das Ceremonialgesetz im Messiasreich* (Schwerin: Verlag der C. Kürschner'schen Buchhandlung, 1845); Salomon Ludwig Steinheim, "Die Messiasidee nach der Bestimmung der Offenbarungslehre", Zeitschrift für die religiösen Interessen des Judenthums 2, 1 (1845), 21–23 and no. 2, 2 (1845), 41–49. For all of these texts in the German original see the anthology by George Y. Kohler, ed., *Der jüdische Messianismus im Zeitalter der Emanzipation: Reinterpretationen zwischen davidischem Königtum und endzeitlichem Sozialismus*, Mar'ot: Die jüdische Moderne in Quellen und Werken, vol. 2 (Berlin and Boston: De Gruyter and Oldenbourg, 2014).

emerge.⁹ The first Reform rabbis recognized quite early that in this second, rationalistic model of messianism lay the potential for a theological-spiritual defense of Judaism's continued existence in modernity; a hope for the future that in its universality could also be understood independently of particularistic loyalty to the Talmud.[10]

Against the Great Confusion about Messianism

Interest in a theological discussion of Jewish messianism, reawakened for the reasons cited above following the Hamburg Temple controversy, was also certainly Samuel Hirsch's motive for the 1843 publication of twenty sermons held between 1839 and 1842 entitled *The Messianic Doctrine of Judaism*. Hirsch regarded the sermons on the Messiah as a mode of introduction to his best-known work *The Religious Philosophy of the Jews* (1842), which contains a longer, source-critical discussion of the character of the messianic era.[11] The first text from 1839 demonstrates that Samuel Hirsch was interested in a theological examination of Jewish messianism even before the Hamburg Temple controversy, as was the Offenbach Rabbi Salomon Formstecher, for example. In 1839, Hirsch preach-

---

9 A comprehensive study of this subject has yet to be written. For obvious reasons, Gershom Scholem's 1959 classic "Toward an Understanding of the Messianic Idea in Judaism", in idem, *The Messianic Idea in Judaism and other Essays* (New York: Schocken, 1971), 1–36 is characterized by a clear emphasis on the apocalyptic aspect. Gilbert Rosenthal, "Messianism Reconsidered", Judaism 40, 4 (1991), 552–568 ignores the 19th century and goes from Hasidism straight to American Reform Judaism's *Pittsburgh Platform* (1885). There is only one short article specifically about early Reform messianism by Michael A. Meyer, "German Jewish Thinkers Reflect on the Future of the Jewish Religion", Leo Baeck Institute Yearbook 51 (2006), 4–10, whose claims are thoroughly supported here. See also Kenneth Seeskin's more recent chapter, "Judaism and the Idea of a Better Future", in Jonathan A. Jacobs, ed., *Judaic Sources and Western Thought: Jerusalem's Enduring Presence* (Oxford: Oxford University Press, 2011), 49–70.

10 In contrast to the Enlighteners, Jewish Reform theologians' messianism was certainly not just a "metaphor for social progress" as assumed by David Myers; it was rather a serious theological challenge. See David N. Myers, *Resisting History. Historicism and its Discontents in German-Jewish Thought* (Princeton: Princeton University Press, 2003), 132.

11 Samuel Hirsch, *Die Religionsphilosophie der Juden oder das Prinzip der jüdischen Religionsanschauung und sein Verhältniß zum Heidenthum, Christenthum und zur absoluten Philosophie dargestellt und mit den erläuterten Beweisstellen aus der heiligen Schrift, den Talmudim und Midraschim versehen* (Leipzig: Heinrich Hunger 1842; reprint Hildesheim, Zurich, and New York: Olms, 1986), esp. ch. 6, § 74–75 und § 80. This essay, however, is limited to Hirsch's discussion of the teachings on the Messiah in his published sermons, which include more explicit statements than his *Religionsphilosophie*.

ed that "it behooves us" to speak of the Messiah and of our messianic expectations precisely at a time in which there is such great confusion about the Jewish messianic teachings. Israel could not exist without its teachings on the Messiah, and Hirsch's justification of that explicit declaration is just as surprising as it is revelatory for the theological reinterpretation of the messianic idea in modernity. Hirsch asks, how can we "condemn" those Jews who no longer want to be Jews, who consider Judaism to be obsolete in 19th century Germany, if we relinquish the messianic teachings? For "our brothers who are renouncing Israel" see one of the main points of criticism against traditional Judaism in the teachings of the Jewish Messiah, because they "are prone to the delusion that holding to the messianic hopes of Israel hinders them from choosing the civic and moral calling for which God had bestowed upon them strength and capacity".[12] For precisely that reason, Hirsch is convinced that the Messiah must be preached and that which Judaism associates with those teachings must be clearly enunciated.

In this preliminary argumentation, several fundamental approaches to Jewish Reform theology were anticipated simultaneously: the purpose of a reform of theological thought in Judaism (not only regarding the Messiah) was always to reclaim *lost brothers*, strengthen Judaism to meet the demands of modernity, and finally to enable the survival of the Jewish religion in the modern era. The intent of the reforms was not to enable the integration of Jews into civil society, which was an unquestioned expectation of the surrounding non-Jewish world. The idea of abandoning traditional elements of Judaism for the goal of emancipation was rejected by Hirsch as an "insane" solution that could only be based on a misunderstanding of Jewish theology, whose actual essence could never stand in the way of civil, and above all moral integration. Hirsch knew well that the simplest and fastest method of acculturation into the Christian state would be the complete renunciation of Judaism. He thus considered it the rabbi's duty to present the main essence of the Jewish tradition, in our case the teachings of the Messiah, in such a way that its theological core emerges surrounded solely by a thin shell of historically determined separatist tendencies. Theological reform for Hirsch was thus not about true innovation within the Jewish religion, but about the reclamation of the actual essence which had for too long remained uncultivated due to persecution and suppression.

Ostensibly, Hirsch first saw faith in the Messiah as a provider of hope for the Jewish people, in which they were meant to find "solace and reassurance for all

---

[12] Samuel Hirsch, *Die Messiaslehre der Juden in Kanzelvorträgen* (Leipzig: Heinrich Hunger, 1843), 2 et seq.

that grieves us". However, it soon became clear that he was also expressly emphasizing the universal aspect of the messianic era, the future unification of all humanity in the worship of "our God". In the messianic era, "humans will live humanely and thus godly", wrote Hirsch. Traditionally this refers to the disappearance of sensible idols, but, as Hirsch expressly emphasizes, also the idols that "we harbor in our hearts, both the fear as well as the love of that which is vacuous". For Hirsch, God's reign over human hearts signifies the realization of universalized ethical life in the messianic era, for then "all of our desires would be godly, all of our ambitions would pursue only noble purposes".[13] This attests clearly to what Hirsch openly stated in a later sermon: for him, as for many other Reform theologians of his time, Jewish messianic thought refers not simply to the political liberation of the Jewish people from foreign rule. Quite the contrary – while liberation of the Jews had already been accomplished by their civic emancipation, for Hirsch the messianic era had not yet dawned: "In our German fatherlands, Israel may no longer complain of undue pressure" he wrote already in 1840, but it was permitted *nonetheless* to hope for a "more beautiful, glorious future."[14] He then added that the Jews themselves would not suppress any other people in this future time – in an obvious attempt to forestall the common argument invoking various Talmudic, but above all medieval statements along those lines.[15] Clearly, according to Hirsch "violent rule" is not compatible with messianic Jewish thought. This view is in stark contrast to the secularized messianic theories with which twentieth century Jewish thinkers had opposed their predecessors. In particular in the cases of Gershom Scholem, Walter Benjamin, and later Jacob Taubes, messianism became a nihilistic-anarchist revolution aimed at forcefully bringing heaven down to earth in an apocalyptic act – a destructive interpretation of messianism built on an antinomian celebration of the pseudo-messiahs.[16] In the 19th century however, the leading view among Jewish theologians was that the messianic pretenders, from Bar Kochba to Shabbatai Zvi, had inflicted damage on biblical messianism by "exploiting the true, biblical promise of the Messiah inherent to the Jewish spirit through mys-

---

13 All citations are found in *Messiaslehre*, 8.
14 *Messiaslehre*, 31 et seq.
15 See for example, *Exodus Rabba* 1:26 when the Messiah takes "revenge upon Edom" (Rome). Particularly as a reaction to the suppression and persecution of Jews in the Middle Ages, numerous legends were constructed of violent vengeance and the militant salvation of Israel from foreign rule. See Raphael Patai, *The Messiah Texts*, especially chapters 15–18.
16 See Scholem's classic text "Redemption through Sin", in *The Messianic Idea in Judaism*, 78–141 and Jacob Taubes, *Abendländische Eschatologie* (München: Matthes und Seitz, 1991).

tification and false interpretation for the purpose of deception", as noted by the Hungarian Rabbi Samuel Schwarz in 1860.[17]

Messianism as Human Progress

Samuel Hirsch's complete de-politicization of messianic teaching is undoubtedly radical and difficult to reconcile with the traditional sources. The societal-historical notion of progress seems particularly significant and novel theologically speaking, as it is rare in rabbinical thought and most probably derives from Hirsch's study of Hegel: "Humankind progresses – that is the first principle of our religion", Hirsch declared in a sermon from 1840, knowing full well that the Talmudic understanding of history and morality up to the time of Mendelssohn presupposes the exact opposite, i.e., a world in present time, in which the will of God must be continuously fulfilled. For the Talmudic sages, the only exception is the teaching of the future coming of the Messiah, undoubtedly modeled on prophetic texts. However, the transition to a better future is also often portrayed as rather abrupt; as the sudden, wonderful pronouncement of God upon which human action has little influence. In contrast, the fundamental concept behind Hirsch's collective thoughts on the Messiah is that humankind is involved in a slow process of learning, bringing them "closer to self-betterment", for that is the historical objective set them by God. For Hirsch, the Messiah acts as a warranty "that the Lord's divine purpose for humankind will be achieved".[18] This understanding of messianism as the guarantee for the attainment of a predestined and worthwhile "objective" had wide-reaching consequences for liberal Jewish theology in the nineteenth century of which Hermann Cohen provides the most striking expression. For Cohen, the biblical prophets with their messianic ideas had above all unambiguously affirmed the complex issue of the possibility of the realization of a moral humankind. Cohen thus wrote seventy years after Hirsch that it is only with messianism that the concept of the one God will be complete; for without it ethical monotheism lacked the

---

17 Samuel Schwarz, *Die Messias-Zeit: Erläuterungen der Talmudstellen, die Bezug auf Israels Zukunft haben, mit Rücksicht auf unsere Zeit* (Lemberg: Piller, 1865, 3rd edition), 26. For the same negative view, especially on Bar Kochba, see Ludwig Philippson, *Die israelitische Religionslehre*, vol. 3 (Leipzig: Baumgärtner, 1865), 136.
18 Both citations: *Messiaslehre*, 86.

sorely needed future perspective.[19] Hirsch applied here what Cohen would later call the *Theodicy of World History*: the religio-philosophical indispensable immortality of the soul, still proposed by Mendelssohn, was thereby exposed as a myth and replaced with Hirsch's "progress of humankind", which identified human moral responsibility with the religious ideas of messianism. With that, as part of an historical process, all doubts about God's righteousness disappeared; the messianic consciousness of the prophets was substantiated in an ideal future for humankind.[20]

Hirsch's concept of messianism thus had wide reaching effects on the status of religious law in Judaism: life's purpose is no longer solely the present fulfillment of God's commandment. Samuel Hirsch, and many Reform theologians along with him, identified an ultimate purpose of religious practice that lay outside of the actual observance of law, and that appeared to overrule the traditional dictum of the Torah as an end in itself. For a theological description and above all defense of this ultimate purpose – namely an ideal future for all humankind – Hirsch enrolled the Jewish teachings on the Messiah as outlined in the books of the prophets, attempting to reshape them according to the requirements of modernity. Without the hope of the Messiah, not only would "our whole presence on earth be a puzzle", Hirsch proclaimed in 1842 in one of his messianic sermons, but also "our sacred history, our singular memories" would be completely incomprehensible without this notion. Clearly, devout adherence to the law as the traditional Jewish life-purpose did not provide Hirsch with an alternative to a messianic future. For Hirsch, even the stories of the Jewish people as presented in the Bible only made sense if they resulted in the messianic era – and so he asks the rabbinical tradition in a nearly polemical way: "What was the purpose of our Exodus out of Egypt, our wandering through the wilderness [...], if the promised land only has milk and honey, thereby only refreshing the body, but failing to revitalize the spirit?" But politics, science, and art also lack real meaning if God delivered Israel from Egypt without finally "accomplishing" his work: if the knowledge of God did not universally spread as described in Isaiah (11:9).[21] Hegel's influence is again felt clearly here, without whose concept of history as a dialectic process of development leading to an ever more complete realization of absolute spirit, the new notion of a specific

---

19 See Hermann Cohen, "Die Bedeutung des Judentums für den religiösen Fortschritt der Menschheit", in idem, *Hermann Cohens Jüdische Schriften*, vol. 1 (Berlin: Schwetschke, 1924), 18–35, here 32 et seq.
20 See Hermann Cohen, "Die Messiasidee", (1892), ibid., 105–124, here 117.
21 All citations: *Messiaslehre*, 396 et seq.

Jewish-messianic mission for the rest of humankind would not be possible.[22] Soon, 19th century Jewish religious philosophy would present prophetic messianism in its mission to disseminate monotheism with all of its social and ethical implications as Judaism's decisive contribution to human civilization. Up until its displacement by Zionist ideology, it remained one of the major components of theological thought of acculturated Western European Judaism.[23]

Personal Messiah or Messianic Era

Using the notion of humankind's messianic goal, Hirsch could also answer the question that made up the central theme of the last of his twenty sermons: the question of an individual *person* as Messiah.[24] In the 19th century, this question increasingly became the focus of debates on the enduring value of Jewish messianism in the modern era and is mostly associated with Hermann Cohen's later work. Cohen's messianic concept is often described as a "messianism without the Messiah", since for him the *person* of the Messiah is replaced by an ideal messianic *era* in history.[25] However, that concept is not new: the rabbinical conferences in the 1840s on the reform of Judaism demanded a new impersonal notion of the Messiah, and the replacement of the national-political call for a return to Israel linked to the messianic age with the concept of a messianic era for all humankind.[26] The reformers refer to traditional sources here as well: while it is true that a personal Messiah is only spoken of in a small portion of the biblical prophetic texts, the Messiah as an individual figure (as a descendant of King David) is commonplace in the Talmud. In addition, another exegetical line of

---

22 On Hirsch's dependence on Hegel, see Emil L. Fackenheim, *Samuel Hirsch and Hegel* (Cambridge: Cambridge University Press, 1964), Gershon Greenberg, "Samuel Hirsch: Jewish Hegelian", Revue des études juives 129 (1970), 205–215, and Dirk Westerkamp, "Platon in Moses. Hegels Kritik der Substanzmetaphysik und die 'Philosophia Haebraeorum'", Hegel-Jahrbuch 7, 1 (2005), 106–113, here 110 et seq.
23 Cf. Max Wiener, "The Concept of Mission in Traditional and Modern Judaism", YIVO Annual of Jewish Social Science 2–3 (1947/1948), 9–24.
24 *Messiaslehre*, 397. See also: David Novak, *Jewish Social Ethics* (Oxford: Oxford University Press, 1992), 228–236.
25 See for example, Rory Schacter, "Hermann Cohen's Secular Messianism and Liberal Cosmopolitanism", Jewish Political Studies Review 20, 1–2 (2008), 107–123; Martin Kavka, *Jewish Messianism and the History of Philosophy* (Cambridge: Cambridge University Press, 2004), 113.
26 See *Protokolle und Aktenstücke der zweiten Rabbiner-Versammlung* (Frankfurt a.M.: E. Ullmann, 1845), 73–86 and 94–106 and the reports in the Allgemeine Zeitung des Judenthums 9, 32 (1845), 485 et seq.

thought had been developing since the Middle Ages. Perhaps as the Jewish answer to the Christological exposition of the "servant songs" in Isaiah, the concept emerged (in Rashi, 11th century at the latest) that the *suffering servant* of God in Isaiah, who re-appeared as the suffering Messiah in Talmudic literature, was in principle a metaphor for the whole people of Israel and its oppression.[27] This interpretation spread rapidly among 19th century liberal theologians and became the biblical foundation of the modern Jewish *mission theology*. In a sermon in 1843, the Rabbi of Brunswick warned his audience about the collective Messiah, "indeed, only a few are of this opinion"[28] – twenty years later in 1863, Heinrich Graetz called out in plain language, "Israel is the messianic people". That would be the most important concept of the exile-Isaiah,[29] and it is again Hermann Cohen who developed this concept thoroughly in his systematic religious philosophy.[30]

In Samuel Hirsch's treatment of the topic, even the formulation of the question about the personal Messiah is unusual: when the earth is full of the knowledge of God, war and hate have ceased, "and the nations have brought us to Zion, and divine services will be held in the right way" – why then was "a rod out of the stem of Jesse" (Isaiah 11:1), the *person* of the Messiah, still necessary?[31] From the start, the question was not in keeping with the Talmudic messianic tradition that views the Messiah as Israel's savior – both politically and even militarily – and thus as the one who would build the ideal kingdom of Zion with the strength of his worldly power. For Hirsch, as revealed in his later answer to this initial question, the situation is the reverse – and certainly, there is a theological innovation concealed here, one that is important to the Rabbi and that accounts

---

27 Cf. bSan 98a and Rashi on Isaiah 53:4: Israel's suffering serves the redemption of other peoples. The ideas are summarized in Samuel Rolles Driver and Adolf Neubauer, *The Fifty-Third Chapter of Isaiah – According to the Jewish Interpreters* (New York: Ktav, 1969). On Rashi: Esra Shereshevsky, "Rashi and Christian Interpretations", Jewish Quarterly Review 61 (1970), 76–86.
28 Levi Herzfeld, *Zwei Predigten über die Lehre vom Messias*, 12.
29 Heinrich Graetz, "Die Verjüngung des jüdischen Stammes", Jahrbuch der Israeliten 10 (5624/1863–1864), 1–13, here 11. This essay resulted in Graetz (but above all the annual's publisher Leopold Kompert) being sued for libel by a Christian zealot. Kompert was even partially convicted by a Viennese court. In the present context, it is interesting to note that positive opinions were voiced by the court-ordered Jewish experts, the Rabbis Isaac Noah Mannheimer and Lazar Horowitz, on the question as to whether Judaism permitted an impersonal view of the Messiah. See Nils Roemer, *Jewish Scholarship and Culture in Nineteenth-Century Germany: Between History and Faith* (Madison: University of Wisconsin Press, 2005), 58.
30 Hermann Cohen, *Religion der Vernunft aus den Quellen des Judentums* (Frankfurt: Kauffmann, 1919), 308 et seq.
31 *Messiaslehre*, 397.

for a meaningful part of his own interpretation of Jewish expectations of the future. This innovation is the key to understanding why Hirsch considered the concept of the Messiah to be the "foundation" of Judaism without which we "distort the whole of our religion, making it incomprehensible".[32] Traditionally, that meaning had rarely been attributed to messianic teachings so that Hirsch's focus on those teachings can thus be seen as groundbreaking for 19th century Reform theology.

Hirsch summarized the main ideas of his Messiah-concept in the following way: The Messiah "shall not denote the beginning but rather the end of salvation". For him, the Messiah was not coming to "plant a new spirit" within the people; he would in fact only come once people already internalized the new spirit. Referring to the *Servant's Song* at the beginning of Isaiah 42, Hirsch argued that the Messiah can only bring justice there "where everybody desires justice and nothing but justice". Hirsch continued to say that if that were not the case then there would be a danger that "someone would be hurt, or someone's wishes would be offended" – as if that were not, at least according to an important part of Jewish tradition, precisely the unavoidable responsibility of a politically understood messianism. However, Hirsch seemed to reject that kind of "violent" understanding so fundamentally that he found himself moving toward circular reasoning here. The Messiah's responsibility was therefore not the establishment of humankind's ideal future kingdom but rather its *preservation*, and from Hirsch's Messiah-King "only instruction would be sought so that love does not stray" – a straying that was obviously a real possibility for Hirsch, even with a sufficiently broad knowledge of God.[33]

The point of this pacifist, even passive interpretation of the Messiah is clear: Hirsch wanted to avoid the concept of some form of miraculous, supernatural salvation at all costs. For him, the path to the ideal future kingdom was much more of a long process of learning and self-education for humankind, and any thoughts of a *sudden* transformation of the moral and social situation was evidently completely foreign to him for theological reasons. "This sprout should not be a wonderful and unfathomable phenomenon to us, nor a God who suddenly comes down from heaven whom we were not expecting and could not have expected", wrote Hirsch.[34] It is unclear whether explicit criticism of the mystical aspect of the Christological concept of the Messiah was made here. Apparent is that Hirsch had recourse to Jewish theology's traditional insistence that

---

32 Ibid.
33 All citations: *Messiaslehre*, 398 et seq.
34 Ibid, 398.

the Messiah is exclusively human in order to formulate a clear counterargument against any sudden, unexpected, unpremeditated and thus supernatural redemption – for that would lie outside of human ability.[35]

For Hirsch, a Messiah who is "the only one who is pious" would be a completely useless redeemer if the rest of humankind remained "estranged from God"; and miracles could only superficially heal "the sickness of the spirit" – seemingly a critique of the Christian concept. With "sickness" Hirsch is obviously referring to the sinfulness that another person could never "remove from my heart". Once again wholly in line with Talmudic teachings, Hirsch claims that people must "come to God themselves wanting to be purified"; then, and only then, would "God help immediately".[36] As though for confirmation, at this point in the sermon he then cited the Talmud, apparently from memory and without providing a reference in the printed version. The citation's point of reference however is the word *purify* (*reinigen*) – Hirsch's cryptic reference was surely to the following words by Resh Laqish in tractate bYoma 38b: "If one wishes to defile himself, the door is opened to him; but he who comes to purify himself, will surely be assisted." That is classic rabbinic theology: the forgiving of sins (primarily on the Day of Atonement – *Yoma*) is accomplished by those seeking God's forgiveness through repentance and return, without mediation by any other person. Hirsch's reference does not only demonstrate that he could cite Talmudic literature without difficulty when it suited his needs. More importantly, it shows that he anticipated another doctrine from later liberal religious philosophy of Judaism: the Day of Atonement's central importance for the definition of the relationship between humankind and God, concisely expressed in the work of Hermann Cohen in particular.[37] Whereas in the biblical description of the ceremonies of the Day of Atonement (Leviticus 16) the idea of atonement by proxy (animal sacrifice) does still occur, the emphasis on the impor-

---

[35] Cf. here Hirsch's representation of Jesus in *Religionsphilosophie*, 623 et seq.: After his death, "in poetic excitement" Jesus was "adorned with attributes that one feels entitled to expect from the Messiah" by his disciples. (The entire fifth chapter of *Die Religionsphilosophie* is of interest here). The debate about Jewish messianism would develop into a sharp dispute with Christianity and its image of the Messiah in the later 19th century. For just one example out of many, see Ludwig Philippson, "Vergleichende Skizzen über Judentum und Christentum", (first 1869 and later) in Ludwig Philippson, *Gesammelte Abhandlungen*, vol. 1, ed. Martin Philippson (Leipzig: Fock, 1911), 199–324, here 316–324.

[36] *Messiaslehre*, 399. Obviously due to his extensive discussion of Christianity in *Religionsphilosophie*, Hirsch names "the sinlessness of all humanity as the foundation of all of the Messiah's teachings" (854), a perspective on which his entire discussion of Jewish messianism is almost exclusively based.

[37] Cf. the chapter "Der Versöhnungstag" in Cohen's *Religion der Vernunft*.

tance of a *direct correlation* between humankind and God is Talmudic in origin (thus post-biblical) and in this form became a core element of Jewish liberal theology. Protestant biblical Criticism in the 19th century had moreover located the historical origin of the Day of Atonement (due to it not being mentioned in Deuteronomy) in the late, religious-historically "less valuable" post-exilic phase of the development of the biblical writings, thereby providing Jewish theologians of the Cohen School with another opportunity to support their claims.[38]

The Messiah and Humanist Ethics

Hirsch then further argued that the alternative to his concept of the Messiah – the traditional, supernatural, miracle-working Messiah – contrasted strongly with the biblical religion. As the word of God, the Bible contains the only and eternal truth, but nowhere does it contain a reference to the Messiah "bringing new knowledge (*Kunde*) of heavenly things, new knowledge that we could never have anticipated, and that would never have reached us without him".[39] Hirsch appears to be once again shifting the discussion away from the direction the debate about the repeal of Torah law in the messianic age would have traditionally taken. In fact, there are many references in post-biblical rabbinic literature to the Messiah bringing a "new Torah" with him, which would obviously contradict the earlier, biblical laws in some instances.[40] Behind this expectation lies the Talmudic notion of the *yoke* of the biblical commandments,[41] a yoke that will be set aside at the end of times in a messianic act of redemption. For upon his arrival, the Messiah will release the devout from the burdens of those limitations based on religious law that have been taken on willingly out of piety.[42]

---

38 See, for example, Julius Wellhausen's *Prolegomena zur Geschichte Israels* (Berlin: De Gruyter, 2001), 106 et seq.
39 *Messiaslehre*, 399.
40 Isa 51:4 ("the Torah will come from Zion"), is interpreted in Midrash LevR 13 as referring to "a new Torah". YalqShim (13th century) claims this Torah will be given directly by the Messiah (see YalqShim on Isa 26). Cf. QohR, ch. 11:18 in which the Torah learned by the people in this world is labeled "void" (*hevel*) in comparison to the Messiah's Torah.
41 *The yoke of the commandments* or the *yoke of the Kingdom of Heaven* – among others, see mBer 2:2. Also see mAvot 3:6 and bBer 61b in which, at the time of his brutal execution, R. Akiva interprets "with all your soul" (Deut 6:5) as the acceptance of the *yoke of the Kingdom of Heaven.*
42 For example, the Talmudic rabbis would sometimes say that those who followed dietary laws would be rewarded with unkosher meals in the Kingdom of the Messiah. Cf. for example LevR 13:3.

Moses Mendelssohn, for whom the function of Jewish "ceremonial law" was above all that of demarcation, could still imagine a miraculous second public revelation, a second prophet on the level of Moses who "would introduce new religious practices", that would make it possible for all peoples to worship their Creator *together*.[43] This traditional idea was later appropriated by radical reformers, primarily Samuel Holdheim, who identified at least the beginning of the messianic era with the civic emancipation of the Jews and sought to use these Talmudic arguments to defend his abrogation of certain laws.[44]

As a classical Reform theologian however, Samuel Hirsch did not see God's commandments as a burdensome yoke, nor did he need Talmudic grounds to repeal outdated regulations. Hirsch's messianic theory is neither about the continued observance of the commandments in the kingdom of the Messiah, nor about legal principles, but about *Herzensangelegenheiten* (matters of the heart), a word that for him served as a metaphor for humanist ethics. In his sermon, Hirsch invoked the verse from Ezekiel (36:26) saying that "God will take our heart of stone from our body and give us a heart of flesh instead";[45] but that would only be in God's own power because "this work is not possible for his anointed one, for a human being the likes of us, nor is it relegated to him".[46] Whether Hirsch is aware of the context of this position in the Christian-Jewish debate is impossible to determine here. The heart metaphor plays a decisive role in the Pauline critique of the Jews' "technical" observance of religious laws, which had been replaced by universal faith after the coming of Christ – while in rabbinical usage the image of "uncircumcised" or "stone" hearts referred exclusively to the struggle with "evil impulses" or more directly in Hirsch's terms, to humankind's due repentance.[47] The rejection of a supernatural transformation of human nature upon the arrival of the Messiah is thus necessarily linked religio-philosophically to universal ethical truths here, as taught in the Bible accord-

---

[43] Mendelssohn, *Schriften zur Philosophie*, 594.

[44] See Samuel Holdheim, *Das Ceremonialgesetz im Messiasreich* (Schwerin: Verlag der C. Kürschner'schen Buchhandlung, 1845), 44–46. See too Hermann Cohen's critical discussion of this topic, *Religion der Vernunft*, 424 et seq.

[45] Ezekiel 36:26, "A new heart also will I give you, and a new spirit will I put within you: and I will take away the stony heart out of your flesh, and I will give you a heart of flesh."

[46] *Messiaslehre*, 399.

[47] See Romans 2:17–4:25. For the Jewish interpretation, see bSukka 52a and Sifra Lev 26:41 (Bechuqotai 2:5). Hirsch considers Jesus (in Matthew's description) to be entirely Jewish, his fundamental teachings corresponding to those of Judaism. For Hirsch, Christianity first begins with the "Pharisee youth" Paul and his consequential misjudgment of the true meaning of the ceremonial laws – a false interpretation that shaped the Christian image of Judaism from then on. (See Hirsch's discussion of Paul's *Epistle to the Romans* in *Religionsphilosophie*, 726–767.)

ing to Hirsch. Within the scope of a religion such as Judaism, one which claims an eternal, divinely sanctified ethic, the Messiah's task can only be to *proclaim* universal moral laws, to turn the eternal divine truth into established justice, as Hirsch writes.

For Hirsch, that was another reason why the coming of the Messiah would occur at the end of this moral reform, and not at its beginning. The beginning was the fall of humankind in Paradise; according to Hirsch's interpretation of the biblical salvation history, it was already there that humankind obtained its heart of stone. God had then transformed the Jews' hearts back into flesh through the proclamation of his eternal word, but also through punishment for non-compliance "until we know and understand that a heart of stone makes us unhappy". This understanding would spread progressively throughout all of humankind: "Only then can the banner from the stem of Jesse be erected before God for all nations so that all can come to him for guidance."[48] Here too Hirsch's Messiah emerges solely as an adviser, as a guarantor of the preservation of his kingdom whose first establishment is manifested in the moral progress of humanity, which must be realized without supernatural assistance.

However, there was still one argument for Hirsch to invalidate: even if his Messiah does not perform miracles or personally usher in the ideal future for all people, that does not necessarily mean that he would only arrive at the very end of the ethical and spiritual *progression* of humankind. It would be quite natural for him to appear at any point in time as a model for humanity, as a moral compass – an argument that Hirsch possibly derived from the contemporary quest for the historical Jesus and the consequential liberal Protestant theology of Jesus as the ideal model for all humans. In 1835, David Friedrich Strauss's *Das Leben Jesu* was published and caused a lot of commotion, including in Jewish circles. The young Abraham Geiger, for example, was excited about the work's consequences, but only in one way, as he enthusiastically expressed in a private letter to Josef Derenbourg: "that has put an end to Christianity" … "with all of its twisting and turning, it will certainly come to a fall!"[49] Samuel Hirsch did not believe that ideal human role models would contribute to securing people's faith either: "as long as we are sinners, we cannot value a holy life", he preached, "much less emulate it." He argued that there were enough examples of that in the history of Israel, one being his interesting interpretation of

---

[48] *Messiaslehre*, 400.
[49] "Abraham Geigers Briefe an J. Derenbourg (1833–42)", Allgemeine Zeitung des Judenthums 60, 14 (1896), 164–166. Geiger's letter was later published in Ludwig Geiger, ed., *Abraham Geiger's Leben in Briefen* (Berlin: Louis Gerschel, 1878), 225–227, here 226. For Hirsch's critique of Strauss, see, for example, *Religionsphilosophie*, 461, 650, 687, 827 among others.

the *Aqedah*, the Binding of Isaac: If even Abraham's much praised willingness to sacrifice his son at God's command was not enough to serve as a model act, "that is proof that an individual human life could never suffice to countermand the obstinacy and sinfulness of the rest of humankind". While Maimonides, for instance, had interpreted the *Aqedah* expressly in relation to the role model function of Abraham's actions, according to Hirsch the meaning of the *Aqedah* is rather "that God only demands complete and active love, not the act itself".[50] Once more it is God who examines hearts or even replaces them, effecting change, not the God-fearing act of a human being.

For Hirsch, the Messiah is not there to judge, guide, or reform evildoers – instead, he only appears to those seeking "nothing but justice and truth". The Messiah cannot take up his position until evil has vanished, wrote Hirsch, "and the kingdom of the good begins". It is clear here that the temporal beginning of the messianic era is related neither to the actual duty of the Messiah, nor even to God: "How close or how far away this kingdom is depends not on God, but on us."[51] Humanity must first destroy evil in order to enable the arrival of the Messiah. Hirsch argues that the means to that end is the universal recognition of the one God; the Messiah can do nothing for those who do not accept God. "His task is to keep us on the path of life, for that, however, we must already be convinced of the glory of that path."[52] This clear and often repeated claim in Hirsch's theology is also a new element, contrasting with Judaism's centuries-long messianic hope, embraced by Jews on account of the yearning for external salvation, if not for revenge against their suppressors that it entailed.

For Hirsch, however, the Messiah's power was subordinate to that of *Keneseth Israel* (כנסת ישראל), a theological concept in Judaism similar to that of the *Holy Catholic Church:* it is comprised of past and future generations of professed Jews who shape traditions and keep the religion alive. As a human, the Messiah remains controvertible and vanquishable as an "individual" for Hirsch. Only the "congregation", and thus the people of Israel, could resist evil, he wrote. Referring to the notion that the biblical "suffering servant" is the people of Israel, Hirsch even went as far as to declare that it had been and still was the very mission of the *Congregation of Jacob* "to cause evil to befall it [Israel] in all places and at all times".[53] If a sole individual opposes evil – even if he be God's anoint-

---

50 All citations: *Messiaslehre*, 400 et seq. Maimonides: *Moreh Nevuchim* (*The Guide for the Perplexed*) III, 24. The idea that God truly wants to or must "test" Abraham had always been rejected by rationalist Jewish religious philosophy.
51 *Messiaslehre*, 401.
52 Ibid., 403.
53 Ibid. (emphasis added).

ed one – that evil is not vanquished, as demonstrated in the biblical stories. Here, the role of the challenger of evil, a conventional role for the traditional Jewish Messiah, is completely transferred to the people of Israel. The expected messianic figure is also categorized as just one in a line of purely human figures who exhibit human weaknesses and strengths just as do the heroes of the biblical narrative.

The Messiah as the Enlightened Monarch

In Hirsch's theology therefore, only a small role remains for the Messiah-King, who is still understood entirely as an individual person: that of a judge rather than of a warrior, albeit the "highest judge on earth" whose mission above all consists of preventing a relapse into the pre-messianic era by proclaiming truth and justice *after* the victory of good and the dawning of the true Kingdom of God. History has taught us that this figure must be an *individual person:* "Everything in history begins with the rule of one person", wrote Hirsch, "and for that reason history will also end with the rule of one person."[54] What then follows is an almost classic argument for enlightened monarchism: the kingship that the people chose purely intuitively at the beginning of their history, that they "acquiesced to based on their feelings of need" would over the course of time be recognized as the most reasonable form of government, prophesied Hirsch in 1842, and the people would "choose [it] again with free judgment at the end of days". Although strictly monarchist, Hirsch's messianism is not restorative; it does not constitute a simple return to some early period of a naturally peaceful, glorified utopia and original human harmony. The element of evolving knowledge, introduced into Jewish eschatology by Maimonides as a defining characteristic of the messianic era, is also indispensable for Hirsch, despite his monarchist end time romanticism. The restoration of the monarchy (obviously meant as an actual alternative to democracy[55]) would only happen "with free judgment" at the end of days according to Hirsch because "humankind had progressed to a state of enlightenment". An enormous amount of moral and intellectual development will have occurred to get to that point, which in turn would prevent a reversion back to the era of "atrocities and vice" situated between the beginning and the end of human history.[56]

---

54 Ibid., 408.
55 On Hirsch and monarchy see the articles of Judith Frishman and Michael A. Meyer in this volume.
56 All citations: *Messiaslehre*, 408 et seq.

At this point, we also find Hirsch's only indication that there were already certain signs of the messianic age during his own time, in the modern era, in which "freedom of thought and speech" had become one of human society's most important objectives. However, despite these liberal ideals, "we all love and truly honor our imperial dynasty, with the deepest and most heartfelt conviction, as we know that it is only under a monarch who receives his glory and office from God that true freedom can prosper over the length of time". In contrast, a democracy is incapable of guaranteeing the uninhibited development of the ideals of freedom, be it today or during the messianic era – as demonstrated by the example of the United States. There, even the most holy of human rights went unobserved, and "restoring the poor slaves' innate human dignity proved impossible, despite the intense strife of the better-minded". Hirsch believed that power struggles were inherent to societies dominated by interest groups while the enlightened monarch (and thus also Hirsch's Messiah-King) would be "an impartial judge and partyless adjudicator". It was precisely his divine mission and the authority stemming from it that would free him from involvement in daily power struggles.[57]

All these characteristics of the "partyless" monarch apply universally to the Messiah; he is the enlightened king of *all* peoples. But, Hirsch asks purely rhetorically at the end of the sermon, why should the nations of the world choose a king specifically from Israel? Because, as we saw, he must be chosen with "free judgment", and in Hirsch's attempt to reconcile the traditional Jewish messianic teachings with the modern era, a Messiah – understood as an individual person – can apparently only arise from the people of Israel. And here once again, the argument of selflessness is brought to bear: just as the ideal monarch should hold no worldly interests, Israel, out of all the peoples, had received solely a spiritual heritage. Their mission was "to carry the doctrine of truth and to prove it everywhere" and to achieve peace between God and those peoples who have become estranged from God. "All other peoples have received a heritage of worldly interests from God, they should become great in the arts and sciences, they should circumnavigate the earth and spread their treasures everywhere ..." For Hirsch, the preservation of the older messianic doctrine in his modern era appeared to be of such great importance at this point that he was more willing

---

[57] All citations: ibid., 409 et seq. Cf. David Einhorn – a radical Reform rabbi and Hirsch's predecessor as rabbi in Philadelphia – and his deliberate involvement in the campaign against slavery in the U.S. Einhorn's celebrated sermon entitled "Response to a Biblical View of Slavery" was printed in Sinai 6 (1861), 2–22 available online: http://www.jewish-history.com/civilwar/einhorn.html. For discussion see Gershon Greenberg "The Significance of America in David Einhorn's Conception on History", American Jewish Historical Quarterly 63, 2 (1973), 160–184.

to deny the Jewish people their part in the arts and sciences than their spiritual claim to leadership in the messianic age of humankind. Carried away by this idea, he even attempted a half-hearted defense of the Messiah's Davidic lineage at the end of the sermon – David, after all, descends from an ancient royal dynasty.[58]

But despite all these attempts at reconciliation, several of Samuel Hirsch's basic principles on the Messiah clearly demonstrate that his theological approach had little to do with any traditional Jewish understanding. Hirsch was simply using the old terminology and motifs to yield the impression of religio-historical continuity, particularly in the case of his theory that the Messiah will only come once the moral self-education of humankind has been completed. While on the one hand this stands in obvious contrast to tradition, even to that of the biblical prophets, on the other hand one could easily comprehend this theory within a modern notion of "spiritual" conceptions of the Messiah, even if the Messiah is still conceived as an individual person in Hirsch's writings. According to him, the Messiah does herald truth and justice to a humankind ready for free judgement and is in no way defined by considerations of political power. Hirsch's Messiah is thus naturally weak and requires the willing recognition of the congregation that itself won the actual battle against evil. But the Messiah must not be a role model, an ideal human being – perhaps Hirsch sees him more as an ideal rabbi – for: "each person, even the most poor and most humble, may come to him and speak out openly and freely demand his justice; for he is a judge of the people, a judge who never tires and never languishes until justice has in truth penetrated everywhere."[59]

In order to deal with the problem of personalization in Jewish messianism, in a bold stroke Samuel Hirsch completely separated the notion of the Messiah from the realization of an ideal future kingdom. For Hirsch, the Messiah remains nothing but the custodian of this kingdom, and that perhaps only to salvage the traditional concept of a messianic individual that plays into Hirsch's own political monarchism. To do so however, he did not refer to the "Mosaism" of the Enlighteners, nor could he completely identify with Talmudic thinking. At points where the Hebrew Bible aligns with his messianic concept it is used and inter-

---

58 Ibid., 411.
59 Ibid., 412. Shortly after its publication, Hirsch's collection of sermons on the Messiah's teachings were extensively discussed in the Literaturblatt des Orients. The reviewer agreed with all of Hirsch's arguments and emphasized for his part that the Messiah's teachings were a cornerstone of Judaism without which the entire building would collapse – therefore, spreading the truth of the Messiah must still be Judaism's responsibility today. See Literaturblatt des Orients 18 (1843), column 274–279, here 274.

preted to that effect; but where Talmudic theology according to Hirsch supersedes it, he follows the Talmud. Other German Reform theologians of his time may have gone farther than Hirsch, completely abandoning the concept of a personal Messiah after having taken his thoughts to their logical conclusion. However, all the approaches of these later Jewish thinkers can be traced to Hirsch: theologically, deliverance from evil must be understood as a human act in Judaism. The Messiah, therefore, cannot suddenly and unexpectedly appear as God's representative. Instead, the messianic age requires humanity to undergo a process of gaining ever increasing knowledge that will in the end lead to a universal and moral kingdom of peace.

Part IV: **Samuel Hirsch's Luxembourg: Industrialization, Emancipation and Community**

Norbert Franz
Mid-19th Century Luxembourg. Nation Building and the Late Industrialization

Samuel Hirsch's activities in both the political and religious sphere in Luxembourg came at a particularly dynamic phase of the country's nation building. In the mid-19th century, the first effects of modern industrialization were gradually being felt, although the Grand Duchy's development into one of the leading iron producers of Europe would not occur until the end of the century.[1] That was also true of the capital city in part, where Samuel Hirsch lived with his family between 1843 and 1866. The process of industrialization was limited there since the city's topography was greatly impacted by a fortress whose grounds confined the municipality.[2]

Despite the fundamental political and economic transformations of the "brief" 19th century, this period of time in Luxembourg City has rarely been the object of historical scholarship.[3] This chapter will illuminate some aspects

---

[1] Michel Pauly, *Geschichte Luxemburgs* (München: C.H. Beck, 2011), 78–80.
[2] Pauly, *Geschichte Luxemburgs*, 66–77; Gilbert Trausch, "Comment faire d'un état de convention une nation", in idem, ed., *Histoire du Luxembourg. Le destin européen d'un "petit pays"* (Toulouse: Éditions Privat, 2003), 201–274, here 207–237.
[3] There are many individual local historical studies, for instance the one by Jean-Pierre Koltz, *Baugeschichte der Stadt und Festung Luxemburg* (Luxembourg: Saint-Paul, 1972) which contains a particularly impressive wealth of material. François Lascombes, *Chronik der Stadt Luxemburg 963–1795*, vol. 1–3 (Luxemburg: Saint-Paul, 1968, 1976, 1988) is helpful for the Middle Ages and early modern period, but without sources or bibliographic references, so that citations are unverifiable. In view of the current state of research, the studies that this paper is based on (Norbert Franz, *Die Stadtgemeinde Luxemburg im Spannungsfeld politischer und wirtschaftlicher Umwälzungen (1760–1890). Von der Festungs- und Garnisonsstadt zur offenen multifunktionalen Stadt*, Trierer historische Forschungen, vol. 40 (Trier: Kliomedia, 2001/Diss. phil. Univ. Trier 1998) and idem, "Assistance municipale des pauvres de la ville de Luxembourg dans la deuxième moitié du XIXe siècle: le Bureau de Bienfaisance luxembourgeois (1850–1880)", in Henri Wehenkel, ed., *Luxemburg - Paris - Luxembourg. Migrations au temps de la Commune. Études d'histoire économique et sociale accompagnant l'exposition*, Publications scientifiques du Musée d'histoire de la ville de Luxembourg, vol. 8 (Luxembourg: Musée d'histoire de la ville de Luxembourg, 2001), 33–42) are related to Michel Pauly's comprehensive analysis (Michel Pauly, *Luxemburg im späten Mittelalter*, vol. 1: *Verfassung und politische Führungsschicht der Stadt Luxemburg im 13.–15. Jahrhundert* and vol. 2: *Weinhandel und Weinkonsum*, Publications de la Section historique de l'Institut grand-ducal, vol. 107 and 109 (= Publications du CLUDEM, tome 3, 5) (Luxembourg: Saint-Paul, 1992, 1994)) but concentrate on laying down some of the structural foundations of Luxembourg's urban history supplemented with microhistorical

of the social transitions in the Grand Duchy of Luxembourg during the time of Samuel Hirsch's activities within that state system. Drawing on prior research 1) it will begin with an outline of the inter- and intrastate frameworks and socioeconomic conditions that affected urban development. 2) An investigation into the causes for Luxembourg's statehood formation and for its continued existence follows. 3) Next is an inquiry into the scope of political participation in the Duchy's rapid succession of constitutions. 4) The chapter will also examine – on both a larger governmental level and a local municipal level – the expansion of the functions of the state beyond its core governmental functions, namely law, order, and national security. In the process, governmental activity regarding religious communities will be analyzed in particular. 5) This chapter will conclude with an analysis of the socioeconomic structure of Luxembourg's urban society and specifically the position of Samuel Hirsch's family within a model of the municipality's social stratification.

---

findings. Regarding the history of the Luxembourgish upper classes in the second half of the 19th century, see the comprehensive study conducted by Josiane Weber, *Familien der Oberschicht in Luxemburg. Elitenbildung & Lebenswelten 1850–1900* (Luxembourg: Édition Guy Binsfeld, 2013), which delves deeper into this field, impressively expanding it. Guy Thewes provides a synthesis of research on the history of Luxembourg governments since the 1848 Revolution (Guy Thewes, *Les gouvernements du Grand-Duché de Luxembourg depuis 1848* (Luxembourg: Édition Guy Binsfeld, 2003)). There are several newer studies on Luxembourg's constitutional history: Wolfgang H. Lorig and Mario Hirsch, eds., *Das politische System Luxemburgs. Eine Einführung* (Wiesbaden: VS-Verlag für Sozialwissenschaften, 2008); Christoph Bumb, *Luxemburgs Weg zur parlamentarischen Demokratie* (Berlin: VS-Verlag für Sozialwissenschaften, 2011); and Norbert Franz, "Luxemburg", in Werner Daum, ed. *Handbuch der europäischen Verfassungsgeschichte im 19. Jahrhundert. Institutionen und Rechtspraxis im gesellschaftlichen Wandel*, vol. 2: *1815–1847* (Bonn: Dietz, 2012), 543–573. Stephanie Schlesier has worked intensively on the history of the Jewish minority in Luxembourg and the neighboring regions of France and Germany (Stephanie Schlesier, "Grenzüberschreitend. Juden in Luxemburg, ihre Kontakte in die Nachbarregionen und ihre Einbindung in das luxemburgische Leben im 19. Jahrhundert", in Norbert Franz and Jean-Paul Lehners, eds., *Nationenbildung und Demokratie. Europäische Entwicklungen gesellschaftlicher Partizipation*, Luxemburg-Studien / Études luxembourgeoises, vol. 2 (Frankfurt am Main: Peter Lang Edition, 2013), 171–192). For the emancipation of the Jews in Luxemburg see Renée Wagener's dissertation, *Die jüdische Minderheit in Luxemburg und das Gleichheitsprinzip. Staatsbürgerliche Emanzipation vs. staatliche und gesellschaftliche Praxis vom 19. bis zum Beginn des 21. Jahrhunderts* (Hagen: FernUniversität in Hagen, 2017), available online https://ub-deposit.fernuni-hagen.de/receive/mir_mods_00001049. See the contributions by Schlesier and Wagener in this volume.

The Formation of the Sovereign State of Luxembourg

Luxembourg's statehood is a result of power constellations in Europe and of the increasing interest of a significant part of the population in managing Luxembourgish matters themselves. The following section will investigate the external and internal interests that determined Luxembourg's state formation in the 19th century and how those interests were reflected in state behavior on an inter- and inner-governmental level, as well as in the governmental activities on a central and local level.

At the Grand Duchy of Luxembourg's inception, there was no one nation that brought the state into being. It was instead the will of European powers, the representatives of which gathered in Vienna in 1814 and 1815 to reorganize large portions of Europe's political landscape after Napoleon Bonaparte's double defeat. In the process, numerous borders were newly drawn and the Grand Duchy was transferred to the head of the House of Orange-Nassau, William I. He treated Luxembourg as an integral component of his newly created United Kingdom of the Netherlands, to which Belgium also belonged. In the Congress' final act,[4] King William I and his descendants were awarded sovereign rights over the Grand Duchy of Luxembourg. This newly created territory comprised most of the area of the former Duchy of the same name. It had belonged to the Austrian Netherlands from 1714 until 1795, when it was captured by French revolutionary forces and became a part of France as the *Département des Forêts*. King William I of the Netherlands joined the German Confederation (that would constitute Central Europe's supranational regime until 1866) in 1815 as the Grand Duke of Luxembourg. The fortress city of Luxembourg became a part of the permanent military organization of this confederation of states, to which numerous monarchs and representatives of free states had loosely associated themselves. Since William I waved his right to have some of his own troops included in the garrison, the Confederation's Luxembourg fortress generally had a garrison made up exclusively of Prussian soldiers.[5]

Despite being a member of the German Confederation, the Grand Duchy of Luxembourg was still governed as a part of the Netherlands during the first

---

[4] Johan Ludwig Klüber, *Acten des Wiener Congresses in den Jahren 1814 und 1815*, vol. 6 (Erlangen: J. J. Palm and Ernst Enke, 2nd edition 1836), 12–96, here 21.
[5] Albert Calmes, *Histoire Contemporaine du Grand-Duché de Luxembourg*, vol 1: *Naissance et débuts du Grand-Duché (1814–1830)* (Luxembourg: Saint-Paul, 1971, 2nd edition); Trausch, "Comment faire d'un état de convention une nation", 209 et seq.

years of its existence. That meant that instead of having its own operating state administration, it had a Dutch provincial administration. Nevertheless, the country and the Grand Duke and his administration in Luxembourg did acquire particular rights and obligations through their membership in the German Confederation. In that way, the Grand Duchy played a similar special role in the United Kingdom of the Netherlands as did the Duchy of Holstein in the Kingdom of Denmark. That would change during the Belgian Revolution of 1830, a part of the first large revolutionary wave in Europe in the 19th century. Starting in Paris, this series of revolutions encompassed large portions of West and Central Europe, including Poland. Significant portions of the Luxembourgish population joined the revolution and within a short period of time almost the entire territory of the Grand Duchy was Belgian. One important reason for the rapid establishment of the Belgian Revolution in Luxembourg must have been the high tax burden, which had peaked with the introduction of a grist tax in the run-up to the revolution.[6] The capital – whose Prussian garrison and the threat of intervention by the German Confederation forestalled Belgian occupation – was alone in remaining under the authority of the Dutch King after the Belgian Revolution.

It was only in 1839 that King William agreed with the London Conference's decision to split up the Grand Duchy. The size significantly reduced, it only maintained its connection to the Netherlands through a personal union;[7] nevertheless, in that form the country was able to develop quickly into a separate state. Over the following years and up until the Revolution of 1848, Luxembourg's sovereign institutions were established predominantly by indigenous or nationalized ministers and officials. In 1841, the country obtained its own state constitution for the first time;[8] in 1842, it joined the Prussian-led German customs union.[9]

The founding of the Apostolic Vicariat of Luxembourg in 1841 constituted the preliminary stage for the establishment of a diocese within the borders of the Grand Duchy and augmented Luxembourgish sovereignty in the territorial organ-

---

6 Albert Calmes, *Histoire Contemporaine du Grand-Duché de Luxembourg*, vol. 2: *Le Grand-Duché de Luxemburg dans la Révolution Belge (1830–1839)* (Bruxelles: L'Édition Universelle, 1939); Trausch, ibid., 209–217.
7 Albert Calmes, *Histoire Contemporaine du Grand-Duché de Luxembourg*, vol. 3: *La Restauration de Guillaume Ier, Roi des Pays-Bas (l'Ère Hassenpflug) (1839–1840)* (Bruxelles-Luxembourg: L'Édition Universelle, Saint-Paul, 1947); Albert Calmes, *Histoire Contemporaine du Grand-Duché de Luxembourg*, vol. 4: *La création d'un état (1841–1847)* (Luxembourg: Saint-Paul, 1954).
8 "Verfassung Luxemburgs vom 16. Oktober 1841", Mémorial du Grand-Duché de Luxembourg, 1841, no. 51, 425–436.
9 Albert Calmes, *Der Zollanschluss des Grossherzogtums Luxemburg an Deutschland (1842)*, 2 vol. (Luxemburg: J. Beffort, 1919).

ization of the Catholic Church.[10] Based on the organizational logic of denominational relations, the foundation of a Chief Rabbinate of the Jewish congregation with Samuel Hirsch as the first Chief Rabbi was in order.[11] The establishment of the Protestant Evangelical congregation in Luxembourg had already been arranged by the Prussian-Dutch military convention on November 8, 1816. It was composed primarily of members of the Prussian garrison that had been joined informally by a civilian community since 1842.[12]

The second large revolutionary wave in Europe in the mid-19th century also included Luxembourg. As in other countries, there were demands for universal voting rights as well as basic rights such as freedom of the press, and the monarch's high level of income drawn from the so-called "civil list"[13] was criticized. Luxembourgish gendarmerie and the Prussian soldiers of the fortress' garrison struck down the at times violent demonstrations in Luxembourg City, just as they did with the uprisings in other regions of the country. Nonetheless, the monarch and the government felt compelled to relent. After the initial riots, King-Duke William II followed the decision of the German Federal Convention and granted freedom of the press and agreed to the election of a constituent assembly. Luxembourg additionally dispatched three delegates to the German National Convention in Frankfurt am Main with the task of advocating for Luxembourg's independence. In July 1848, a new and liberal constitution of the Grand Duchy went into effect.[14] Religious freedom was not one of the new basic rights, as it had been granted from the inception of the Grand Duchy – first by the Dutch constitution of August 24, 1815 and then through the first Luxembourgish

---

10 Trausch, "Comment faire d'un état de convention une nation", 209 et seq., 219 et seq.; Norbert Franz, *Durchstaatlichung und Ausweitung der Kommunalaufgaben im 19. Jahrhundert. Tätigkeitsfelder und Handlungsspielräume ausgewählter französischer und luxemburgischer Landgemeinden im mikrohistorischen Vergleich*, Trierer historische Forschungen, vol. 60 (Trier: Kliomedia, 2006 / Habilitationsschrift Univ. Trier 2005), 103 et seq.
11 Laurent Moyse, *Du rejet à l'integration. Histoire des Juifs du Luxembourg des origines à nos jours* (Luxembourg: Édition Saint Paul, 2011), 83.
12 Klaus Loetsch, "Zwischen vielen Stühlen. Geschichte des Protestantismus in Luxemburg", in Forum, Luxemburg 254 (March 2006), 33–40, here 34.
http://www.forum.lu/pdf/artikel/5440_254_Loetsch.pdf.
13 Pauly, *Geschichte Luxemburgs*, 72–74; Albert Calmes, *Histoire Contemporaine du Grand-Duché de Luxembourg*, vol. 5: *La Révolution de 1848 au Luxembourg* (Luxembourg: Saint-Paul, 1982, 2nd edition); this is in reference to the income drawn out of Luxembourg's national budget by the monarch.
14 "Verfassung Luxemburgs vom 9. Juli 1848", Mémorial du Grand-Duché de Luxembourg, 1848, no. 52, 389–414.; Thewes, *Les gouvernements du Grand-Duché de Luxembourg*, 12–14.

constitution of October 12, 1841.¹⁵ In the early 1840s the administrative implementation of the fundamental equality of religions and denominations commenced, as demonstrated in part by the financial support provided to non-Catholic congregations.

As in almost all of the other states of the German Confederation, an "age of reaction" followed the revolutions of 1848 and 1849. In the process, some of the progress made during the course of the revolution regarding participation rights was reversed.¹⁶ In 1856, King-Duke William III (who had succeeded his father after the latter's death in 1849) re-imposed a *landständische* constitution based on resolutions by the German Confederation. This constitution once again limited the possibilities for the population and its elected representatives to take part in the organization of policy and strengthened the monarchical principle.¹⁷

Just a few years after the crisis-laden beginnings of its sovereignty, Napoleon III's annexation goals newly endangered Luxembourg's existence as a state. Due to this Luxembourg Crisis of 1867 marking the end of the German Confederation, the government of the conservative Victor von Tornaco fell after having been in office since September 26, 1860.¹⁸ Another conference of European powers in London resolved to neutralize Luxembourg and withdraw the Prussian garrison from the former Federation fortress. As part of a broad petition movement in support of attaining Luxembourgish sovereignty, the affected parties initially became involved in those debates. However, it was only following the renewed danger of annexation in the 1870/71 war that the population of Luxembourg spoke up in the form of a petition movement in which almost all adult male citizens participated.¹⁹ Tornaco's successor, the industrialist Emmanuel Servais, led the Luxembourgish government beginning in December 1867 and set a cautious liberal course.²⁰ This is reflected in particular in the revised state constitution of 1868.²¹ In those decisive decades of Luxembourgish state formation, it became

---

15 Norbert Franz, "Luxemburg", in Daum, *Handbuch der europäischen Verfassungsgeschichte im 19. Jahrhundert*, vol 2, 543–573, here 555–556.
16 Pauly, *Geschichte Luxemburgs*, 74.
17 "Verfassung Luxemburgs vom 27. November 1856", Mémorial du Grand-Duché de Luxembourg, Première Partie: Actes législatifs et d'administration générale, Luxemburg 1856, no. 28 (30. November 1856), 209–248; Pauly, *Geschichte Luxemburgs*, 74; Thewes, *Les gouvernements du Grand-Duché de Luxembourg*, 20–25.
18 Thewes, ibid., 30–34.
19 Pauly, *Geschichte Luxemburgs*, 75.
20 Ibid., 74 et seq.
21 "Verfassung Luxemburgs, Revision vom 17. Oktober 1868", Mémorial du Grand-Duché de Luxembourg, Première Partie: Actes législatifs et d'administration générale, Luxemburg 1868, no. 23, 213–242.

apparent that the existence of the Grand Duchy was dependent on the will of the great powers of Europe – as it always had been.

The above analysis has shown that Luxembourg's very existence as a state was decidedly marked by its function within the system of European powers: primarily in terms of its importance for the German Confederation and its armed forces. Later, it would become a plaything to be tossed about in the interest of the Great Powers' strategic goals, France and Prussia in particular. Nonetheless, Luxembourgish nation building had made great strides in the three decades since the founding of the state: the Grand Duchy of Luxembourg and its inhabitants were no longer just pawns to be used in the great European forces' power play.

State Constitutions Marked by Restricted Participation Rights

The balance of state authority between the parliament and monarchical heads of state was the one major constitutional policy question during this era. The other point of conflict regarding constitutional policy concerned the extent of participation in the political decision-making process by not only the political, cultural, and economic elite, but also by the broader population. These questions can be answered for the most part based on an analysis of the Luxembourgish constitutions, exchanged in rapid succession during this period. The relationship between the state and religion will also be examined in the following section.

The Grand Duchy of Luxembourg has an unusually erratic constitutional history. During the last years of the 18th century and the first two decades of the 19th century, three French constitutions were in effect here – that of the Directory of the French Republic, of the Consulate, and of the first French Empire. In the officially established Grand Duchy of 1815, an 1815 revised version of the Dutch constitution of 1814 was initially applied; and from 1830 to 1839 it was the Belgian constitution of 1830 that was used for the entire Grand Duchy excepting its capital city, the German Confederal Fortress.

The Dutch constitution that came into effect after the founding of the Grand Duchy allocated the majority of governing rights to the monarchy and only granted participatory rights to the parliament for legislation and the establishment of the budget. The first Luxembourgish constitution of 1841[22] did nothing to change

---

22 "Verfassung Luxemburgs vom 16. Oktober 1841", Mémorial du Grand-Duché de Luxembourg, 1841, no. 51, 425–436.

that in any fundamental way. The monarch in particular maintained a dominant position; the government was answerable to him. The *Ständeversammlung* (estates assembly) had only limited decision-making power in regard to legislation and the creation of a state budget.

As had already been the case with the Dutch constitution, the Luxembourgish constitution excluded middle and lower classes from active political participation through instituting a high minimum tax qualification for voting. Active voting rights were held by only one tenth of adult male citizens.[23] All of these constitutional state structures did maintain the fundamental right to freedom of religion already established in the American Revolution and the French Revolution. The Calvinist leaders of the House of Orange-Nassau were particularly interested in maintaining that right due to their relationship with their numerous Catholic subjects. And in contrast to the neighboring Prussian Rhineland, the emancipation of the Jews was no longer restricted in the Kingdom of the Netherlands, Belgium or in the first Luxembourgish constitution.

As with the other liberal state constitutions of this era, the revolutionary constitution of 1848[24] broadened the spectrum of the basic rights of the individual, of freedom of speech, of the press and of assembly. Responding to the pressure of numerous petitions, pamphlets, assemblies, and demonstrations, the monarch conceded to one of the revolutionaries' principle demands, i.e., the freedom of the press, as early as March 20, 1848.[25] That led to the rapid flourishing of the Luxembourg press. Alongside the *Diekircher Wochenblatt*, the liberal *Courrier du Grand-Duché de Luxembourg* and the *Echternacher Grenzbote*, which had already emerged amidst the fight against censorship, more newspapers were founded in quick succession: the *Luxemburger Wort für Wahrheit und Recht* – which remains the most important newspaper today – as the institution of ultramontanist and social-reformist oriented political Catholicism and the conservative-liberal *Volksfreund*. Samuel Hirsch was majorly involved in the creation of the latter, which was very short-lived, being discontinued in June 1849. Both the paper's orientation and the composition of its contributors pro-

---

[23] Statec Luxembourg, *Statistiques historiques: 1839–1989* (Luxemburg: Statec, 1990). Thanks to my colleague Michel Dormal at the RWTH Aachen University for the calculation of the share of the population's eligible voters; Franz, "Luxemburg"; Bumb, *op. cit.*, 40 et seq.

[24] "Verfassung Luxemburgs vom 9. Juli 1848", Mémorial du Grand-Duché de Luxembourg, 1848, no. 52, 389–414.

[25] Norbert Franz, "Nation oder Partikularismus: Die Revolution von 1848/49 in Luxemburg", in Elisabeth Dühr, ed., *"Der schlimmste Punkt in der Provinz". Demokratische Revolution 1848/49 in Trier und Umgebung* (Trier: Selbstverlag des Städtischen Museums Simeonstift Trier, 1998), 644–661, here 649.

vide a clear picture of the Luxembourg Chief Rabbi's political position and social milieu. Two of the individuals working on the paper were: Nicolas Martha, a secondary school instructor and later the first director of the Luxembourg *Sparkasse*; and an employed businessman named Joseph Seelhof. A close colleague of the governor named Pierre-Antoine Schou was a part of the editing department of the *Volksfreund*, as was the lawyer Mathieu-Lambert Schrobilgen, a high state and municipal official who had headed the pro-government *Journal de Luxembourg* until his appointment in 1844, and written for the *Courrier* until 1851. And finally, the lawyer Charles Simonis, who was later to become the mayor of Luxembourg, also played a leading role in the editing of *Volksfreund*. Many of the members of the editorial board were members of the Luxembourg Masonic Lodge, as was Samuel Hirsch. Politically, they were aligned with the Orangists, the supporters of the House of Orange. This constituted an anticlerical, conservative-liberal and Germanophile orientation, which particularly opposed the "progressive" liberal francophile "Partei Metz", political Catholicism, and any democratic tendencies.[26]

The representatives of the former Orangist elite were unable to prevent the new constitution from strengthening the population's rights to political participation: for example, parliament deputies were now voted in directly, instead of being indirectly elected using electoral delegates. The sphere of eligible voters was broadened to almost a quarter of the male population by means of a considerably reduced minimum tax qualification.[27] However, the participation rights of the middle and lower classes were still seriously limited: the democrats' demand for universal male suffrage was not met. Nevertheless, the parliamentarization process went forward. Although the government was still appointed by the King-Grand Duke, it was de facto accountable to the chamber of deputies. The institution of unlimited budgetary powers further strengthened the parliament. On the whole, the new constitution significantly restricted the rights of the monarch: Luxembourg had completed its first step toward a parliamentary monarchy.[28]

In the 1850s however, the old powers would have a reaction that would correct these steps toward democratization: In 1856, King-Grand Duke William III issued a constitution[29] that signified a clear break from that of 1848. It imple-

---

26 Calmes, *La Révolution de 1848 au Luxembourg*, 50 et seq. Further research is needed here.
27 "Wahlgesetz von 1848", Mémorial du Grand-Duché de Luxembourg, 1848, no. 64, 497–515, Art. 1.
28 Bumb, *op. cit.*, 56–61.
29 "Verfassung Luxemburgs vom 27. November 1856", Mémorial du Grand-Duché de Luxembourg, Première Partie: Actes législatifs et d'administration générale, Luxemburg 1856, no. 28 (30. November 1856), 209–248.

mented the German Confederation's resolutions, limiting the parliament's budgetary powers just as it limited the population's participation rights. Deputies, considerably diminished in number, were now elected in part based on a high minimum tax qualification, in part indirectly through cantonal assemblies based on a lower minimum tax qualification. Along with the state council, a second chamber was established whose members were appointed by the monarch instead of being elected. In 1860, the minimum tax qualification was generally fixed at thirty francs. The number of eligible voters was thereby reduced to such a degree that it fell decisively below that of the *Vormärz* period: just eight percent of adult male citizens who lived in the Grand Duchy were entitled to vote, about thirty percent less than in the *Vormärz* period and only around a third of those eligible to vote in 1848.[30] The 1856 constitution substantially limited freedom of press and association, based likewise on the German Confederation's resolutions.[31]

After the end of the German Confederation, it was once again necessary to revise the constitution: the constitution of 1868[32] further weakened the position of the monarch. He nevertheless maintained his sovereignty and the parliament still had to share legislative powers with him. All the men in Luxembourg who held civil rights, had reached the age of twenty five, lived in the country, and paid an amount of direct tax of between ten and thirty francs were enfranchised. The precise minimum tax qualification was determined in each case based on a special electoral law. The strengthening of the parliamentarian principle meant that the parliament had complete budgetary and financial power, as all of the state's financial affairs required an ordinance. The constitution transferred a portion of the budgetary power to the local municipalities; they had decision-making authority over municipal tax increases. Any law that involved revisions to the constitution had to be accepted by the monarch and a two-thirds majority of the chamber.[33] The comparatively liberal constitution of 1868 significantly limited eligible voters in the long term: until 1890, the participation of eligible male voters remained at a maximum of 15 percent, corresponding to 7.4 percent of the entire adult population. At the turn of the 20th century, still only a third of adult

---

30 "Wahlgesetz von 1860", Mémorial du Grand-Duché de Luxembourg, Première Partie: Actes législatifs et d'administration générale, Luxemburg 1860, no. 28, 157–176.
31 Bumb, *op. cit.*, 63–69.
32 "Verfassung Luxemburgs, Revision vom 17. Oktober 1868", Mémorial du Grand-Duché de Luxemburg, Première Partie: Actes législatifs et d'administration générale, Luxemburg 1868, no. 23, 213–242.
33 Bumb, *op. cit.*, 71–77.

Luxembourgish men were eligible to vote.³⁴ Broad sections of the middle classes, all lower classes, and all women remained barred from any formation of political will via participation in the electoral process.

The parliament's rights and political clout were remarkably enhanced vis-à-vis the monarchs in the four decades around the middle of the century. Yet the broader public's participation in political decision-making processes – in particular regarding the election of parliamentary representatives – was remarkably restricted during the entire period under observation. The percentage of eligible voters in the adult population lagged at the same low level characteristic of the conservative and liberal state systems of 19th century Europe.³⁵

The Expansion of State Activity at the Governmental Level

While the state constitutions provide information about the basic principles of each state system, the national finances reflect the scale and prioritization of governmental activity. Using examples of selected budgets from this time period, the following section will examine whether the tendency seen by the Berlin economist Adolph Wagner toward a broadening of governmental activity in the area of public services can also be observed in Luxembourg. The question of what kinds of services were focused upon and what that means for the evaluation of the character of a political system in Luxembourg during this time will also be addressed in particular.

The 1844 budget³⁶ put forward by the de la Fontaine³⁷ administration (which came into office in 1841) stipulated one third of government expenditure for the maintenance of the civil state power structure. Over one-tenth of the budgetary expenses went to the so-called "civil list", funneled directly to the monarch, and the remainder was put into the judicial system and general public administration. For the armed portion of the power structure – the militarily organized gen-

---

34 "Wahlgesetz von 1868", Mémorial du Grand-Duché de Luxembourg, Première Partie: Actes législatifs et d'administration générale, Luxemburg 1868, no. 26, 269 f.
35 Peter Brandt, Martin Kirsch, and Arthur Schlegelmilch, eds., *Handbuch der europäischen Verfassungsgeschichte im 19. Jahrhundert. Institutionen und Rechtspraxis im gesellschaftlichen Wandel*, vol. 1: *Um 1800* (Bonn: Dietz, 2006).
36 Converted total expenditures: 3.2 million francs. Mémorial du Grand-Duché de Luxembourg, 1843, 530–550.
37 Christian Calmes and Danielle Bossaert, *Geschichte des Großherzogtums Luxemburg* (Luxemburg: Saint-Paul, 1996), 74–77; Thewes, *op. cit.*, 12–15.

darmerie, the militia, and the Grand Duchy's allotment of armed forces to the German Confederation – just under one fifth of the budget was allocated. All in all, the government dedicated more than half of its financial resources to the core sovereign functions of the state. In the area of government services, the so-called *Leistungsverwaltung* (service management) carried the largest weight, being responsible for transportation, communication, and public structures. It received just under a quarter of the funds, thus occupying second place for funding. Most of these resources went into road construction, a smaller portion into other building projects of the state and the post office. In contrast, only one tenth of the governmental budget was allocated to the cultural sector: over three fourths of these funds were expended on the salaries of Catholic clergy, the remainder went to public education and subsidies to the municipalities for church and school buildings. Among the rest of the state expenditures were the costs of public enterprise (the state salt monopoly and forest management), as well as those of the social sector of which expenditures on former state officials' pensions made up the largest portion. Governmental aid for the poor, however, remained negligible – and this in the face of mass poverty during that time, on the cusp of industrialization. All of the above point to the start of an evolving expansion of state activity regarding public service management, as will be advanced in the following section.

An important question for this analysis is also the precise economic weight and evolution of the appropriations to the clergy. The budget drawn up in 1847 for the year 1848, and thus before the revolution, included 126,985 guilder or 268,751 francs for the Catholic clergy's wages – a total of about 8 percent of the entire budget.[38] No payments were designated to the clergy of other religions, with the exception of the Jewish congregation: the Chief Rabbi obtained a state salary of 1,000 guilder or 2,117 francs.[39] The post-revolutionary Willmar Ministry's budget for 1850[40] allocated 245,585 francs for the wages of the Catholic clergy, 2,000 francs for the Rabbi. Over the course of the revolution there were thus slight reductions in the clergy's salaries, but nothing that represented any significant lowering of their income level. Overall, this budget features some obvious lasting effects of the revolution. In particular, the expenditure allotment for the

---

[38] Mémorial du Grand-Duché de Luxembourg, 1847, 391–431, here 420 et seq.

[39] The annual income of a day laborer was 200 to 500 francs; a minister's income was 6,000 francs; Franz, "Assistance municipale des pauvres de la ville de Luxembourg", 251.

[40] Total expenditures: 2.9 million francs; Mémorial du Grand-Duché de Luxembourg, 1849, 933–941, 949–951, 1003–1011, 1027–1029; Mémorial du Grand-Duché de Luxembourg, 1850, 43–45, 52–57, 63–71; Thewes, *op. cit.*, 19. On the incomes of Catholic clergy and rabbis, see Mémorial du Grand-Duché de Luxembourg, 1849, 1008–1010.

state apparatus lowered considerably. That is in part attributable to the substantially reduced disbursement to the monarch's "civil list". However, military expenses also sank considerably, as the government diminished the contingent contributed by Luxembourg to the German Confederation's armed forces. By contrast, spending on road construction, schools, and care of the poor increased. These changes are to be interpreted as resulting from the 1848 revolutionaries' demands. State budget disbursements for social assistance, however, remained rather marginal.

During the reaction era of the 1850s, the tendency toward a broadening of public service management stagnated. Minister of State Simon's budget for the year 1855[41] was only slightly larger than the comparable example from the Willmar Ministry. The focus of his budget had shifted slightly in favor of civil administration, for minimal losses in the budget for public buildings. However, the focus of state activities would undergo a vast transformation in subsequent years: the Tornaco Ministry apportioned a budget for 1862[42] whose volume had almost doubled in comparison to the budgets discussed thus far. The total expenditures for sovereign state functions as well as for public services in the areas of public enterprises, social issues, culture, and economic promotion had barely been altered. The expenditures for Catholic clergy salaries added up to 270,000 francs, and 700 francs for the Protestant clergy. Rabbi Samuel Hirsch's wages remained precisely at the same 1850 level, namely 2,000 francs. Additional state financial allocations were funneled primarily into the expansion of the transportation infrastructure: the road and path network was improved and the first railroads and train stations were built.[43]

The budget that Minister Servais produced for 1868[44] exhibits a distinct shift in the focus of public service administration; it was certainly at a considerably lower level than that of the comparable budget from 1862. This was primarily due to the more than fifty percent reduction in disbursements for transportation and communication infrastructure as well as for public buildings. In contrast,

---

41 Total expenditures: 3.1 million francs; Mémorial du Grand-Duché de Luxembourg, 1854, 141–147, 165–173, 175–179, 181–185; Mémorial du Grand-Duché de Luxembourg, 1855, 1–9, 191, 224, 256.
42 Total expenditures: 5.7 million francs; Mémorial du Grand-Duché de Luxembourg, 1861, 202–225. On the costs of supporting the Catholic clergy, the Protestant clergy and the rabbis, see 255.
43 For transportation, communication and public buildings, the budget allocated a total of 2.6 million francs. Of that, 1.2 million were for the railway and 0.8 million for road and path construction.
44 Total expenditures: 4.9 million francs; Mémorial du Grand-Duché de Luxembourg, 1854, 141–147, 165–173, 175–179, 181–185.

cultural and social expenditures grew significantly. Here, the government's increased efforts in public education promotion, healthcare, and poverty aid had an effect. However, the largest portion of social spending was allocated for the pensions of former civil servants. This expansion of state activity in the sectors of transportation infrastructure, public education, and social issues in the 1860s was financed in part through increased internal revenue, but primarily through the incurrence of an abruptly rising national debt. Including the short-term loans and cash advances made by the *Banque Internationale à Luxembourg* (founded in 1856), the national debt made up over 22 percent of the budget, occupying second place in state spending after civil government expenditures.

Considering the extensive exclusion of the wider population from political participation, as demonstrated by the historical constitutional analysis provided above, an examination of the state budgets from this time period produces surprising results: This state – characterized by its conservative-liberal orientation – increased activities in the service of its citizens quite remarkably. This was reflected in a relative decrease in the share of government spending for the state power structure. According to my hypothesis, the broadening of state activity in the area of education and transportation infrastructure – as well as in the social sector to a much lesser extent – was an important reason for the identification of ever larger segments of the population with the Luxembourg State. The educational sector was a particularly strong driving force in the development of a Luxembourgish identity that quickly took on the form of nation building typical of that time. This is reflected in the powerful petition movements of 1867 and 1871 for the preservation of the Grand Duchy of Luxembourg's statehood.

The Economy and Populace in the Country and City of Luxembourg

The initial signs of modern industrialization first became noticeable in Luxembourg during this observed time period. The country had additionally entered a phase of demographic transition marked by high population growth, as had many other European countries. The following section will outline Luxembourg's economy and its population development during this period.

In the year that the country was divided as a consequence of the Treaty of London between the Great Powers of Europe, the Netherlands, and Belgium on April 19, 1839, the downsized Grand Duchy of Luxembourg included 169,920 people on its territory of now 2,586 square kilometers. It grew significantly in following years however: ten years later, there were already 189,783 inhabitants. The country only maintained a relatively modest iron, fabric, and leather industry – it was mainly oriented toward an agrarian economy barely capable of supporting the swiftly growing population. The insufficient supply was due to agricultural operation methods with low productivity. Property relations dominated by small business holders prevented the improvement of those methods based on the English example. Luxembourg therefore exhibited an especially high level of emigration at this time, particularly before the 1848 Revolution. In 1846 alone, 1,587 people left the country.[45]

The driving force of that development was real mass poverty, something that was widespread in Luxembourg as in other parts of Central Europe up until the 1860s. It was not until after that period that improvements to the economic situation and public infrastructure in the education and transportation sectors led to a strong decrease in the amount of people receiving public assistance. While 12.3 percent of the 184,099 citizens of the Grand Duchy were in need in 1847, that number decreased to 3.2 percent by 1868. At the same time, the country's population rose to 203,664.[46]

The fortress city of Luxembourg – excluding the members of the Prussian garrison – also grew substantially during this time:[47] from circa 9,500 inhabitants in 1806 to some 10,500 inhabitants in 1839 despite the crowded conditions in the fortress city. In the following quarter century, the population rate accelerated, reaching roughly 14,000 residents in 1865 shortly before the defortification of the city. From the opening up of the fortress until the end of the period under consideration here it rose to about 18,000. As of the 1840s, the demographic development can be differentiated on the basis of city districts: It becomes clear that there was only an insignificant change in the amount of people per district. The low level of population of Limpertsberg and Siechenhof remained almost unchanged; the number of inhabitants of Clausen and Pfaffenthal decreased slightly; only Grund and Petrusbachtal experienced a distinct increase. The Ville Haute or "Upper City" consolidated its dominant position. This result is surprising in that one could have expected the overpopulated Ville Haute's significance to decrease after the garrison's withdrawal and the beginning of defortification. However, the rapidly growing populace clearly first occupied the spaces

---

45 Calmes, *La Révolution de 1848 au Luxembourg*, 396–417; Calmes, *La création d'un état (1841–1847)*, 430 et seq.

46 Simone Kayser, *La lutte contre la pauvreté au Grand-Duché de Luxembourg 1839–1880* (Luxembourg: Unpublished typescript 1996 located in the Bibliothèque Nationale du Grand-Duché de Luxembourg), 22–23, 88–91, 106–109, 139–14; Franz, "Assistance municipale des pauvres de la ville de Luxembourg", 33–42.

47 Franz, ibid., 184–200.

vacated by the military within the former fortress city. The population of the districts beyond the former fortress walls only began to grow substantially in the following decades.

On the whole, the economic and population development of Luxembourg was marked by a structural socioeconomic crisis that can be traced back to the distinct, rapid development of industry and agriculture on the one hand, and of the population on the other. Its most important characteristic was the widespread poverty of the urban but above all rural population. During that period poverty was a mass phenomenon. That would not begin to change until the 1860s, when the results of government support for education and transportation infrastructure as well as the emergence of modern industrialization led to a general improvement of material conditions for the people of Luxembourg.

The Municipality of Luxembourg: Municipal Activity and Social Inequality

Significant components of state activity were not conducted at the state level, but at a local governmental level. The modern political administrative municipality was and still is today the *Staat vor Ort* ("local city") and carries particular weight in the small state of Luxembourg, in which the intermediate levels of state organization are of little significance. The following section will therefore use the example of Luxembourg City to sketch the activities of the political-administrative municipality of Luxembourg during the observed period. This will help answer the question of whether the expansion of the state's role as public service provider can also be found at the local level. The outline of the municipality's political-administrative side will be augmented by a summary of the socioeconomic structure of Luxembourg's urban community and the development of social inequality. The position of Samuel Hirsch and his family within this social structure will also be examined as a part of this analysis.

As the local level of the modern bureaucratic *Anstaltsstaat* (institutionalized state), the administration of the Luxembourg municipality fulfilled official duties, as did all other municipal administrations. That included the municipal administration structure, the city police, and the fire department. The city additionally maintained its own staff for the collection of local taxes and customs duties. Out of the total expenditures, the share of funds allotted to this sector decreased considerably over the course of the 19th century. The relative importance of the city government in its role as public authority continued to diminish vis-à-vis the municipality's other functions, some of which were entirely new. This development corresponds in principle to the tendency towards a relative decrease in the financial support allotted for these official duties, which we have already noted at the governmental level.

Duties in the area of social and health care ministration had already been assigned primarily to the municipalities by the legislative body since the French Revolution; these and additional duties were taken on by the city municipality during the observed time period. The *Bureau de Bienfaisance* (Welfare Office), which assumed the largest responsibility of caring for the poor,[48] was merely overseen by the municipality and occasionally received regional assistance and subsidies from the government. Alongside poor relief the municipality allocated funds for public health care – something that was relatively seldom, certainly up until the mid-19th century. Financing poor relief directly through the municipal budget had already become significantly more widespread during the *Ancien Régime*. Particularly in the late 1780s and early 1790s, the political and socioeconomic crisis had escalated to such an extent that more and more orphans and abandoned children, and eventually the destitute and ailing elderly as well, were assigned by the city to be fostered by private individuals.[49]

There was an especially high rate of social spending in 1831. In the face of inflation associated with the Belgian Revolution, the municipal administration bought substantial amounts of grain to provide aid to the city's poor.[50] The share of funds provided for poor relief thus reached a zenith, making up 46 percent of total expenditures in 1831, also expressed in relative terms. By the end of the 1850s, it decreased significantly. In the 1860s and 70s, this percentage stabilized at between 5–7 percent of the municipality's total expenditures.

The scope of city municipality expenditures for public health (hospitals, nursing homes, and other hospices, but also for all forms of disease prevention and control) was marginal as a norm – but in some exceptional cases, it took on a massive scale. The 1832 and 1866 cholera epidemics required the city council[51] to take special measures. On the whole, spending in the social sector remained one of the municipal administration's observable but rather marginal activities. In contrast, the municipality did increase its activity particularly intensively in two sectors: culture and transportation infrastructure. Alongside the maintenance of bridges and roads, the largest construction project undertaken by Lux-

---

[48] Franz, ibid., 33–42.
[49] During the observed period, these expenditures went from 15,000 to 30,000 francs annually.
[50] For 20,000 Dutch guilder (42,000 francs).
[51] The epidemic claimed the lives of 215 Luxembourg civilians and 57 Prussian soldiers. Out of the 10,000 who fell ill throughout the country, about 3,500 individuals died. Calmes and Bossaert, *op. cit.*, 110.

embourg City up until the end of the 19th century was of particular importance: the building of the *Passerelle* (also known as the Luxembourg Viaduct), a bridge that began at the *Heiliggeistplateau* and connected the Ville Haute district to the new railway station. Erected in 1859, the bridge's cost of around 585,000 francs was felt by the municipal budget the following year. Thus debt service became increasingly important, as the municipality financed its investments to a significant extent through loans. Following the financing of the *Passerelle* at the beginning of the 1860s, its share in the total expenditures of the city rose to one third, while it otherwise amounted to between 5–15 percent.

The municipality expanded its activities even more intensively in the cultural sector, including the funds designated for religious congregations. Subsequent to the Concordat of 1801 between the French Republic and the Vatican, the municipality was responsible for the accommodation costs of parish vicars and pastors. It furthermore provided financial assistance for the repair and construction of churches.[52] Its allocations to the Jewish community were comparatively modest, and only mentioned for the first time in 1851.[53] As the municipality's activities within other areas of the cultural sector grew, the relative financial importance of municipal responsibility towards religious groups tended to diminish, despite Luxembourg's ecclesiastical elevation to an apostolic vicariate and eventually a diocese.

In contrast, municipal expenditures for the advancement of science and the arts, and in particular for the educational sector, became increasingly significant; the promotion of primary and higher education schools became especially important in that process. During the observed time period, the municipality dedicated about one fourth of its total expenditures to this sector. This sphere of activities developed from one of comparatively negligible scale during the *Ancien Régime* into one of the primary municipal fields of activity and the most significant expenditure in the city budget.

Around mid-century, this urban society – one still characterized by a preindustrial socioeconomic structure – profited from the intensified public adminis-

---

52 Based on a French National Assembly resolution on November 2, 1789, the Catholic Church's property in France was nationalized, that is, it was declared a *bien national*, or a "national good". The concordat of July 15, 1801 and the "organic articles" of April 8, 1802 provided a new and cooperative foundation for state-church relations in France. François Lebrun, *Histoire des catholiques en France du XVe siècle à nos jours* (Paris: Hachette, 1985), 303–320; Jean Thill, *Documents et textes relatifs aux Constitutions et Institutions politiques luxembourgeoises* (Luxembourg: Centre de documentation communale, 1978, 2nd edition), 36, 49.
53 In 1851, the municipal collector paid 150 francs into the "subside à la communauté Israélite". See Norbert Franz, *Die Stadtgemeinde Luxemburg*, 117.

tration activities and the substantially improved infrastructure in the education and transportation sector. This can be demonstrated by a look at the occupational structure:[54] in 1852, about 4,500 of the roughly 13,000 inhabitants of the municipality of Luxembourg were involved in administrative work. Those in skilled trades dominated the working population at 42 percent; among them, textiles were the most represented.[55] The second largest category also had to do with clothing: the leather trade. The numerous glovemakers, many of them women, worked for the glove factory in the former refugium of the Abbey of Echternach – evidence of an (early) industrial element within the population of Luxembourg craftsmen. The third group of tradespeople who also dedicated themselves to supplying basic human needs was in the food trades. There are observable influences of industrialization here as well: Heintz, the tobacco manufacturer in the Neutorgasse, employed many tobacco spinners, all in all surpassing the share of bakers in this occupational branch. The woodworking trades were dominated by joiners, the building trades by masons, painters, roofers, and carpenters. The smallest skilled trade subcategory was the book and printing trade and was made up of bookbinders, typesetters, printers, lithographers, a stitcher, and an embroidery printer.

The largest of the remaining occupational groups – manual laborers, day workers, and servants – made up over 21 percent of the workforce. Of these domestic servants – among whom young women were particularly well represented – formed the great majority. The merchant trades – with a share of almost eleven percent of the labor force, making it the third largest occupational category – also feature a comparatively high percentage of women. Over six percent were employed in public service – teachers, government officials, and the staff of judicial authorities. More than three percent worked in gastronomy; they were especially numerous in the lower cities. Over two percent of the employed were in fishing, forestry, and agriculture occupations; the majority were gardeners.

Four percent of the labor force lived off capital investments, retirement benefits, and pensions. A similar share was in service occupations – messengers, midwives, carousel operators, musicians, ironers, washerwomen, clerks, nurses, and wet nurses. Two percent belonged to the clergy. A particularly numerous sector was made up of members of the seminary, incremented by the regular clergy,

---

54 Franz, "Assistance municipale des pauvres de la ville de Luxembourg", 318–327.
55 The extremely delayed mechanization of weaving emerged slowly in *Vormärz* Germany in comparison to that of spinning, and only made substantial advancements in production in the last quarter of the century; Jürgen Kocka, *Arbeitsverhältnisse und Arbeiterexistenzen. Grundlagen der Klassenbildung im 19. Jahrhundert, Geschichte der Arbeiter und der Arbeiterbewegung in Deutschland seit dem Ende des 18. Jahrhunderts*, vol. 2 (Bonn: Dietz, 1990), 449.

who mostly belonged to the St. Sophie congregation in the Kongregationsgasse. The remaining clergy consisted of a pastor and a parish vicar from the municipal church, priests and sextons, as well as the apostolic pro-vicar Nicolas Adames who would become the bishop's secretary and, years later, the first diocesan Bishop of Luxembourg (1870–1883). There must have been at least one Protestant minister amongst the priests. The Jewish community was represented by the Chief Rabbi Samuel Hirsch and the sexton Salomon Picard.

Only between 0.5 and 1.5 percent of the workforce was made up of clerks, self-employed individuals, workers in the transport business, or members of the militia who were not part of the fortress occupation. The occupational structure of the Luxembourgish urban population in the mid-19th century was much like that of the beginning of the century. However, some initial effects of the new forms of industrialization were beginning to emerge. These were more clearly felt in the neighboring municipalities of Hollerich and Eich, which only became districts of Luxembourg in the 20th century.[56]

The final outline of the social stratification of Luxembourg's urban society in 1852 is based on a complex model that qualitatively links any assignation to a particular social stratum with quantitative criteria.[57] This analysis has resulted in the finding that the large majority of the urban population was a part of the lower classes (64.2%), just under a third belonged to the middle classes (30.5%), and about one twentieth of the populace was a member of the upper class (5.2%).[58] This result complies closely with the percentages listed in the local historical research for this time.[59] It is important to note here that this methodology for the analysis of the social stratification of urban societies in the 19th century is in no way standardized.

---

56 Jean-Pierre Koltz, *Baugeschichte der Stadt und Festung Luxemburg*, 595.
57 Franz, *Die Stadtgemeinde Luxemburg*, 328–354.
58 Compare 1806: lower classes 75.8%, middle classes 22.6%, upper classes: 1.6%; Franz, ibid., 290.
59 The percentage given for the portion belonging to the lower classes in Cologne in 1852 is 64.4%, in Aachen 75.5%; similar numbers are listed for Trier and Bonn around mid-century; Jürgen Herres, *Städtische Gesellschaft und katholische Vereine im Rheinland 1840–1870* (Essen: Klartext, 1996/Diss. phil. Univ. Trier 1991), 64, 66, 69, 71. For select German cities between 1815 and 1850, Wehler provides the following statistics for the portion of the urban population consisting of the lower-classes: Cologne 78%, Bonn 73–87%, Hamburg 75–80%, Flensburg 90%, Göttingen 65–70%, Magdeburg 70–80%, Weimar 68–78%, Wismar 69%, Bielefeld 67–69%, Barmen 90%. Hans-Ulrich Wehler, *Deutsche Gesellschaftsgeschichte*, vol. 2 (München: C.H. Beck, 1987), 279; Wehler's data on urban upper and middle classes are in the same range as that ascertained for Luxembourg; ibid., 182.

Close to half of the members of the lower classes were tradespeople (49.1%) and about a third were manual laborers (31.5%). Tradespeople dominated the middle classes (30.4%) much less than they did the lower classes. Here, merchant trade (17.9%) and public service (16.9%) were well represented. The upper classes were dominated by those in the merchant trade (33%). The share of people drawing on capital investments and retirement benefits was also comparatively high (18.5%), as was that of the skilled trades (16.2%), independent professions (11.9%) and those in public service (10.6%).

Mid-19th century Luxembourg City's social stratification thus proves to be typical of other contemporary urban societies on the eve of high industrialization. According to this model of social stratification, Samuel Hirsch belonged to the upper classes. The decisive criterion here is not his fairly average income, but rather criteria associated with the political and cultural dimensions of social change: as shown above, Samuel Hirsch belonged on the one hand to the country's former Orangist elite milieu; on the other hand, and looking at it from a socio-analytical perspective, he must be considered a member of the Luxembourg upper classes given his role as leader in the Jewish religious community and his significant intellectual weight.[60]

The previous section demonstrated that the Luxembourg municipality exhibited a typical social stratification for Central European cities of this era, combined with another typical aspect of this period: substantial population growth. Nearly two-thirds of all inhabitants lived on the margins of a minimum subsistence level, or under it; they performed all possible forms of manual labor. Only about every third urban Luxembourger belonged to the middle classes; their living conditions were shaped by occupational autonomy and good to very good education. As for the upper class, only one out of every twenty inhabitants was a member and played a significant role in the economic system, administration, or cultural life. Luxembourg's military impact as a fortress and garrison city was a feature shared by many other European cities.

Public services (the service administration) were of growing importance both on the central governmental level and the local municipal level.[61] This was primarily true for the social sector, whose share of the municipality's financial expenditures remained nevertheless meager. The trend observed at the governmental level is thus also reflected here in municipal administrative behavior. In contrast, the municipal administration's main areas of focus were transportation

---

60 Franz, ibid., 352.
61 As also in the analysis results of select Luxembourgish and French rural municipalities; Franz, *Durchstaatlichung und Ausweitung der Kommunalaufgaben im 19. Jahrhundert*.

infrastructure and especially culture. In the following decades, that trend would come to an end.

Conclusion

Samuel Hirsch's activities in both the political and religious sphere took place during a historical phase marked by particularly rapid and fundamental changes in the city and Grand Duchy of Luxembourg – and this accelerated social transformation was influenced by Hirsch himself. He lived in an urban society characterized by two contradictory basic tendencies: on the one hand, its socioeconomic structure had not changed much compared to the beginning of the 19th century; it was shaped by manual labor and poverty. Due to the role of Luxembourg as a fortress city, modern industrialization (already visible to some extent at this point) was put into effect primarily in the fortress city's neighboring municipalities, which were only incorporated after World War I. The immediate socioeconomic consequences of defortification for the social stratification and occupational structure of the municipality of Luxembourg did not become explicit until after the period analyzed here. However, domestic and political power politics displayed a strong dynamism that confronted the fortress city's socioeconomic stagnation. Samuel Hirsch appeared on the stage during the liberal-democratic revolution of 1848 and 1849 on the side of the adroit supporters of the ruling regime who opposed political Catholicism. He was thus a member of the upper classes – and not only of the municipality, but of the entire Grand Duchy of Luxembourg.

Demands for Luxembourg's sovereignty and the evolution of its nation building played no role in the struggles of the Great Powers that was characterized by revolutions, periods of reaction, the fight for hegemony in Europe, and Belgian, Polish, Italian, and German nation building. But despite the instability in foreign affairs, one can assume that the Luxembourgish population profited significantly in the medium-term from the construction of their own state administration. The state of Luxembourg greatly expanded the range of services it provided to the country's inhabitants during the observed time period, on both a national and local level. Together with the economic revival of the 1860s, this led to a clear decline in mass poverty throughout the country. The expansion of governmental activity did not only bind the functionaries and officials active in the state power structure to this new state, but also the growing number of those who worked in national public service administration. However, this growing identification with the state was not limited to officials and public service employees. Although most citizens were excluded from direct political participation, everybody profited from the improvement of schools, roads and paths, waterways and railways. The effect was heightened by a political discourse that increasingly linked the traditional loyalty of subjects to their monarch with nationalism. The result of the 1871 petition movement, in which a great majority of the Grand Duchy's adult male inhabitants spoke out for state sovereignty, can be interpreted as such. With that, the Luxembourgish citizens took their first step on the path to nation building.

Renée Wagener
Between Recognition and Exclusion. The Effects of the *Décret Infâme* on Jewish Emancipation in Luxembourg

> I am far from arguing that no measures are necessary to make my brothers in faith worthy of becoming citizens. Yet one cannot attain a laudable goal by engaging in dishonorable treatment, thereby crushing every seed of goodness. To the contrary: the good must be stimulated and the bad eradicated at its roots.

The Jewish lawyer Heinrich Marx wrote the above in his "Memorandum on the 1808 Law of Exception Against Jews" in 1815 in Trier.[1] During that time period, Napoleon's *décret infâme* – a set of separate legal regulations imposed on the Jewish population that invalidated the equality principles of the French Revolution – had already been abolished in Prussia with the Jewish Edict of 1812. In Luxembourg, it was replaced by William I's legislation, which was modeled on the unconditional emancipation of the Dutch Jews in 1796. Nevertheless, the short time frame from the beginning of the French Revolution in 1789 to the end of Napoleon's reign in Luxembourg in 1814 was a key period in the development of the Jewish community in Luxembourg, with the *décret infâme* serving as a decisive instrument for the social classification of Jews, the consequences of which were not solely legal.

This period of time also formed a dense chapter in the history of Luxembourg. Within a quarter of a century, not only did Luxembourg experience two conquests, it also went through four different political systems. This contribution will be structured around these ruptures in its discussion of the *décret infâme*'s effect on the development of Jewish emancipation in Luxembourg. After a brief discussion of the situation of Jews during the *Ancien Régime*, I will illuminate the situation of Jews in Luxembourg during the French Revolution, particularly during the era of Napoleon I. The question to be addressed is whether the *décret infâme* was an abandonment of the French Revolution's egalitarian project or simply one further step in the revocation of accorded rights that had commenced at the time of the Revolution. This analysis makes use of general and specific Luxembourgish documentation of Jewish history, as well as of sources from

---

1 Cited in Detlev Claussen, *Vom Judenhaß zum Antisemitismus. Materialien einer verleugneten Geschichte* (Darmstadt: Luchterhand, 1988, 2nd edition), 78.

the municipal archive of Luxembourg and from the Luxembourgish and French national archives.

There is a reasonable amount of literature available on the history of the Luxembourgish Jewish community for this period. Nevertheless, during the research process the impression that some of the source material had not yet been thoroughly examined was confirmed. This depreciation can be explained in part by the political complexity of this epoch, but it might also have something to do with a fixation on both mainstream history and the role of the Catholic resistance against the agents of the French Revolution. However, this was not the only era in which Jewish history was neglected. This accounts for the fact that there is as yet no in-depth knowledge about the history of Jews in and around Luxembourg – and this is true for this chapter as well – and many historical contentions remain unconfirmed.

Jewish Life in the *Ancien Régime*

The sporadic Jewish settlement in the Duchy of Luxembourg reached a peak of ten to eleven households from the mid-15th century up to the beginning of the 16th century.[2] The absence of Jews was caused by pogroms and expulsion and, as most scholars concur, particularly by "a settlement prohibition" ordered by Charles V in 1532 that, aside from short business trips, forbade them from settling permanently in the Duchy.[3] Under the reign of Charles V, there were in fact

---

[2] Jean-Marie Yante, "Heurs et malheurs des établissements juifs dans le Luxembourg (XIIIe siècle – début XVIe)", in Laurent Moyse and Marc Schoentgen, eds., *La présence juive au Luxembourg : du moyen âge au XXe siècle* (Luxembourg: B'nai Brith, 2001), 11–20, here 14; Jean-Marie Yante, "Les Juifs dans le Luxembourg au Moyen âge", Bulletin trimestriel de l'Institut archéologique du Luxembourg 62, 1–2 (1986), 3–22.

[3] According to Gilbert Trausch, for example: "All Jews were expelled in the 16th century (1532 edit)." Gilbert Trausch, *Le Luxembourg sous l'Ancien Régime (17e, 18e siècles et débuts du 19e siècle)*, Manuel d'histoire luxembourgeoise, vol. 3 (Luxembourg: Bourg-Bourger, 1986, 2nd edition), 79; Paul Wynants: "Struck by the edit of Charles Quint (1532), they were soon forbidden to stay in our provinces, so they disappeared once again." See Paul Wynants, *Autres Cultes (1598–1985)* (Namur: Fondation Meuse-Moselle, 1986), 61; Charles and Graziella Lehrmann: "In 1532, the Jews of Luxembourg were struck by Charles V's edict that forbade them from staying in the Netherlands." See Charles Lehrmann and Graziella Lehrmann-Gandolfi, *La Communauté Juive du Luxembourg dans le passé et dans le présent* (Esch-sur-Alzette: Luxembourg cooperative printer, 1953), 30. In footnote 35, they reference Alexandre Henne, *Histoire de la Belgique sous le règne de Charles-Quint*, vol. 3 (Bruxelles: Rozez and Paris: Borrani, 1865), 397. They also remark however that the prohibition may have applied to Marranos. If Henne is the source that all these authors are referencing, an error has indeed been made. Henne writes on p. 397: "In 1532 an August 14th

several texts that had legal significance for the Netherlands, i.e. the ordinances and letters from 1532, 1538, 1544, 1549 and 1550 revoking the privileges of the so-called New Christians – those Jews who had formally converted to Christianity due to the Inquisition and subsequently fled, mainly from Portugal. The title of the one from 1532, for example, reads: "by which the Emperor, seeing that the new Christians of Portugal are secretly arriving in the Netherlands in large numbers, and from there going to Salonica and to other areas of Turkey, bans them entry into these provinces and forbids merchants from handling the transportation of their goods and chattels."[4]

If the "New Christians" were no longer tolerated, then the question remains how the ordinances were applied to those remaining Jews who were more or less established in the area, or to those who had migrated there from the East. Through their reinforcement of the Inquisition, Charles V's 1532 criminal legislation *Constitutio Criminalis Carolina* and Pope Paul IV's 1555 papal bull *Cum nimis absurdum* led to a deterioration of the living conditions of members of the Jewish faith.[5] Aline Goosens refers to the shift in the understanding of heresy against which the Inquisition was taking action: "One cannot be a heretic without having been baptized; yet the papacy ordained that Jews and Arabs be prosecuted."[6] Yet in contrast to the statements of many long-established historians, other more recent authors claim that there was never a proper legal public ban in the Netherlands[7] and qualify the earlier assumption that all Jews left the area. Antoinette

---

announcement [...] forbade them from staying in the Netherlands and ordered everyone to take any Marrano Jew or unbaptized person to the local authority. This edict was initially executed with severity, but soon became obsolete because Jewish industry had become indispensable to the host of great lords burdened with debt as a result of wars and lives of luxury." He also points to the fact that in 1563 14 Jews attained permission to settle in the lower city of Luxembourg for nine years. According to Cilli Kasper-Holtkotte, those edicts were referring to Marranos. She also cites the city authorities of Brussels, who claim not to have executed the edict. Cilli Kasper-Holtkotte, *Im Westen Neues: Migration und ihre Folgen: Deutsche Juden als Pioniere jüdischen Lebens in Belgien, 18./19. Jahrhundert* (Leiden and Boston: Brill, 2003), 20 and 23.

4 Commission royale pour la publication des anciennes lois et ordonnances de la Belgique, *Règne de Charles-Quint, 1506–1555*, Liste chronologique des édits et ordonnances des Pays-Bas 1 (Bruxelles: Fr. Gobbaerts, 1885), 332.

5 Through the introduction of the ghetto system and the segregation of the members of Christian and Jewish faiths.

6 Aline Goosens, "Mourir pour sa foi au temps des réformes dans les Pays-Bas méridionaux", in Wim Blockmans and Nicolette Mout, *The World of Emperor Charles V.*, Koninklijke Nederlandse Akademie van Wetenschappen, Verhandelingen, Afd. Letterkunde, Nieuwe Reeks, 188 (Amsterdam: Royal Netherlands Academy of Arts and Sciences, 2004), 227–245, here 231.

7 For instance, Jean-Philippe Schreiber, p. 40, speaks of an "imaginary decree" for Belgium in the 14th century. He is referring to Jean Stenger's statement: "If the legal practitioners of the 17th

Reuter emphasizes that, "The range of edicts and ordinances that reject all Jewish presence in the former Duchy of Luxembourg do not in fact reflect the reality of everyday life."[8] There is after all evidence that Jews settled in surrounding cities, such as Trier, Metz, Sierck and Charleville in the 16th century. Reuter also notes the role of horse-trading for the army, which was often fulfilled by Jewish traders at the Fortress of Luxembourg at the end of the 17th century. There were also exceptions to the non-admission regulation, in the case of Jewish soldiers abiding in Luxembourg as part of one of the military occupations. Hannick and Muller, for example, point to the fact that there were Jewish soldiers in the Spanish regiment during Louis XIV's wars of conquest.[9]

Records of an unsevered chain of contacts and at least temporary residencies demonstrate the inaccuracy of the claim that Jews were completely absent from the region at the time. Moreover, they indicate that for a long time the forms of Jewish presence were different than those of a domestic settlement. This was a consequence of the repressive politics, at times in the form of expulsions. The economic activities and the specific lifestyles – perhaps a cultural non-sedentariness – may also have played a role. Cilli Kasper-Holtkotte underscores that Jewish traders, bankers, rabbis and teachers had a propensity for travel.[10] Above all, the traditional perception disregards the fact that the Jewish social structure did not only consist of traders wealthy enough to pay the high transit taxes; there were also peddlers, vagabonds and other "losers of the system" who lived on the edge or outside of society. Vagabonds, Jewish or not Jewish, were rarely recorded in official lists and registers and, other than in the case of prosecution, do not appear in any written documents because their survival depended precisely on remaining unregistered. Kasper-Holtkotte records that paupers and wandering Jewish beggars made up ten percent of the electorate in Trier in the 18th century: "The latter were deemed to be without rights; if

---

century solemnly pronounced that there was a decree of perpetual banishment, they actually knew no more than we did of such an act by Jeanne and Wencelas, and are only reproducing an unfounded assertion by a historian." Jean-Philippe Schreiber, *L'immigration juive en Belgique du moyen âge à la Première Guerre mondiale* (Bruxelles: Edition de l'Université de Bruxelles, 1996).

8 Antoinette Reuter, "Présence juive dans les forteresses louis-quatorziennes, l'exemple de Luxembourg", www.cdmh.lu, n.d., https://www.cdmh.lu/resources/pdf/_base_3/9781683124009.pdf?ac=1400484551 [accessed: 02.06.2022]. This article points to some new interesting perspectives.

9 Pierre Hannick and Jean-Claude Muller, "Juifs de passage dans les duchés de Luxembourg et de Bouillon, avant leur émancipation en 1808", Annales de l'Institut archéologique du Luxembourg, 136 (2005), 241–254, here 245.

10 Kasper-Holtkotte, *Im Westen Neues*, 68 et seq.

they wanted to survive, they were forced to move from one Jewish community to the next."[11]

As a result of persecution, "Eastern Jews" started emigrating from Eastern Europe to Germany in the 17th century. This led to renewed growth in the communities in Western Europe, despite continued confrontation by the trade guild system. The trade guilds represented one of the most important factors of the centuries-long social marginalization of Jews; and their exclusion from them led to the strong development of Jewish itinerant trade (the social role of which has been little examined to date). In the final decades of the 18th century Jewish bands of thieves appeared in the Rhineland and in both the Northern and the Southern Netherlands, often recruiting members from Polish or German regions.

The question of whether the history of the Jewish community in Luxembourg is primarily a new history of immigration that began with the French Revolution, or one in which the newcomers encountered long-established residents, may therefore not yet be quite as fully answered as previously conceived. Moreover, perhaps it would be better for the time being to join Jean-Philippe Schreiber in speaking of *geographic mobility* rather than immigration.[12] Supporting that view is the fact that settled Jews also engaged substantially in mercantile expeditions after this period.[13]

The Age of Tolerance and the Politics of Joseph II

The Theresian-Josephinian era represents the relatively short transition from the categorical exclusion of Jews to the tolerance of a few based on their financial status, and finally to the implementation of the principle of equality. However, there was officially a very sparse population of settled Jews in all of the southern Netherlands in comparison to the other European regions: in 1756, 76 individuals

---

11 Cilli Kasper-Holtkotte, *Juden im Aufbruch. Zur Sozialgeschichte einer Minderheit im Saar-Mosel-Raum um 1800* (Hannover: Hahn, 1996), 17.
12 Jean-Philippe Schreiber, *L'immigration juive en Belgique*, 10, 12.
13 Marianne Bühler points to the Trier passport registry from the French era, which demonstrates a high level of regional mobility. The "Département des Forêts" was among the Trier Jewish travelers' preferred destinations. Marianne Bühler, "Die jüdische Gemeinde Triers zur Zeit der Franzosen", in Elisabeth Dühr and Christl Lehnert-Leven, eds., *Unter Der Trikolore: Trier in Frankreich, Napoleon in Trier* (Trier: Städtisches Museum Simeonstift, 2004), 437–459, here 441.

were counted, none of whom lived in Luxembourg.[14] As a contrasting example: in 1689, there were already 23 families (166 people) officially residing in Trier, a city where Jews were tolerated.[15]

Initially, the taxes applied specifically to Jews were maintained in the states of the southern Netherlands. A high yearly tax instituted in 1756 enabled only the rich Jews to stay in Brussels, Namur, Charleroi and Luxembourg.[16] The city of Luxembourg opposed the decree, albeit not out of kindness to the Jews: they were worried about an influx of Jews wealthy enough to pay the taxes.[17] However, in cities such as Ostend and Brussels, there were certainly some families who were domiciled there, and at least some individuals demonstrated social advancement. Their limited citizenship makes it clear that "the Emperor's decree admitting Jews into the bourgeoisie of the cities of the Netherlands does not render them capable of holding public office, nor does it ascribe to them the right to vote on public affairs".[18] Citizenship was yet again the key to gaining access to the trade guilds, but there was continued insistence on the requirement of being a Christian. However, in the 1780s at the latest, the privy council of the southern Netherlands also spoke out in support of opening up the trade guilds.[19]

After Joseph II's Patent of Toleration on October 13, 1781, which only mentioned the Protestant faith, charters were published for the Jews of Bohemia, Silesia, Moravia, Vienna, and Lower Austria.[20] Jews were allowed to attend public (i.e. Christian) schools, practice trade and manufacturing and were liberated from all discriminatory taxes.[21] There was no specific version of this patent in the Netherlands, but according to Jean-Philippe Schreiber there was a de facto

---

14 Kasper-Holtkotte, *Im Westen Neues*, 10, 20.
15 Bühler, "Die jüdische Gemeinde Triers", 438.
16 Kasper-Holtkotte, *Im Westen Neues*, 20. Out of 76 people, 74 lived in Brussels and two in Antwerp, ibid., 451; Hannick and Muller, "Juifs de passage", 243.
17 Wynants, *Autres cultes*, 61.
18 From 30.9.1782. Commission royale pour la publication des anciennes lois et ordonnances de la Belgique, *Liste chronologique des édits et ordonnances des Pays-Bas autrichiens, de 1751 à 1794*, part 2: *1781–1794* (Brussels: Em. Devroye, 1858), 32. The decree from 3.8.1785 made access to the middle class dependent on the consent of the governor. For more on this, see Schreiber, *L'immigration juive*, 47. Kasper-Holtkotte discusses how it was possible for some individual Jews to attain citizenship as of the second half of the 18th century. Kasper-Holtkotte, *Im Westen Neues*, 28 et seq., 50 et seq.
19 Kasper-Holtkotte, *Im Westen Neues*, 64 et seq.
20 Michael Graetz, *Les Juifs en France au XIXe siècle: de la Révolution française à l'Alliance israélite universelle* (Paris: Éd. du Seuil, 1989), 26.
21 Paula E. Hyman, *The Jews of Modern France*, Jewish Communities in the Modern World, vol. 1 (Berkeley, Los Angeles: University of California Press, 1998), 19.

application of it in those provinces as well.²² However, in Luxembourg at least, it was systematically ignored. In 1782, Luxembourg's city council asked the governor to prevent Jews from settling in Schleiden or Cobreville.²³ In 1792, Leopold II overturned the Edict of Tolerance in light of the Brabant Revolution.

Luxembourg as a French Department

The revolutionary French constitution of 1791 secured the equality of all citizens. Having not participated in the revolution in large numbers however, Jews only had a few vocal advocates in the legislative assemblies. In January 1790, equal rights were initially only accorded to Sephardic Jews. On September 27 1791, the entire Jewish population obtained access to civil liberties.²⁴ This decision was preceded by an intense dispute between liberal deputies insisting on the principle of equality and conservative Alsatian opponents, backed by anti-Jewish riots in Alsace.²⁵ The first years of the revolution, which Paula Hyman describes as "a state of institutional anarchy",²⁶ are marked by the debate on the particularism vs. assimilation of the Jewish population. There was increased pressure on the members of a partially unassertive Jewish community to relinquish their local autonomy and to become "useful" citizens by giving up moneylending in favor of other professions. With the Terror starting in 1793, religious suppression was broadened to also include Judaism. Jews were violently persecuted, especially in the German regions.²⁷ After the end of the Terror, the 1795 separation of Church and State relegated the supervision of religious communities to public authorities.²⁸

At first, Luxembourg remained under Austrian rule. After France declared war on Austria in 1792, it took until the end of 1795 for the Fortress of Luxembourg to fall, at a time when the *Directoire* was already emerging. The territory of the Duchy of Luxembourg would be integrated for the most part into the "Dé-

---

22 Schreiber, *L'immigration juive en Belgique*, 48.
23 Wynants, *Autres cultes*, 62; Reuter, *Présence juive*, 10; Hannick and Muller, *Juifs de passage*, 249 et seq.
24 The decision was affirmed by a law passed on 13.11.1791. Wynants, *Autres cultes*, 124.
25 Hyman, *The Jews of Modern France*, 25 et seq.
26 Ibid., 37.
27 Heinrich Graetz, *Geschichte der Juden vom Beginn der mendelssohnschen Zeit (1750) bis in die neueste Zeit (1848)*, Geschichte der Juden von den ältesten Zeiten bis auf die Gegenwart, vol. 11 (Darmstadt: Wissenschaftliche Buchgesellschaft, 1998, 2nd augmented and improved edition), 212 et seq.
28 Wynants, *Autres cultes*, 124 et seq.

partement des Forêts". It was not until 1797 that the revolutionary French law system, and along with it the principle of equality, was implemented there.[29] The 1791 abolition of trade guilds was another fundamental transformation with enormous economic and social consequences. Its importance for the development of the Jewish community is underestimated in my opinion.[30] This economic freedom and the freedom of establishment opened new avenues for migrant settlement in the areas surrounding Luxembourg. For example, in Metz, the center of Ashkenazic Jewry in France, the community had lived in ghetto-like conditions before the revolution, locked up at night in one quarter. As in many other regions, in Lorraine they were forbidden to own land, to become members of a trade guild or to sell newly manufactured goods. For that reason, they returned to peddling, dealing in second-hand goods, cattle and horse trade, intermediary trade, brokering, and moneylending. Moreover, their right of residence often depended on their paying higher taxes.[31]

While new families were moving here from abroad, the longtime residents were settling in the neighboring area – and the city of Luxembourg was certainly an attractive new center.[32] Some of the Jews from the surrounding region were already acquainted with the city of Luxembourg because of their occupational activities. One such individual was the metal engraver Pinhas Godchaux, who was likely the first to settle in Luxembourg in 1798. As was later reported, "he had already visited this city to practice his craft long before the former province of Luxembourg was reunited with France".[33] According to Paul Wynant, the first members of the Jewish community in Luxembourg came from Lorraine, primarily from Metz and Thionville, and a few isolated individuals originated from the Saar Department.[34] Based on the sources analyzed so far, in addition to Pinhas Godchaux, Isaac Lazare, and the families of both men settled first in Luxembourg city in 1798; more families followed starting in 1801.

It is unknown how relations with the newcomers were managed in practice. What can be asserted about this era, however, is that the Catholic population

---

29 Gilbert Trausch, *Histoire du Luxembourg* (Paris: Hatier, 1992), 62.
30 On the role of trade guilds in the marginalization of Jews since the Middle Ages, see also: Nicolas Van Werveke, *Kurze Geschichte des Luxemburger Landes mit besonderer Berücksichtigung der Kulturgeschichte: Urgeschichte bis Ende des XIV. Jahrhunderts* (Luxemburg: Worré-Mertens, 1909), 234 et seq.
31 Hyman, *The Jews of Modern France*, 9 et seq.
32 Robert Anchel, *Napoléon et les Juifs* (Paris: Les presses universitaires de France, 1928), 39.
33 14.7.1806. ANL, B-74.
34 Wynants, *Autres cultes*, 160. Metz counted 440 Jewish families at the beginning of the revolution, more than 2,000 people. In Thionville, there were in contrast only 2 families in 1789, and 40 in 1812. Wynants, *Autres cultes*, 142.

was primarily concerned with its own treatment by those newly in power. Dissatisfaction with the new French policies including antireligious measures, tax burdens and, starting in 1798, compulsory military service for men between the ages of 20 and 25 (unfamiliar to Luxembourgers) led to what is known as the Klëppelkrich or Peasants' War of the same year.[35]

Luxembourg under Napoleon

At the close of 1799, Napoleon Bonaparte put an end to the revolutionary era with a coup d'état. At that point in time, French statistics registered 77,162 people of the Jewish faith in the entire Napoleonic Empire, and only 852 in the so-called "Belgian" departments.[36] While those of the Catholic faith in Luxembourg were to be affiliated with the Diocese of Metz, one of the three decrees from March 17, 1808 established the creation of a Jewish consistory in every department containing at least 2,000 Jews. That was not the case for the "Département des Forêts".

The synagogue in Luxembourg, which had evolved out of the house of prayer established in 1798, was affiliated with the Trier consistory. Voted in on March 2, 1809, the Trier consistory included the Departments of "Saar", "Forêts", and "Sambre-et-Meuse" and out of the total of thirteen consistories, it was the tenth largest.[37] It counted 3,553 people in the Department of "Saar",[38] but initially only 75, and then 79 individuals in the "Département des Forêts" (78 of whom were located in the capital city of Luxembourg), and two in the Department of "Sambre-et-Meuse". In 1810, 84 people were counted in the city of Luxembourg, and then 126 in 1814. Although other documents attest to the settlement of additional Jews in Arlon and Ettelbruck, they are not mentioned in these registries.[39]

---

35 Up until 1810, there is only one record of a Jewish man being drafted into the army: Léon Ruben. That suggests that most of the men of the community were too young or too old to be inducted. ANF, F/19/1840.
36 Schreiber, *L'immigration juive en Belgique*, 49, 52.
37 Bühler, "Die jüdische Gemeinde Triers", 448.
38 At the Sanhedrin of 1806, the Saar Department had two representatives, one from Trier and one from Saarbrucken. Wynants, *Autres cultes*, 147.
39 Jourdan, the prefect of the "Département des Forêts", mentions in a letter to the minister of religion on April 18, 1809, for example, that a Jew from "Saarguion", from the Bas-Rhin Department had settled in Ettelbruck with his wife and five children, as a reseller.

The *Décret Infâme*

It was not until some years after his seizure of power that Napoleon I more specifically addressed the question of the Jewish population's position within French society. His wish to provide the Jewish community with a unitary structure was more about strengthening the prospects of state control than about according them equal rights. After the large meeting of Jewish notables at the Sanhedrin of 1806, a pre-existing May 30, 1806 decree declaring a moratorium on all debts owed by peasants to Jewish creditors in the Saar, Ruwer, Rhine, and Mosel regions was nonetheless upheld. The three subsequent decrees issued in 1808 were clearly of the same spirit; it was a slap in the face to all who had hoped for more recognition of the Jewish people after the Sanhedrin.

Alongside the two decrees on the organization of the Jewish community, there was a third, the actual *décret infâme*, which addressed the Jews' trade activities and military duties. The decree, which applied to all regions except the city of Bordeaux and the Gironde and Landes Departments, forbade any new Jewish migration to Alsace. Furthermore, it secured a series of general measures:

1. Only those buying agricultural property were permitted to settle.
2. A patent for all trade activities was required, and lending was restricted to that specific sector. In order to obtain a patent from the prefects, a yearly letter of reference from the municipal council had to be submitted attesting that the applicant had never practiced usury, and one from the responsible consistory testifying to that person's morality.

Alfons Bürge points out that the introduction of the patents "opened up ample room for the public authorities to make arbitrary decisions".[40] However, the consistories also gained a lot of influence over their members in the process.

3. Debts already owed to Jews were retroactively reduced or pardoned if the interest had been set at more than 5 percent. The effect of the moratorium of 1806 was thereby further intensified.[41]
4. The decree required Jewish men to personally serve in the army, whereas other citizens had the right to have someone replace them.

---

[40] Alfons Bürge, *Das französische Privatrecht im 19. Jahrhundert: zwischen Tradition und Pandektenwissenschaft, Liberalismus und Etatismus*, Ius commune, Sonderhefte, Studien zur Europäischen Rechtsgeschichte 52 (Frankfurt a.M: V. Klostermann, 1995, 2nd edition), 317.

[41] The decree of 1806 was renewed in 1807 until the implementation of the new decree.

5. Finally, another decree from July 20, 1808 forced all Jews to acquire a fixed family name and a first name from either the revolutionary calendar or Greek antiquity.[42] Names from the Hebrew Bible or town names were forbidden. Violations of the decree resulted in expulsion.

By applying certain aspects of the decree specifically to Jewish communities from Alsace while exempting those from Paris and the Gironde, Napoleon effected a geographical division between "good" and "bad" Jews. This was clearly based on the distribution of the financially weaker Ashkenazic Jews and the more affluent Sephardic Jews. The decree was perhaps also a xenophobic reaction to the influx of Jews from conquered territories. Napoleon formulated his first thoughts about reducing usury and revoking Jewish people's civil rights in a memorandum to the *Conseil d'État* on March 6, 1806: "All of these provisions could be applied particularly to Jews who arrived here ten years ago, and originating from Poland or Germany."[43] The so-called *décret infâme* from March 17, 1808 had a profound symbolic consequence. It clearly demonstrates how far-removed Napoleon was from the revolution's principles of equality and the extent to which he fed on the influence of the anti-Jewish currents dominant in Catholic agrarian circles, particularly in Eastern France.

The fact that the *Conseil d'État* explicitly rejected any implementation of the *décret infâme* demonstrates, however, that egalitarian principles still carried weight at that time. For example, in the following citation, the *Conseil d'État* presents its argument regarding the problem of usury in its opinion on the 1806 moratorium: "(for) the solution to this evil cannot be found in a measure applicable to only a portion of the territory, nor in a measure applicable to only a portion of the Empire's citizens. This measure must be for the entire state and for all those who reside in it."[44]

In his memorandum, the aforementioned Heinrich Marx, Karl Marx's father, enumerated several of the "monstrous decree's" deviations from the "axioms of law":[45]

1. The decree punishes people based on uncommitted offenses.

---

[42] The decree was implemented in Luxembourg by an "order from the prefect of the *Forêts*" from 19.9.1808, but not according to the letter of the law.
[43] Quoted in: Pierre Birnbaum, *L'Aigle et la Synagogue : Napoléon, les Juifs et l'Etat* (Paris: Fayard, 2007), 104.
[44] Quoted in: Birnbaum, *L'Aigle et la Synagogue*, 181. The *Conseil d'État* also asks the following delicate question for the first time: "How do you prove Jewishness?" The question has concrete relevance. For instance, cases of conversions are consistently depicted that may in part have utilitarian causes. See for example Kasper-Holtkotte, *Juden im Aufbruch*, 404.
[45] Quoted in: Claussen, *Vom Judenhaß zum Antisemitismus*, 79 et seq.

2. It denies the accused the possibility of proving their innocence.
3. It has retroactive power against actions that were not punishable earlier.
4. Regarding the question of usury, it imposes the burden of proof on the accused.
5. It applies to a group of people based on their religion, instead of making the criminal offense, namely usury, universally punishable.
6. The decree falls short of its goal, namely the improvement of the Jews, because it exposes the contempt for them.

The specific impact of the decree remains unclear. According to Jean-Philippe Schreiber, for instance, the decree threatened numerous small creditors with financial ruin in the consistory of Trier (affiliated with the "Département des Forêts" together with the consistory of "Sambre-et-Meuse").[46] In any case, a wave of applications for exemption from the ordinance (as granted to the Departments of "Gironde" and "Landes") poured in from the consistories immediately after the decree was implemented. These were met with partial success: In the same year, the first decrees of exemption were accorded to several states and departments, and to a further 15 departments in April 1810.[47] In the end, out of the 130 departments existing in 1811, 20 of them (14.6 percent) were exempt. According to Anchel this amounted to one sixth of the Jewish population at that time.[48]

In the intervening period, a further twelve departments requested the exemption. In his March 13, 1811 report on the "Regeneration of the Israelites", the Interior Minister Jean-Pierre de Montalivet was struck by this: "Everywhere they are hastening to deserve the paternal generosity of His Majesty; they are attempting to render themselves worthy of the same favor obtained by their coreligionists [...]". Based on the possibilities for expansion contained in the new decree, De Montalivet proposed including a further four departments: "Rhône", "Montenotte", "Rome", and "Forêts".

On September 21, 1808, the interior minister presented a report on the implementation of the decree, in which the Napoleonic government's pedagogic discourse is clearly demonstrated:

> Your Majesty [...] rightly thought that it was necessary to improve the Jews' minds, to perfect their mores, to make them adopt customs common to the other citizens of the Empire, thereby raising them up to the same level of civilization and blending them in with the

---

46 Robert Anchel also reports this more generally, although neither statement is supported by any sources. Schreiber, *L'immigration juive en Belgique*, 55; Anchel, *Napoléon et les Juifs*, 352.
47 Imperial Decree of April 11, 1810.
48 Except Holland and the new departments of the north.

crowds, thus making at least the sharpest differences, if not the nuances – something that is quite difficult – disappear. Until then, Your Majesty in his wisdom thinks that [...] the ways of love should not be used [...] to the contrary, it would be better to present examples to follow and exceptions to envy. It would be more natural to take that direction, as it has generally been recognized that the state of the Jews is caused almost as much by the subjugation under which almost all the governors had held them, as by the particularistic practices, with the help of which their profound Legislator created a people apart, so to speak, from the rest of humankind.[49]

This discourse is not new: in Napoleon's (in)famous address at the *Conseil d'État* on May 7, 1806, in which he equated the Jewish people with grubs and locusts looking to infest France, he declared: "There would be weakness in driving out the Jews, there will be strength in improving them."[50] However, it appears as though this "regeneration" potential, implicit in the fulfillment of the request for exemption from the decree, was only recognized in retrospect. In this regard, Anchel speaks of a "shift that took place in Napoleon's mind between 1808 and 1813".[51] It is possible that Napoleon's ministers also discerned an opportunity to at least diminish the decree's inherent deviation from the principles of equality. In any case, guidelines for the submission of applications for exemption were circulated to the prefects from the remaining departments.

The Jewish Community in Luxembourg and the *Décret Infâme*

Before the creation of the Trier Consistory, on June 1, 1808, Luxembourgish Jews campaigned for a dispensation from the *décret infâme* in a petition supported by the prefect and the mayor of the city of Luxembourg.[52] The "Département des

---

49 ANF, F/19/1838.
50 Joseph Pelet de la Lozère, *Opinions de Napoléon sur divers sujets* (Paris, 1833), 214–215, quoted in Pierre Birnbaum, *L'Aigle et la Synagogue*, 83.
51 Anchel, *Napoléon et les Juifs*, 366.
52 The attitude of the non-Jewish officials, for example the pro-regime mayor Jean-Baptiste Servais, and that of the various judges who had to deliver legal opinions, was thoroughly positive in this case. It is unclear what motivated these men: the spirit of Enlightenment, the fact that they were free thinkers or maybe even anti-clericalism. Servais' behavior sets itself far apart from that of other mayors, for instance in the Saar Department. See, for example, Kasper-Holtkotte, *Juden im Aufbruch*, 227 et seq., who states that "the community representatives and mayors of Mosel and Hunsrück had barely anything positive to say about the Jews". However, "good leadership"

Forêts" is the only "Belgian" department that acted accordingly.[53] In contrast to some of the other departments, there were no official complaints about usury in the "Département des Forêts". In their answer to a circular letter from the prefects, all of the arrondissements' district attorneys denied Jewish involvement in usury.[54] The attorney for the arrondissement of Neufchâteau even underscored that, "never in this arrondissement have Jews been engaged in usury, they were always replaced by Christians, with regard to whom the law of the third of September 1807 was illusory up to this day since the moneylenders took double precautions due to the risks they run".[55] However, a fatal change occurred for the Jewish community of the "Département des Forêts" shortly afterward. The prefect Jean-Baptiste Lacoste, who had been well-disposed toward them, was replaced by André Joseph Jourdan. His letter to the interior ministry on August 27, 1808[56] presents a negative bias: According to the prefect, up until that point the army conscripts had had Christians replace them; other than a metal examiner and a private teacher, two innkeepers and a haberdasher, all the other adult men were peddlers; none were land holders; none of the children went to a public school.

> There is nothing to prevent them being accorded the favor requested by my predecessor. Only one circumstance would incline me towards a limited adjournment, the so-called Jewish petition addressed to my predecessor is nothing but a letter from a metal examiner at the guarantee office *signing for his brothers*. It is likely that he acts without authority, that he acts as if he were a public official, that he was persuaded to do so due to the constraints of his subordinate position. Even if the Jews of Luxembourg are not guilty of any offense, they also do nothing that could inspire confidence and it is reasonable to believe that their opinion about everything that can frustrate our legislation and our customs has not changed.[57]

---

was attributed to the Jews of Trier, which points to a discrepancy between the urban and rural situations.

53 Schreiber, *L'immigration juive en Belgique*, 54.
54 For example, Bas Rhin or Alsace, Seine and Meurthe. According to Kasper-Holtkotte, there were ten processes against Jews regarding the rescinding of debt in the Saar Department from March 1806 to April 1808. Kasper-Holtkotte, *Juden im Aufbruch*, 280.
55 Letter from July 6, 1808. ANL, B-74.
56 The list of the 75 Jews established in Luxembourg was first compiled on October 4, 1808. Charles and Graziella Lehrmann trace this long lapse of time to problems ensuing from the decree's requirements concerning Jewish naming practices, Lehrmann and Lehrmann-Gandolfi, *La Communauté juive du Luxembourg*, 47. They likely did not have access to the document mentioned here, dated August 27, 1808, which refutes that thesis.
57 Letter from 27.8.1808 to the interior minister. ANF, F/19/1838. Author's italics.

The Jewish community did not want to allow the matter to rest with Jourdan's deprecating opinion. On October 16, 1808, their representatives turned to the interior minister in order to refute his assertions, about which they had been "indirectly informed". Silence ensued. It was only on August 20, 1810 that another letter was sent to the interior minister. Two years had passed at this point without Luxembourgish Jews receiving the favor ardently desired by them. The following points against the refusal were delineated:

1. The children of the families who have only settled in Luxembourg in recent years are still too young for the boys to be eligible for the compulsory military service.
2. Even if, to this day, none of the signatories are managing an estate or operating a factory, six of them are indeed in a position to support themselves with new occupations or income; the nine others have been able to develop fixed establishments as traveling merchants.
3. As soon as the signatories' children reached the age of compulsory education, they attended public schools, to which the enclosed attestations from the respective teachers will corroborate.
4. Although it is true that only one individual, Pinchas Godchaux, has been able to hold public office, it is also difficult for Catholics to fulfill that kind of function; moreover, the French who newly arrived in Luxembourg were not granted the same privileges enjoyed by the local inhabitants.
5. There is not one signatory who was not already established in France prior to the revolution; none of them have ancestors from Alsace, only one from Lothringen; all signatories supported the *consulat à vie*.
6. There is documentation to the effect that the Jews who settled in the "Département des Forêts" have not been guilty of usury or any other crimes.[58]

On that day, however, all the Jews of the city of Luxembourg would sign the petition due to the question of mortgages. Only Lazarre Levi from Grevenmacher had outstanding debts to report, but he was not one of the signees. The Jews of the city of Luxembourg thus asked the interior minister "to place their plea at the feet of the throne so that the Emperor could deign to distinguish them from their coreligionists who had incurred such severity", for the Luxembourgish Jews "belong to him heart and soul, as do the most excellent French people of

---

[58] On July 3, 1808, the imperial public prosecutor mentions at the tribunal of the Luxembourg arrondissement that only foreign Jews had been legally convicted: "According to my findings, two other Jews were also convicted to three months imprisonment for having been arrested as beggars and vagabonds at Arlon. One of them, Abraham Behr, was originally from the Haut-Rhin, the other, Meyer Zettig, was from Alterheim close to Warsbourg." ANL, B-65.

which they are a part". It becomes clear here that the Luxembourg Jews not only conceived of themselves as decidedly French, in contrast to the local Catholics, but that they wished to distance themselves from the Jews of Alsace, who had indeed "incurred the severity of the decree".

In the meantime, however, Prefect Jourdan underwent a profound change of heart. In a letter to the Interior Ministry dated August 10, 1810, he wrote that the behavior of the Luxembourg Jews was exemplary, and that he had not seen the attestations inserted into the initial 1808 request owing to administrative issues during a temporary absence. He added: "If I caused the suspension of this act of justice due to the report that I had the honor of submitting to you on August 27, 1808, it was because I was not yet in a state to sufficiently appreciate their conduct, it was on account of having only spent a brief amount of time in the department." The Interior Ministry's request to provide further and more current documents was fulfilled by Jourdan on October 5th; and on November 6, 1810 he wrote again, insisting.[59] In December 1810, an Interior Ministry internal report stated that the "Département des Forêts" and three others would receive the dispensation. On March 5, 1811, even the president of the *Députation du collège électoral* of the "Départements" intervened. As attested by the minister on March 12th, Jourdan's additional information "would be examined by the minister very shortly". After that, the correspondence came to an end.

On March 13, 1811, Interior Minister de Montalivet proposed that the "Départements" of "Rhône", "Montenotte", "Rome", and "Forêts" receive a dispensation from the *décret infâme*.[60] A succinct response quickly followed on March 19, 1811, stating that His Majesty had suspended the decision. No explanation was provided and the Emperor never addressed the suspension again. In fact, after April 11, 1810, no further departments or cities were exempt from the decree.[61] Due to Jourdan's initially negative appraisal, the "Département des Forêts" may have missed the opportune moment to obtain their dispensation.

The Consequences of the *Décret Infâme*

As the developments in Luxembourg indicate, the incidental – but subsequently instrumentalized – introduction of possible dispensation from the *décret infâme*, initially contributed to an enormous pressure to conform in the empire. The Lux-

---

59 ANL, B-74.
60 He delivered the corresponding report to Napoleon on that same day. ANF, F/19/11007.
61 Anchel, *Napoléon et les Juifs*, 371.

embourg Jewish community's desire to be exempt from the decree may have been motivated by material concerns, but also resulted from the psychological need to belong to the group of those exempt and thus recognized as citizens. The amount of energy expended by communities including that of Luxembourg toward procuring a dispensation is remarkable at any rate.

One telling example is the behavior of the Trier Central Consistory, of which the Luxembourg congregation was a member. In a circular letter to the coreligionists of the consistorial district, the issue of charity for Jewish beggars and vagabonds is discussed. Although solidarity with poor coreligionists was self-evident in Jewish tradition, in a bilingual tract Chief Rabbi Samuel Marx demanded that people refrained from such actions: "Do you want to be rightfully accused of fostering robberies through illegal assistance?"[62] In 1809, the Trier Consistory even called on their fellow Jews to enlist in the military;[63] in 1810 it reported people who disobeyed the decree to the authorities. An undated circular letter states the following: "How greatly satisfied we would be should the throne one day acknowledge that the Israelites of our district are worthy of seeing the bonds imposed upon them by the Emperor's decree of March 17, 1808 broken; that they – like the citizens of other faiths – are finally worthy of becoming members of the great family."[64] In this context, Kasper-Holtkotte speaks of a "disciplinary measure whose goal it was to transform the Jews into a homogeneous group 'worthy of emancipation'".

We know little about the concrete material effects in the areas where no dispensation was granted, other than through an analysis of the substantial bureaucratic time and effort that was involved in fulfilling the decree. The annually required Jewish patent for the practice of trade involved the yearly issuance of certificates from local councils and synagogues. The city of Luxembourg performed this duty conscientiously, issuing 10–14 patents each year between 1809 and 1813. The discrepancy in number primarily reflects shop closures, bankruptcies, etc. In 1811, collective patents were issued for Grevenmacher, Arlon and for the "Arrondissement Dickrich".[65] However, the issuing of a collective patent for Arlon is questionable, for after several complaints about Jewish merchants,

---

[62] Kasper-Holtkotte, *Juden im Aufbruch*, 399. The Central Consistory applied pressure on the departmental consistories in this regard.
[63] Schreiber, *L'immigration juive en Belgique*, 59 et seq.
[64] ANF, F/19/1840.
[65] Contrary to other information, according to which Jewish families only settled in the city of Luxembourg and Grevenmacher, there were clearly Jewish families who were not included in the statistics. Letter from 4.4.1812, ANL, B-621.

in 1812 the Mayor of Arlon noted that he was obligated "to notify them of the order to stop their commerce until they have their patent".[66]

Luxembourg as the Grand Duchy: William I of the Netherlands

After Napoleon's defeat in 1814, Jewish emancipation in the German regions was once again either completely or partially rescinded in many of the states and cities of the German Confederation founded in 1815.[67] Luxembourg fell to the King of the Netherlands in 1814. Although Luxembourg was also part of the German Confederation, it was subject to the laws of the Netherlands,[68] whose August 24, 1815 constitution secured religious freedom and the protection of religious communities.[69] Under King-Grand Duke William I, there was no longer any legal differentiation between Jewish and non-Jewish citizens.

Gilbert Trausch optimistically wrote the following about Luxembourg:

> The French Revolution is opening Luxembourg up to the modern world. Certainly, it has been a forced opening, rather brutal, but inevitable and advantageous in the long run. The realized reforms represent an irreversible phenomenon. There is no longer any serious question of reconsidering concepts of legal equality, of religious tolerance, and rational administration. Even in a country as pious as Luxembourg, the secularization of the state remains an asset.[70]

---

[66] Letter of 4.4.1812. ANL, B-621.
[67] Graetz, Les Juifs en France, 36 et seq.
[68] The "Mémorial administratif du Grand-Duché de Luxembourg" – the administrative memorandum for the Grand Duchy of Luxembourg – appeared in 1815. It contained both Luxembourg-specific provisions as well as general Dutch provisions that were also valid for Luxembourg.
[69] According to Schreiber, immediately after the defeat of Napoleon a decree by William I repealed the Napoleonic legislation effectuating the unfavorable status conferred upon the Jews through the implementation of the *décret infâme*. Schreiber, *L'immigration juive en Belgique*, 67.
[70] Gilbert Trausch, "Les Luxembourgeois devant la Révolution française", in Raymond Poidevin and Gilbert Trausch, eds., *Les relations franco-luxembourgeoises de Louis XIV à Robert Schuman: Actes du colloque de Luxembourg, 17–19 novembre 1977* (Metz: Centre de recherches Relations internationales de l'Université de Metz, 1978), 83–117, here 115.

Conclusion

According to Cilli Kasper-Holtkotte, "The March 1808 *décret infâme* once again imposed special, discriminatory provisions on Jews, not unlike those of the *Ancien Régime*. The crucial point, however, was that it did not fundamentally revoke the constitutional status of Jews as French citizens."[71] Regarding the *décret infâme*, Paula Hyman writes that Napoleonic policies contributed to the inner strengthening of the Jewish community: "Its ultimate goal was the complete assimilation of the Jews within French society, but the adopted methods paradoxically reinforced Jewish solidarity, which Napoleon deemed necessary to suppress in the name of French national identity."[72]

Scholars have not always evaluated the effects of the *décret infâme* so positively. Due to the pressure induced by the decree to conform, Jewish particularism was undermined. Yet it was the governmental rather than the social integration of the Jews that was stimulated. The impact of the *décret infâme* was felt only through the founding of the consistories. These consistories were not only integrated into one centralized system for the implementation of governmental measures, but in turn integrated Jews on a local level into one community – or excluded them from it, as the case may be. Schreiber describes the Consistories of Krefeld and Trier as "conduits of imperial ideology".[73]

The rising population of the French Jewish community commencing with the French Revolution indicates that the Napoleonic system was considered appealing by at least some of the members – or as the lesser evil. The settlement of new coreligionists, observed throughout all of France, also took place in the "Département des Forêts".[74] It is plausible that Jews living under less favorable conditions elsewhere in Europe attempted to emigrate to the Netherlands, Belgium, France or Luxembourg at a later stage.

The emancipation process in the "Département des Forêts", implemented in 1797, was at least temporarily interrupted by the decree. It generated distinctions that were perceived by the local administration as troublesome but normal. So far, however, no documents have been found requesting prolongation of the *dé-*

---

71 Kasper-Holtkotte, *Juden im Aufbruch*, 4.
72 Hyman, *Jews of Modern France*, 38.
73 Schreiber, *L'immigration juive en Belgique*, 57.
74 In Luxembourg in 1818, there were already 34 households. This growth is perhaps also related to an urban phenomenon observable in several formerly southern Dutch states. Kasper-Holtkotte refers to Brussels and Gent, for instance, where the Jewish population doubled between 1808 and 1818. Kasper-Holtkotte, *Im Westen Neues*, 439 et seq.

cret infâme or challenging the principle of equality more generally. Quite the contrary: the above-cited assessments made by the administration's local representatives suggest that the principle of equality was already being taken into consideration. However, the French central administration clearly showed no preference to the Department in the allocation of dispensations. The economic potential of this small, thoroughly poor Ashkenazic community gave Napoleon no grounds to do so.

Stephanie Schlesier
Between Acceptance and Aversion. Jews and Christians in Luxembourg in the 19th and Early 20th centuries

This chapter will examine the daily lives of the Jews who settled in Luxembourg, including their religious practice and the ways in which they were able to participate in social life. When relevant it will also address any similarities between the situation of the Grand Duchy's Jewish inhabitants and that of those living in the neighboring French and Prussian regions. In order to shed light on the conditions of Jewish life in Luxembourg, a brief outline of the demographic development and occupational distribution of the Jewish minority will be presented. Against that background, the chapter will describe the places where Jews and Christians encountered one another and how their social coexistence was structured. The final sections will examine the development of Jewish religious life in Luxembourg, the forms of contact between Jews and Christians at familial or church-related events and celebrations, and their involvement in the country's political and social life.

The Development and Occupational Distribution of Luxembourg's Jewish Population

In contrast to neighboring regions in the 17th and 18th centuries, Jews were not permitted to settle in the Luxembourg territory; they were only allowed to enter temporarily to conduct business. Jews began to settle there permanently only as a consequence of French rule.[1] They originated primarily from adjacent regions, namely Lorraine, Alsace, and the later Prussian Mosel area and Saar Basin. In 1808, the city of Luxembourg counted 78 Jewish inhabitants, and the rest of

---

[1] Charles Lehrmann and Graziella Lehrmann-Gandolfi, *La communauté juive du Luxembourg: Dans le passé et dans le présent* (Esch-sur-Alzette: Impr. coop. luxembourgeoise, 1953), 30–41; Joseph Goedert, "L'émancipation de la communauté israélite luxembourgeoise et l'administration du culte dans la première moitié du 19ᵉ siècle (1801–1855)", Galerie: Revue culturelle et pédagogique 11, 3 (1993), 345–384, here 347–349; Pierre Hannick and Jean Claude Muller, "Juifs de passage dans les duchés de Luxembourg et de Bouillon avant leur émancipation en 1808", Annales de l'institut archéologique du Luxembourg 136, 1 (2005), 241–254.

the country only one.² In the following decade, that picture gradually changed due to an increase in immigration: in 1818, alongside the 27 Jewish families in the capital, there were nine more dispersed throughout the rural areas.³

Out of the 52 Jewish families counted as part of the Jewish religious community in Luxembourg, 30 lived in the capital and five others lived in the neighboring Schleifmuhl in 1850. The remaining families were spread out over 13 villages, although the majority lived in Ettelbruck, Frisange, Dudelange, and Esch-sur-Alzette.⁴ In 1871, the Grand Duchy's Jewish inhabitants numbered 523, which amounted to 0.26 percent of the entire population.⁵ Following the Franco-German War more Jews emigrated from eastern France and the Rhine Province to Luxembourg, so that their number increased to 777. They were now even more dispersed: over 21 different areas, in 11 of which only one Jewish family was living. This led to the formation of new Jewish centers, above all in Esch-sur-Alzette and Ettelbruck. Out of the 1,212 Jews living in the Grand Duchy in 1900, about a third lived in the center of the country.⁶

There were various motives for the Jewish immigration to Luxembourg. In the first half of the century, an immigrant was moved to settle primarily based on economic motives: After the lifting of the settlement ban, Jewish business people who had already conducted business in Luxembourg before the begin-

---

2 Jean Claude Muller, "Le registre de prise de noms des Juifs de Luxembourg (département des Forêts) en 1808. Edition en fac-similé de l'original conservé aux Archives de la Ville de Luxembourg", Annales de l'institut archéologique du Luxembourg 136, 1 (2005), 255–286; Emile Krier, "Les Juifs au Grand-Duché au XIXᵉ siècle", in André Neuberg, ed., *Le choc des libertés: L'église en Luxembourg de Pie VII à Léon XIII (1800–1880)* (Bastogne: Musée en Piconrue, 2001), 119–128, here 119.
3 Liste des familles juives établies dans l'arrondissement de Luxembourg, 14.3.1818, état nominatif des Juifs dans l'arrondissement de Diekirch, 16.2.1818, Archives Nationales de Luxembourg [subsequently: ANL] C386. Krier, "Les Juifs au Grand-Duché", 120. To be included are the Jewish inhabitants of Arlon, which was part of Belgium after 1839. Angélique Burnotte, "La communauté juive d'Arlon au XIXe siècle", Bulletin trimestriel de l'Institut archéologique du Luxembourg 81, 3/4 (2005), 72–82, here 73 et seq.; Jean-Philippe Schreiber, *L'immigration Juive en Belgique du Moyen Âge à la Première Guerre Mondiale* (Bruxelles: Edition de l'Université de Bruxelles, 1996), 159 et seq.
4 Etat des répartitions faites sur les israélites de la communauté israélite du Grand Duché de Luxembourg, 11.8.1850, ANL G128. The number of Jews living in the country was certainly higher, since not all were included in the list. Marc Schoentgen, "Die jüdische Gemeinde in Medernach. Einwanderung, Integration und Verfolgung", in Vic Molitor, ed., *Fanfare Miedernach. 1930–2005* (Mersch: Faber, 2005), 299–366, here 300 et seq.
5 Statec Luxembourg, *Statistiques historiques: 1839–1989* (Luxemburg: Statec, 1990), 574.
6 Conseil administratif de la communauté israélite de Luxembourg, 13.9.1880, ANL H78. Lehrmann, *La communauté juive du Luxembourg*, 65, 76.

ning of French rule were able to become residents. One demographic factor that favored immigration to the Duchy was the natural increase in the Jewish population in Lorraine and in the Rhine Province, which led to heightened competition in "classical" Jewish occupations and thus to migration. Jews who moved to Luxembourg were able to use their business experience to create a new existence, which in turn led to the influx of more coreligionists of the same origins.[7]

An additional reason for immigration to Luxembourg was marriage. In the first half of the 19th century, the number of Luxembourgish Jews was still very small, so the majority of brides and grooms came from neighboring countries.[8] Due to the limited selection of appropriate marriage partners locally, most of the Jews working as merchants married someone from across the border by way of their extensive business networks in the neighboring countries.[9] Jewish emigration out of the neighboring regions during and after the Franco-German War demonstrates that political motivations were sometimes a decisive factor for settling in the Grand Duchy. It is possible that a desire for emancipation was what prompted Jews to immigrate to Luxembourg from the Prussian Rhine Province starting in 1815. However, the fact that Prussian or German citizenship was often maintained for a long time afterwards speaks to the contrary.[10]

Trade represented the focus of Jewish business activity in Luxembourg. Jewish business people distributed a variety of goods, from second-hand goods and fabric, to livestock and horses, to leather, meat, and grain. Over the course of the 19th century, different kinds of trade developed and the selection of wares changed. The Jewish inhabitants, however, continued to be active primarily in

---

[7] Recensement de la population d'Ettelbruck, 1851, 1864, ANL Rpop 221 et seq. and 505 et seq.; Will Dondelinger and Arthur Muller, "Jüdische Bevölkerung in Ettelbrück: Zum Gedenken an eine einst blühende Religionsgemeinschaft", De Reider. Informatiounsblad vun der Gemeng Ettelbréck, part II, 11, 24 (1998), 23–28, here 24–26 and part III, 12, 25 (1999), 24–37, here 24; Mémorial législatif du Grand-Duché de Luxembourg, 35 (18.5.1881), 429. For further information see the article of Renée Wagener in this volume.
[8] Bevölkerungszählung von Ettelbrück, 1852, ANL Rpop 221 et seq.; Dondelinger and Muller, "Jüdische Bevölkerung in Ettelbrück", part II, 24–26; Daniel Thilman, La présence juive à Mondorf-les-Bains et à Mondorff: Des origines à 1953 (Nancy: Self-published, 2005), 36.
[9] Schoentgen, "Die jüdische Gemeinde in Medernach", 304; Jean Daltroff, Les Juifs de Niedervisse: Naissance, épanouissement et déclin d'une communauté (Strasbourg: Self-published, 1992), 46–71; Cilli Kasper-Holtkotte, Juden im Aufbruch: Zur Sozialgeschichte einer Minderheit im Saar-Mosel-Raum um 1800 (Hannover: Hahn, 1996), 409.
[10] Thilman, La présence juive à Mondorf-les-Bains, 25–42, 74–78; Jakob Segall, "Die Juden im Großherzogtum Luxemberg" [sic], Zeitschrift für Demographie und Statistik der Juden [subsequently abbr.: ZDSJ] 6, 2 (1910), 24–27, here 24–26. "Ergebnisse der Volkszählung in Luxemburg am 1./12. 1905", ZDSJ 3, 6 (1907), 94.

the commercial sector. In 1907, 68 percent of the employed Jewish population was in commerce. They were otherwise in the skilled trades for the most part, often working as butchers or bakers, as was also the case in the neighboring regions. A small group of industrialists made up the Jewish upper class, among them were the families Godchaux and Lippmann who were active in textile and glove manufacturing.[11]

Points of Contact between Jews and Christians

Neighborhoods

Since Jews only represented a small minority of Luxembourg's population, frequent contact with the Christian inhabitants was unavoidable. The following will examine the specific points of Jewish-Christian contact; the term "contact" here will address various aspects, including neighborhoods, business life, schools, and taverns.[12]

Due to their scattered settlement, Jewish inhabitants usually had Christian locals as immediate neighbors.[13] Based on the situation in the bordering regions, one can presume that if Jews and Christians lived together in one house it was for economic reasons: either as a result of poverty or in the case of Christian servants living on the grounds of more affluent Jews.[14] Jews and Christians had neighborly relations of varying intensity with each other. They were mostly

---

[11] "Die Ergebnisse der Berufszählung vom 12. Juni 1907 im Großherzogtum Luxemburg", ZDSJ 7, 2 (1911), 30; Segall, "Juden", 25. Hubert Marx, "Die Tuchfabrik auf der Schleifmillen: Entstehung, Entwicklung, Untergang", in Klaus Schneider and Jan Nottrot, eds., *Schläifmillen: Geschichte und Gegenwart* (Luxembourg-Schläifmillen: Inter-Actions, 2007), 31–61; Marc Jeck, "De 'simples tisserands' aux 'barons de drap': Les Godchaux", Die Warte: Kulturelle Wochenbeilage des Luxemburger Worts 55, 17 (2003), 1; No author, "Den ale Juddekürfech", Ons Stad 1, 2 (1979), 10–12.
[12] Instead of "points of contact", the term "contact zones" can be used. Alexandra Binnenkade, *Kontaktzonen: Jüdisch-christlicher Alltag in Lengnau*, Industrielle Welt 75 (Köln: Böhlau, 2009).
[13] For example, see the population census for Ettelbruck from 1852 and 1864, ANL Rpop 221 et seq. and 505 et seq.; Steven M. Loewenstein, "Anfänge der Integration 1780–1871", in Marion Kaplan, ed., *Geschichte des jüdischen Alltags: Vom 17. Jahrhundert bis 1945* (München: Beck 2003), 125–224, here 126–134.
[14] For the Rhine Province and Lorraine, see for example the Gemünden population census for the years 1840, 1843, 1852 and 1864, Landeshauptarchiv Koblenz [subsequently abbr.: LHAK] Best. 655,12 Nr. 46, the population census for Boulay, 28.6.1851 and the occupation and industry census for Boulay, 14.6.1895, Archives Départementales de la Moselle [subsequently abbr.: ADM] E-dépôt 100 1F1 and 1F4.

peaceful, but by no means were they always free of conflict. Beginning at the end of the 19th century at the latest, it was customary for Jewish and Christian women to assist each other if they needed something for the household. They exchanged recipes on occasion in Ettelbruck; and in close-by Medernach, the Jewish woman Henriette Herz regularly visited a neighboring Christian family in order to bake her cake bases along with theirs in the first half of the 20th century. During those times, they would usually chat for a bit about their daily cares or the preparations for particular celebrations. In small localities where only a few families had their own well, doing the laundry also provided an opportunity to exchange village news.[15] At the end of the 19th century, it was the custom for Jewish inhabitants to present their Christian fellow citizens with a gift of matzah at Passover. Since Passover often fell at the same time as Easter, the Christian inhabitants showed their appreciation by giving their Jewish neighbors Easter eggs. In Ettelbruck, Christians reciprocated with a gift of horseradish, and in Medernach Jewish inhabitants even handed out Easter eggs to Catholic children.[16]

The Christian servants employed by Jewish families represented the Christian section of the population that was most familiar with the Jewish residents' religious practices. Due to the close spatial proximity in villages and small cities, some Jewish religious ceremonies were also familiar to the rest of the inhabitants – although that awareness did not necessarily include any deeper understanding of their meaning.[17] Some cultural differences to the Christian lifestyle that were linked to practicing Judaism even led to expressions of disapproval on occasion. In Medernach in the first half of the 20th century for instance, Christian women who took a short-cut across a Jewish family's property to return to the village

---

15 Dondelinger and Muller, "Jüdische Bevölkerung in Ettelbrück", part III, 28; Schoentgen, "Die jüdische Gemeinde in Medernach", 305–308; Daltroff, *Juifs*, 135; Erhard Roy Wiehn, ed., *Interessante Zeitgenossen: Lebenserinnerungen eines jüdischen Kaufmanns und Weltbürgers* (Konstanz: Hartung-Gorre, 1998), 20.
16 Daltroff, *Juifs*, 115. Loewenstein, "Anfänge der Integration", 219; Dondelinger and Muller, "Jüdische Bevölkerung in Ettelbrück", part III, 28; Schoentgen, ibid., 319 et seq.; Thilman, *La présence juive à Mondorf-les-Bains*, 73 et seq.
17 Christof Pies, *Jüdisches Leben im Rhein-Hunsrück-Kreis*, Schriftenreihe des Hunsrücker Geschichtsvereins 40 (Simmern: Hunsrücker Geschichtsverein, 2003), 67; Claudia Ulbrich, *Shulamit und Margarethe: Macht, Geschlecht und Religion in einer ländlichen Gesellschaft des 18. Jahrhunderts*, Beiheft Aschkenas: Zeitschrift für Geschichte und Kultur der Juden 4 (Wien: Böhlau, 1999), 265; Daltroff, *Juifs*, 107, 112; Ulrich Baumann, *Zerstörte Nachbarschaften: Christen und Juden in badischen Landgemeinden 1862–1940*, Studien zur jüdischen Geschichte 7 (Hamburg: Dölling und Galitz, 2004), 24.

after fieldwork on Saturdays criticized the fact that the Jews there were just sitting around inactive on that day.[18]

In Luxembourg, as in the neighboring regions, tension between Jewish and Christian neighbors often concerned the usage of one's own property. For example, in 1873 in Ettelbruck, Nicolas Wagner complained that the enlargement of the Godchaux family's factory dam was responsible for the flooding that had demolished his garden wall. Although an investigation demonstrated that the wall in question had not been destroyed as a consequence of the heightening of the dam, Wagner initiated another complaint in which he and over 20 property owners who had land above the Godchaux's dam demanded that it be lowered to its original height. In the end, an agreement was made that it would be lowered slightly. There was no specific anti-Jewish line of attack in the conflict, as there had already been similar disputes between Christian inhabitants there in the 1850s.[19] Conflicts between neighbors that were directly linked to religious practices were rare in Lorraine, and even more so in the Rhine Province, due, among other reasons, to the Jewish inhabitants' cautious behavior. They often placed high value on not offending their Christian fellow citizens. However, that also meant that if they did publicly live out their religious otherness beyond what may have been deemed acceptable by the Christian majority, they could expect a confrontation.[20]

Trade

Since Jewish merchants, tradespeople and factory owners had primarily Christian clients – and the manufacturers had almost exclusively Christian employees – contact between Christians and Jews was a matter of course in business life. Due

---

18 Albert Mic, "Plazen, Gaassen, Weeer a Pied", in Molitor, ed., *Fanfare Miedernach*, 221–247, here 223.

19 Joseph Flies, *Ettelbrück: Die Geschichte einer Landschaft* (Luxemburg: Imprimerie St. Paul 1970), 1564, 1608; Fabien Godchaux, "Barrage à Ettelbruck",
Internet: https://godchaux-fe.pagesperso-orange.fr/page-13.html [accessed: 02.06.2022].

20 Henri Schumann, *Mémoire des communautés juives de Moselle* (Metz: Édition Serpenoise, 1999), 23; Daltroff, *Juifs*, 135, 146; Volker Boch, *Juden in Gemünden: Geschichte und Vernichtung einer jüdischen Gemeinde im Hunsrück* (Konstanz: Hartung-Gorre, 2003), 32 et seq., 217; Monika Richarz, "Die Entdeckung der Landjuden. Stand und Probleme ihrer Erforschung am Beispiel Südwestdeutschlands", in Karl-Heinz Burmeister, ed., *Landjudentum im südeutschen und Bodenseeraum: Wissenschaftliche Tagung zur Eröffnung des Jüdischen Museums Hohenems 1991*, Forschungen zur Geschichte Vorarlbergs 11 (Dornbirn: Vorarlberger Verlagsanstalt, 1992), 11–21, here 18 et seq.

to the occupational distribution, Jews in turn had to make use of Christian services.[21] These business relations between Jews and Christians did not come about as a result of reforms owing to emancipation; they had already existed during the *Ancien Régime* – even though Jewish business people had not yet been allowed to become residents in Luxembourg at that time.

Like neighbor relations, business relations between Jews and Christians were not free of conflict. In the first decade of the 19th century, Jews and Christians occasionally took each other to court, but there were no lawsuits concerning any illegal business practices of Jewish merchants. Presumably, the suits were about the same issues as in neighboring regions, namely disputes about back payments or the quality of goods. What is important to underscore here is that the conflict constellation was varied in those disputes: Jews also sued Jews for late payments and Christian creditors also litigated Jewish debtors.[22]

Conflicts based on economic competition did not play any particular role in Luxembourg, most likely due to the relatively small number of Jewish inhabitants. After the turn of the century, right-wing circles were openly critical, but these complaints were voiced more frequently by members of the antisemitic group "Letzebuerger Nationalunio'n" (founded by students in 1910) rather than by Christian merchants. This group sought to use antisemitism as a mainstay for a national identity that would bridge the social gaps between Luxembourgers. They struck out at the Jewish merchants, accusing them of "engaging in outrageous competition against the Luxembourg business world".[23] But the large majority of the Luxembourg population did not support the calls by the "Nationalunio'n" for a boycott of Jewish businesses.[24]

---

21 "Die Ergebnisse der Berufszählung vom 12. Juni 1907 im Großherzogtum Luxemburg", ZDSJ, 7, 2 (1911), 29–30; Lehrmann, *La communauté juive du Luxembourg*, 125; Will Dondelinger, "200 Jahre Marktgeschehen", in idem, ed., *1780–1980: 200 Jahre Marktgeschehen* (Ettelbrück: Gemeindeverwaltung, 1980), 47–109, here 58.

22 A close evaluation of court records has yet to be conducted for Luxembourg. Goedert, "L'émancipation de la communauté israélite luxembourgeoise", 349; Friedrich L. Kronenberger, *Die jüdischen Vieh- und Pferdehändler im Birkenfelder Land und in Gemeinden des Hunsrücks*, Schriftenreihe der Kreishochschule Birkenfeld 8 (Birkenfeld: Kreisvolkshochschule, 1983), 17; Gilbert Roos, *Les Juifs de France sous la monarchie de juillet*, Bibliothèque d'études juives 30 (Paris: Champion, 2007), 106 et seq., 353; idem, *Les relations entre le gouvernement royal et les Juifs du nord-est de la France au XVIIe siècle*, Bibliothèque d'études juives 10 (Paris: Champion, 2000), 114, 265, 354; Pierre Mendel, *Les Juifs de Bionville en pays messin: Du 17e siècle à nos jours* (Metz: Association Mosellane pour la Conservation du Patrimoine Juif, 1995), 14.

23 Lucien Blau, "Antisémitisme au Grand-Duché de Luxembourg de la fin du XIXe siècle à 1940", in Laurent Moyse and Marc Schoentgen, eds., *La présence juive au Luxembourg: Du moyen âge au XXe siècle* (Luxembourg: B'nai Brith, 2001), 57–70, here 62.

24 Ibid., 62–67.

Regarding the Jewish manufacturers in Luxembourg, it should be mentioned here that there were no serious conflicts with their mostly Christian workforce. One reason for that is that they had been attempting to improve the social conditions of their workers since the 1848 revolution at the latest, as had some of the Christian employers, with the goal of binding the workers to them, maintaining social peace and out of paternalistic welfare considerations.[25]

Although Jewish-Christian economic relations in Luxembourg functioned without too much conflict, Jews were still confronted with the stereotypical accusation of *Wucher* – a term for exorbitant interest rates ("usury"), but also used for the reprobation of any kind of Jewish commerce. When trade authorizations were required of Jews as a consequence of the 1808 *décret infâme*, the local Luxembourger authorities did declare that the settled Jews in their areas enjoyed a good reputation. However, some level of suspicion remained nonetheless,[26] as evidenced in part by the Dutch minister De Thiennes' 1816 directives requiring Jewish peddlers in the southern provinces of the realm – and thus in Luxembourg as well – to be monitored especially closely because he assumed they were often guilty of handling stolen goods.[27] An article series inspired by the antisemitic writings of August Rohling, Alphonse Toussenel and Édouard Drumont and published in the *Luxemburger Wort* in 1888 demonstrates the fact that eco-

---

[25] Guy Thewes, "Das Leben der Arbeiter der Schleifmillen im 19. Jahrhundert", in Schneider and Nottrot, eds., *Schläifmillen* 12–30, here 23–25; Denis Scuto, "1848 – Die erste Revolution des industriellen Zeitalters: Zum Geburtsakt der Luxemburger Arbeiterbewegung", Forum fir kritsch Informatioun iwer Politik, Kultur a Relioun 13, 185 (1998), 42–47, here 43–46; Luxembourg city tourist office, *Der Godchaux-Rundweg: Auf den Spuren der industriellen Revolution* (Luxemburg: city tourist office, n.d.), 2–7.

[26] Deputy administrator of Luxembourg to the governor of the Grand Duchy of Luxembourg, 14.3.1818, ANL C386. Prussian and Lorrainese administrative records from the 1840s can be found in: Manfred Jehle, ed., *Die Juden und die jüdischen Gemeinden Preußens in amtlichen Enquêten des Vormärz*, vol. 2: *Enquête des Ministeriums des Innern und der Polizei über die Rechtsverhältnisse der Juden in den preußischen Provinzen 1842–1843: Rheinprovinz, Enquête des Ministeriums der geistlichen, Unterrichts- und Medizinal-Angelegenheiten über die Kultus-, Schul- und Rechtsverhältnisse der jüdischen Gemeinden in den preußischen Provinzen 1843–1845: Berlin, Provinzen Brandenburg, Preußen, Pommern*, Veröffentlichungen der Historischen Kommission zu Berlin 82, 2 (München: Saur, 1998) 495–547 and Rina Neher-Bernheim, *Documents inédits sur l'entrée des Juifs dans la société française (1750–1850)*, vol. 2, Publications of the Diaspora Research Institute 5 (Tel Aviv: Diaspora Research Institute, 1977), 350–392. See the article of Renée Wagener in this volume.

[27] Secretary of state to the governors of the southern provinces, 8.5.1816, ANL C386. Krier, "Les Juifs au Grand-Duché", 121 et seq. For Lorraine and the Rhine Province, see Jean-Bernhard Lang and Claude Rosenfeld, *Histoire des Juifs en Moselle* (Metz: Edition Serpenoise, 2001), 110 and Kasper-Holtkotte, *Juden im Aufbruch*, 348–371.

nomic assumptions about the Jewish minority over the course of the 19th century did not just disappear. The newspaper attacked Jews, saying that their community was attempting to use their economic activities to hurt Christians.[28] The fact that these accusations were at least partially linked to discussions stemming from neighboring regions is demonstrated by both the reference to the named antisemitic authors and the declaration by the article's author, Verlter, that "foreign campaigns against the Jews, especially those led by the German press, had motivated him".[29]

It is difficult to estimate the extent to which the readers of the widely distributed *Wort* shared the newspaper's negative attitudes. An 1889 article in the newspaper *Allgemeine Zeitung des Judenthums* attests that they were not shared by the entire Luxembourgish population. However, it is important to note here that Jewish Germans in part idealized the situation of Jews in the Grand Duchy.[30] Anti-Jewish stereotypes persisted in Luxembourg as well, as demonstrated by the successful 1920 village theater piece "Zwé Judden als Schmoggler" published by Louis Biren, which disseminated the cliché of "profiteering Jews" trying to ruin the poor honest farmer.[31] However, anti-Jewish stereotypes appear to have played a rather subordinate role in daily business relations around the turn of the 20th century. As in the neighboring regions, it was customary in rural Luxembourg for Jewish merchants and Christian customers to forgo the signing of a contract in livestock sales, sealing the deal with a handshake instead. This presupposes a certain amount of trust in the honesty of one's trade partners.[32]

---

28 At the request of the public prosecutor, one court imposed the highest possible penalty for defamation in a case involving the slandering of the Jewish religion and the incitement of one class of citizens against another. Allgemeine Zeitung des Judenthums [subsequently abbr.: AZJ] 52, 28 (1888), 395 et seq.; 52, 28 (1888), 811 et seq.; 53, 4 (1889), 55 et seq.; 53, 5 (1889), 72; 53, 6 (1889), 86 et seq.; 53, 13 (1889), 196 et seq.; 53, 15 (1889), 235; 53, 22 (1889), 340; Der Israelit, Beilage 30, 9 (1889), 160. On antisemitism in the *Luxemburger Wort*, see Thorsten Fuchshuber's chapter in this volume.
29 AZJ, 52, 25 (1888), 395.
30 The AZJ wrote: "The *Lux. Wort* itself declared that 'the people, both the educated and the common people, would be surprised by its messages [concerning the Jews]'. The Luxembourgers must have been surprised by this incrimination of the Jews, as they [...] had never sensed anything of it in reality." AZJ 53, 6 (1889), 86.
31 Schoentgen, "Die jüdische Gemeinde in Medernach", 308, 323, 362.
32 Dondelinger and Muller, "Jüdische Bevölkerung in Ettelbrück", part III, 38; Flies, *Ettelbrück*, 1632. Kronenberger, *Die jüdischen Vieh- und Pferdehändler*, 7–19. Daltroff, *Juifs*, 127.

The Schools

In addition to commerce, schools represented a point of contact between Jews and Christians, albeit a controversial one – for government officials as well as for the Catholic clergy and parents. In general, Jewish children attended Catholic schools. In Ettelbruck, there was collaboration between Christians and Jews in the educational sector that went even further: in the sewing workroom of the so-called *Gemeindearmenschule* (municipal charity school), a Jewish woman worked alongside several nuns in the second half of the 19th century. From time to time, she and a Catholic nun taught poor village girls sewing and tailoring together.[33]

In the early 1840s, it became clear that educating children of different religious affiliations in the same classroom was viewed critically by many of the parents in the capital, as both Jewish residents and Christian city leaders expressed that it would be wise to separate the children of different faiths out of consideration for religious sensitivities. However, once the municipality was expected to participate financially in the Jewish school's maintenance, consideration for the religious sensitivities of the minority ended abruptly.[34] At that point Rabbi Samuel Hirsch objected, saying that there were good reasons for a separate Jewish school: The Jews, who "are barely freed from the pressures of the Middle Ages, require special education in order to understand what it meant to be a citizen of a free state, to comprehend their responsibilities as such, something that cannot be taught to them by a Christian teacher who has never known the humiliation that Jews had to suffer, and who knows nothing of the effects that it has had on the disposition of the Jews".[35] The rabbi was greatly influenced by the ideas of Christian Wilhelm von Dohm – but those arguments proved insufficient, as the Jewish school was forced to close in 1847 due to financial problems after only having been open a few years, and despite a subsidy accorded by the municipality by order of the government. The Jewish children then attended the Catholic school for elementary instruction once again.[36]

---

33 Dondelinger and Muller, "Jüdische Bevölkerung in Ettelbrück", part II, 23 et seq.; Flies, *Ettelbrück*, 1446, 1467, 1472; Correspondence about Jewish schools at the beginning of the 1840s, ANL F68.
34 Bourgmestre et échevins de la ville de Luxembourg au Régence du Pays, 17.12.1841, ruling by the Luxembourg city town, 2.4.1844, ANL F68.
35 Chief Rabbi Samuel Hirsch to the Luxembourg *Regierungsrat*, 9.5.1844, in ANL G128.
36 Israelite consistory of Metz to the prefect of Moselle, 4.9.1830, ADM 1T23; Britta L. Behm, "Moses Mendelssohn und die Frage der 'bürgerlichen Verbesserung' der Juden – Ansätze zur jüdischen Integration zwischen 'Gleichheit' und 'Mannigfaltigkeit'", in idem, ed., *Jüdische Erzie-*

Jewish parents' concerns about the influence of the many religious teachers were not completely unfounded, as demonstrated by the baptizing of a young Jewish girl in the village of Strassen in 1866. Henriette Levy attended the local Catholic school run by nuns, and they "as it appears, could not resist their pious wish to present the beloved Lord with a Christmas present of a baptized Israelite soul".[37] It is important to emphasize here that apparently the girl was not forced to change religions by the priest or by the attending members of the municipality administration; it appears rather as though she was moved to this decision by the teachings in her school classes. That this situation was an extraordinary one is evidenced by the transnational media response generated by the case, and the comparisons made to the so-called "Mortara Affair".[38] After the event, Henriette Levy was sent to a boarding school in France with the aid of donations collected through the Jewish community administration. The reactions on the Christian side were contradictory: The liberal *Courrier du Grand Duché de Luxemburg* regretted that it had happened, while the *Luxemburger Wort* highlighted the fact that the young Jewish woman had been ready to convert voluntarily and that the mother had put pressure on her daughter and had thus violated her freedom of conscience.[39]

In the neighboring Prussian Rhine and Lorraine regions, both Jewish and Christian parents supported separating the schools according to faith, particularly in rural areas. However, due to Jewish emigration, many Jewish village schools closed at the end of the 19th century.[40] The fact that a Jewish school was founded in 1889 in the Luxembourg city of Ettelbruck, where the Jewish community had grown to 30 families, and continued to function beyond the turn of the century went against the general trend. In the other areas of Luxembourg, Jewish chil-

---

hung und aufklärerische Schulreform: Analysen zum späten 18. und frühen 19. Jahrhundert, Jüdische Bildungsgeschichte in Deutschland 5 (Münster: Waxmann, 2002), 269–289, here 275–279.
37 AZJ 31, 3 (1867), 50.
38 Luxemburger Wort 20, 1 (1867), 1 et seq; Der Israelit, Add. 8, 2 (1867), 27. The "Mortara Affair" was about the secret baptizing of a Jewish child – Edgardo Mortara – in Bologna and his abduction from his family by the papal police. A discussion ensued in the European public sphere and various state governments appealed to the Vatican in the name of the child's parents. On this affair, see Thomas Brechenmacher, *Der Vatikan und die Juden: Geschichte einer unheiligen Beziehung vom 16. Jahrhundert bis in die Gegenwart* (München: Beck, 2005), 113–121.
39 AZJ 30, 3 (1867), 50; Luxemburger Wort 20, 1 (1867), 2.
40 Jean Daltroff, "L'histoire des communautés juives rurales de Moselle", Cahiers des pays de la Nied: Revue des recherches spécifiques aux pays de la Nied 11, 24 (1994), 12–26, here 20; Andreas Brämer, *Leistung und Gegenleistung: Zur Geschichte jüdischer Religions- und Elementarlehrer in Preussen 1823/24 bis 1872*, Hamburger Beiträge zur Geschichte der deutschen Juden 30 (Göttingen: Wallstein, 2006), 340–344.

dren went to the local elementary schools after mandatory schooling was introduced in 1881 without the occurrence of any incident comparable to that in Strassen.[41]

Taverns

As in the Rhine Province and Lorraine, taverns in Luxembourg represented places of contact between Jews and Christians, most predominantly since the last decades of the 19th century. In the neighboring regions, it was initially Jewish cattle merchants and their customers who would often go to one of these taverns after the closing of a deal to have a drink or a cup of coffee. In the second half of the 19th century, it became customary to meet at taverns for reasons of a more social nature, particularly association meetings. In addition, Jews also frequented Christian establishments together. In Medernach, Jewish men regularly went to the Kieffer tavern. Some of the Christian-managed places accommodated the requests of their Jewish guests. The proprietor of the above tavern made allowances for his Jewish guests' religious customs by keeping special "*Juddeglieser*" (Jew glasses) at hand, as due to dietary regulations they only ingested coffee at his locale.[42]

Jewish Religious Practice

It is only possible to portray fragments of the religious life of Jews in Luxembourg due to the state of the source material. What is fundamentally clear, however, is that religion had a very important place in daily life, as it did in the neighboring regions during the 19th century. The Christians' churchgoing, the Jews' synagogue attendance, weddings and funerals: none of these events

---

[41] Dondelinger and Muller, "Jüdische Bevölkerung in Ettelbrück", part III, 26; Flies, *Ettelbrück*, 1630; Schoentgen, "Die jüdische Gemeinde in Medernach", 314–317. Thilman, *La présence juive à Mondorf-les-Bains*, 48.

[42] Schoentgen, "Die jüdische Gemeinde in Medernach", 318 et seq.; Dondelinger and Muller, "Jüdische Bevölkerung in Ettelbrück", part III, 31; Kronenberger, *Die jüdischen Vieh- und Pferdehändler*, 14–19; Daltroff, *Juifs*, 149, 161; Wiehn, ed., *Interessante Zeitgenossen*, 25; Tobias Dietrich, *Konfession im Dorf: Westeuropäische Erfahrungen im 19. Jahrhundert*, Industrielle Welt 65 (Köln: Böhlau, 2004), 316–318.

were private matters. They were a component of living together in a community and were thus subject to social control.⁴³

Focusing on the Luxembourg Jews' religious institutions, it would seem that Judaism in the 19th century was a religion largely located in the capital. The first synagogue was erected in the 1820s in the city of Luxembourg and was financed through the selling of reserved synagogue seats, contributions, donations, as well as a small grant from the municipality. Rural Jews also visited the religious site, as they did not have the mandatory ten male participants for a service in their villages in the first half of the century.⁴⁴ Some of the Jews who lived on the border of the Grand Duchy would visit synagogues in the neighboring regions, such as Lazarus Levy from Grevenmacher who went to Trier.⁴⁵

The first Jews to independently celebrate services outside of the capital were the Jewish inhabitants of Ettelbruck in the 1840s, together with coreligionists from the surrounding area. They took on the construction of their own synagogue in the mid-1860s, once their small community had experienced significant growth. The Jews contributed the majority of the costs themselves, but after petitions were written highlighting the state's guarantee of both religious and civil equality, they received 900 francs in government grant money towards a total of 9,850 francs in cost.⁴⁶ Subsequently other Jewish communities in Luxembourg built synagogues or small houses of prayer in their own cities, namely Esch-sur-Alzette and Mondorf-les-Bains, Medernach and Grevenmacher.⁴⁷

---

43 Dietrich, ibid., 177–194. Colette Mechin, "Fêtes et saisons", in Jean Lanher, ed., *Encyclopédie illustrée de la Lorraine*, vol. 4: *La vie traditionnelle* (Metz: Edition Serpenoise, 1989), 83–126. Hansgeorg Molitor, "La vie religieuse populaire en Rhénanie francaise, 1794–1815", in Bernard Plongeron, ed., *Pratiques religieuses: Mentalités et spiritualités dans l'Europe Révolutionnaire (1770–1820)* (Turnhout: Brepols 1988), 59–68, here 59–66.

44 According to Lehrmann, the synagogue was erected in 1823, but older reports date it to 1827 and 1828. Levy, secretaire de relevé, 29.9.1855, ANL H78; Lehrmann, *La communauté juive du Luxembourg*, 53; Goedert, "L'émancipation de la communauté israélite luxembourgeoise", 356–358; Dondelinger and Muller, "Jüdische Bevölkerung in Ettelbrück", part II, 25.

45 Lazarus Levy to the governor of the Grand Duchy of Luxembourg, 19.1.1842, ANL E55.

46 Dondelinger and Muller, "Jüdische Bevölkerung in Ettelbrück", part II, 26 et seq. Correspondence between the Luxembourg authorities and the Ettelbruck Jews about the building of a synagogue, 1865–1871, ANL H1024, 1000; Administration of the Israelite community of Ettelbruck to the secretary of state, 26.8.1881, ANL H 78. It is occasionally falsely assumed in the literature that the state took on all of the costs. See Dondelinger and Muller, ibid., part III, 28.

47 Thilman, *La présence juive à Mondorf-les-Bains*, 54–58; Schoentgen, "Die jüdische Gemeinde in Medernach", 313 et seq.; Claude Marx, "Jüdisches Leben in Luxemburg", in Antoinette Reuter, ed., *Ansichten jüdischen Lebens zwischen Maas, Mosel und Rhein im Spiegel alter Postkarten (vom Ende des 19. bis Anfang des 20. Jahrhunderts): Eine Ausstellung des Centre de documentation sur*

Until the final decades of the 19th century, there was also only one Jewish cemetery in Luxembourg, located in Clausen at the capital's border. Starting in 1818, the majority of Jews who lived in Luxembourg buried their dead at this cemetery, with an occasional exception, as in the case of the above-mentioned Lazarus Levy, who was put to rest in Trier. Other than the 1897 burial of a couple that was part of the religious community's elite, the Clausen cemetery was used by Luxembourgish Jews only until 1883. At that time, the community purchased another burial site, as the first had become too small.[48] At the beginning of the 1880s, another Jewish cemetery was constructed in Ettelbruck. It was used by the Jews living in the north of the country, due to the high transport costs and major effort involved in burying coreligionists in the capital's cemetery. In fact, Ettelbruck's small religious community had already expressed the desire to build another cemetery there at the end of the 1850s. However, it was only in the context of the issues with the Clausen cemetery that an additional cemetery became possible, as the number of Jews in Luxembourg had greatly increased and the government recognized the necessity of another Jewish graveyard.[49] Aside from Ettelbruck, a Jewish cemetery was built in 1895 in Grevenmacher, and another in 1905 in Esch-sur-Alzette.[50]

Compared to synagogues and cemeteries, the existence of *mikvahs* is difficult to substantiate. The religious community's budget suggests that there was a ritual bath for the capital's Jewish inhabitants in the 1820s, as there is a listing for the item "women's bath rent" in its accounts in 1822. As far as the Jews living in rural areas are concerned, it has been reported that the remains of structural fea-

---

les migrations humaines Düdelingen (Dudelange: Centre de documentation sur les migrations humaines, 2005), 42–43.

48 Claude Marx kindly made his manuscript available: "Visite du cimetière de Clausen Malakof"; Marcel Kaiser, "Der alte Judenfriedhof in Clausen", Luxemburger Tageblatt 81, 171 (1993), 3; Lehrmann, *La communauté juive du Luxembourg*, 66. General administration of municipal concerns to the mayor and deputy burgomaster of the city of Luxembourg, 15.5.1852, ANL G128; Lazarus Levi au gouverneur du Grand-Duché de Luxembourg, 19.1.1842, ANL E55.

49 Administrators of the Israelite community of Luxembourg to the secretary of state, 23.4.1859; Secretary of state to the general director of the interior, 27.4.1859, ANL H78. Dondelinger and Muller, "Jüdische Bevölkerung in Ettelbrück", part III, 24 et seq.; Flies, *Ettelbrück*, 1432, 1613.

50 Laurent Moyse, "Les cimetières juifs", in Claude Geudevert, Micheline Gutmann and Laurent Moyse, eds., *Les Juifs du Luxembourg* (Paris: Association de Généalogie Juive Internationale, 1999). Paul Cerf and Isi Finkelstein, *Les Juifs d'Esch / Déi Escher Judden. Chroniques de la communauté juive de 1837 à 1999* (Luxembourg: Editions des cahiers luxembourgeois, 1999), 20; Lehrmann, *La communauté juive du Luxembourg*, 66 et seq., 77.

tures relating to ritual baths were discovered a few decades ago in Esch-sur-Alzette.[51]

The establishment of Jewish religious institutions in different areas around Luxembourg shows that over time the Jewish communities living outside of the city became more independent from coreligionists in the capital. That is also demonstrated by the fact that a community such as Ettelbruck had its own chairman of the board by 1870 at the latest.[52] This undeniable, increasing autonomy was not reflected in the official organization of the Jewry however, since the government did not alter the law that stated that "all of the Israelites of the Grand Duchy are members of the synagogue of Luxembourg".[53] Moreover, all Jews remained linked to one another by virtue of their being under one rabbi's responsibility. Until 1815, the Luxembourgish Jews were under the supervision of the Rabbi of Trier, and after that the Rabbi of Maastricht, who, however, did not concern himself with the Luxembourgish community.[54] The Jews of Luxembourg appointed a cantor to lead the services, one who sometimes also carried out the duty of *shochet* (ritual slaughterer) in order to supplement the meager salary, as in the case of Nathan Schuster who was employed at the beginning of the 1840s.[55]

It was only after the separation of Belgium and independence from the Netherlands that Jews in Luxembourg sought the appointment of their own rabbi. In 1841, the Jewish community leadership addressed the Grand Duke, linking the request for a rabbi with a demand for a regular state subsidy for the Jewish congregation. In light of the Jews having been granted equal status to the Christian population, the community was granted a subsidy for the appointment

---

51 Account of revenues and expenses of the Luxembourg Israelite community for the fiscal year 1823, ANL E55; Lehrmann, ibid., 77.
52 Joseph Cahen to the general director of the interior, 7.3.1870, ANL H1024, 100.
53 Government of the country to the King-Grand Duke, 25.12.1841, ANL E55. On the discussions about a new organization of the Jewish religion, see: Goedert, "L'émancipation de la communauté israélite luxembourgeoise", 380 et seq.
54 Verdeeling van de Resorten der Israelitsche Hoofdsynagogen in 't Koningrijk der Nederlanden in Synagogale Ringen of Kerkgangen, Anhang an einen Brief des Commissaris-Generaal, provisioneel belast met de Zaken der hervomden en andere eerediensten. Behalve dien der Roomsch-Catholyken, 21.8.1816; Godchaux to the governor of the Grand Duchy of Luxembourg, 10.12.1819, ANL C654; Goedert, "L'émancipation de la communauté israélite luxembourgeoise", 351. Cilli Kasper-Holtkotte, *Im Westen Neues: Migration und ihre Folgen: Deutsche Juden als Pioniere jüdischen Lebens in Belgien, 18./19. Jahrhundert* (Leiden and Boston: Brill, 2003), 395 et seq.
55 Number of non-Catholics currently established in the Grand Duchy of Luxembourg, ca. 1815, ANL C654; Rabbi Samuel Hirsch, 28.3.1844, administration of the Luxembourg Israelite community to the mayor and deputy burgomaster of the city of Luxembourg, 30.11.1843, 26.6.1844, ANL F68.

of a rabbi in 1842.[56] After Samuel Hirsch's appointment as Rabbi of Luxembourg in 1843, he pursued many different activities. One particularly exceptional duty that he took on was the occasional fulfillment of the cantor's responsibilities. Such was the case when the Jewish teacher and prayer leader Oberndörfer left in 1847, and nobody was able to take over the reading of the Torah. In 1852, a new prayer leader was appointed, but Hirsch continued to perform some of the responsibilities that actually fell under the new leader's purview. He preached regularly in the synagogue and prepared the young boys for their bar mitzvah in so-called confirmation courses. He also supervised the education of the Jewish children and after the closing of a short-lived Jewish school in the capital, he taught the children living there biblical history and Hebrew. Hirsch also spent copious amounts of time on his studies, something that can be observed based on the list of works he completed during these years.[57]

In the beginning, the small religious communities outside of the capital did not appoint any religious staff for financial reasons. Congregation members took on the duties of prayer leader and, when necessary, *shochet*. For instance, Léon Cahen, a brother of the Trier Rabbi Kahn, was a prayer leader in Ettelbruck and instructed the local children in religion as well. In 1864, the Ettelbruck Jewish congregation appointed a cantor named Jacob Bocclinger, who also worked as a teacher and *shochet*. In contrast to the rabbis, these office holders did not receive any subvention from the government. In 1881 in Ettelbruck, the Jewish community's petition for regular government assistance for a trained religious teacher was denied.[58] The reason provided for the refusal was the fear that "a favorable decision (…) would lead to great inconvenience if it had to be applied to other religions and to all of the sufficiently large number of Israelites living in

---

56 Administration of the Luxembourg Israelite community to the King Grand-Duke, 15.11.1841; State chancellor to the governor of Luxembourg, 4.8.1842, 26.9.1842; State chancellor to the King Grand-Duke, 21.2.1843, 21.3.1843, ANL F 68; Krier, "Les Juifs au Grand-Duché", 122 et seq.; Goedert, "L'émancipation de la communauté israélite luxembourgeoise", 362.

57 Administration of the Luxembourg Israelite community, 22.5.1843; Samuel Hirsch to the Grand-ducal government and to the minister of state, respectively, 14.7.1848, 22.4.1858; Samuel Hirsch to the Luxembourgish general administrator of religions and the president of the general administration, 2.1.1854, ANL H78; Marginal note, 15.10.1847 (on one of the writings by the mayor and judges of Luxembourg city, 9.11.1846), ANL G128. Lehrmann, *La communauté juive du Luxembourg*, 55; Gershon Greenberg, "The Historical Origins of God and Man: Samuel Hirsch's Luxembourg Writings", Leo Baeck Institute Year Book 20, 1 (1975), 129–148.

58 Dondelinger and Muller, "Jüdische Bevölkerung in Ettelbrück", part II, 26 et seq. and part III, 24. Ettelbruck population census, 1864, ANL Rpop 505 et seq. Petition by the Jewish community of Ettelbruck to the assembly of the estates of Luxembourg, 23.11.1866, ANL H1024, 100. Petition of the Jewish community of Ettelbruck to State Minister Blochausen, 26.8.1881, ANL H78.

the cantons of Echternach, Esch s/Alz., Grevenmacher and Remich".⁵⁹ The children of the Jewish inhabitants living in the countryside who were unable to attend religion classes were taught by their parents. The Jewish elite was critical of their knowledge, as demonstrated by the catechism published by Hirsch with support from the congregation leadership, meant in part as an aid for those parents.⁶⁰

The religious practice of Jews in Luxembourg was similar to that of those in the Rhine Province and in eastern France, the areas from which the Luxembourgish Jews often originated. The celebration of the Sabbath and holidays connected the members of the Jewish community to each other, but simultaneously separated them from the Christian segment of the population. In rural areas and in small cities, Jewish rites were strictly followed for the most part up until the end of the 19th century. The divergent ways of separating the week into workdays and days of rest led to differing rhythms of life – and although they were accepted in the surrounding Christian world, they were not always viewed favorably (as noted above in the case of Christian women in Medernach criticizing the Jews for resting on the Sabbath).⁶¹ In regards to livestock trade however, market days were postponed if they fell on Jewish holidays, since the remaining attendees lost interest in taking part if the Jewish merchants were not present.⁶²

---

59 State minister to the commissioner of the Diekirch district, ANL H78.
60 Samuel Hirsch, *Systematischer Katechismus der israelitischen Religion, auf Beschluß des Vorstandes der israelitischen Gemeinde zu Luxemburg* (Luxemburg: V. Bück, 1856), i. See also, Bernd Schröder, "Jüdische Katechismen in Deutschland am Beispiel eines Katechismus aus der Feder von Samuel Hirsch (1815–1889)", in Klaus Herrmann, Margarete Schlüter, and Giuseppe Veltri, eds., *Jewish Studies Between the Disciplines - Judaistik zwischen den Disziplinen: Papers in Honor of Peter Schäfer on the Occasion of His 60th Birthday* (Leiden and Boston: Brill, 2003), 456–478 and the article by Ken Koltun-Fromm in this volume.
61 Flies, *Ettelbrück*, 1630; Lehrmann, *La communauté juive du Luxembourg*, 76 et seq.; Jacob Toury, *Soziale und politische Geschichte der Juden in Deutschland 1847–1871: Zwischen Revolution, Reaktion und Emanzipation*, Schriftenreihe des Instituts für deutsche Geschichte 2 (Düsseldorf: Droste, 1977), 122 et seq.; Karl Erich Grözinger, "'Schaddaj' – Hüter der Türen Israels: Jüdische Frömmigkeit in Alltag und Schabbat im 19. Jahrhundert", in Haus der Geschichte Baden-Württemberg, ed., *Nebeneinander – Miteinander – Gegeneinander? Zur Koexistenz in Süddeutschland im 19. und 20. Jahrhundert*, Laupheimer Gespräche 1 (Gerlingen: Bleicher, 2002), 65–79, here 66; Daltroff, *Juifs*, 112–135; Pies, *Jüdisches Leben im Rhein-Hunsrück*-Kreis, 79 et seq.
62 Lehrmann, *La communauté juive du Luxembourg*, 125; Dondelinger, "200 Jahre", 58; Dieter Kastner, ed., *Der Rheinische Provinziallandtag und die Emanzipation der Juden 1825–1845: Eine Dokumentation*, vol. 1 (Köln: Rheinlandverlag, 1989), 34; Paula E. Hyman, *The Emancipation of the Jews of Alsace: Acculturation and Tradition in the Nineteenth Century* (New Haven: Yale University Press, 1991), 34.

Presumably, Jews in Luxembourg did business on Sundays just as the Jews in the neighboring regions did – even though it was not necessarily well-regarded by public authorities, churches and some of the Christian citizens.[63] For example, one reader of the *Luxemburger Wort* complained in 1889 that Jewish traveling salesmen had been working on All Saints' Day in Grevenmacher, and had offered their wares to resident business people. He doubted that there was any contact with Christians, as he assumed, "that surely no Catholic businessman would receive the young men today".[64] That cannot be considered a definitive answer to the question however: As early as 1816, the Luxembourgish governor reported that the Catholic population was greatly inconvenienced by the regulation forcing all businesses to remain closed on Sundays and holidays, since those days were always considered profitable for business. In the 1880s therefore, once doing business on Sundays and holidays was no longer prohibited, it is highly likely that people chose to exercise that option.[65]

The Jews of Luxembourg, who for the most part originated from villages in the neighboring regions in the first half of the 19th century, practiced a kind of "popular Judaism"[66] as did their counterparts in those areas. In this form of practice, great value was placed on compliance with religious customs, but the knowledge of religious texts was rather poor. That is also made clear by Hirsch when he states that his catechism "was not just to be considered necessary [for rural inhabitants], [but also] for many Israelite fathers and mothers, [although] the same principles and teachings had been presented from the pulpit for years on every Sabbath and on every holiday".[67]

Attendance of religious services does not represent concrete evidence of religiosity or devoutness, as the pressure to conform must be taken into consideration in this context. This was especially the case for the small Jewish communities outside of the capital, in which the services were only possible when all of the men who were of age were present – as was the case in Ettelbruck in mid-

---

[63] Ulbrich, *Shulamit und Margarethe*, 261; Daltroff, *Juifs*, 128, 161–166; Newspaper reports by the mayor of Gemünden, October and November 1838, LHAK Best. 655, 12 Nr. 161; LAS Dep. Illingen Nr. 986, 11 et seq.
[64] Luxemburger Wort 42, 306/307 (1889), 3.
[65] State minister to the governor of Luxembourg, 7.11.1816, ANL C386; Flies, *Ettelbrück*, 1358–1360.
[66] Loewenstein, "Anfänge der Integration", 227; Patrick Girard, *Les Juifs de France de 1789 à 1860: De l'émancipation à l'égalité* (Paris: Calmann-Lévy, 1976), 218 et seq.
[67] Heinz Monz, "Samuel Hirsch (1815–1889). Ein jüdischer Reformator aus dem Hunsrück", Jahrbuch für westdeutsche Landesgeschichte 17, 1 (1991), 159–180, here 171. Hirsch, *Systematischer Katechismus der israelitischen Religion*, i et seq.

19th century.⁶⁸ At the same time, the situation in central Luxembourg was different. There, the elite attempted to be available to their Christian business partners on the Sabbath as well, meaning that they were often not present at services, leading Hirsch to regret that the "main day of enterprise [...] [is] now Saturday and [...] the well-educated [are] practically forced to miss out on the public service".⁶⁹

The members of the Jewish community leadership began campaigning notably early for the institution of a "contemporary" prayer service that would include aesthetic reforms inspired by the ideas of the German Reform movement. In the 1820s, for instance, the auctioning of inherited synagogue honors during services was temporarily abolished.⁷⁰ As in the neighboring regions, religious reforms were initially met with resistance: While the Jewish community leadership was eager to innovate, Luxembourgish Jews were mainly opposed. This came explicitly to the fore during the conflict about the rabbinical candidate in the 1840s, in which the community leadership expressly demanded a rabbi who "belongs to a Reform party".⁷¹ However, the majority of Jews living in the Grand Duchy did not consider that a requirement and supported the local born Isaias Levy. His father pointed out that the only people who were against his son were the community board members, since "he is too religious for them"⁷² and that they preferred someone "who enlightens religion".⁷³ In fact, one of the leadership's criticisms was that Levy was the wrong man for the position due to his "traditional" education: "all of his quite contestable expertise [...] consists of knowledge of Talmudic commentaries and the outdated principles of the rabbis of yore, which he has come to display in the temple at times, to the horror of the enlightened men of the community."⁷⁴ In the end, the elite succeeded in

---

68 Susanne Zittartz-Weber, *Zwischen Religion und Staat: Die jüdischen Gemeinden in der preußischen Rheinprovinz 1815–1871*, Düsseldorfer Schriften zur Neueren Landesgeschichte und zur Geschichte Nordrhein-Westfalens 64 (Essen: Klartext-Verlag, 2003), 273–285; Dondelinger and Muller, "Jüdische Bevölkerung in Ettelbrück", part II, 25 et seq.
69 Samuel Hirsch to the general administrator of religions, 7.11.1853, ANL H78.
70 Israelitische Annalen 1, 25 (1839), 198.
71 Petition by 43 Jewish community members to the King, ANL F68. On the neighboring regions: Zittartz-Weber, *Zwischen Religion und Staat*, 252–302 and Schumann, *Mémoire des communautés juives de Moselle*, 23–27.
72 Isaac Levy to the mayor and the judges of the city of Lützemburg, 22.1.1843, ANL F68.
73 Isaac Levy to the King, 18.1.1843, ANL F68.
74 Administration of the Luxembourg Israelite community to the mayor and deputy burgomaster of the city of Luxembourg, 23.1.1843, ANL F68.

appointing Hirsch, the man recommended to them by the Trier rabbi, since they could count on the support of the government for their choice.[75]

With the selection of Hirsch, Jews obtained a reform-oriented rabbi, who saw himself as taking on the role of their ameliorator: They were not "to remain at the lowest ranks of civilization", but instead "be guided towards the cultural refinement of our century".[76] Right after his appointment, Hirsch advocated changing elements of the prayer service, which some members rejected.[77] The resistance was not unanimous however, and in 1848 the leadership was able to declare that "the majority of Luxembourgish Israelites also understand the requirements of this century and our honored Rabbi is endeavoring to lead us on this path of improvement".[78] The fact that Hirsch was able to convince the members to accept reforms was possibly due to his having demonstrated a certain tolerance for traditional members of the congregation in spite of his personal convictions: "Should somebody desire to observe medieval Judaism with all of its excesses, I would not have anything against that; [...] I have never been authoritarian or controlling. [...] Freedom of conscience is my motto."[79] The traditionally minded congregation members thus proved more open to changes than they otherwise would have been. Léon Cahen of Ettelbruck, for example, was "personally strictly Orthodox, [...] but was not averse to contemporary improvements in the area of synagogue life".[80] Hirsch was successful at implementing moderate reforms in Luxembourg, but not more radical measures such as shifting the Sabbath to Sunday.[81]

---

[75] Luxembourg council of state to the King Grand-Duke, 7.3.1843, ANL F68; Governor of Luxembourg to Samuel Hirsch, 13.4.1843, ANL H78; Monz, "Samuel Hirsch", 170 et seq.

[76] Samuel Hirsch to the governor of Luxembourg, 8.4.1844, ANL F68.

[77] Der Orient 5, 48 (1844), 370; Luxembourg council of state to the King Grand-Duke 24.7.1844, ANL F68; Mayor and deputy burgomaster of the city of Luxembourg to the secretary of foreign affairs, of justice and religion, 13.9.1848; Samuel Hirsch to the royal grand-ducal goverment, 14.7.1848, ANL H78.

[78] Nathan and Bonn to the mayor and deputy burgomaster of the city of Luxembourg, 7.9.1848, ANL H78. Despite personal conflicts between Hirsch and the Godchaux family, they always agreed on the necessity of dignified religious worship services. Goedert, "L'émancipation de la communauté israélite luxembourgeoise", 376.

[79] Samuel Hirsch to the royal grand-ducal government, 14.7.1848, ANL H78.

[80] AZJ 45, 49 (1881), 815; Dondelinger and Muller, "Jüdische Bevölkerung in Ettelbrück", art II, 27.

[81] Israelite governing board to the mayor and judges of the city of Luxembourg, 24.9.1866, ANL H78; Monz, "Samuel Hirsch", 174 et seq.; Lehrmann, La communauté juive du Luxembourg, 61 et seq; Goedert, "L'émancipation de la communauté israélite luxembourgeoise", 366; Jacob Katz, "Samuel Hirsch: Rabbi, Philosopher and Freemason", Revue des études juives 125 (1966), 113–126.

Prior to Hirsch's appointment, only individual prospective rabbis who were passing through or who had come from the Prussian Rhine neighboring regions had preached in the Luxembourgish capital. After the establishment of the rabbinate, it was a regular occurrence there and occasionally in rural areas, as in the case of the consecration of the Ettelbruck synagogue or at funerals. After Hirsch's departure, prayer services were not modified until Isaac Blumenstein's appointment, coinciding with the opening of the capital's new synagogue in 1893. One of the innovations was the enhancement of prayer services by organ and choral music on a regular basis. The musical accompaniment itself did not constitute a reform however, since there had already been a choir that sang occasionally, at times backed by the organ. Interestingly, it was only after 1900 that any opposition to the musical accompaniment arose in the congregation.[82]

Mutual Mourning and Celebration in the Community

The religious lives of Jews in Luxembourg and the neighboring regions were not limited to prayer services; they also involved family celebrations such as weddings. In the first decades of the 19th century, these kinds of events often took place exclusively within the circle of the Jewish community, yet this did change gradually.[83] Up through the 1830s, Christians – above all street children and poorer residents – repeatedly disturbed Jewish funerals. However, it became established practice in the 1840s for the Christian public to attend Jewish mourning events in sympathy, at least when members of the upper class were concerned. For instance, the coffin of Cerf Godchaux, a Belgian state prosecutor from Luxembourg, was accompanied by a large group of people.[84] The same practice became common in the countryside after the construction of a local Jewish cemetery, for example in 1881 in Ettelbruck, when Léon Cahen "was carried to his grave escorted by much of the local community".[85]

---

[82] Israelitische Annalen 1, 25 (1839), 199. Der Orient, 4, 31 (1843), 244. AZJ 35, 10 (1871), 198. Dondelinger and Muller, "Jüdische Bevölkerung in Ettelbrück", part III, 26; Lehrmann, *La communauté juive du Luxembourg*, 53, 64–71, 127.
[83] Richarz, "Die Entdeckung der Landjuden", 18; Daltroff, *Juifs*, 39, 108, 135, 146.
[84] AZJ 8, 11 (1844), 159; Lehrmann, ibid., 32.
[85] AZJ 45, 49 (1881), 815.

There is evidence that Christians in the neighboring regions occasionally attended the wedding celebrations of their Jewish acquaintances at the end of the 19th century. Similarly, Christians sometimes took part socially in family celebrations in Luxembourg during that time: Christian dignitaries, fellow citizens and employees were also among the well-wishers at the golden wedding anniversaries of Jewish couples. For example, when the factory owner Samson Godchaux celebrated his 1887 wedding jubilee, a great deal of his staff participated and organized a program of celebratory activities.[86] In the case of civil marriages between Jewish couples and the registration of Jewish children in the birth registry or of deceased individuals in the death registry, Christian fellow citizens often appeared as witnesses. Although this action may only constitute participation in bureaucratic formalities, one can conclude that most Jews would not have been able to involve Christian citizens in these matters if relations between them had been highly fraught. It can therefore be assumed that Schuster, a day laborer from Medernach, enjoyed a good relationship with his Jewish fellow citizens, seeing that he appeared as a witness for the Jewish families Herz and Kahn at nine births, two marriages and one death.[87]

Jewish-Christian intermarriages were a rarity in Luxembourg and the neighboring regions until the late 19th century. They were viewed negatively by both Christians and Jews, not least because they often involved religious conversion (despite the possibility of a civil marriage). The marriage mid-century between a Catholic woman and a Jewish man living in the town of Strassen was an extraordinary case, especially considering the fact that she converted to Judaism for her husband.[88] Another piece of evidence that supports the view that intermarriages were met with little acceptance, is the observation that Jewish and Christian couples kept their relationships secret for the most part: in Lorraine, the number of children born outside of marriage to interreligious couples was higher than the number of marriages.[89] It was not until the end of the 19th century that

---

86 Landesarchiv Saarbrücken, Dep. Illingen, Nr. 33, 3–7; Der Israelit, supplement 28, 71 (1887), 1307.
87 Schoentgen, "Die jüdische Gemeinde in Medernach", 306 et seq.; Pies, *Jüdisches Leben im Rhein-Hunsrück-Kreis*, 70; Lang and Rosenfeld, *Histoire des Juifs en Moselle*, 254.
88 Luxemburger Wort 20, 1 (1867), 2; Francoise Job, *Les Juifs à Lunéville aux XVIIIe et XIXe siècles* (Nancy: Presse Université de Nancy, 1989), 262; Karl Heinz Debus, "Das Verhältnis zu den christlichen Religionsgemeinschaften", in Landesarchivverwaltung Rheinland-Pfalz, ed., *Dokumentation zur Geschichte der Juden in Rheinland-Pfalz und im Saarland*, vol. 4: *Das Verhältnis der Juden zu den christlichen Religionsgemeinschaften* (Koblenz: Landesarchivverwaltung Rheinland-Pfalz, 1974), 227–242, here 238.
89 For example, in 1818 in Prussian Gemünden, the relationship between a Christian woman and a Jewish man was only discovered after the birth of their child; the village community pun-

the number of intermarriages rose in the Rhine Province and Lorraine, although the phenomenon was concentrated in the large cities.⁹⁰

It has already been mentioned in the context of Christian-Jewish neighbor relations that small gifts were occasionally exchanged during specific celebrations. It should be emphasized here, however, that religious celebrations were of an ambivalent nature, as they could also provide an opportunity for conflict between members of the different religions. In contrast to neighboring regions, there was no violent form of ritualized anti-Judaism (such as the throwing of stones at synagogues during Easter week) before the 19th century due to the lack of continuous Jewish settlement in the Grand Duchy up until then. However, in the capital city of Luxembourg in the first decades of the 19th century, where Jews had also come to do business during the *Ancien Régime*, the custom of humiliating Jews through verbal abuse or similar acts lived on, in particular among children and the more impoverished sections of the Christian population.⁹¹ An event that took place in 1821 is worth mentioning here: Having been invited by a Catholic colleague, a Jewish teacher wanted to attend a Christian service on Easter. He ended up having to leave upon the sexton's request and "outside of the church, he was pursued by idlers who cursed and threatened him and threw stones at him".⁹² The Jewish community leadership protested to the township administration, aware of the danger that the entire Jewish community could be submitted to worse treatment in the future due to the "furor of prejudice"⁹³ held by one section of the Christian public. The subsequent police investigation came to the conclusion that the Jewish community's fears were unfounded.⁹⁴

In the SaarLorLux region in the 19th century, the consecration of a synagogue was an event followed by many of the Christian inhabitants; and by mid-

---

ishment was the banishment of the mother. Gemünden Catholic parish register, 1812–1931; Ravengiersburg Catholic parish register, Job, 261.
90 Segall, "Juden", ZDSJ 2, 10 (1906), 159; statistical article on marriages in Alsace-Lorraine from 1900–1906, ZDSJ 4, 4 (1908), 63.
91 Krier, "Les Juifs au Grand-Duché", 120 et seq; Goedert, "L'émancipation de la communauté israélite luxembourgeoise", 355 et seq.; Stefan Rohrbacher, *Gewalt im Biedermeier: Antijüdische Ausschreitungen in Vormärz und Revolution (1815–1848/49)*, Schriftenreihe des Zentrums für Antisemitismusforschung 1 (Frankfurt a. M.: Campus-Verlag, 1993), 50–53; Prefect councillor to the mayor of Boulay, 29.3.1818, ADM E-dépôt 100 3P1; Daltroff, *Juifs*, 135 f.
92 Goedert, "L'émancipation de la communauté israélite luxembourgeoise", 355 et seq.; Krier, "Les Juifs au Grand-Duché", 120 et seq.
93 Jewish community notables to the municipal administration of the city of Luxembourg, 26.4. 1821, ANL C639. In regard to the Jewish teacher, the Jewish community leadership thought that he had made a mistake in attending the service.
94 Police commissioner to the mayor of the city of Luxembourg, 29.4.1821, ANL C639.

century it was not uncommon for municipality representatives to participate. Everything generally went peacefully, but there were some conflicts: A synagogue consecration in Ettelbruck in 1870 in which the mayor took part and at which the local Philharmonic Society (whose members were of mixed religious backgrounds) provided musical accompaniment, afforded the Catholic pastor the opportunity to berate his parishioners in a sermon, calling upon them to renounce all contact with Jews. However, the priest's behavior was met with repudiation for the most part. His prohibition against the Philharmonic Society entering the church was considered particularly incomprehensible, as its members – including the Jews – had frequently helped to organize Christian celebrations.[95] The fact that the prevailing associations between Jews and Christians in Ettelbruck were sometimes considered bewildering and not at all self-evident by some Catholics is demonstrated by a commentary in the *Luxemburger Wort* claiming that Catholic participants at the consecration celebration were attempting to "dignify the religious celebrations of the Jewish religion"[96] through their involvement.

Life in Society: Between Integration and Independence

Based on the records of Jewish participation in society life in terms of politics and associations, it is possible to determine that there was some involvement as early as the mid-19th century, but that it was not until after that time that it intensified in any notable way.[97] The majority of Luxembourg's Jewish population did not demonstrate any political ambition in the 19th century. Most Jews retained their former citizenship for decades, meaning that they were unable to vote. In addition, the electoral procedure in the first half of the 19th century intermittently excluded the unprosperous majority of residents – Jews as well as Christians – from political participation. The Godchaux family, which supplied several town councillors and mayors, was an anomaly. While the Jewish town

---

95 AZJ 35, 24 (1871), 477; Luxemburger Wort 23, 304 (1870), 2.
96 Luxemburger Wort 23, 304 (1870), 2.
97 For a more detailed discussion, see Stephanie Schlesier, "Grenzüberschreitend: Juden in Luxemburg, ihre Kontakte in die Nachbarregionen und ihre Einbindung ins luxemburgische Leben im 19. Jahrhundert", in Norbert Franz and Jean-Paul Lehners, eds., *Nationenbildung und Demokratie: Europäische Entwicklungen gesellschaftlicher Partizipation*, Luxemburg-Studien / Études luxembourgeoises, vol. 2 (Frankfurt am Main: Peter Lang Edition, 2013), 171–192, here 177–192.

councillors were not a matter of complaint, there were some individuals on the Catholic side who expressed their discontent at Samson Godchaux being named mayor of Hamm. A section of the Catholic population as well as the government supported him against any challenges however, so it is clear that the Christian population did not reject Jews in political office as a rule.[98]

Members of the Jewish upper class gained entrance into the Luxembourgish Masonic lodges in the 1830s.[99] The Ettelbruck Philharmonic Society mentioned above was founded at the beginning of the 1850s and was an early example of the combined activities of Jews and Christians in a rural association. There were numerous secular associations in the capital of the Grand Duchy in the second half of the century, which made it possible for Jews to have social interactions with Christians, such as in the chorus, at shooting clubs, and at the casino. Jewish citizens were also sometimes the co-founders of associations of varying focus, including the "Public Company Theater Society of Luxembourg" whose aim it was to furnish the capital with a theater. Among its founders were Louis Godchaux and his father-in-law Gabriel Mayer. In Ettelbruck, Isaac Cahen advocated for the establishment of a local secondary school in the name of a parents' association.[100] In comparison to the capital, there were fewer opportunities in rural areas for Jews and Christians to come together in the context of a club or association, as more of the groups there were of a religious nature. At the end of the 19th century, however, gymnastics associations and shooting clubs increasingly provided the opportunity for social meet-ups, such as in the case of the gymnastics association established in 1894 in Ettelbruck.[101]

It is important to note that not all the religious associations were exclusively Catholic. The Jewish inhabitants of Luxembourg also maintained their own

---

98 Schlesier, "Grenzüberschreitend", 187 et seq.
99 According to Paul Rousseau's information, the declaration in the AZJ 8, 11 (1844), 158 – namely that the Luxembourgish Freemasons and the Prussian military lodges did not unite due to different attitudes concerning Jewish involvement – is not wholly correct; the different orders of both groups were not in agreement with one another regardless.
100 Fabien Godchaux, *Activités sociales*, https://godchaux-fe.pagesperso-orange.fr/page-7.html [accessed: 02.06.2022]; Ettelbruck parents' association, 18.10.1848, Scharff, Schmitt and Vikar Müllendorff to the general administrator of the interior, 20.10.1848, ANL H620.
101 Paul Cerf, "Les Juifs de Mondorf", in Martin Gerges, ed., *Mondorf, son passé, son présent, son avenir* (Luxembourg: Publications mosellanes, 1997), 309–312; Thilman, *La présence juive à Mondorf-les-Bains*, 70–74; Schoentgen, "Die jüdische Gemeinde in Medernach", 317; Arthur Muller, "Jüdische Bevölkerung in Ettelbrück", in Administration Communale d'Ettelbruck, ed., *Ettelbruck: 100 Joer Stad 1907–2007* (Ettelbruck: Administration communale, 2008), 267–272, here 270; Dondelinger and Muller, "Jüdische Bevölkerung in Ettelbrück", part III, 28–36.

societies or were involved in international Jewish organizations. A *Chevrah Kaddishah* – a pious association of men for the caring of the sick and the final services for the dead[102] – was founded by Rabbi Blumenstein, who was appointed in 1871. The entry "funeral costs" appears repeatedly in the Jewish congregation's account books, revealing that members of the Jewish congregation were already providing for the burials of their fellow members in the first half of the 19th century. Based on knowledge about neighboring regions, one can assume that there were informal *chevrot* whose members recited the *kaddish* for the dead in all rural areas with Jewish cemeteries.[103] Alongside the funeral brotherhood that was reserved for men in the capital city, there was a Jewish women's association. There was also a women's association in Ettelbruck that crafted a curtain for the local synagogue.[104]

It is unclear whether there was a specifically Jewish charitable society in the 19th century in Luxembourg, but it is certain that the Jewish congregation recorded sums dispersed to local members living in poverty as well as to wayfaring Jews.[105] The supposition that a Jewish institution for Jews in need existed at the beginning of the 20th century at the latest is supported by the founding of the "Lorraine and Luxembourg's Central Association of Jewish Migrant Welfare" in 1911 in Metz.[106] Even before that, transnationally active Jewish associations had already been established and Luxembourg Jews were participating in them. For instance, there was the "Society for the Promotion of the Arts and Trades among the Israelites of Metz", established in Lorraine in 1823 whereby a segment of the Jewish elite sought to make certain members of the community more productive. In the 1820s, Jews from cities in neighboring regions or countries participated in the society (which also had Christian dignitaries), among them five individuals from the Jewish upper class of Luxembourg. The members

---

102 Lehrmann, *La communauté juive du Luxembourg*, 71.
103 Budget de la synagogue paroissale des israélites à Luxembourg pour l'exercice 1833, ANL F149; Daltroff, *Juifs*, 155.
104 Lehrmann, ibid., 71. Dondelinger and Muller, "Jüdische Bevölkerung in Ettelbrück", part III, 28.
105 Budget de la synagogue paroissale des israélites à Luxembourg pour l'exercice 1833, ANL F149; Compte des recettes et des dépenses de la Communauté israélite pour l'exercice 1835, ANL E55.
106 Max Dienemann, "Die jüdischen Gemeinden in Elsaß-Lothringen 1871–1918", Zeitschrift für die Geschichte der Juden 7, 2 (1937), 77–85, here 85.

of the association who were not Lorrainese quickly lost interest however, and by 1844 there were no more members from abroad.[107]

The *Alliance Israélite Universelle*, founded in 1860 in Paris, was far more successful. Its aim was to assist oppressed Jews on a global scale, advocating for the rights of Jews in different countries and establishing schools for their "moral improvement". Eastern Europe and countries with a majority Muslim population constituted the main sphere of activity for the organization, which quickly outgrew its national framework and whose idea of civilization reflected a tendency of French imperialism.[108] Not all of its members were located in the capital of the Grand Duchy; it also attracted members from outside during the first 25 years of its existence, such as Joseph Cahen in Ettelbruck.[109] One way in which Jews demonstrated their support for the Alliance's concerns was through their willingness to donate. When the organization collected money in Europe in 1912 for the victims of anti-Jewish attacks in the Moroccan city of Fez, the Jewish congregations from Esch-sur-Alzette, Ettelbruck, and Luxembourg contributed.[110] Moreover, the Jewish couple Adèle and Albert Israel were active in the *Alliance*: they moved to Tangiers in the 1880s, where she worked as the director of the school at which they were both teachers.[111]

A Growing Closeness

The Jewish inhabitants of Luxembourg cultivated relationships with the Christian inhabitants in numerous spheres of life, partly based on necessity due to their limited number. Although relations appear to have been generally harmonious, there were also some instances of conflict. As a part of daily life, there was contact within the domestic realm, in trade, schools, and taverns. One element that separated the Jewish and Christian worlds was religious life, but even

---

107 Unterlagen der Gesellschaft und Schriftwechsel mit der französischen Verwaltung, 1823–1852, ADM M270; Société d'Encouragement pour les arts et métiers parmi les israélites de Metz, Metz 1844, 7–11.
108 Lisa Moses Leff, *Sacred Bonds of Solidarity: The Rise of Jewish Internationalism in Nineteenth-century France* (Stanford: Stanford University Press, 2006), 154–164; Hyman, *The Emancipation of the Jews of Alsace*, 83–90.
109 Central-comité der allgemeinen israelitischen Allianz, *Die allgemeine israelitische Allianz: Bericht des Central-comités über die ersten Fünfundzwanzig Jahre 1860–1885* (Berlin: Kauffman in Comm., 1885), 63–66; Bulletin de l'Alliance israélite universelle 1 (May 1862), 142.
110 Ost und West, 12, 7 (1912), 676.
111 Adèle and Albert Israel personnel files 1881–1898, Archiv der Alliance israélite universelle, côte Moscou 100–1–52/08 and 13.

there the separation was not total. Over the course of the 19th century, the boundaries between Jewish and Christian circles narrowed: Christian participation in Jewish family celebrations and obsequies became more frequent and there were individual cases of people of differing religions following or even helping to organize the other's religious celebrations. In addition, interdenominationally oriented associations provided Jews and Christians with the opportunity to socialize. The fact that there were Jewish associations should not be seen as a reaction to any exclusion on the part of the majority Christian society. They were analogous to the ecclesiastical associations whose existence did not strictly prevent the existence of non-religious associations. However, the fact that there was a good deal of contact did not mean that Jews always enjoyed a peaceful coexistence with their neighbors. Not everyone had a positive view of this growing closeness – as demonstrated by comments made in the *Luxemburger Wort* and the behavior of some of the Catholic clergy and sections of the Christian population.

Part V: **From Luxembourg to Philadelphia. Samuel Hirsch's Transnational Reform Judaism**

Thorsten Fuchshuber
"One Always Panders to the Basest Jew-Hatred". Samuel Hirsch, *Der Volksfreund* and *Luxemburger Wort*'s Campaign against Secularization and Jewish Emancipation 1848–50

Samuel Hirsch was not just a religious philosopher and important representative of the Jewish Reform movement in the mid-19th century;[1] he was also a passionate participant in the sociopolitical debates of his time. Hirsch desired a widespread audience for his opinions on pressing areas of social transformation and a daily publication would enable him to comment at will on the events of the day. It was therefore only logical for him to contribute to the founding and publication of a newspaper while in Luxembourg following the lifting of the censorship in 1848.

One of the most important issues for Hirsch was the progress of the emancipation movement, which was not only of existential importance for the Jews. He had a keen awareness of reactionary argumentation strategies that aimed to turn questions of general social relevance into mere "Jewish issues" with the goal of stigmatization. He moreover opposed attempts to blame the Jews for the failure of emancipation efforts, as his 1843 argumentative essay against the anti-Jewish polemics of the former Left Hegelian Bruno Bauer attests.[2]

Having arrived in Luxembourg from Dessau, Hirsch continued to be confronted with Jew-hatred. However, the political and social circumstances differed from those of the other parts of the German Confederation (*Deutscher Bund*), and the precise form of hostility against Jews was affected by those differences. First, after the end of Napoleonic rule in 1815 and under the subsequent reign of the King of the Netherlands as Grand Duke of Luxembourg, Jewish political and legal equality was not rescinded – in contrast to all other member states in the German Confederation. Second, Hirsch found himself in the Grand Duchy (which became independent in 1839) at a time when the local Catholic Church was struggling to preserve its considerable influence on government and society

---

[1] Cf. Christian Wiese's contribution in this publication.
[2] See Samuel Hirsch, *Das Judenthum, der christliche Staat und die moderne Kritik: Briefe zur Beleuchtung der Judenfrage von Bruno Bauer* (Leipzig: Heinrich Hunger, 1943) and the article by Judith Frishman in this volume.

during the era of transition from estate-based, feudal forms of commerce to bourgeois-capitalist structures. The clergy was thus also eager to use the newly won freedom of the press for its own interests. The *Luxemburger Wort für Wahrheit und Recht*, founded for that very purpose, often drew on anti-Jewish patterns of argumentation. These were met with strong criticism by Samuel Hirsch and his colleagues at *Der Volksfreund*.

In what follows I will document Samuel Hirsch's struggle against Jew-hatred in Luxembourg as reflected in the debates between the *Luxemburger Wort* and *Der Volksfreund* between March 1848 and December 1850.[3] Additionally, I will demonstrate how the Catholic Church's efforts to maintain power in a developing modern state provided an opportunity[4] for the articulation of anti-Jewish sentiments. While the sentiments are fundamentally irrational, they still served as a functional element within the Church's power struggle. Finally, I will elucidate the ongoing transformation of Jew-hatred that accompanied each and every change within societal rule in the 19th century.

Samuel Hirsch's Ultramontane Opponent

In order to better situate the context of the debate between the two papers it is necessary to recall the situation in the Grand Duchy of Luxembourg at mid-century. In 1848, the forces of the revolution were having an impact in many places around Europe. In France the revolts began in February; in the states of the German Confederation, including Luxembourg, the unrest ran its course in March. It was in that context that the Luxembourgish government announced an amend-

---

[3] My analysis encompasses all issues of Der Volksfreund from April 7, 1848 to June 29, 1849 (180 issues), as well as all issues of Luxemburger Wort from March 23, 1848 to December 29, 1850 (409 issues).

[4] The word "opportunity" is purposefully chosen here. This essay makes no attempt to "explain" the phenomenon of antisemitism. A critique of antisemitism must approach the matter in the manner discussed by Jean Améry in 1945 who posited that while antisemites could indeed be analyzed, they are far from being understood. Cf. Jean Améry, "Rasende Verbrecher" (Anhang zu *Jenseits von Schuld und Sühne*), in Gerhard Scheit, ed., *Jean Améry. Werke*, vol. 2 (Stuttgart: Klett-Cotta, 2002), 505–513, here 510. Every attempt at finding a rational "explanation" of a phenomenon that is irrational amounts to its rationalization. Thus, there is no way for light to be shed on antisemitism solely through the presentation of the context of its emergence. No direct correlation between cause and effect, between an event and the antisemitic reaction to it should therefore be assumed. Cf. Shulamit Volkov's claim: "Der Antisemitismus war keine direkte Reaktion auf reale Umstände." Shulamit Volkov, *Antisemitismus als kultureller Code: Zehn Essays* (Munich: Beck, 2000, 2nd edition), 25.

ment to the constitution on March 20th. Freedom of the press was also declared, which immediately led to the establishment of various newspapers. Just three days after the abolishment of censorship, the first edition of *Luxemburger Wort* was published on March 23, 1848. According to the editor's avowal, the paper counted "the issue of religion as not the most insignificant of the issues that affect the true welfare of the country".[5] Eduard Michelis, professor of dogmatic theology at the Luxembourg seminary, was chief editor and the driving force[6] behind the paper's publication. At this point in time, Michelis already had a remarkable career behind him: as the former privy secretary of the Archbishop of Cologne, he was one of the main protagonists in the 1837 Cologne dispute about mixed marriage. According to the historian Olaf Blaschke, this dispute represented a "strong turning point for the implementation of ultramontanism".[7] Michelis, who even spent time in a Prussian prison for his conviction, served as a symbol of political Catholicism and the ultramontane movement. This man was to become Samuel Hirsch's journalistic opponent.

Shortly after the advent of the *Luxemburger Wort*, the first edition of *Der Volksfreund* was published on April 7, 1848. Although Samuel Hirsch was not the sole founder of the paper,[8] he was supposedly the "actual editor".[9] Since there is no attribution of authorship to the individual contributions, it is generally difficult to identify for certain which texts were written by Hirsch. The debate between the two papers occurred at the same time as government circles were calling for the removal of Bishop Theodor Laurent, the Vicar Apostolic of Luxembourg. One of the accusations against him was that he had incited the March Revolution. Members of the government used this accusation to pressure King-Duke William II to dismiss the cleric, and with success: the monarch finally appealed to the Pope and on May 1, 1848, Laurent permanently left the country.

---

5 Luxemburger Wort 1 (23.03.1848), 2. In the so-called sample edition the editors note: "Wir achten und ehren jede Überzeugung, und werden uns nie erlauben, die religiöse Meinung eines Andern zu kränken oder zu beeinträchtigen. Wir werden Protestanten, Juden und Freimaurer friedlich neben uns bestehen lassen." ("We respect and honor all convictions and would never take license to offend or besmirch the religious opinion of others. We will countenance the peaceful coexistence of Protestants, Jews and Freemasons.") ibid.
6 See Pierre Grégoire, *Das Luxemburger Wort für Wahrheit und Recht: Die Geschichte einer Zeitung in der Geschichte eines Volkes* (Luxembourg: Sankt Paulus, 1936), 267.
7 Olaf Blaschke, *Katholizismus und Antisemitismus im Deutschen Kaiserreich* (Göttingen: Vandenhoeck & Ruprecht, 1997), 32.
8 Concerning the persons involved, see the article by Norbert Franz in this volume.
9 Romain Hilgert, *Zeitungen in Luxemburg 1704–2004* (Luxembourg: Service information et presse du gouvernement luxembourgeois, 2004), 64.

That dismissal represented a serious defeat for Luxembourg Catholicism. Just as in the case of Eduard Michelis, Laurent was a major figure in ultramontanism. He was above all a man who was attributed with the institutional renewal of the Catholic Church of Luxembourg (an organization that had been weakened by the French Revolution and Josephinism) and its tight tethering to Rome within a few years.[10] At this time Rome stood with Pope Pius IX for a forced ultramontanization of the Church and a "reactionary and emphatic anti-liberal course [...] in line with the traditional alliance between throne and altar".[11] So too in Luxembourg Laurent had no mind to stand back idly and watch the trend of increased secularization and the threat of the separation between Church and State.

For the *Luxemburger Wort*, the dismissal of the symbolic figure of Laurent was the prelude to its journalistic battle against any loss of influence by the Church after the March unrest. According to the newspaper, it was clear that the dismissal was due to the "persecution of the Catholic religion instigated by the Freemasons".[12] It was no coincidence that all the opponents named in the *Wort* could also be found in the ranks of *Der Volksfreund*. According to an official correspondence to the State Chancellor Friedrich Georg Baron von Blochausen in Den Haag dated March 30, 1848, the much-hated government – some of whose members had organized the attack against Laurent and ultramontanism – had suggested the founding of a newspaper.[13] According to that letter, after the lifting of the censorship, the government found itself confronted with an "all-round hostile press",[14] not least the *Luxemburger Wort*. This was clearly a situation that the government needed to change. Whether or not this set of events was indeed the reason for the foundation of *Der Volksfreund* will never be known. At any rate, there were several government officials working alongside Samuel Hirsch at the paper, including some of Hirsch's fellow masons.

Luxemburger Wort did not hold long to its assertions that it would "respect and honor" all convictions, and "never permit impeding or offending the reli-

---

10 See Georges Hellinghausen, *Kampf um die Apostolischen Vikare des Nordens J. Th. Laurent und C.A. Lüpke: Der Hl. Stuhl und die protestantischen Staaten Norddeutschlands und Dänemark um 1840* (Rome: Pontificia Università Gregoriana, 1987), 79.
11 Aram Mattioli, "'So lange die Juden Juden bleiben...': Der Widerstand gegen die jüdische Emanzipation im Grossherzogtum Baden und im Kanton Aargau (1848–1863)", in Olaf Blaschke and Aram Mattioli, eds., *Katholischer Antisemitismus im 19. Jahrhundert: Ursachen und Traditionen im internationalen Vergleich* (Zürich: Orell Füssli, 2000), 287–315, here 293.
12 Luxemburger Wort 16 (14.05.1848), 2.
13 See Hilgert, 62.
14 Cited in Hilgert, 62.

gious views of others", whether they be "Protestants, Jews or Freemasons".¹⁵ Barely a week after the first edition of *Der Volksfreund*, the *Luxemburger Wort* reported that the public was aware that the "Jew Rabbi Mr. Hirsch" was also among the publishers of the paper.¹⁶ The *Wort* further remarked that in its second edition *Der Volksfreund* had already begun to count the "gold threads in the liturgical gowns" of the Catholic Church and that the Bishop's income had not been cited accurately.¹⁷ *Der Volksfreund* reacted immediately. It criticized the *Wort* for making an issue out of an editor's personal background: "We are weaponless against this kind of polemic. We hope that our readers put great stock in what we provide, and that who we are will be of no importance to them."¹⁸

However, other Luxembourg newspapers also thought that it was of particular interest that Samuel Hirsch worked at *Der Volksfreund*. In the *Courrier du Grand-Duché de Luxembourg* on May 3, 1848 for example, an anonymous letter writer complained about how much Luxembourg had to suffer as a member of the German Confederation.¹⁹ In that context, the writer criticized a *Der Volksfreund* article about the upcoming National Assembly in Frankfurt am Main as being too German-friendly²⁰ and suspected that this love of Germany could stem from the fact that the author was probably not born in Luxembourg.²¹ *Der Volksfreund*'s reaction to this letter leaves little doubt that the anonymous letter writer's accusations were directed at Samuel Hirsch. At the end of a substantive debate on the relationship of Luxembourg to the German Confederation, comes a fiery speech against the lack of rights for Jews in the other German Confederation member states:

> At the end, the writer points to the German, not Luxembourgish, birth of the assumed composer of our article. We have the following to say to him in that man's name: Luxembourg suffered from the German Confederation only in that it too suffered from the collective pressure on all German countries. This man, however, suffered from something else in particular: up until a few weeks ago,²² he belonged to those pariahs of the whole society of Ger-

---

15 Luxemburger Wort 1 (23.03.1848), 2.
16 Luxemburger Wort 7 (13.04.1848), 2.
17 Ibid.
18 Der Volksfreund 3 (14.04.1848), 2.
19 Courrier du Grand-Duché de Luxembourg 38 (03.05.1848), 2.
20 Cf. Der Volksfreund 7 (28.04.1848), Extrablatt.
21 "[...] l'amour pour votre chère Allemagne à laquelle vous avez, en naissant, tendu une main qui n'était peut-être pas Luxembourgeoise [...]." Courrier du Grand-Duché de Luxembourg 38 (03.05.1848), 2.
22 The County of Hessen-Homburg had granted Jews voting rights and full legal equality on March 6, 1848; other German Confederation member states followed suit over the course of

many who have no rights. For him, Luxembourg was the only green oasis in the sad desert of rightlessness and shame. Reason enough for him to love his new fatherland that has adopted him, above all and with all the thankfulness of which he is capable. Also reason enough for him to foster less sympathy than any for the German Confederation.[23]

Threats of Violence and Pogroms

While the tone was kept conciliatory in the above response to the letter writer's allusions to Samuel Hirsch, Joseph Seelhof, one of the editors of *Der Volksfreund*, lost his composure in his reply to a *Luxemburger Wort* article a few days later: "Oh you ignominious newspaper! What righteous man, what honorable citizen, for whom the maintenance of inner calm must be so dear in these unsettling times, can read such distasteful things. Things that would disgust any free man, written in the guise of a correspondence article from Vienna, aimed at stirring up the uneducated class and perhaps inciting them to all kinds of dishonorable violent acts!"[24]

Seelhof's enraged outburst might be astonishing at first glance – but his intense reaction was triggered by his immediate recognition of the perfidious method that the *Luxemburger Wort* would use in the coming months and years for anti-Jewish muckraking and the incitement of pogroms. The essence of this simple method consisted of presenting texts with antisemitic content as alleged reprints from foreign newspapers. On May 7, 1848, the paper applied this technique for the first time when reporting on an anti-Jewish pogrom in Pressburg (present day Bratislava) in a short announcement. Many had died according to the article – but the article also included the supposed cause of the pogrom:

> The persecution of the Jews is due to those Jewish youth and Jewish rabbis without faith who, due to their watered-down Enlightenment, are abhorred by their own coreligionists, and who are always getting involved in the affairs of Christians, writing newspapers, and insulting and vilifying the Christian religion.[25]

One recognizes in the above the use of a rhetorical figure that forms a classic topos ubiquitous in modern antisemitism: the Jews are themselves responsible

---

the year. These rights were at least in part officially repealed with the counter-revolution and the legal discrimination of Jews was reimplemented in several of the Confederation's countries.
23 Der Volksfreund 9 (05.05.1848), 7.
24 Der Volksfreund 10 (09.05.1848), 3.
25 Luxemburger Wort 14 (07.05.1848), 5 et seq.

for the hatred of Jews.[26] The text most notably contains the barely veiled threat of what should be expected by a "Jewish rabbi" who gets involved in social debates that are ultimately solely the "affairs of Christians". Samuel Hirsch understood that threat very well. In one of his rarely signed texts, he exposed the truth behind this report that was supposedly reprinted from another newspaper: "There is no rabbi writing in a newspaper in Pressburg or anywhere else in Hungary."[27] Concerning the anti-Jewish threat itself, he appealed to his fellow citizens' good sense: "Incidentally, I confidently put myself and my family, as well as all my Jewish coreligionists, under the protection of my fellow Luxembourgish citizens! You are too honorable and too good willed to tolerate any of the incitement for scenes such as those in Hungary here."[28]

Consequently, Hirsch remained highly sensitive about who was preparing to make common cause with "the party" – "in fact a Catholic party" – involved in the *Luxemburger Wort*.[29] On May 10th therefore, he wrote an "open missive"[30] "in the morning hours"; it was a passionate indictment of the lawyer Charles Théodore André. In 1848, André was known as "the red André", whose "call to the workers of the country of Luxembourg" was regarded as the "birth of the Luxembourgish workers' movement".[31] Although he and Hirsch were friends, André had distanced himself from him and migrated over to the Catholic milieu.[32] At least that was what Hirsch feared. He suspected that André wanted to be elected Luxembourg Delegate to the Frankfurt National Assembly at any cost. Known for his impulsive reactions,[33] Hirsch accused André of treason: "I therefore charge you of betraying that which is holy to the workers; you have sold their free-

---

26 The cited text from the *Luxemburger Wort* includes a whole range of anti-Jewish arguments: The Enlightenment, clearly a societal development, is attributed to and identified with the Jews in whom it is personified. Moreover, they are reproached for embracing the faithless, Godless and corrosive field of journalism and even accused of scoffing at Christianity. The latter is a traditional, age-old motif of Christian anti-Judaism: hatred incurred upon the Jews as Jews because of their refusal to recognize Christ as the Messiah.
27 Der Volksfreund 10 (09.05.1848), 3.
28 Ibid.
29 Der Volksfreund 11 (12.05.1848), 2.
30 It is signed with "H" (Der Volksfreund 11 (12.05.1848), 3), presumably standing for Hirsch. In any event the contents of the missive seem to point to Samuel Hirsch as author.
31 *Luxemburger Autorenlexikon*, Gast Mannes' entry for Charles Théodore André. http://www.autorenlexikon.lu/page/author/766/766/DEU/index.html, last consulted on 05.05.2022.
32 Hirsch's article indicates that the two were planning to found a liberal association whose program Hirsch was to design. Hirsch records André's reaction as follows: "… and when I had designed the program and wanted to present it to them, they simply did not show up; they were evasive …" (Der Volksfreund 11 (12.05.1848), 2).
33 Cf. the article by Michael A. Meyer in this volume.

dom."³⁴ The primary reason for this reaction, however, was not a disappointing friendship:³⁵ Behind André's lack of principles, which according to Hirsch was responsible for his migration over to the "Catholic party", the Rabbi recognized above all a willingness to once again accept Jew-hatred as a negligible societal problem, or in any event not a problem that concerned non-Jews:

> Thus you let the workers – who wish to gain equality for themselves, and whose cause is only fair and viable if there are no slaves among us, no more pariahs – form an alliance with a party that could not exist without pariahs and zealots, without slaves, and the very least without the Jews as slaves. It is a party that preached mass murder and destruction in May 1848 because Jews considered the affairs of Christians to be their own affairs! Is this the fraternization of people, the foundation of all the efforts for the working class? You, sir, are permitting the workers to make an alliance with a party whose every third word is Jewish youth and Jewish rabbis; that rants about 'the Enlightenment' and calls it 'watered-down'; a party that would like to re-institute ghettos and locked gates, the identificatory yellow badge, and body tax (*Thorgeld*) for the Jews, who aside from a few nabobs have had an even worse fate than the workers in society thus far. For according to this party's political creed, all political affairs of this world are exclusively the affairs of Christians and any Jew who dares to involve himself in Christian affairs will be massacred.³⁶

Hirsch thus left no doubt that he thought it necessary to combat the clergy active in Luxembourg who were "opponents of all freedom and education of humankind",³⁷ and whose position could in short be understood as "Jesuitism" and thus contrary to Catholicism.³⁸

The *Luxemburger Wort* did not appear affected in any way by the accusations of inciting anti-Jewish sentiments. In fact, in its May 14, 1848 issue, it published

---

34 Der Volksfreund 11 (12.05.1848), 2.
35 The conflict clearly included this dimension as well. In the opening of his accusation Hirsch writes: "But you ask, who is he? Who is this plaintiff? ... It is he who has loved and respected you for years. And do you know why he loved you? Because already at our first meeting three years ago you grasped the problem of the working class and like me were convinced that the working class must gain its rights; ..." (Der Volksfreund 11 (12.05.1848), 2).
36 Ibid.
37 Ibid.
38 Ibid., 2f. In the same article Hirsch notes that "Catholic is an ecclesiastical and therefor a holy name. Catholic for me implies distance from the world and its affairs. The epithet Catholic represents love. But that party sows poison and hatred. Its motto is: defamation and besmirching of a good reputation" (Der Volksfreund 11 (12.05.1848), 2). Eight days later he adds: "Until recently we too considered the episcopal party to be sincere. However, since they have ceased opposing us with spiritual arms and instead have encouraged the people to literally kill us ... preach none other than hate against religious denominations ... yet consider none of this to be beneath their dignity, we can no longer deem them worthy of the esteem of any self-respecting person" (Der Volksfreund 13 (20.05.1848), 3).

an entire series of articles with anti-Jewish invectives; some were directed specifically at Samuel Hirsch, attacking the "Jewish Rabbi Herr Hirsch"[39] by name, no longer bothering with anonymity. As for the accusation that they had fabricated accounts in the abovementioned article on the anti-Jewish pogroms in Pressburg, the *Wort* writes "concerning the cause of the persecution of Jews that has broken out in all areas":

> It [*Der Volksfreund*; T.F.] believes that we invented the reasons provided. If *Der Volksfreund* so wishes, we are ready to print ten articles from various newspapers on the sinister activities committed by the badly enlightened Jews. Among others, an article from a Dutch paper concerning the activities of enlightened Jews with which our writer from the so-called *Volksfreund* is perhaps familiar. There is also mention of a Jew in Luxembourg in it. [...] There is no doubt that aside from some other known causes, the impudent and knavish language of watered-down Enlightenment that Jewish youths and Jewish rabbis have used against the Christian religion has significantly contributed to the doubling of the hatred of the people against the entire Jewish population, which is to a large part innocent of its leaders' wicked activities.[40]

In another article in the same issue, the *Wort* even escalates its threat against the "Jewish Rabbi Mr. Hirsch": "We can only acquiesce if the Jewish rabbi promises to no longer involve himself in Christian affairs, that would be first of all and above all in his own interests."[41] Subsequent to this overt threat, the *Luxemburger Wort* plays on Hirsch's membership in the Freemasons, presumably to link him to the rumors of their supposed conspiratorial plans for world domination that were circulating in the 19th century: "We will not disturb his peace and will simply leave it to his congregation to decide whether or not they wish to be content with his participation in the Freemasons."[42]

The following issue of *Der Volksfreund* published a response (most likely written by Samuel Hirsch) to the allusion made by *Luxemburger Wort* to Jews or Freemasons respectively as exchangeable protagonists of a conspiracy. In a few short words, the author demonstrated that there was indeed a link between Jews and Freemasons, albeit a rationalist and humanist one:

---

[39] Luxemburger Wort 16 (14.05.1848), 1. In the issue of *Der Volksfreund* of May 9th Joseph Seelhof, co-editor, criticized the pejorative nature of the pleonasm "Jewish rabbi" and noted: "Who will not recall this stylistically incorrect expression, that has solely and frequently been employed by our lying press (meaning the *Luxemburger Wort* whose full name bears the words "for Truth and Justice"- T.F.) To which author may this be attributed? Let the reader judge for himself" (Der Volksfreund 10 (09.05.1848), 3).
[40] Luxemburger Wort 16 (14.05.1848), 1.
[41] Ibid.
[42] Ibid.

> A Jew can be a Jew and a Freemason with all his heart, and do you know why? Because the Jewish religion and Freemasonry share the same objective when it comes to their confessors: unlimited philanthropy, without regard for belief, class or nationality. To set up a temple in which God dwells and that includes every person as a building block. That is why a famous rabbi in a large and famous area of Germany has named Judaism the revealed Freemasonry and Freemasonry the secret Judaism.[43]

"A Higher Equality"

There are additional articles, presumably written by Samuel Hirsch, in which the rabbi attempts to shed light on his concept of the Jewish religion and its reconcilability with Christianity, the Enlightenment and the contemporary emancipation movements. So too a two-part article published under the title "Thoughts of a Sleepwalker" (*"Gedanken eines Nachtwandlers"*):

> That which once drove Christ to sacrifice himself for the salvation of humankind, this divine-human trait, which was personalized in Christ and which filled his entire being [...] the same divine-human trait lies at the core of every human being, it is just underdeveloped; it strives towards its own development and evolution. [...] Christ, this archetype for humankind, should take shape in every individual.
> This one truth is not only acknowledged by every person – whether he be called Jew or Christian (for only the form, if you will, only the name separates today's Jews from today's Christians. The Christian's understanding of Christ as the example and archetype of all that is sublime and divine is the same as the Jew's understanding of the pure image of God to which he is called to aspire: the two are one and the same) – it is the truth that determines the life story of every person.[44]

In the second part of his text Hirsch broadens his argument, approaching it from a religio-historical perspective regarding notions of egalitarian principles. The idea that all human beings are equal had been completely foreign to the "old paganism", while pre-Christian Judaism had basically recognized this concept. Christianity, however, was the first to make the "great concept of the equality of all people a more general one".[45] Hirsch notes, however, that in this so-called first period "equality existed solely in religious spheres [...], while class distinctions dominated in the secular areas".[46] The second period had thus begun at

---

43 Der Volksfreund, 12 (16.05.1848), 2.
44 Der Volksfreund, 40 (06.08.1848), 1.
45 Der Volksfreund, 46 (20.08.1848), 2.
46 Ibid.

the end of the 18th century and more specifically with the French Revolution: "It is the period of governmental equality, equality before the law."[47]

While many considered this the non plus ultra of all possible progress, the article's writer considered this view erroneous. "Humanity", he averred, "can no more retire at this stage of political equality than it could at religious equality or than it could at the inequality of paganism; the concept of equality must instead be realized completely and totally, as in the case of every global historical concept."[48] Hirsch remarked further that even political equality would not yet mean that every person's "abilities and assets" could be fully developed.

> That is the goal of today's movement. Behind equality before the law, there is a higher equality that must be attained. Even if all socialist systems created up until now are utopias and thus impracticable, that does not change the fundamental question. It is not possible for equality to halt at the political level any more than it was able to halt at the religious level; it must become whole and real.[49]

Hirsch made it clear that the clerical politics, as propagated by the *Luxemburger Wort*, were diametrically opposed to that goal. In a three-part article series entitled "Intolerance and Tolerance", he wrote that the "Jesuit Catechism" projected an image of people as a "cadaver, a corpse with no will" while "today's popular movement" believes in the enlightenment of human beings and assumes "that people will not always have to be under police supervision, that that was only for the notorious criminal".[50]

He described the clerical milieu of Luxembourg as a "system completely dependent on medieval intolerance".[51] "One can see that the system is fighting for its sovereignty, and it fights well, it is only that the weapons are a bit rusty."[52] In so saying, Hirsch knew full well that Jew-hatred was one of those rusty weapons the Luxembourg clergy were using to maintain power and to establish the developing Luxembourg state as a theocratic one. The Catholic anti-Judaism expressed in the *Luxemburger Wort* at that time was rusty because it ignored the fact that legal and political equality had long been a reality there, in contrast to most of the other states of the German Confederation. The usual polemic, namely that Jews were neither worthy nor capable of equality, thus failed to take hold. Hirsch intimates this in the article cited:

---

47 Ibid.
48 Ibid.
49 Ibid.
50 Der Volksfreund, 55 (10.09.1848), 1.
51 Ibid.
52 Ibid.

[...] in our country, where civil institutions have sanctioned the equality of all people before the law for fifty years now, notwithstanding any difference in belief and where this equality sanctioned by law has passed over into the morals of our honest and lawfully minded people, any intolerance or mistrust based on faith ... is simply an anachronism.[53]

A reading of the *Luxemburger Wort* allows us to observe the attempts to give anti-Judaism's "rusty weapons" a contemporary polish. Misunderstood social phenomena and processes of transformation – some resulting in fundamental social changes – were identified as "Jewish".[54] This development from traditional anti-Judaism to what is described today as modern antisemitism must be understood as a consequence of social change that affected all social phenomena as well as forms of thought and consciousness – thereby also influencing the form of Jew-hatred.

New Strategies of Anti-Jewish Practices

One may simultaneously observe how actively new strategies for effective anti-Jewish practices were sought. In the case discussed here, the enemies of the Jews were trying to circumvent the fact that so-called "Jewish emancipation" – the legal and political equality of the Jews in Luxembourg – had long been realized. Any attempt to use the methods of agitation most common in the other states of the German Confederation to prevent such emancipation, could have no real damaging effect. Therefore, although Jews were formally capable of participating in society, their adversaries increasingly aimed to hinder any productive participation on their part. They commenced to argue that now that the Jewish people had been granted equal rights, they were planning on usurping all the institutions essential to community life, be they economic, social or national. All of the extant, well-established institutions (shaped not least by Christianity and

---

53 Ibid.
54 The fundamental transformation of traditional anti-Judaism into modern antisemitism can be observed here: All the phenomena of modernity that, unlike relations of personal dominion, can no longer be directly grasped, and seemingly exist only in abstract principles, remain unexplained. Antisemitism unmasks all of them as "Jewish": be it capitalism and liberalism, be it communism, be it Enlightenment and Freemasonry. Antisemitism turns into an explanatory model of the world, an "everyday religion" (*Alltagsreligion*), seemingly providing an explanation for all these inscrutable social phenomena. So too Detlev Claussen states: "It is bourgeois society that turns into the antisemitic society par excellence." Detlev Claussen, *Aspekte der Alltagsreligion: Ideologiekritik unter veränderten gesellschaftlichen Verhältnissen* (Frankfurt am Main: Verlag Neue Kritik, 2000), 124 f.

Catholicism in Luxembourg) were to that end being robbed of their substance: "corroded", "diluted", "destroyed".

The *Luxemburger Wort* presents the Enlightenment as one of the methods used in this "Jewish strategy". The danger of this Enlightenment, identified as essentially Jewish, is a recurring motif in the *Luxemburger Wort* – as is the personification of both phenomena in Samuel Hirsch. As noted above, in the May 14, 1848 edition, the *Wort* wrote that the "impudent and knavish language that Jewish youths and Jewish rabbis with a diluted form of Enlightenment" employed made them responsible for the anti-Jewish pogroms. The same issue included the following quote from the book *Athanasius* by the Catholic journalist Joseph Görres:

> Judaism also had to spume that garlic-like sharpness, which the depravity of modern times breeds in the blood of the most degenerate in its midst. And as often as this spirit spills out over something time-honored, this knavishness finds, alongside numerous silent worshippers, those among the rabble who shout out their approval.[55]

The *Luxemburger Wort* expanded on the above with the following statement: "The readers will easily be able to apply this to the so-called *Volksfreund*."[56] The "depravity", which is descending with the "modern times" upon that which is "time-honored" is thus, according to Görres – and particularly to the *Luxemburger Wort* – of a "Jewish" nature. Since Samuel Hirsch published in *Der Volksfreund* and, as far as the authors of the *Luxemburger Wort* were concerned, the liberal paper stood for the Enlightenment and secularization, without further ado *Der Volksfreund* itself was also identified as "Jewish". Not only did they write in general about the "*Schmutzblätter* (smutty papers) edited by Jews, Protestants and Freemasons",[57] they also commented about the formerly independent *Echternacher Grenzbote* upon its merging with the *Der Volksfreund*: "You already had half-Jewish flesh on you that was not entirely kosher, and now – oh, I really fear for you."[58]

An attack allegedly directed at Samuel Hirsch can also be found in the following text:

> Long enough have we been mocked by a Jew, and that which we hold most dear and holy has been spoken of in such impudent and provocative ways that we will suffer it no longer.

---

55 Luxemburger Wort 16 (14.05.1848), 1.
56 Ibid.
57 Luxemburger Wort 39 (03.08.1848), 2.
58 Ibid.

> Fellow citizens! Let us show in the next election that *Der Volksfreund* has not yet succeeded at turning us into Jews.[59]

The sociologist Detlev Claussen understands this link between antisemitism and the Enlightenment, which is also observable in the *Luxemburger Wort*, in the following way: "Antisemitic practice and the rejection of the Enlightenment coincide."[60] Therefore, it is not that a hatred of Jews continued despite the Enlightenment, it is more that antisemitism represents the limits of the Enlightenment's implementation. Antisemitism is an indication of a failed, incomplete process of Enlightenment. It is, as Margherita von Brentano accurately phrased it, an index of the failure of social emancipation.[61] Antisemitism, therefore, is "a moment in the social process that can only be isolated artificially", Detlev Claussen concludes.[62] As this process demonstrates, the societal subconscious, articulated in anti-Jewish obsession, merged with the functional aspect of hostility against Jews: in this case as an instrument in the Catholic Church's struggle for the maintenance of power in light of Luxembourg's developing modern state. So too in its November 19, 1848 issue the *Luxemburger Wort* attacked the founding of *Der Volksfreund*, which allegedly occurred at the government's initiative. The *Wort* accuses the *Volksfreund* of the "most hollow Enlightenment" and exclaims: "and that the government selects such a paper as its organ!"[63] Religion, it claims, must "always and under every circumstance be sacred to the government". But with the *Volksfreund*'s and Samuel Hirsch's significant participation, the Luxembourg government surely had the "undermining of religion and morality" in mind: "Are not Jews and Protestants hired to defile the faith of the Luxembourgish people, a faith preserved with fidelity and valor by our fathers, and to trample it into the dust?"[64]

In the November 24th issue, the *Luxemburger Wort* reinforced the point that the Catholic Church was a "legal [...] force" alongside the state, but that the latter

---

59 Luxemburger Wort 58 (17.09.1848), 1.
60 Detlev Claussen, *Grenzen der Aufklärung: Die gesellschaftliche Genese des modernen Antisemitismus* (Frankfurt am Main: Fischer, 2005, expanded new edition), x.
61 "Antisemitism is an index of the failure of emancipation and liberalism to realize the ideals of the Enlightenment and the revolution, namely liberty, equality and fraternity rather than a measure of the partial difficulties of one specific group in relationship to the whole of society." Margherita von Brentano, *Akademische Schriften* (Göttingen: Wallstein, 2010), 249. Cf. Shulamit Volkov, *Die Juden in Deutschland 1780–1918* (München: Oldenbourg Wissenschaftsverlag, 2000, 2nd corrected edition), 106.
62 Claussen, *Grenzen der Aufklärung*, 66.
63 Luxemburger Wort 84 (19.11.1848), 1.
64 Ibid.

had "undermined its own foundation" by fighting against the power of the Church: "By tolerating and encouraging the degradation of respect for Church authority and the unpunished vilification and blasphemy against the Most Holy, it [the state; T.F.] has compromised its own authority. What can save us from such hopeless circumstances? Only a return to the Church."[65]

The Impersonal State

The state is thus accused here (among other things) of encouraging the damage inflicted upon the Church's authority by Samuel Hirsch and others, but also of having undermined its own authority in the process. From a socio-theoretical perspective, the transformation into a so-called modern state – which the *Luxemburger Wort* had depicted as a threat of total disintegration – must be seen in the context of the universalization of the production of commodities. The circulation of commodities and money became the leading principle of societal relations. The fact that the capitalist mode of production, as abstract and anonymous as it seems, can only work because everyone actively participates in this form of socialization based on wage labor and private property, remained and remains misunderstood. On an individual level of experience, the developing modern state thus appeared faceless, impersonal, and unprincipled to many of Hirsch's contemporaries. Where once decisions were left to the personal whims of the sovereign – who, however was at least visible and nameable – it was increasingly about the inhuman rule of material constraints, as articulated by the impersonal bureaucratic character of the modern state, the "rule of the office", as the *Luxemburger Wort* called it.[66] While these above-characterized relations fail to be understood, antisemitic delusion (as it can be observed here avant la lettre[67]) finds itself certain of the truth about the changing world: it traces these incomprehensible, apparently abstract-inhuman relations back to the alleged conspiratorial power of the Jews. It is they who purportedly dominate or are striving to dominate the economy – not to mention the modern secularizing

---

65 Luxemburger Wort 86 (24.11.1848), 1.
66 Luxemburger Wort 87 (26.11.1848), 1.
67 The term "antisemitism" as used today was popularized by the Berlin journalist Wilhelm Marr in 1879. Marr, who proudly characterized himself as an "anti-Semite", used the word as a battle term that could replace the outdated, religiously grounded term anti-Judaism. "Antisemitism" transformed Jew-hatred into a seemingly "universalist" concept and therefore "rational" political form and "social problem".

state – and that is why they are responsible for the "decomposition" of traditional structures.

In the context of a debate about a new constitution, the *Luxemburger Wort* wrote as early as May 1848 "by means of the new constitution a meaningless minority in the country is (trying to gain) a lawful dominating influence on the Catholic Church". Not only do "these people stipulate freedom and independence from every religion for themselves, they also no longer want to recognize the Catholic religion as the leading religion of the country". Moreover, they also want "Jews, Protestants and Freemasons to have the right to exercise the highest state offices".[68] If from an economic perspective the Jews had become the agents and dominators of the now universal circulation of commodities and money, considered the essence of the capitalist mode of production,[69] then from a political perspective they were envisioned as being the power seeking to usurp the state as an instrument of domination, and along with this state – and the money – one more abstract medium: the law.

In 1848 and the beginning of 1849, there are examples of this train of thought in the *Luxemburger Wort*. They coincide timewise with a few important debates on the sovereignty of the state, that were also conducted in the two newspapers examined here. In addition to the new constitution, there were primarily discussions about educational authority for primary schools and the future financing of religious communities. All three topics were important areas in the debate about the separation of Church and State. For example, when the new constitution was adopted on July 9, 1848, an article in the *Luxemburger Wort* on June 1, 1848 criticized the secularizing measures associated with the draft of the constitution as comprising the "subjugation of the Church". In addition, they explain that *Der Volksfreund*'s standpoint on the constitution draft is "the long since superseded position of the Old Testament intermingled with modern superficialities"[70] – in other words: a Jewish standpoint.

There are more articles in which legal aspects of social secularization are traced back to an allegedly "Jewish" influence. In an article on "The Education Act and the Demands of the Catholic Church" from September 3, 1848, the *Wort* claims regarding *Der Volksfreund:*

> It would seem that those newspaper articles coming from those rotten Jews – articles that cast their disgusting spawn out across all the lands – have also found a permanent insti-

---

68 Luxemburger Wort 19 (25.05.1848), 1.
69 The *Luxemburger Wort* pointed to England as an example of exploitive "Handelsjuden" (Luxemburger Wort 41 (05.04.1850), 2).
70 Luxemburger Wort 21 (01.06.1848), 3.

tution here in the respectable lands of Luxembourg through which they can spread their filth and slime out over our pastures.⁷¹

During the remaining months of 1848, Samuel Hirsch's stamp was infrequently detectable in the *Volksfreund* articles and responses to the attacks of *Luxemburger Wort* were rare. Nevertheless, the latter continuously returned to the topos of identifying the *Der Volksfreund* and other liberal newspapers (along with the standpoints associated with them) as "Jewish".⁷² To that end, they made use of the three elements discussed above: alongside direct anti-Jewish attacks, they resorted to anti-Jewish citations from well-known authors,⁷³ as well as anti-Jewish articles that were supposedly or actually derived from other newspapers. According to Samuel Hirsch and the *Der Volksfreund* however, these articles had clearly been "forged" by the *Luxemburger Wort* itself.⁷⁴

This relentlessly constructed identification of Jews with liberalism and republicanism, with secularization and the emancipation movement, with the Enlightenment and the press, was then instrumentalized as a "warning" with respect to Luxembourg. While rhetorical figures were often used when directly referencing Luxembourg, thus requiring the readers to have a certain skill in the translation of antisemitic codes,⁷⁵ Jew-hatred was expressed bluntly in the texts and book citations characterized as "correspondence articles". That was the case in an issue of the *Luxemburger Wort* from June 1, 1848 already cited above in a report on the unrest in Vienna, which was supposedly instigated "primarily by Jewish literati": "almost no one but Jews are at the top of the political central committee"; it is "Jewish" editors who dared to "proclaim the Republic"

---

71 Luxemburger Wort 52 (03.09.1848), 1.
72 So too in in the July 9, 1848 issue the *Echternacher Grenzbote* is described as "filled with cursing and mocking like the Jews" (Luxemburger Wort 32 (09.07.1848), 2).
73 The Freiburger lawyer Joseph von Buß is quoted as saying: it is the "ludicrous press, made ludicrous by the Jews", that "by eternally singing the praises of emancipation ... have ruined our good people and slowly led to its death" (Luxemburger Wort 48 (25.08.1848), 2).
74 Der Volksfreund 10 (09.05.1848), 3.
75 According to Shulamit Volkov, as a cultural code, antisemitism has not only become a permanent aspect of language: by means of simple intimations or reference to familiar symbols an "entire system of ideas and attitudes" is transmitted (Volkov, *Antisemitismus als kultureller Code*, 23). Nicoline Hortzitz points to the mimetic elements in the language of the Jew-hater: "In texts anti-Jewish 'historical images of Jews' are often implied." All are "intended to be persuasive in so far as they desire to influence those addressed and aim at consensus between the writer/speaker and the reader/audience". See Nicoline Hortzitz, "Die Sprache der Judenfeindschaft", in Julius H. Schoeps and Joachim Schlör, eds., *Bilder der Judenfeindschaft: Antisemitismus – Vorurteile und Mythen* (München: Piper, 1995), 19–40, here 20. Antisemitism as a cultural code is a "sign of belonging" and thereby forms identity (Volkov, *op. cit.*, 69).

and "Jewish money that is freely distributed to students and workers". A threat of consequences – allegedly in reference to Vienna – was noted as follows:

> The persecution of this godforsaken race is unfortunately! inevitable here as well; but they [the Jews; T.F.] must also admit that they have invited this storm over their own heads. Devoid of any religious belief, avaricious, selfish and intrusive, they only use their talents and money to cause embarrassment to both themselves and us everywhere.[76]

Once again, it is "the Jews" who are made responsible for their own suffering. The alleged avarice refers to the accusations of usury, and the alleged selfishness to the fidelity to biblical law for which they are reproached. At times *Der Volksfreund* resigned itself to such vehement and persevering anti-Jewish defamation. However, in the July 7, 1848 issue the following statement was published in reaction to anti-Jewish articles:[77] "One always panders to the basest Jew-hatred, invoking it with the greatest possible force, because it – thank God – cannot be found among our good people. To fight against such crudeness would be a vain endeavor indeed!"[78]

Polemic Concerning Hirsch's Income

Over the further course of *Der Volksfreund*'s publicist battle against the *Luxemburger Wort*, Samuel Hirsch spoke up personally one last time when the polemic against his supposedly excessive income as rabbi refused to draw to a close. In May 1848, the *Luxemburger Wort* had already written in the context of the secularization debate: "Notwithstanding his [Samuel Hirsch; T.F.] limited activities, Christians have paid him a disproportionally high wage, to which he would certainly have difficulty laying claim in a constitutional state."[79] By referencing familiar motifs such as "disproportionally high wage" and "limited activities" in the formulation of the above claim, the *Wort* is counting on anti-Jewish resentment of the Jews' "parasitic existence". As the historian Olaf Blaschke demonstrates with reference to Shulamit Volkov, Jew-hatred already functioned as a cultural code in ultramontane Catholicism. Samuel Hirsch, who naturally recog-

---

76 Luxemburger Wort 21 (01.06.1848), 4. The article is signed at the bottom with "(Süddeutsche Ztg.)".
77 This time referring to an article in the *Diekircher Wochenblatt*.
78 Der Volksfreund 27 (07.07.1848), 4.
79 Luxemburger Wort 16 (14.05.1848), 1.

nized the anti-Jewish nature of the claim, reacted very tersely initially. Two days after the article was published, *Der Volksfreund* countered the *Luxemburger Wort*:

> And how do you know that the local rabbi has so little to do? In any case, he has not found time to preach misanthropy, or to go around to homes carrying petitions; instead, he preaches every week and teaches religion every day, so that the youth can grow up to be civilized and, above all, to have love for all people regardless of faith.[80]

However, as the attacks relentlessly continued and were published in other newspapers as well, Hirsch found it necessary to come out with a position statement in his own name in November of the same year:

> The *Luxemburger Wort* has often threatened me with a wage reduction, and now so does the *Courrier*, based on the same alleged disputes in the local community and on who knows what else. [...] This is my sixth year here, I am naturalized and have therefore no homeland other than Luxembourg. [...] As far as my pecuniary circumstances are concerned, I am the head of a family and without fortune.[81]

Hirsch then followed that relatively extensive description of his personal circumstances with the argument that it was the state after all that had summoned him to Luxembourg to be Chief Rabbi:

> If the state wants to provide the local Jews with a rabbi, namely a man who must complete grammar school, university and Talmudic studies, then it must settle on a wage for him so that he can live a decent life with his family, as Jews do not observe celibacy. [...] As it [the Luxembourg Parliament; T.F.] would surely not consider reducing the wages of the Catholic clergy, it would be hard pressed to plunge me and my family into misery; I, who receives 980 guilder out of state funds per year, out of which I still must pay my taxes.[82]

At the end, Hirsch speculates about the motivations behind the attacks against him:

> My participation at the *Volksfreund* provoked all this wrath. Everyone knows that I am not the founder of that paper, but simply a collaborator; and I have and still do collaborate with the purest of patriotic intentions. I have not written and will not write one line that I could not defend with honor in front of Christians and Jews alike. I think that the *Volksfreund* has become dear to the country and that is the only payment that I expected for my participation.[83]

---

80 Der Volksfreund 12 (16.05.1848), 2.
81 Der Volksfreund 86 (22.11.1848), 4.
82 Ibid.
83 Ibid.

The last issue of the embattled *Volksfreund* was published on June 29, 1849. The reason given by the paper was "circumstances of the time", meaning the success of the Restoration within the German Confederation. At the same time, this issue expressed the hope that "that sooner or later, action will once again follow reaction".[84]

Over the course of 1849 in the *Luxemburger Wort*, expressions of hostility against Jews were primarily to be found in reports from abroad. As always, those articles presented liberal, emancipatory and revolutionary movements as Jewish dominated or as "Jewish" identified; the "rabble-rousing" Jews strove to overthrow the existing order, their goal was immorality and anarchy. The associated accusation of "corrosive" activities was increasingly personified in the form of the "enemy within" – a Jewish form (which they never tired of emphasizing) – that was allied with the external enemy. In the case of the Hungarian uprising against Austria for instance, *Luxemburger Wort*'s February 23, 1849 issue speaks of the "Jews, who have been the principle instigators of all treachery against Church and State",[85] and that "it is precisely the Israelites who have (allowed themselves) to be used as spies and messengers for the rebels".[86] On June 3rd it was reported that "the entire mob of enlightened Jews in Hungary, who are as morally corrupt and treacherous as Jews everywhere, will encourage revolution at any rate".[87]

Toward the end of 1849, the *Luxemburger Wort* began reporting about the upcoming vote on the Jewish emancipation law in Bavaria. It wrote about the state parliament's adoption of the draft law, the ensuing campaign against Jewish emancipation and – with great satisfaction – about the Imperial Council of the Crown of Bavaria's rejection of the law.[88] On March 1, 1850, they published the following: "We consider any emancipation of the Jews as an irruption of demoralization and as an immense danger to law and order and peace. The Jews are a strange and foreign people who according to the laws of their own religion can never ever merge and become one with a Christian people."[89]

The *Luxemburger Wort* continued to confront the issue of Jewish emancipation in several articles, as if it were still to be negotiated in Luxembourg. Samuel

---

84 Der Volksfreund 77 (29.06.1849), 1.
85 Luxemburger Wort 23 (23.02.1849), 1.
86 Luxemburger Wort 23 (23.02.1849), 4.
87 Luxemburger Wort 65 (03.06.1849), 2.
88 For the events in Bavaria see Hannes Ludyga, *Die Rechtsstellung der Juden in Bayern von 1819–1918: Studie im Spiegel der Verhandlungen der Kammer der Abgeordneten des bayerischen Landtags* (Berlin: Berliner Wissenschafts-Verlag, 2007), 241 et seq.
89 Luxemburger Wort 26 (01.03.1850), 3.

Hirsch thus felt compelled to take a personal position once again in this regard. As the *Der Volksfreund* no longer existed, he wrote a letter to the *Courrier du Grand-Duché de Luxembourg*, which was published on March 6, 1849. In it, Hirsch wondered about the "purposes of these articles" in *the Wort*. He concisely pointed out that the Jews of Luxembourg had already been "emancipated for about 50 years, and thus not as a result of the 1848 Revolution".[90] In turn, the *Luxemburger Wort* assured that it had "never tried to provoke animosity towards the Jews as such, much less hatred". They instead claimed that it was in "the interests of more general questions delving into the deepest aspects of the life of the people. [...] But for all that, it is all the more staunchly that we oppose the emancipation of the Jews in a Christian state".[91]

This citation, and the assertion that no animosity had been directed against any Jew as a concrete person, or against any of "the few Jews living here in the country",[92] explicitly illustrate one of the main features of modern antisemitism: indifference.[93] The assertion of having nothing "personal" against the Jews suggests disinterested analysis, objectivity and rationality. It can similarly be found in many of the publications exhibiting modern antisemitism, for example in Johann Gottlieb Fichte's *Writings on the French Revolution* and in Richard Wagner's works. This position, however, would not become leading until the second half of the 19th century.

---

90 Courrier du Grand-Duché de Luxembourg 19 (06.03.1850), 2.
91 Luxemburger Wort 29 (08.03.1850), 1. The second half of the article deals mainly with Samuel Hirsch as advocate of emancipation of the Jews and ends with an assortment of accusations: "In conclusion we can point to the hostile behavior of the emancipated Jews towards Christianity; to their influence on the press; to their role in undermining society. Yes, you may ask, who is he who interferes so hostilely in Christian affairs here in Luxembourg? Who as speaker in the Freemasons lodge spread unchristian tenets? Who allowed himself in excellent fashion to be used as a persecutory instrument against the bishop and of enmity against the ardent and faithful priests? Who more than all others took part in the *Volksfreund*, this vehicle of socialism? We have referred to these personal considerations to illustrate the general question of the resistance to the emancipation of the Jews, and prefer avoiding discussions regarding individuals, in as much as we would like to give full recognition to Dr. Hirsch's well-balanced epistle" (ibid., 2).
92 Luxemburger Wort 29 (08.03.1850), 1.
93 Cf. Detlev Claussen, *Vom Judenhaß zum Antisemitismus: Materialien einer verleugneten Geschichte* (Darmstadt: Luchterhand 1987, 2nd edition), 12 et seq. Claussen illustrates this by way of Fichte, who denied bearing any personal animosity towards Jews despite his Jew-hating attitude.

Conclusion

Essential elements of modern antisemitism are clearly recognizable in *Luxemburger Wort*'s reporting. It functions as a cultural code, thereby establishing identities. It understands "Jewishness" as a principle that is just as abstract as it is dominating, personified in the Jews; antisemitism thus becomes an explanatory model of the world. Although it was not yet understood under this term, antisemitism had taken to the political stage. Its representatives claimed to be acting in the common interest. This can also be seen as a reaction to liberalism's claim to rationality, as was called for in the social debates at the time.

The analysis of the generalization of commodity exchange in Europe and in the U.S., of the capitalist mode of production, as well as of the creation of the modern state is relevant for an examination of the distinguishing characteristics of this period in Luxembourg, a time that has been described by Detlev Claussen as "so revealing for the history of antisemitism". According to Claussen "it is in this period that a transformation from traditional Jew-hatred to antisemitism occurred – prior to the existence of the word antisemitism".[94] At the end of the 19th century, it was presented as a political movement by authors such as Wilhelm Marr and Paul de Lagarde, as an "antisemitic movement", whose beginnings Jacob Toury saw in the constellation of events surrounding the revolutionary years of 1848/49.[95]

The change in the manifestations of hostility towards Jews cannot therefore only be seen as a delusional, unconscious reaction to the transformation of societal relations. It can also be analyzed in terms of the antisemites' search for an effective anti-Jewish practice, since it was necessary to find other ways and means to harm the Jews after they had successfully attained political and legal equality in Luxembourg. The political form of antisemitism is manifested on the one hand on a structural-systematic level, in measures such as discrimination, marginalization and rejection of equal status – i.e. through mediated forms of violence. However, the key factor of anti-Jewish fervor is obscured behind this political form. It is the hatred of Jews, rooted in the antisemites' psyche, that wants to exercise anti-Jewish violence for its own catharsis, and this violence can only be enacted on concrete individuals. As already shown, the *Lux-*

---

94 Claussen, ibid., 17.
95 Quoted from Volkov, *Die Juden in Deutschland 1780–1918*, 109 et seq. As is known, the revolt of 1848 was accompanied from the start by antisemitic violence that by far surpassed the 1819 Hep-Hep riots. Cf. Helmut Berding, *Moderner Antisemitismus in Deutschland* (Frankfurt am Main: Suhrkamp Verlag, 1st editon, 1988), 74.

emburger Wort asserts in a sober and objective tone that the paper's fight against Jewish emancipation and social participation only had to do with "more general questions penetrating the deepest aspects of the life of the people" – this alongside tirades of unbridled furor and barely encoded calls to pogroms.

For the *Luxemburger Wort*, it is clear that the battle against Jewish emancipation was simultaneously a pars pro toto of the battle for a Christian, Catholic, non-secular state. The historian Olaf Blaschke, who published a book of comparative studies on the so-called Catholic antisemitism in the 19th century, points to the close link between ultramontanism and antisemitism, and speaks of a "logical systemic connection, in terms of the history of mentality, between anti-liberal ideology, the fear of emancipation and anti-Jewish behavior".[96] As a form of reaction to social change, the ultramontane movement opposed any tendency within the Catholic Church "attempting to come to terms with the modern world".[97] A characteristic structural feature of ultramontanism was a dualism within which Judaism constituted the antithesis of Catholicism.[98] Ultramontane antisemitism functioned as a defensive self-understanding for Catholics, one that was "against the accelerated transformation processes in economy, culture and society".[99]

It is in this context that the delusional, antisemitic identification of Jews with social and governmental secularization tendencies, as well as with the legal system, must be analyzed. Among other things, one can see that the clerics of Luxembourg discussed here understood that emancipation – which they always attempted to reduce to a supposedly "Jewish question" – is in truth an issue for society as a whole, and one that results in the actual separation of Church and State. Once the official universal application of civil rights was implemented, the Church's political power would surely be at an end. On March 6, 1850 in the *Courrier du Grand-Duché de Luxembourg*, Samuel Hirsch stated this very clearly:

> The *Wort* knows quite well, or so at least we think, what the question of Jewish emancipation signifies. It is not a question that applies to the Jews alone. If the state says that the Jews, because they are Jews, shall not share in all civil rights, then it will soon be forced to see that what logically follows is to only accord those who are true Christians civil rights. [...] It is not without reason that Protestants and Freemasons always figure alongside Jews

---

96 Olaf Blaschke, "Die Anatomie des katholischen Antisemitismus. Eine Einladung zum internationalen Vergleich", in Blaschke and Mattioli, eds., *Katholischer Antisemitismus im 19. Jahrhundert*, 3–56, here 26.
97 Ibid., 26.
98 Ibid., 33.
99 Ibid., 10.

in the *Wort*. For, from the *Wort*'s perspective, how do the Protestant and the Freemason stand any closer to the true church than the Jew? Consequently, the state in the end must be only the domain of the true believers.[100]

In the same article, Hirsch concisely quashes the *Luxemburger Wort*'s efforts to once again challenge "Jewish emancipation" in Luxembourg:

> The principle of the freedom of conscience is included in our constitution and the *Wort* is not going to deprive us of our heritage of the last well-nigh sixty years. We are therefore going to allow it, unperturbed, to inveigh and rant against the Jews as much as it desires. It is not our responsibility to see to it that publications leading to hatred and scorn for an entire category of citizens should be disapproved.[101]

Hirsch thus makes it quite clear that it was not primarily the Jews' responsibility to combat Jew-hatred and its protagonists, just as society's emancipation was not simply a "Jewish question". Unfortunately, what he was trying to communicate to his fellow citizens with those words has yet to be realized in society today.

---

[100] Courrier du Grand-Duché de Luxembourg 19 (06.03.1850), 2.
[101] Ibid.

Michael A. Meyer
A Sense of Loneliness. Samuel Hirsch's American Years

European Baggage

Rabbi Samuel Hirsch did not have an easy career in America. Both his intemperate relations with others and his location on the radical extreme of Reform Judaism alienated him from other rabbis and from his own congregation. After only two years in Philadelphia, he confessed to one of the few rabbinical associates with whom he could be frank: "Am I then alone among my colleagues struck by blindness?"[1] Personal conflict was not new to Hirsch when he crossed the ocean to the United States in 1866. In Dessau he had been at odds with the Jewish educator David Fränkel and with his congregation there, which voted not to retain his services; in Luxembourg, following a dispute, he had resigned from the Masonic Lodge.[2] He also entered into a hostile exchange with a rival Jewish philosopher, Salomon Formstechter, after Hirsch had severely criticized Formstecher's work.[3] The protocols of the Brunswick rabbinical conference of 1844 record Hirsch's "fierce" reaction when colleagues displayed the "audacity" to ignore a proposal he had brought to them.[4] Intellectual or religious compromise in a matter of principle was entirely foreign to Hirsch's way of thinking. Cordial relations were not his highest priority. In America he would quarrel not only with rabbinical colleagues standing to his religious right but also with adherents of his own Reform persuasion and with the majority in his own congregation. His proposals for reforms would be questioned if not actually rejected. And yet beyond the vituperation and sharp differences of opinion, there were also alliances formed on individual issues. Opponents even evinced a measure of respect for this man

---

[1] Hirsch to Bernhard Felsenthal, January 1, 1869. Bernhard Felsenthal Letters, MS-153, American Jewish Archives, Cincinnati. Subsequent citations from Hirsch letters to Felsenthal are all from this collection.
[2] Elmar P. Ittenbach, *Samuel Hirsch. Rabbiner-Religionsphilosoph-Reformer* (Berlin: Hentrich & Hentrich, 2014), 19–20, 31.
[3] Christian Wiese, "Von Dessau nach Philadelphia: Samuel Hirsch als Philosoph, Apologet und radikaler Reformer", in Giuseppe Veltri and Christian Wiese, eds., *Jüdische Bildung und Kultur in Sachsen-Anhalt von der Aufklärung bis zum Nationalsozialismus* (Berlin: Metropol, 2009), 381 n. 62.
[4] *Protocolle der ersten Rabbiner-Versammlung abgehalten zu Braunschweig* (Braunschweig: Friedrich Bieweg, 1844), 88. The quoted words in the original are *heftig* and *Keckheit*.

whose Jewish and secular knowledge were rare in the American context of his time.

It was entirely due to the recommendation of Rabbi David Einhorn, who also had felt intellectually isolated in America, that Hirsch was invited to accept the pulpit of Reform Congregation Keneseth Israel.[5] The combination of an attractive salary with a life contract, the character of the congregation, and the freedom America offered attracted him to the Philadelphia position. In his youth Hirsch had been very poor and upon his departure from Luxembourg he was deeply in debt. Despite his castigations of materialism, references to his salary, enviously compared with those of his colleagues, would appear even in his polemical writings.[6] Keneseth Israel was the largest Philadelphia congregation, had recently built a handsome temple, and had begun to reform its liturgy and customs well before Hirsch's arrival.[7] It had adopted Einhorn's Reform prayerbook and shortly after Hirsch assumed its pulpit required that men attend services without a head covering.[8] Hirsch would remain at Keneseth Israel for twenty-two years until its governing board decided that its aging rabbi, who was able to preach only in German and spoke English with a decided accent, was no longer appropriate for an Americanizing younger generation. Hirsch's view, like Einhorn's, had been that German constituted an essential vehicle for serious religious discourse. On one occasion he remarked: "I don't write for schoolboys who understand no German."[9] He had dismissed the idea of a younger associate rabbi capable of delivering sermons in English, believing that conflict would inevitably result. After that it was not long until he was retired against his will in 1887. According to the recollection of his son Edward, his father arrived home one day with stooped shoulders and ashen face. When he was finally able to speak, he

---

[5] Samuel Hirsch, *Rev. Dr. David Einhorn, Gedächtniß-Rede* (Philadelphia: E. Hirsch, 1879), 5–6. For Einhorn's experience in the United States see Gershon Greenberg, "The Significance of America in David Einhorn's Conception on [sic] History", American Jewish Historical Quarterly 63 (1973), 160–184.

[6] See, for example, Samuel Hirsch, *Dr. Jastrow und sein Gebaren in Philadelphia. Ein ehrliches, leider abgenöthigtes Wort* (N.p., terminus post quem 17 February 1868), 1–2, 9, 25.

[7] Henry Samuel Morais, *The Jews of Philadelphia: Their History from the Earliest Settlements to the Present Time* (Philadelphia: Levytype Company, 1894), 91–92.

[8] The rule against head covering was so strongly enforced that a congregant had to petition the Board of Directors to make an exception for him "for reasons of health". *Reform Congregation Keneseth Israel: Its First 100 Years, 1847–1947* (Philadelphia, 1950), 15–16; Malcolm H. Stern, "National Leaders of Their Time: Philadelphia's Reform Rabbis", in Murray Friedman, ed., *Jewish Life in Philadelphia* (Philadelphia: Institute for the Study of Human Issues, 1983), 184.

[9] Hirsch, *Dr. Jastrow und sein Gebaren in Philadelphia*, 4.

said: "I have been fired, like a clerk, without a minute's notice."[10] Hirsch spent the last two years of his life in Chicago, where his rabbinical son, Emil, served as the rabbi of the large radical Reform congregation, Temple Sinai. There he gave an occasional German sermon and there he died and was buried in 1889.[11]

It was, however, not only his attachment to the German language that proved increasingly a barrier to his career in America. There was also his political philosophy. Unlike the admired scholar Leopold Zunz, who had once recommended Hirsch for a prize, and some of his German rabbinical colleagues, Hirsch had not been a democrat but a monarchist when he lived in Europe. In the United States this position, influenced by his early attraction to Hegel, came to haunt him. Opponents could claim that with such views he simply did not belong in a democratic United States, and especially not as a spiritual leader. It was the conservative rabbi of Baltimore, Benjamin Szold, who used this argument most effectively by simply citing his European writings. Such sentences as "The king is not chosen as a servant of the people, but the king is the anointed of God, called by God to be a true shepherd of humanity" could only damage Hirsch in the eyes of American Jewry. Hirsch had at one time indeed been convinced that absolute monarchy was the best system – as opposed to the British limited monarchy – since the king was thus above parties and special interests.[12] With such a platform, Szold taunted, how could one come to America? According to Szold, politically at least, Hirsch was an absolutist and a toady, a servile *Speichellecker*. Perhaps most damaging was that Hirsch had elevated monarchy into the realm of religion. He had written: "What the king does as king is ... the deed of God." And the messianic age that Hirsch envisioned – following Maimonides – was to be a monarchy.[13]

Hirsch had no choice but to defend his ability to be a good American despite his earlier views. He chose to do so in Isaac Mayer Wise's German-language newspaper, *Die Deborah*. Claiming that he had no reason to blush for anything he had written in Europe, Hirsch pointed out how in the preface to his major philosophical work, *Die Religionsphilosophie der Juden*, he had not idolized the Prussian king but criticized the Prussian policy of tolerating Jews while refus-

---

10 Leo Kaul, *The Story of Radical Reform Judaism* (Los Angeles: Leo Kaul, 1951), 27–28.
11 The tall obelisk erected above his grave in Rosehill Cemetery in Chicago is pictured in The Reform Advocate 49 (1915), 539.
12 See the article by Judith Frishman in this volume for Hirsch's views on the state and the monarchy.
13 Benjamin Szold, *Auch ein Wort über Jastrow & Hirsch* (Baltimore: C.W. Schneidereith, 1868), esp. 10–15. Cf. Gershon Greenberg, "Samuel Hirsch's American Judaism", American Jewish Historical Quarterly 62, 4 (June 1973), 372–373; Wiese, "Von Dessau nach Philadelphia", 397 n. 106.

ing to recognize Judaism in the manner that it recognized the Christian denominations. Moreover, the law of the state was God's law only when the king acted in accordance with the constitution. And yet at the same time Hirsch was at pains to point out the shortcomings of American democracy in which a tyrannous majority could oppress a subservient minority, witness especially America's history of black enslavement. To be sure, he now no longer believed that the king stands fully above his subjects. Kings too sometimes follow their private interests. There were good and bad kings as there were good and bad republics. But Hirsch would not call himself a republican either. At least during his first American years he did not entirely abandon the monarchical idea. The messianic ruler would be a king, but a kind of Platonic ruler and one fully receptive to the highest ideals of Judaism.[14]

In Hirsch's view, whether monarchical or republican, the state possessed religious sanctity. Like his mentor Rabbi Samuel Holdheim, who had given him his rabbinical certificate, Hirsch frequently cited the Talmudic saying that for Jews the law of the state is law. But it was more than just law: it was God's law. In Hirsch's words: "Reform declares that the law of the state is also religious law, without qualification." It is sacrosanct.[15] However, it is worth noting that Hirsch's sanctification of the state did not imply that Jews needed to compress their identity into a denomination on the Christian model. In Europe he had defined the Jews as a "spiritual nationality", not a *Konfession*, and he continued to hold that view in America though he no longer believed, as he had in Dessau, that one day the Jews would return to Palestine.[16] Now Hirsch held up that belief as irreconcilable not so much with American patriotism as with religious honesty. Orthodox Jews in America continued to pray for the return, but they did not really want it. Their prayers were therefore hypocritical. The hope of return, which was sincerely wished for in ages of persecution, was meaningless babble in a free country. He termed it *golus* Judaism, a religion of exile inappropriate in a land of freedom for all. Hirsch also used this argument to dismiss the Ortho-

---

14 Die Deborah 13 (1868), 187, 190, 194–195.
15 Ibid., 126.
16 Samuel Hirsch, *Die Religionsphilosophie der Juden oder das Prinzip der jüdischen Religionsanschauung und sein Verhältniß zum Heidenthum, Christenthum und zur absoluten Philosophie dargestellt und mit den erläuterten Beweisstellen aus der heiligen Schrift, den Talmudim und Midraschim versehen* (Leipzig: Heinrich Hunger 1842; reprint Hildesheim, Zurich, and New York: Olms, 1986), viii. Still three years later at the rabbinical conference in Frankfurt am Main in 1845, Hirsch argued for the legitimacy and political innocuousness of the belief in return to Zion. See *Protokolle und Aktenstücke der zweiten Rabbiner-Versammlung zu Frankfurt am Main* (Frankfurt am Main: E. Ullmann, 1845), 79. He stressed the distinction between religious confession and spiritual nationality again in Der Zeitgeist 1 (1880), 202.

doxy of American Jews. "You are good American citizens", he wrote, "and you feel as such. But just for that reason you are not Orthodox."[17] The traditional rabbis who sought to hold on both to American patriotism and to a hope of return to Zion Hirsch termed "amphibians", neither land nor sea animals, neither fully Orthodox nor fully Reform. As for their laity, they merely called themselves Orthodox.[18]

The Rabbi and (Mixed) Marriages

The relationship of Judaism to the state came up for open discussion when the American Reform rabbis met in Hirsch's Philadelphia study in November of 1869. The question before them was the relative roles of state and rabbinate regarding marriage and divorce. Like Holdheim, Hirsch expressed his opinion that all legal matters should be in the hands of the states. Divorce should be regulated entirely by civil law. The legal aspects of marriage should likewise be in the hands of the state with clergy adding only a religious ceremony that sanctified the marriage but possessed no legal effect.[19] However, there was one exception. Should the state grant a divorce for reasons that conflicted morally with Jewish tradition, the rabbi should feel free to refuse a remarriage.[20] In a concrete instance Hirsch extended this right of the rabbi to refuse officiation on moral grounds when he turned away an individual seeking to remarry very soon after the death of his spouse.

Hirsch's views on marriage resulted in the most painful conflict of his American years since it involved a colleague whom he greatly respected, David Einhorn. Following the precedent of Samuel Holdheim but almost alone among his American colleagues, Hirsch believed it acceptable for a rabbi to sanctify a mixed marriage. It was a view he had already held in Europe and in at least one instance had acted upon it. In 1853 he had conducted a wedding in France for a gentile groom and a Jewish bride from the Fould family when no French rabbi was willing to do so. However, he castigated Rabbi Jacob Mayer of Cleve-

---

17 Die Deborah 13 (1868), 118.
18 Ibid., 110, 130.
19 Der Zeitgeist 1 (1880), 203.
20 *Protokolle der Rabbiner-Conferenz abgehalten zu Philadelphia, vom 3. bis zum 6. November 1869* (New York: S. Hecht, 1870), 29, 32, 33, 35.

land for marrying a couple where the bride was a believing Catholic and the Jewish groom gave her a breviary as a wedding gift.[21]

In his articles in American Jewish periodicals and in personal letters Hirsch sought to justify his position based on the Talmud and later rabbinic literature. He would not sanctify the marriage with a believing Christian. However, if a Christian had given up his faith even though he had not converted to Judaism, Hirsch considered him to be in the traditional category of the *ger toshav*, the resident alien, not yet a Jew, but also no longer a Christian. It would, however, have to be a gentile man and a Jewish woman, not vice versa, as Hirsch believed that only the woman could insure that the children would be raised as Jews, and the Jewish education of the children was a condition that Hirsch set for his blessing such weddings.[22] Yet despite these limitations, the laymen of his congregation for a long time were decidedly opposed to his officiation at a mixed marriage.[23] Only in 1887, shortly before his move to Chicago, did its Board of Directors give him permission to perform a marriage between a Miss Meyer and a Mr. McIlvaine on the condition that the groom, while apparently not formally converting, renounce Christianity and accept Judaism in the presence of the president and vice president of the congregation.[24]

However, it was not the opposition of the laity on this issue that caused Hirsch the most anguish. It was the sharp rejection of his colleagues. At the Philadelphia conference Hirsch had brought in a radical suggestion, printed in the protocols but not acted upon, which in effect brought non-Jews into the synagogue. It read in part: "The non-Jew, who has come to God without adopting Judaism, is as close to God as the Jew, for the non-Jew is not obligated to Israel's priestly calling ... The congregations are therefore justified in granting even to non-Jews the rights of seat-holders in the synagogue or of passive member-

---

[21] Hirsch to Felsenthal, December 21, 1868 and February 21, 1870. Hirsch writes: "Dr. Maier in Cleveland". The reference is to Jacob Mayer, rabbi of the Tifereth Israel Congregation in Cleveland from 1867 to 1874. For a partial listing of rabbis who performed mixed marriages at this time see Michael A. Meyer, *Response to Modernity: A History of the Reform Movement in Judaism* (New York: Oxford University Press, 1988), 458 n. 91.

[22] Emil G. Hirsch, "My Father and Teacher", Reform Advocate (1925), 503. In 1842, Hirsch had complained of the fact that the Prussian government did not allow children of mixed marriages to be raised as Jews. *Die Religionsphilosophie*, vii.

[23] Einhorn writes: "Hirsch is living in deep division with his congregation, which has rejected his request for a raise in salary and is decisively opposed to his consecrating mixed marriages." David Einhorn to Kaufmann Kohler, April 29, 1874, David Einhorn Papers, MS-155, American Jewish Archives.

[24] *Reform Congregation Keneseth Israel*, 18.

ship."²⁵ The most severe and hurtful blow on the marriage issue – over which Hirsch obsessed in his correspondence – came from the man whom he could not but respect, whose prayerbook he used in his services, and to whom he owed his position in Philadelphia, David Einhorn. For all his religious radicalism, on this crucial issue Einhorn sharply differed from Hirsch. After Hirsch had written his extended article in *Die Deborah* in support of rabbinical officiation at mixed marriages – articles that Hirsch claimed Einhorn hadn't even read – came Einhorn's sharp reply in which he famously called officiation at mixed marriages "supplying a nail for the coffin of Judaism".²⁶ Hirsch simply could not get over being called in essence the undertaker of his faith. It turned him from admirer of Einhorn to his deprecator, and not on the mixed marriage issue alone. To his most intimate friend among his fellow American rabbis, Samuel Adler, he wrote: "This scandalous and totally unprovoked attack by Dr. Einhorn has, without your telling me, hurt you as much as it did me. Sadly the scandal is great enough. Orthodoxy and Moderate Reform are exulting. All of that was to be expected." For his part, Hirsch would follow the rabbinic dictum to be among the offended but not among the offenders.²⁷ But that was not easy for him to do. In his letters Hirsch now depicted Einhorn as a tyrant, who felt he had the right to make all the significant decisions himself. That had been especially true at the meeting of Reform rabbis held in Hirsch's home, where Hirsch had been allowed to preside, but Einhorn ruled the proceedings. His colleague insisted on wielding "the scepter of autocracy" and refused to recognize "that there were men who understand the subject [of Judaism], who don't need to bow before him and don't wish to do so".²⁸ Had Einhorn himself been the first to introduce the concept of the *ger toshav,* all would have been well. "But that another should be independent of him, the great man – that he must not tolerate."²⁹ Yet paradoxically, when earlier Einhorn had apparently failed to play

---

25 *Protokolle der Rabbiner-Conferenz,* 68.
26 The words appeared in a footnote to an Einhorn article in The Jewish Times 1, 45 (January 7, 1870), 11. The text reads: "Extending one's hand to consecrate mixed marriages, according to my firm conviction, means supplying a nail for the coffin of the tiny Jewish race with its lofty vocation ..." Hirsch replied with an article entitled "Der Nagel zum Sarge der winzigen Rasse". It appeared two weeks later in The Jewish Times 1, 47 (January 21, 1870), 10–11.
27 Hirsch to Samuel Adler, February 3, 187[0], Samuel Adler Papers, MS-423, American Jewish Archives. Whereas Hirsch's letters to Felsenthal remain formal in character, those to Adler, whom he knew from the rabbinical conferences in Germany, address him as "Dear Friend" and use the informal "Du". Subsequent citations from Hirsch letters to Samuel Adler, unless otherwise indicated, are all from this collection.
28 Hirsch to Adler, February 15, 1870.
29 Hirsch to Felsenthal, February 21, 1870.

an active role in furthering reform, Hirsch was disappointed: "Noblesse oblige. Him to whom God has given such great gifts is obliged to accomplish a great deal and may not, like Achilles, without cause withdraw to his tent."[30] Although he was scarcely a democrat in religious matters, Hirsch was less of an elitist than Einhorn. At the Brunswick conference of 1844 he had argued for paying due regard to the submissions of the laity and held that sharp distinctions between rabbi and laymen were uncharacteristic of Judaism.[31] At the Philadelphia rabbinical meeting Hirsch disagreed with Einhorn, who believed that members of congregations were not yet ready to rise to the loftiness of Judaism and hence to be included in religious decision-making. To be sure, unlike Isaac Mayer Wise, Hirsch was not in favor of an immediate assembly of congregations, and in that respect agreed with Einhorn, but he did explicitly indicate his support of the idea in principle.[32] Even Einhorn's sermons became the subject of Hirsch's private critique. He admired their form, their colorful use of images, which provided his listeners with exquisite aesthetic pleasure. But, as he claimed, Einhorn was – implicitly unlike himself – not a philosopher. Philosophical depth was lacking in his sermons as well as in his prayerbook. Hirsch's own maxim was more ambitious: "No idea is too difficult for the people to grasp, provided that the form comes to the aid of the cognitive capacity without causing it confusion."[33]

A decade later, in 1880, the issue of mixed marriage was still very much alive. Kaufmann Kohler, his own son's brother-in-law and also Einhorn's son-in-law, now termed Hirsch's Talmudic justifications for mixed marriage "outrageous pilpulism". Shocked, Hirsch could only respond that his arguments were based on "simple, logical thinking and a correct reading and comparison of texts". Moreover, in Europe he had met hundreds of non-Jews who were neither believing Christians nor indifferent to religion, and some of them had become his most intimate friends. Marrying such a person to a Jew could not be considered an insult to Judaism, at least not to Reform Judaism. Even Orthodox Jews regarded the children of a Jewish bride as Jews, even if the husband had not become a Jew on account of the pain and possible danger accompanying adult circumcision. And it was the fate of the children that mattered. Jews should fol-

---

30 Hirsch to Felsenthal, January 1, 1869.
31 *Protocolle der ersten Rabbiner-Versammlung*, 10, 55.
32 *Protokolle der Rabbiner-Conferenz*, 43.
33 Hirsch to Felsenthal, January 1, 1869. The previous fall Einhorn had published *Zwei Predigten gehalten im Tempel der Adath-Jeshurun-Gemeinde zu New York* (New York: New York Engraving, Lithographing & Printing Co, 1868). These sermons do indeed display Einhorn's ability to present dramatic images.

low the example of Ruth, who had been married to a non-Jew, rather than the restrictions imposed by Ezra and Nehemiah.[34]

Just as his position on mixed marriages placed Hirsch on the far extreme of Reform Judaism, so did his advocacy of Sunday religious services. Although unable to attend the Breslau rabbinical conference of 1846, where Holdheim argued in favor of Sabbath observance on Sunday, Hirsch had published an essay intended to sway his colleagues.[35] In true radical fashion, Hirsch rejected any partial, patchy solution (*Stückwerk*) to the problem of maintaining Sabbath rest for a Jewish community fully integrated into a gentile society. He did not believe that the world was created in six days, but he did stress the notion of rest, which on Saturday was not an acceptable option for an increasing number of German Jews. And since the Sabbath symbolized the perfection of God's creation, resting once a week was of the essence of Judaism.

In the United States Hirsch continued to be an active proponent of Sunday services. Here he even expressed his view in favor of the biblical six days of labor and opposed the notion of resting for two days.[36] Since there were laws in America prohibiting Sunday labor, their religion, in effect, called upon Jews to work on Saturday. Writing to his colleague Bernhard Felsenthal in Chicago in 1869, he supplied a further argument: "I don't know whether it [the Sunday service] is not really imperative on account of the mission of Israel. Very many Christians and freethinkers would surely attend our services if they were regularly to take place on Sundays." As for the Orthodox, "they could not object provided that we do not in our prayers declare [Sunday] as the Sabbath, which should and can be avoided".[37] However, Hirsch did not want to force such a fundamental reform upon his own congregation: "Only when the demand for it arises from a genuinely felt desire would I consent. The novelty may entice. But after a while the sanctuary may stand empty on Sundays, and on Saturdays, as well."[38] In reality, there was little support for a Sunday service at Keneseth Israel. Hirsch had to admit that there were only a few isolated individuals that favored the change

---

34 Samuel Hirsch, *"Unerhörte Pilpulistik". Offenes Sendschreiben an Rev. Dr. K. Kohler, Rabbiner der Beth-El Gemeinde in New York* (Philadelphia, 1880); Hirsch, "Offenes Sendschreiben an Herrn Dr. K. Kohler", Der Zeitgeist 1 (1880), 202–203.
35 Samuel Hirsch, *Die Sabbathfrage vor der dritten Rabbinerversammlung* (Berlin: self-publishing, 1846), esp. 5–6, 11, 17–19; Gershon Greenberg, "The Historical Origins of God and Man: Samuel Hirsch's Luxembourg Writings", Leo Baeck Institute Year Book 20, 1 (1975), 129–148, here 132.
36 Der Zeitgeist 2 (1881), 273; Joseph Krauskopf, *Obituary-Address in Honor of the Late Dr. Samuel Hirsch* (Philadelphia: S. W. Goodman, 1889), 6.
37 Hirsch to Felsenthal, February 8, 1869.
38 Ibid.

and he was not even certain that they meant it in earnest. In the winter of 1872–73, Hirsch's son Emil delivered a series of Sunday lectures at the congregation in the English language every fourth week.[39] But regular Sunday services were not introduced until the tenure of Hirsch's successor, Joseph Krauskopf, and to Hirsch's deep dismay Kaufmann Kohler, once an advocate of Sunday services, retreated to Saturday.[40] As with his position on mixed marriages, Hirsch's views on Sunday services did not quickly prevail and his frustration was palpable.

Rabbis to His Right

Less surprising than Hirsch's disputes with his Reform colleagues and his own congregation are his strained relations with more traditional rabbis, especially Benjamin Szold in Baltimore and Marcus Jastrow, a neighbor who lived only a few blocks away from Hirsch in Philadelphia.[41] These men were not hostile to the notion of a Judaism responsive to changing historical circumstances and were even willing, to some extent, to make common cause with the Reformers. But they strongly opposed what they believed were radical changes that would tear the fabric of traditional Judaism. For a time, both participated in the work of the Reform-oriented Union of American Hebrew Congregations and Hebrew Union College, as did Hirsch himself.[42] In Philadelphia there were personal contacts between Jastrow and Hirsch. They were both among the speakers in a lecture series whose proceeds went to a charitable cause; Jastrow provided Hirsch with complimentary tickets for another series of lectures that he was giving on the age of the Maccabees. And all three men, possessors of a formal advanced German secular education, shared a disregard for the demagogic but organizationally successful Isaac Mayer Wise, who could display no doctorate of his own. Jastrow charged that an unprincipled Wise was widely feared for his influence and that he was willing to engage in lies in order to make an argument. On one occasion he cited the words of "a radical reformer" who had con-

---

39 Hirsch to Adler, March 24, 1873.
40 Hirsch, *Unerhörte Pilpulistik*, 16.
41 Hirsch notes that "Jastrow and Szold are one heart and one soul. Every second Szold is here or Jastrow there." Hirsch to Felsenthal, January 1, 1869.
42 On Jastrow see Mirjam Thulin, "Experience and Epistemology: The Life and Legacy of Marcus M. Jastrow (1829–1903)", European Judaism 45, 2 (Autumn 2012), 32–58 and Michał Galas, *Rabbi Marcus Jastrow and His Vision for the Reform of Judaism* (Boston: Academic Studies Press, 2013).

demned Wise's "unworthy practices".⁴³ On the subject of Wise, Jastrow associated himself easily with the judgment of "the most outstanding Reform rabbis of our country, everywhere respected for their character and knowledge, Drs. Adler, Einhorn, Felsenthal, and Hirsch".⁴⁴ When at a conference called by Wise in 1871 in Cincinnati, Rabbi Jacob Mayer questioned the existence of a personal God and the efficacy of prayer and Wise seemed to lean in the same direction, fourteen both more and less traditional rabbis joined in a collective protest while Jastrow and Hirsch issued a joint statement of their own.⁴⁵

However, with their differing attitudes to the authority of Jewish tradition and their shared intemperance toward rivals, conflicts were bound to arise between Hirsch and the rabbis to his religious right.⁴⁶ The harsh exchange between Hirsch and Szold over the nature of political authority has been noted above. In the strictly religious realm, Hirsch showed little regard for the compromise he thought characteristic of those who – he believed falsely – claimed the mantle of Orthodoxy. One example was the liturgy. The Szold prayerbook, revised by Jastrow, though to some degree differing from tradition, did not fully eliminate reference to the reestablishment of the temple in Jerusalem. But by way of compromise that portion of the liturgy was said only silently. In Hirsch's eyes this product of indecision was an untenable position.⁴⁷ More vicious, because it involved morals as well practice, was the dispute that arose between Hirsch and Jastrow on the question of family seating in the synagogue. Isaac Mayer Wise claimed that the family pew was his idea and that he had already introduced it while serving in Albany, New York. From there it had spread to other congregations including that of Hirsch in Philadelphia. Jastrow's congregation, howev-

---

43 M. Jastrow, *Offene Erklärung an Herrn I. M. Wise* (Philadelphia: Stein u. Jones, 1867). The unnamed radical reformer (p. 27) could well be Hirsch.
44 M. Jastrow, *Gegenerklärung auf die "Erklärung" des Herrn I. M. Wise* (Philadelphia: Stein u. Jones, 1867), 5.
45 The Jewish Times 3 (1871/72), 280–282. For Hirsch's reasons in declining to sign the collective statement, see his letter to Adler, June 26, 1871, SC-5054, American Jewish Archives.
46 The modern Orthodox Isaac Leeser died not long after Hirsch's arrival in Philadelphia, but he had helped to establish a rather traditional rabbinical seminary, Maimonides College, whose faculty included himself but not Hirsch. In a reply to an article Leeser wrote in his *Occident* and with bitter sarcasm, Hirsch repeatedly referred to him as "Professor of Homiletics and Comparative Theology", a title Hirsch surely believed he did not deserve. Die Deborah 13 (December 27, 1867), 98.
47 Hirsch, *Dr. Jastrow und sein Gebaren*, 17, 25. On the Szold-Jastrow prayerbook see Eric L. Friedland, "Marcus Jastrow and *Abodath Israel*", in Michael A. Fishbane and Paul R. Flohr, eds., *Texts and Responses. Studies Presented to Nahum N. Glatzer on the Occasion of His Seventieth Birthday by His Students* (Leiden: Brill, 1975), 186–200.

er, continued to divide men and women during worship. When his Rodeph Shalom congregation was thinking of constructing a new building in 1867, Jastrow felt some pressure to conform to this new practice. He not only resisted it but got into an extended dispute with Isaac Mayer Wise, who had recently written in favor of the practice in his *Die Deborah*. In a written response Jastrow now noted correctly that even in Samuel Holdheim's radical congregation in Berlin men and women sat separately.[48] And on February 15, 1868, Jastrow delivered a sermon in which, according to what was conveyed to Hirsch, he had intimated that the new practice was a violation of proper morality and that he would sooner lay down his rabbinate than succumb to its acceptance. Samuel Hirsch took this as a severe personal attack upon himself and the practices of Keneseth Israel. He soon responded that in Jastrow's congregation men and women might be sitting apart, but the women and girls were clearly "on show" to the men. Moreover, sitting by themselves during an almost entirely Hebrew service of which they understood little, the latter were also more likely to gossip than when they sat with male members of their family. As for the reference to Holdheim, in Germany separating men and women during worship was simply the universal practice among both Jews and Christians. Had he lived in America, Holdheim would surely have adopted family seating.[49]

The dispute over family seating mingled with the argument over the compatibility between American patriotism and praying for return to Palestine (Jastrow) versus allegedly not being fully a republican and immorally mingling the sexes (Hirsch). Each side accused the other of *rishus*, exposing the Jewish community to antisemitic charges whether of disloyalty or immorality. Both sides held nothing back, their polemics moving easily from the substantive to the personal. Sarcasm became the rule; respect cast aside. Charges of Jesuitism[50] and casuistry were thrown in both directions. It was at this point that Szold entered the fray, declaring Hirsch's political views un-American and thereby undermining him even as Hirsch was undermining Jastrow. The strain on Hirsch was great; he was convinced that his colleagues were out to destroy him. Writing to Felsenthal he wondered: "Did Jastrow really have the right to denounce my article [on Jewish restoration in Palestine] to his congregation from his pulpit as attacking

---

48 Jastrow, *Offene Erklärung*, 21–24. Jastrow followed up with *Antwort an Herrn I. M. Wise in Cincinnati* (n.p., n.d.) and *Gegenerklärung auf die "Erklärung"*.
49 Hirsch, *Dr. Jastrow und sein Gebaren*, 8–10.
50 Jesuits had been Hirsch's "deadly enemies" during his Luxembourg years (see the article of Thorsten Fuchshuber in this volume) and he continued to rail against them in America. To accuse a rival of Jesuitism was a severe charge. See Die Deborah 13 (1868), 138. Jastrow accused Wise of Jesuitism in his *Offene Erklärung*, 18.

Jewish civil equality? Were his motives really of a pure nature? Was it for him nothing but an urgent duty and, as he had put it, following the principle (cited in Hebrew) 'where there is a profanation of [God's] name one does not pay honor to the rabbi'? Clear it up for me, I ask for nothing else." Hirsch went on to suggest that, in his opinion, Jastrow's only motive was to draw members away from Hirsch's congregation and to his own. He also noted that Einhorn (of all people!), on a visit to Philadelphia offered to mediate between him and Jastrow.[51] It is not known whether that occurred. Yet the common statement on the personal God issue only two years later and the lack of any public disputes in the following years suggest the establishment of a modus vivendi between the two men, despite their religious and personal differences, was eventually achieved.

In general, it seems fair to say that Samuel Hirsch was not a happy man in America. Initially, he had expressed his hope that American Jewry would be different from its European counterpart, which followed the Christian example in staying away from the house of worship.[52] But not only were the disputes distasteful, he also tended toward despair regarding the success of his own work and that of his colleagues. "Our Reform congregations are the product of religious indifference and drag this disease of their progenitor with them. Religion, synagogue, sermon – show!" Things had begun to look up when the rabbinical conference was in view. But when they came together, the colleagues displayed their differences. Einhorn came out against Hirsch whereupon, according to Hirsch, people began to say: "Is religion anything more than humbug?" To Adler and then also to Felsenthal Hirsch cited in despair the words from Heinrich Heine's poem: "Whether the rabbi or the Capuchin monk may be right I do not know. And yet I think – that both of them do stink." That, Hirsch believed, is what the Jewish public had come to think, as well.[53]

---

[51] Hirsch to Felsenthal, January 1, 1869.
[52] Samuel Hirsch, *"Die Lehre, die uns Moscheh anbefohlen, ist Erbbesitz der Gemeinden Jakobs." Predigt gehalten am [Shemini atseret] 5628, in der Synagoge der Ref. Gem. Keneseth Israel, in Philadelphia* (Philadelphia: Stein u. Jones, 1867), 16.
[53] Hirsch to Adler, February 15, 1870; Hirsch to Felsenthal, February 21, 1870. The lines, not precisely quoted, are the last verse of Heine's late poem "Disputation". In both instances Hirsch rendered the word *stinken* politely simply as "*st...*".

Tenets

Still, it would be unfair to dismiss Hirsch's career in America as consisting simply of disputes and a battle against despair. Hirsch the religious thinker and Hirsch the rabbi played their role in the United States as they did in Europe. Although he did not write any major philosophical works during his American years as he had in Europe, Hirsch continued to express his views through the periodicals then issued by the Reform Jewish community. One subject on which he liked to write was the relationship of Judaism to Christianity.[54] Unlike Felsenthal and some others, Hirsch was not greatly concerned about the efforts of Christian missionaries in America to bring Jews into their fold. "The Jew who wants to become a Christian, if there is such a person, requires no missionary", he wrote. "And the missionaries have scarcely ever convinced anyone, but have bought souls, and what is the value of such purchasable souls?"[55] Believing in the possibility of a common faith, Hirsch was open to lowering barriers between the two religions, even while making sharp distinctions between them. Like Wise and unlike Einhorn, he was eager to gain proselytes for Judaism and wanted to make conversion an easy process. But even a Christian who had not gone through a full conversion was to be welcomed into the Jewish fold except "out of precaution", such an individual should not be given the right to vote on the management of congregational matters. Although not taking on the priestly mission of Israel, he or she could be regarded as a "passive member".[56] In the most radical of the Reform periodicals, *Der Zeitgeist*, and in contradiction to the views of Isaac Mayer Wise, Hirsch also argued in favor of a rabbi's right to eulogize a Jew being buried in a Christian cemetery and, complementarily, he had no problem with Christians being buried next to their Jewish spouses in a Jewish cemetery.[57] After all, belief in God and morality was not unique to Judaism, but inscribed universally upon the human heart.

Nonetheless, in his American writings Hirsch did not seek to equate Judaism with Christianity, as if there were no significant differences between them. And

---

[54] For a more comprehensive treatment of Hirsch's views on this subject see Judith Frishman, "Good Enough for the Goyim? Samuel Hirsch and Samuel Holdheim on Christianity", in Marcel Poorthuis et. al, eds., *Interaction between Judaism and Christianity in History, Religion, Art and Literature* (Leiden: Brill, 2009), 271–287.
[55] Hirsch to Felsenthal, February 8, 1869.
[56] *Protokolle der Rabbiner-Conferenz*, 68; Samuel Hirsch, "Report of the Committee on the Initiatory Rites of Proselytes", Central Conference of American Rabbis Year Book 3 (1893), 69–73. Hirsch wrote his responsum toward the end of his tenure in Philadelphia, June 21, 1886.
[57] Samuel Hirsch, "Theorie und Praxis", Der Zeitgeist 1 (1880), 162.

indeed, Hirsch repeatedly stressed those differences. Unlike Judaism, Christianity in his eyes had no choice but to regard itself as a revealed supra-rational religion.[58] In Judaism, Christian supernatural revelation had its counterpart not in a similar doctrinal message, but in the providentially guided and hence sacred history of the people of Israel and its divinely ordained mission to the nations.[59] Whereas one became a Christian only by accepting the faith's fundamental doctrine, one was a Jew by birth. For Hirsch, from his European writings to his American ones, the specific doctrine that separated the two faiths was the Pauline teaching of Original Sin. Hirsch believed that it was Paul who had launched Christianity on a distinctly non-Jewish course that set it sharply apart from Judaism. More than that, the notion of inherited human depravity had led to Jewish suffering: "The Jew, because not miraculously redeemed from Original Sin, is necessarily [regarded as] a morally less good person. The consequences of such a view we have gotten to know through seventeen hundred years of persecution."[60] Only by giving up its Pauline doctrine could Christianity re-approach the faith out of which it had emerged. Judaism, because it lacked the idea of Original Sin, stood in advance of Christianity. It was Judaism that pointed toward a religious future rooted in unconstrained moral choice, in love and tolerance. In Europe, Hirsch had argued, Christianity too could play a salvific role. Divested of its Pauline burden, it could spread the essentially Jewish message of Jesus to the nations.[61] Christianity was a force for the extension of an intensive Judaism.[62] Shortly after his arrival in America, however, Hirsch wrote more exclusively: "Whatever has occurred in the world for the past two thousand years that is great, noble, and beautiful is Judaism and nothing but Judaism ... Judaism

---

58 Samuel Hirsch, "Revelation and Judaism", The Jewish Reformer 1, 2 (January 8, 1886), 4.
59 Die Deborah 13 (1868), 142–143. Hirsch had already expressed this idea in his earliest publication: Samuel Hirsch, *Was ist Judenthum und was dessen Verhältniss zu andern Religionen?* (Berlin: Carl Heymann, 1838), 12. See also his *Die Reform im Judenthum und dessen Beruf in der gegenwärtigen Welt* (Leipzig: Heinrich Hunger, 1844), 36–37, 60, 64 and Greenberg, "The Historical Origins of God and Man", 136–137.
60 Samuel Hirsch, *Das Nothwendigste aus der Formen-Lehre der Hebräischen Sprache* (Philadelphia: Grassman & Goodman, 1867), iv-v.
61 Hirsch had expressed these ideas most directly during his Luxembourg period. See his *Die Humanität als Religion* (Trier: C. Troschel, 1854), vi note, vii.
62 Hirsch, *Die Religionsphilosophie*, 530, 834; Gershon Greenberg, "*Religionswissenschaft* and Early Reform Jewish Thought: Samuel Hirsch and David Einhorn", in Andreas Gotzmann and Christian Wiese, eds., *Modern Judaism and Historical Consciousness: Identities, Encounters, Perspectives* (Leiden: Brill, 2007), 126; Julius Guttmann, *Philosophies of Judaism: The History of Jewish Philosophy from Biblical Times to Franz Rosenzweig* (Philadelphia: Holt, Rinehart and Winston, 1964), 320–321.

alone is the religion of progress and therefore alone the religion of the present, and even more of the future."[63]

In addition to expressing opinions regarding Judaism's relation to Christianity and Christians, Hirsch's American writings deal with a variety of theological and practical issues. As he had in Europe, Hirsch rejected the standard view of revelation, regarding it as an un-Jewish, Christian doctrine. Belief in God could be attained by human reason; it required no divine intervention. Influenced perhaps by the strong individualism of American culture, Hirsch now recognized moral authority neither in any revelation nor in the pretensions of any religious institution, but as resting squarely in individual conscience. "The first principle of Reform is: The truth is written in the heart of men. ... The truth guides us, not the authority of men."[64] In acting freely, the Jew was imitating God, for God, according to Hirsch, was "freedom itself".[65]

Hirsch's universalism and rationalism did not cause him to reject the chosenness of Israel. He had affirmed this particularizing concept in his early writing and he continued to do so in the United States. Like his colleagues to his religious left and right, Hirsch believed that Israel was in possession of a "lofty world-historical vocation". Without it there was no Judaism. What made Hirsch's conception unique, however, was his belief that Israel's mission consisted not in spreading monotheism, which was a completed task, but primarily in disabusing non-Jews of their belief in Original Sin.[66]

As both a scholar and a preacher, Hirsch necessarily related to Jewish sources. Although in his sermons he cited and expounded upon biblical passages (and rabbinic ones), he did not regard the Bible as revelation. He believed that as a Reformer he had no right during a religious service solemnly to lift the Torah scroll into the air and call out "This is the Torah which Moses placed before the Children of Israel". However, with due interpretation he could recite "the good old honest 'Blessed be the One who has given Torah to His people Israel in His holiness'".[67] Hirsch had no difficulty with biblical criticism. His son Emil relates that the book he was studying on his deathbed was none other than Wellhausen's *Prolegomena* to which he had added comments in the margins within an hour before his death.[68] However, the religious meaning of the

---

[63] Samuel Hirsch, "*Die Lehre, die uns Moscheh anbefohlen*", 14.
[64] Hirsch, "Revelation and Judaism", 5. Cf. Die Deborah 13 (1868), 134. However, Hirsch had already much earlier associated individual freedom with religion. See his *Die Sabbathfrage*, 5.
[65] Der Zeitgeist 2 (1881), 273.
[66] Die Deborah 12 (1867), 103; 13 (1868), 142.
[67] Hirsch to Felsenthal, December 21, 1868; Hirsch to Adler, February 3, 1870.
[68] Reform Advocate 49 (1925), 500.

Bible, in Hirsch's eyes, did not rest upon its origins. As he once put it during the last years of his life: "The real question [for Reform Judaism] is what did the writer, whoever he may have been, seek through his tales for us and for posterity to lay upon our hearts."[69]

As for the Talmud, Hirsch's attitude to it was not one of complete rejection. His arguments with his colleagues were almost invariably backed up by citations from rabbinic texts. He appreciated the role that the Talmud had played in preserving the Jewish people even if its outlook in general had been superseded.[70] And on at least one occasion in Philadelphia he covered his head and taught Talmud to a group of young people that included the conservative lay leaders, Cyrus Adler and Solomon Solis-Cohen.[71] With regard to the observance of religious rituals, in his major European work Hirsch had stressed the "absolute necessity" of restoring ceremonies and customs to Jewish hearts as vital deeds, essential to preserving Jewish uniqueness.[72] Although less attached to religious forms in America, when he republished his catechism in 1877, he stressed that he had not changed his views. To be sure, Judaism for Hirsch was strictly teaching and not law and the meaning of the rite mattered more than the rite itself; but he did not argue for abandonment of all rituals, finding significance even in the dietary laws. The child needed to learn about *kashrut, tefilin* and *tsitsit*, even if the practices themselves were no longer required for the dramatization of their moral message.[73] In his submission to the Philadelphia conference he wrote that although symbolic commandments had lost their collective binding force, their practice remained acceptable where an individual felt that they continued to have sanctifying power and elevated that person to God.[74] Hirsch did not find intrinsic value in circumcision since Jewishness was determined by

---

69 Der Zeitgeist 2 (1881), 356.
70 Greenberg, "Samuel Hirsch's American Judaism", 379–381. Wiese, "Von Dessau nach Philadelphia", 399.
71 Jacob Rader Marcus, *United States Jewry 1776–1985*, vol. 3: *The Germanic Period*, part 2 (Detroit: Wayne State University Press, 1993), 595–596.
72 Hirsch, *Die Religionsphilosophie*, ix-x.
73 Samuel Hirsch, *Systematischer Katechismus der israelitischen Religion* (Philadelphia: S.M. Larzelere, 1877, 2nd. improved and expanded edition), 56–66. The catechism first appeared in Luxemburg in 1856. Hirsch noted that its proper study required 3.5 hours per week. On the catechism see Bernd Schröder, "Jüdische Katechismen in Deutschland am Beispiel eines Katechismus aus der Feder von Samuel Hirsch (1815–1889)", in Klaus Herrmann et al., eds., *Jewish Studies Between the Disciplines: Papers in Honor of Peter Schäfer on the Occasion of his 60th Birthday* (Leiden and Boston: Brill, 2003), 456–477.
74 *Protokolle der Rabbiner-Conferenz*, 68.

birth. However, he advised its practice since the son, upon growing up and perhaps finding meaning in the rite, might regret his parents' decision.[75]

Unlike some of his Reform colleagues and with uncharacteristic conservatism, Hirsch believed in the importance of teaching and using Hebrew. In contrast to Abraham Geiger, he was averse to knowledge of the language contracting to the sphere of rabbis and scholars alone. At the Brunswick conference in 1844, he had justified his insistence upon broadly based knowledge of Hebrew by reference to the non-existent division in Judaism between rabbis and laity.[76] Very soon after his arrival in Philadelphia, Hirsch issued a brief Hebrew grammar to assist congregants in following the Hebrew prayers. In its preface he argued that Reform congregations had a great interest in advancing Hebrew knowledge because it was their principle that all prayers should be fully understood. In addition to the prayers, a good Jew should also be able to read the Bible in its original language.[77] At the Philadelphia conference Hirsch argued that for historical reasons the basic prayers remain in Hebrew and that Hebrew should therefore be taught in the religious school.[78] When Felsenthal, who liked to write to his colleagues in Hebrew, congratulated Hirsch on his seventieth birthday, Hirsch replied that although he was not a master of Hebrew style, as a young man he had written a Hebrew poem on the subject of the Sabbath. When it fell into the hands of his Talmud teacher, the latter expressed his admiration for it.[79]

We know of only two Jewish organizational projects in which Samuel Hirsch was involved. Early in 1868, not long after his arrival in Philadelphia, he was instrumental in founding a society, composed mostly of members of Keneseth Israel, who took responsibility for looking after orphans within a family setting as well as providing them with education and vocational training. The society was Hirsch's idea; he wrote its constitution; and he served briefly as its first president, later as its secretary.[80] Hirsch also took the initiative in forming an American chapter of the French *Alliance Israélite Universelle*, through which he especially hoped to aid Russian Jews.[81] For Hirsch, acting for the welfare of civil society was part of the religious life and stood higher than the practice of any

---

75 E. G. Hirsch, "My Father and Teacher", 502.
76 *Protocolle der ersten Rabbiner-Versammlung*, 55.
77 Hirsch, *Das Nothwendigste aus der Formen-Lehre der Hebräischen Sprache*, iv-v.
78 *Protokolle der Rabbiner-Conferenz*, 14.
79 Hirsch to Felsenthal, July 1, 1885.
80 Krauskopf, *Obituary Address*, 4; Reform Advocate 49 (1915), 541; *Reform Congregation Keneseth Israel*, 16
81 Hirsch to Adler, February 3, 1870; Cf. Ittenbach, *Samuel Hirsch*, 37–38.

symbolic religious ceremony.[82] In his sermons he discussed the Mosaic social welfare laws and dwelt upon the reform of contemporary social abuses and of class and creed injustices.[83]

Conclusion

In sum, it seems correct to conclude that, on the whole, Samuel Hirsch's American years were not happy ones. His ideas were repeatedly rejected both by his colleagues and by his congregation. At the Philadelphia rabbinical conference he resigned his presidency when his colleagues ignored what for him was a vital distinction between teaching (*Lehre*) and law (*Gesetz*). Against his wishes, they voted to accept a wedding formula that included the words "law of God" instead of his proposal, the "teaching of God".[84] Other votes, too, went against Hirsch's opinion. The gathered rabbis rejected Hirsch's proposal regarding Hebrew, preferring Einhorn's formulation instead. And when Hirsch suggested that the conference need not oppose resurrection of the dead since the doctrine allowed of a spiritual interpretation, his colleagues followed Einhorn in rejecting that view.[85] As we have seen, his congregation resisted his Sabbath proposal and his officiation at mixed marriages. And ultimately, they forced his retirement.

Samuel Hirsch was a man of considerable amour-propre. In introducing his major European work he had pointed to himself obliquely as "a proficient and in every respect well-trained spiritual leader".[86] These American setbacks hurt his self-estimation. His bitter disputes left bad feelings on both sides, which could be patched over only with difficulty. Though there may have been some, we know of no close friends outside the rabbinical community, either Jew or Gentile. Surely, he must have been struck with a sense of loneliness in an America with whose republicanism he could not fully identify, whose materialism he abhorred even as he envied Jastrow's higher income,[87] and whose language he could not fully master. Most of all perhaps, it was the rejection of his radical reform ideas that set him apart. In his day he was indeed the most extreme among the prominent Jewish religious reformers in America. Faced with rejection, he could only

---

[82] Die Deborah 13 (1868), 114.
[83] Hirsch, "Die Lehre, die uns Moscheh anbefohlen", 5; The Reform Advocate 49 (1915), 750.
[84] *Protokolle der Rabbiner-Conferenz*, 22–25.
[85] Ibid., 10–11, 15.
[86] Hirsch, *Die Religionsphilosophie*, x. The puffed-up self-image recurs in *Dr. Jastrow und sein Gebaren*, p. 4, where Hirsch refers to himself in the third person.
[87] Hirsch, *Dr. Jastrow und sein Gebaren*, 25.

look straight ahead, hoping that one day his views would gain broader support.[88]

---

[88] Chicago Sinai Congregation, *In Memory of Dr. Samuel Hirsch, Rabbi Emeritus Reform Congregation Keneseth Israel, Philadelphia* (Chicago: S. Ettlinger, 1889), 11, 21. Appropriately enough, engraved into his monument is the citation: "Look neither to the right, nor to the left, but confident of the invincible power of truth, advance, those who now lag behind will follow, and those who now oppose will sooner or later endorse our movement."

Bibliography

Primary Sources

1. Archives and Historical Documents

American Jewish Archives (Cincinnati)
Archive of the University of Leipzig
Archives de la Ville de Luxembourg
Archives Départementales de la Moselle [ADM]
Archives Nationales de France [ANF]
Archives Nationales de Luxembourg [ANL]
Jewish National University Library, manuscript division (Jerusalem)
Landeshauptarchiv Koblenz [LHAK]
Commission royale pour la publication des anciennes lois et ordonnances de la Belgique, *Règne de Charles-Quint, 1506–1555, Liste chronologique des édits et ordonnances des Pays-Bas*, part 1 (Bruxelles: Fr. Gobbaerts, 1885).
Commission royale pour la publication des anciennes lois et ordonnances de la Belgique, *Liste chronologique des édits et ordonnances des Pays-Bas autrichiens, de 1751à 1794*, part 2: *1781–1794* (Brussels: Em. Devroye, 1858).
"Die Ergebnisse der Berufszählung vom 12. Juni 1907 im Großherzogtum Luxemburg", Zeitschrift für Demographie und Statistik der Juden 7, 2 (1911), 29–30.
"Ergebnisse der Volkszählung in Luxemburg am 1./12. 1905", Zeitschrift für Demographie und Statistik der Juden 3, 6 (1907), 94.
Jehle, Manfred, ed., *Die Juden und die jüdischen Gemeinden Preußens in amtlichen Enquêten des Vormärz*, vol. 2: *Enquête des Ministeriums des Innern und der Polizei über die Rechtsverhältnisse der Juden in den preußischen Provinzen 1842–1843: Rheinprovinz, Enquête des Ministeriums der geistlichen, Unterrichts- und Medizinal-Angelegenheiten über die Kultus-, Schul- und Rechtsverhältnisse der jüdischen Gemeinden in den preußischen Provinzen 1843–1845: Berlin, Provinzen Brandenburg, Preußen, Pommern*, Veröffentlichungen der Historischen Kommission zu Berlin 82, 2 (München: Saur, 1998).
Mémorial du Grand-Duché de Luxembourg, 1841, 1843, 1847, 1848, 1849, 1850, 1854, 1855, 1856, 1860, 1861, 1865, 1868 online via: https://legilux.public.lu/.
Muller, Jean Claude, "Le registre de prise de noms des Juifs de Luxembourg (département des Forêts) en 1808. Edition en fac-similé de l'original conservé aux Archives de la Ville de Luxembourg", Annales de l'institut archéologique du Luxembourg 136, 1 (2005), 255–286.
Neher-Bernheim, Rina, *Documents inédits sur l'entrée des Juifs dans la société française (1750–1850)*, vol. 2, Publications of the Diaspora Research Institute 5 (Tel Aviv: Diaspora Research Institute, 1977).
Statec Luxembourg, *Statistiques historiques: 1839–1989* (Luxemburg: Statec, 1990).
Thill, Jean, *Documents et textes relatifs aux Constitutions et Institutions politiques luxembourgeoises* (Luxembourg: Centre de documentation communale, 1978, 2nd edition).

"Verfassung Luxemburgs, Revision vom 17. Oktober 1868", Mémorial du Grand-Duché de Luxembourg, Première Partie: Actes législatifs et d'administration générale, Luxemburg 1868, no. 23, 213–242.

"Verfassung Luxemburgs vom 9. Juli 1848", Mémorial du Grand-Duché de Luxembourg, 1848, no. 52, 389–414.

"Verfassung Luxemburgs vom 16. Oktober 1841", Mémorial du Grand-Duché de Luxembourg, 1841, no. 51, 425–436.

"Verfassung Luxemburgs vom 27. November 1856", Mémorial du Grand-Duché de Luxembourg, Première Partie: Actes législatifs et d'administration générale, Luxemburg 1856, no. 28 (30. November 1856), 209–248.

"Wahlgesetz von 1848", Mémorial du Grand-Duché de Luxembourg, 1848, no. 64, 497–515, Art. 1.

"Wahlgesetz von 1860", Mémorial du Grand-Duché de Luxembourg, Première Partie: Actes législatifs et d'administration générale, Luxemburg 1860, no. 28, 157–176.

"Wahlgesetz von 1868", Mémorial du Grand-Duché de Luxembourg, Première Partie: Actes législatifs et d'administration générale, Luxemburg 1868, no. 26, 269f.

2. Newspapers

Courrier du Grand-Duché de Luxembourg
Das Luxemburger Wort für Wahrheit und Recht
Diekircher Wochenblatt
Der Volksfreund
Echternacher Grenzbote
Journal de Luxembourg

3. Samuel Hirsch Publications

Books

Hirsch, Samuel, *Das Judenthum, der christliche Staat und die moderne Kritik: Briefe zur Beleuchtung der Judenfrage von Bruno Bauer* (Leipzig: Heinrich Hunger, 1843).

Hirsch, Samuel, *Das Nothwendigste aus der Formen-Lehre der Hebräischen Sprache* (Philadelphia: Grassman & Goodman, 1867).

Hirsch, Samuel, *Der rechte Kampf für die Wahrheit: Gast-Predigt in der Synagoge zu Schwerin in Mecklenburg gehalten den 31 October 1846* (Schwerin: Kürschner, 1847).

Hirsch, Samuel, *Die Humanität als Religion in Vorträgen, gehalten in der Loge zu Luxemburg* (Trier: C. Troschel, 1854).

Hirsch, Samuel, *"Die Lehre, die uns Moscheh anbefohlen, ist Erbbesitz der Gemeinden Jakobs." Predigt gehalten am [Shemini atseret] 5628, in der Synagoge der Ref. Gem. Keneseth Israel, in Philadelphia* (Philadelphia: Stein u. Jones, 1867).

Hirsch, Samuel, *Die Messiaslehre der Juden in Kanzelvorträgen. Zur Erbauung denkender Leser* (Leipzig: Heinrich Hunger, 1843).

Hirsch, Samuel, *Die Reform im Judenthum und dessen Beruf In der gegenwärtigen Welt* (Leipzig: Heinrich Hunger, 1844).
Hirsch, Samuel, *Die Religionsphilosophie der Juden oder das Prinzip der jüdischen Religionsanschauung und sein Verhältniß zum Heidenthum, Christenthum und zur absoluten Philosophie dargestellt und mit den erläuterten Beweisstellen aus der heiligen Schrift, den Talmudim und Midraschim versehen* (Leipzig: Heinrich Hunger 1842; reprint Hildesheim, Zurich, and New York: Olms, 1986); also referred to as *Das System der religiösen Anschauung der Juden und sein Verhältniß zum Heidenthum, Christenthum und zur absoluten Philosophie*: Erster Band: *Die Religionsphilosophie der Juden oder das Prinzip der jüdischen Religionsanschauung und sein Verhältniß zum Heidenthum, Christenthum und zur absoluten Philosophie dargestellt und mit den erläuterten Beweisstellen aus der heiligen Schrift, den Talmudim und Midraschim versehen* (Leipzig: Heinrich Hunger, 1842).
Hirsch, Samuel, *Die Sabbathfrage vor der dritten Rabbinerversammlung. Ein Votum* (Berlin: self-published, 1846).
Hirsch, Samuel, *Dr. Jastrow und sein Gebaren in Philadelphia: Ein ehrliches, leider abgenoethigtes Wort* (Philadelphia: n.p., terminus post quem 17 February 1868).
Hirsch, Samuel, *Friede, Freiheit und Einheit: Sechs Predigten gehalten in der Synagoge zu Dessau* (Dessau: Hermann Neubürger, 1839).
Hirsch, Samuel, *Predigt zur hundertjährigen Geburtsfeier Sr. Hochfürstl. Durchlaucht unseres hochseligen Herzogs Leopold Friedrich Franz, am 10. August 1840 in der Synagoge zu Dessau gehalten und zum Besten der israel. Franzschule herausgegeben* (Dessau: Hermann Neubürger, 1840).
Hirsch, Samuel, *Rev. Dr. David Einhorn, Rabbiner der Beth-El Gemeinde, New York. Gedächtniss-Rede, gehalten vor seinem Sarge in der Synagoge obiger Gemeinde, den 6ten November 1879, und dem Inhalte nach wiederholt, den 8. November, 1879 in der Keneseth Israel Synagoge in Philadelphia* (Philadelphia: Congregation Keneseth Israel, 1879).
Hirsch, Samuel, *Systematischer Katechismus der israelitischen Religion, auf Beschluß des Vorstandes der israelitischen Gemeinde zu Luxemburg* (Luxembourg: Bück, 1856; Philadelphia: S.M. Larzelere, 1877, 2nd improved and expanded edition).
Hirsch, Samuel, *"Unerhörte Pilpulistik". Offenes Sendschreiben an Rev. Dr. K. Kohler, Rabbiner der Beth-El Gemeinde in New York* (Philadelphia: s.n., 1880).
Hirsch, Samuel, *Was ist Judenthum und was dessen Verhältniss zu andern Religionen? Predigt zur Einsegnungsfeier seiner beiden Zöglinge Theodor und Oskar Heymann gehalten am 17. Juni 1838* (Berlin: Heymann, 1838).

Articles

Hirsch, Samuel, "Bibelkritik und Reformjudenthum", Der Zeitgeist 2 (1881), 143.
Hirsch, Samuel, "Darf ein Reformrabbiner Ehen zwischen Juden und Nichtjuden einsegnen?", The Jewish Times 1, 27 (1969/70), 9–10; no. 28, 10–11; no. 30, 9–10; no. 31, 10; no. 32, 10; no. 33, 10; no. 34, 10; no. 35, 11; no. 36, 13.
Hirsch, Samuel, "Das Judenthum, der Freiheit und die Offenbarung", Die Deborah 13 (1870), 130–131, 134, 138, 143.

Hirsch, Samuel, "Der Nagel zum Sarge der winzigen jüdischen Race", The Jewish Times 1, 47 (1869/70), 10–11.
Hirsch, Samuel, "Die amerikanische Orthodoxie und das mosaische Erbrecht", Die Deborah 13 (1867), 146–147, 150–151.
Hirsch, Samuel, "Die amerikanische Orthodoxie: Hut auf oder Hut ab", Die Deborah 13 (1867), 110, 114, 118, 122, 126, 158–159.
Hirsch, Samuel, "Die Bibel und das moderne Judenthum", Die Deborah 13 (1867), 158–159.
Hirsch, Samuel, "Die Bibel und die freie Forschung", Die Deborah 13 (1867), 162–163.
Hirsch, Samuel, "Die Humanitarier und das Reformjudenthum", Jewish Times 1, 15 (1869), 10–11; no. 16, 10–11.
Hirsch, Samuel, "Die rabbinische Ehescheidung, der Get", Die Deborah 14 (1868), 6, 10–11, 14.
Hirsch, Samuel, "Die Speisegesetze (Aus einem demnächst erscheinenden Handbuch für israelitische Religionslehrer)", Der Israelit des neunzehnten Jahrhunderts 7, 18 (1846), 137–140; no. 19, 145–148; no. 20, 154–159.
Hirsch, Samuel, "Die talmudische Auffassung des Judenthums nicht falsch sondern nur ein überwundener Standpunkt", The Jewish Times 1, 14 (1869/70), 10–11.
Hirsch, Samuel, "Freiheit und Judenthum", The Jewish Times 1, 3 (1869/70), 11–12; no. 4, 12; no. 5, 12–13; no. 6, 11–12; no. 7, 11–12; no. 8, 12–13.
Hirsch, Samuel: "Herrn Dr. Jastrow", The Jewish Times 5 (1874/75), 542–543, 559, 574–575.
Hirsch, Samuel, "La Verité du Dieu-Un et la Mission d'Israel", Archives israélites 26 (1864), 194–200.
Hirsch, Samuel, "Offenes Sendschreiben an die Herren Aeltesten zu Dessau", Allgemeine Zeitung des Judenthums 6, 15 (1842) (supplement).
Hirsch, Samuel, "Offenes Sendschreiben an Herrn Dr. K. Kohler", Der Zeitgeist 1 (1880), 202–203.
Hirsch, Samuel, "Rechte und falsche Orthodoxie", Die Deborah 13 (1867), 130.
Hirsch, Samuel, "The Reform Worship", The Jewish Times 1, 18 (1869/70), 3–4; no. 19, 3–4; no. 20, 4; no. 21, 5–6; no. 22, 3–4; no. 23, 4.
Hirsch, Samuel, "Report of the Committee on the Initiatory Rites of Proselytes", Central Conference of American Rabbis Year Book 3 (1893), 69–73.
Hirsch, Samuel, "Revelation and Judaism", The Jewish Reformer 1, 2 (January 8, 1886), 4.
Hirsch, Samuel, "Samuel Holdheim, *Ueber die Autonomie der Rabbinen und das Princip der jüdischen Ehe. Ein Beitrag zur Verständigung über einige das Judenthum betreffende Zeitfragen (Schwerin: C. Kürschner, 1843)*" (Kurze Anzeigen), Literaturblatt des Orients 44 (31 October 1843), cols. 696–699.
Hirsch, Samuel, "Sermon, Delivered on Sunday, May 14th, the Opening Day of the German Peace Festival", The Jewish Times 3 (1871/72), 196–198.
Hirsch, Samuel, "Staatrechtliches", Die Deborah 13 (1867), 190, 194–195.
Hirsch, Samuel, "Theorie und Praxis", Der Zeitgeist 1 (1880), 162.
Hirsch, Samuel, "Was ist Frömmigkeit im Sinne des Judenthums?", Der Zeitgeist 2 (1881), 244, 258, 273.

4. Primary Literature

A., "Die Messiaslehre der Juden in Kanzelvorträgen. Zur Erbauung denkender Leser herausgegeben von Dr. Samuel Hirsch, Rabbiner. Leipzig 1843. 8. Heinrich Hunger", Literaturblatt des Orients 18 (2 May 1843), cols. 273–279; no. 19 (9 May 1843), 291–296; no. 20 (16 May 1843), 309–313.
"Abraham Geigers Briefe an J. Derenbourg (1833–42)", Allgemeine Zeitung des Judenthums 60, 14 (1896), 164–166.
"Aufruf zu einer Rabbiner-Conferenz", The Jewish Times 1, 14 (1869/70).
Bauer, Bruno, *Das entdeckte Christentum* (Zürich: Verlag des Literarischen Comptoirs, 1843).
Bauer, Bruno, *Das Judenthum in der Fremde* (Berlin: F. Heinicke, 1863).
Bauer, Bruno, "Die Fähigkeit der heutigen Juden und Christen frei zu sein", in Georg Herwegh, ed., *Einundzwanzig Bogen aus der Schweiz* (Zürich and Winterthur: Verlag des Literarischen Comptoirs, 1843), 56–71.
Bauer, Bruno, *Die Judenfrage* (Braunschweig: Otto, 1843).
Bauer, Bruno, *Kritik der evangelischen Geschichte der Synoptiker*, 2 vol. (Leipzig: Otto Wigand, 1841).
Bauer, Bruno, *Kritik der evangelischen Geschichte der Synoptiker und des Johannes* (Berlin: Friedrich Otto, 1842).
Bauer, Bruno, *Kritik der Geschichte der Offenbarung: Die Religion des Alten Testaments*, vol. 1 (Berlin: Dümmler, 1838).
Bendavid, Lazarus, *Über den Glauben der Juden an einen künftigen Messias* (Berlin: Trowitzsch, 1823).
Chicago Sinai Congregation, *In Memory of Dr. Samuel Hirsch, Rabbi Emeritus Reform Congregation Keneseth Israel, Philadelphia* (Chicago: S. Ettlinger, 1889).
"Des Dr. Hirsch Votum über die Sabbathfrage", Der Israelit des neunzehnten Jahrhunderts 7, 34 (1846), 266–268.
Dohm, Christian Wilhelm, *Über die bürgerliche Verbesserung der Juden: Kritische und kommentierte Studienausgabe*, ed. Christoph Seifert (Göttingen: Wallstein Verlag, 2015).
Einhorn, David, "Gutachtliche Äußerung eines jüdischen Theologen über den Reformverein an einen sich dafür interessierenden Christen", Allgemeine Zeitung des Judenthums 8, 7 (1844), 87–89.
Einhorn, David, "Holdheim's Religionsbuch: Haemuna wehadea", Sinai 4 (1859/60), no. 2, 33–38; no. 3, 65–71; no. 4, 97–102; no. 5, 129–137.
Einhorn, David, "Noch ein Wort über gemischte Ehen", The Jewish Times 1, 48 (1869/70), 10–13.
Einhorn, David, "Prinzipielle Differenzpunkte zwischen altem und neuem Judentum", Sinai 1 (1856/57), no. 6, 162–164; no. 7, 193–197; no. 10, 290–294; no. 11, 333–335; no. 12, 365–371; 2 (1857/58), no. 1, 399–404; no. 5, 540–544; no. 6, 572–576; 7 (1862/63), no. 12, 320–327.
Einhorn, David, "Response to a Biblical View of Slavery", Sinai 6 (1861), 2–22, http://www.jewish-history.com/civilwar/einhorn.html.
Einhorn, David, "Stein's Thora umizwah und Holdheim's Haemuna wehadea", Sinai 1, 4 (1856/57), 507–511.
Einhorn, David, *Zwei Predigten gehalten im Tempel der Adath-Jeshurun-Gemeinde zu New York* (New York: New York Engraving, Lithographing & Printing Co, 1868).
Eisenmenger, Andreas, *Entdecktes Judenthum* (Frankfurt: n.p., 1700).

Felsenthal, Bernhard, "Gedächtnisrede", in Chicago Sinai Congregation, *In Memory of Dr. Samuel Hirsch, Rabbi Emeritus Reform Congregation Keneseth Israel, Philadelphia* (Chicago: S. Ettlinger, 1889), 23–25.

Feuerbach, Ludwig, *Das Wesen des Christentums* (Leipzig: Otto Wigand, 1841).

Feuerbach, Ludwig, *The Essence of Christianity*, trans. George Elliot [Marian Evans] (London: John Chapman, 1854).

Feuerbach, Ludwig, "Zur Kritik der Hegel'schen Philosophie", in Arnold Ruge and Theodor Echtermeyer, Hallische Jahrbücher für Deutsche Wissenschaft und Kunst 208 (1839), 1157–1160; no. 209, 1165–1168; no. 210, 1673–1677; no. 211, 1681–1684; no. 212, 1689–1693; no. 213, 1697–1702; no. 214, 1705–1709; no. 215, 1713–1718; no. 216, 1721–1725.

Formstecher, Salomon, *Religion des Geistes: Eine wissenschaftliche Darstellung des Judenthums nach seinem Charakter, Entwicklungsgange und Berufe in der Menschheit* (Frankfurt am Main: Hermann, 1841).

Geiger, Abraham, Abhandlungen aus den "Programmen der jüdischen Religionsunterrichts-Anstalt in Breslau 1844–1863", in Ludwig Geiger, ed., *Abraham Geiger's Nachgelassene Schriften*, vol. 1 (Berlin: Louis Gerschel, 1875), 305–351.

Geiger, Abraham, "Bruno Bauer und die Juden. Mit Bezug auf dessen Aufsatz: Die Judenfrage", Wissenschaftliche Zeitschrift für jüdische Theologie 5, 2 (1844), 199–234; 325–371.

Geiger, Abraham, *Was hat Mohammed aus dem Judenthume aufgenommen?* (Bonn: F. Baden, 1833).

Geiger, Ludwig, *Abraham Geiger: Leben und Lebenswerk* (Berlin: Georg Reimer, 1910).

Geiger, Ludwig, ed., *Abraham Geiger's Leben in Briefen* (Berlin: Louis Gerschel, 1878).

Graetz, Heinrich, "Die Verjüngung des jüdischen Stammes", Jahrbuch der Israeliten 10 (5624/1863–1864), 1–13.

Graetz, Heinrich, *Geschichte der Juden vom Beginn der mendelssohnschen Zeit (1750) bis in die neueste Zeit (1848)*, (1870), Geschichte der Juden von den ältesten Zeiten bis auf die Gegenwart, vol. 11 (Darmstadt: Wissenschaftliche Buchgesellschaft, 1998, reprint, 2nd edition).

Hegel, Georg Wilhelm Friedrich, "Der Geist des Christentums und sein Schicksal", in Hermann Nohl, ed., *Hegels Theologische Jugendschriften. Nach den Handschriften der Kgl. Bibliothek in Berlin* (Tübingen: J.C.B. Mohr, 1907), 241–342.

Hegel, Georg Wilhelm Friedrich, *Grundlinien der Philosophie des Rechts*, ed. Georg Lasson (Leipzig: F. Meiner, 1911).

Hegel, Georg Wilhelm Friedrich, *Introduction to the Philosophy of History*, trans. Leo Rauch (Indianapolis: Hackett Publishing, 1988), 22, 92–98.

Hegel, Georg Wilhelm Friedrich, *Lectures on the Philosophy of Religion*, vol. 1: *Introduction and the Concept of Religion*, ed. Peter C. Hodgson, trans. Robert F. Brown et al. (Oxford: Oxford University Press, 2007).

Hegel, Georg Wilhelm Friedrich, *Lectures on the Philosophy of Religion*, vol. 2, ed. Peter C. Hodgson, trans. E.B. Speirs and J. Burdon Sanderson (London: Routledge and Kegan Paul; New York: The Humanities Press, 1968).

Hegel, Georg Wilhelm Friedrich, *Lectures on the Philosophy of Religion*, vol. 2, ed. Peter C. Hodgson, trans. Robert F. Brown et al. (Berkeley: University of California Press, 1984–1987).

Hegel, Georg Wilhelm Friedrich, *Vorlesungen über die Philosophie der Religion* (1832), parts 1–3, ed. Walter Jaeschke (Hamburg: Meiner, 1983–85, 1993–1995).
Hegel's Phenomenology of Spirit, trans. Arnold Vincent Miller (Oxford: Clarendon Press, 1977).
Hegel's Philosophy of Mind, trans. William Wallace and Arnold Vincent Miller (Oxford: Clarendon Press, 1971).
Herzfeld, Levi, *Zwei Predigten über die Lehre vom Messias* (Braunschweig: Friedrich Bieweg, 1844).
Hess, Mendel, "Der Frankfurter Reformverein", Der Israelit des neunzehnten Jahrhunderts 4 (1843), no. 46, 183–185; no. 47, 187–188; no. 48, 191–192.
Hess, Moses, "Briefe über Israels Mission in der Geschichte der Menschheit", in Theodor Zlocisti, ed. and intr., *Moses Hess. Jüdische Schriften* (Berlin: Lamm, 1905), 16–49.
Hess, Moses, "Die europäische Triarchie", in Wolfgang Mönke, ed., *Moses Hess. Philosophische und sozialistische Schriften, 1837–1850. Eine Auswahl* (Vaduz: Topos Verlag, 1980, 2nd edition), 75–168.
Hess, Moses, "Noch ein Wort über meine Missionsauffassung", in Theodor Zlocisti, ed. and intr., *Moses Hess. Jüdische Schriften* (Berlin: Lamm, 1905), 68–69.
Hess, Moses, "Notiz- und Tagebücher 1837", in Wolfgang Mönke, *Neue Quellen zur Heß-Forschung. Mit Auszügen aus einem Tagebuch, aus Manuskripten und Briefen aus der Korrespondenz mit Marx, Engels, Weitling, Ewerbeck, u.a* (Berlin: Akademie-Verlag, 1964).
Hess, Moses, *Rom und Jerusalem, die letzte Nationalitätenfrage: Briefe und Noten* (Leipzig: Eduard Wengler, 1862).
Hess, Moses, "Über das Geldwesen", in Wolfgang Mönke, ed., *Moses Hess. Philosophische und sozialistische Schriften, 1837–1850. Eine Auswahl* (Vaduz: Topos Verlag, 1980, 2nd edition), 329–347.
Hirsch, Emil, "My Father and Teacher", The Reform Advocate (29 May 1915), 497–503.
Holdheim, Samuel, *Das Ceremonialgesetz im Messiasreich* (Schwerin: Verlag der C. Kürschner'schen Buchhandlung, 1845).
Holdheim, Samuel, *Die Erhaltung des Judenthums im Kampfe mit der Zeit: Ein Bild aus der Vergangenheit belehrend für die Gegenwart. Predigt gehalten im Gotteshause der jüdischen Reformgemeinde zu Berlin (am 11. Mai 1851)* (Berlin: L. Lassar, 1851).
Holdheim, Samuel, *Gemischte Ehen zwischen Juden und Christen. Die Gutachten der Berliner Rabbinatsverwaltung und des Königsberger Konsistoriums beleuchtet* (Berlin: L. Lassar, 1850).
Holdheim, Samuel, *Ha-emunah veha-deah: Jüdische Glaubens- und Sittenlehre. Leitfaden beim Religionsunterricht der jüdischen Jugend. Zunächst für die Religionsschule der jüdischen Reformgemeinde zu Berlin* (Berlin: Julius Springer, 1857).
Holdheim, Samuel, *Ueber die Autonomie der Rabbinen und das Princip der jüdischen Ehe. Ein Beitrag zur Verständigung über einige das Judenthum betreffende Zeitfragen* (Schwerin: Kürschner, 1843).
Jastrow, Marcus, *Antwort an Herrn I. M. Wise in Cincinnati* (n.p., n.d.).
Jastrow, Marcus, *Gegenerklärung auf die "Erklärung" des Herrn I. M. Wise* (Philadelphia: Stein u. Jones, 1867).
Jastrow, Marcus, *Offene Erklärung an Herrn I. M. Wise* (Philadelphia: Stein u. Jones, 1867).

Jellinek, Hermann, "Die Judenfrage. Teil 1", Literaturblatt des Orients 25 (20 Juni 1843), 385–390; "Die Judenfrage. Teil 2", Literaturblatt des Orients 26 (27 Juni 1843), 401–408; "Die Judenfrage. Teil 3", Literaturblatt des Orients 27 (4 Juli 1843), 423–430.

Kant, Immanuel, *Die Religion innerhalb der Grenzen der bloßen Vernunft* (1793) (Berlin: Akademie Ausgabe, 1914, VI).

Kohler, Kaufmann, "Leichenrede für Dr. Samuel Hirsch gehalten von Dr. K. Kohler, Rabbiner der Beth El Gemeinde, New York. Chicago, 17. Mai 1889", in Chicago Sinai Congregation, *In Memory of Dr. Samuel Hirsch, Rabbi Emeritus Reform Congregation Keneseth Israel, Philadelphia* (Chicago: Ettlinger, 1889), 18–22.

Kohler, Kaufmann, "Über Mischehen. Ein Gutachten", Der Zeitgeist 1 (1880), 76–78, 180–182.

Kohler, Kaufmann, and Isidore Singer, "Bauer, Bruno", https://www.jewishencyclopedia.com/articles/2668-bauer-bruno.

Krauskopf, Joseph, *Obituary-Address in Honor of the Late Dr. Samuel Hirsch* (Philadelphia: S.W. Goodman, 1889).

Levi, Gerson B., *Samuel Hirsch: Address at Tempel Keneseth Israel, Philadelphia, at the Celebration of the Centenary of the Rev. Dr. Samuel Hirsch, November 7, 1915* (Cincinnati, OH: n.p., 1916/17).

Maimonides, "Kings and Wars", in idem, *Mishneh Torah*, ch. 12. https://www.sefaria.org/Mishneh_Torah%2C_Kings_and_Wars.12.1?ven=Laws_of_Kings_and_Wars._trans._Reuven_Brauner,_2012&vhe=Torat_Emet_363&lang=bi.

Marx, Karl, and Friedrich Engels, *Die heilige Familie oder Kritik der kritischen Kritik Gegen Bruno Bauer & Consorten* (Frankfurt a.M.: Literarische Anstalt, 1845).

Mendelssohn, Moses, *Jerusalem oder über religiöse Macht und Judentum*, ed. David Martyn (Bielefeld: Aisthesis, 2001).

Mendelssohn, Moses, *Schriften zur Philosophie, Aesthetik und Apologetik*, ed. Moritz Brasch, (repr. Hildesheim: Olms, 1968).

Nitzsch, Karl Immanuel, *System der christlichen Lehre* (Bonn: Adolph Marcus, 1851).

Oko, Adolph S., *Bibliography of Dr. Samuel Hirsch (b. June 8, 1815; d. May 14, 1889)* (Cincinnati, OH: n.p., 1916).

Philippson, Gustav, *Die Judenfrage von Bruno Bauer näher beleuchtet* (Dessau: Fritsche, 1843).

Philippson, Ludwig, *Die israelitische Religionslehre*, vol. 3 (Leipzig: Baumgärtner, 1865).

Philippson, Ludwig, "Vergleichende Skizzen über Judentum und Christentum", (1869) in idem, *Gesammelte Abhandlungen*, vol. 1, ed. Martin Philippson (Leipzig: Fock, 1911), 199–324.

Philippson, Ludwig, "Wohin?", Allgemeine Zeitung des Judenthums 7, 34 (1843), 502–503.

Protocolle der ersten Rabbiner-Versammlung abgehalten zu Braunschweig (Braunschweig: Friedrich Bieweg, 1844),

Protokolle der Rabbiner-Conferenz abgehalten zu Philadelphia, vom 3. bis zum 6. November 1869 (New York: S. Hecht, 1870).

Protokolle und Aktenstücke der zweiten Rabbiner-Versammlung (Frankfurt a.M.: E. Ullmann, 1845).

Ruge, Arnold, and Ernst Theodor Echtermeyer, *Der Protestantismus und die Romantik: Zur Verständigung über die Zeit und ihre Gegensätze: Ein Manifest* (1839) (Hildesheim: H. A. Gerstenberg, 1972 reprint).

Sachs, Michael, "Gutachten über den Reformverein", Zeitschrift für die religiösen Interessen des Judentums 1, 2 (1844), 49–60.
Salomon, Gotthold, *Bruno Bauer und seine gehaltlose Kritik über die Judenfrage* (Hamburg: Perthes-Besser & Mauke, 1843).
Segall, Jakob, "Die Juden im Großherzogtum Luxemberg", Zeitschrift für Demographie und Statistik der Juden 6, 2 (1910), 24–27.
Stahl, Friedrich Julius, *Die Philosophie des Rechts nach geschichtlicher Ansicht*, vol. 2: *Christliche Rechts- und Staatslehre*, Abtheilung 2 (Heidelberg: Mohr, 1837).
Steinheim, Salomon Ludwig, "Die Messiasidee nach der Bestimmung der Offenbarungslehre", Zeitschrift für die religiösen Interessen des Judenthums 2, 1 (1845), 21–23; no. 2, 2 (1845), 41–49.
Steinthal, Heymann, "Ein jüdischer Religionsphilosoph unseres Jahrhunderts", Allgemeine Zeitung des Judenthums 59, 10 (1895), 126–128; 59, 11 (1895), 138–140.
Strauss, David Friedrich, *Das Leben Jesu* (Tübingen: C. F. Osiander, 1838).
Szold, Benjamin, *Auch ein Wort über Jastrow & Hirsch* (Baltimore: C.W. Schneidereith, 1868).
Trier, Salomon Abraham, ed., *Rabbinische Gutachten über die Beschneidung. Gesammelt und herausgegeben von Salomon Abraham Trier, Rabbiner, Als Manuskript gedruckt* (Frankfurt am Main: Bach, 1844).
"Über die Judenfrage", Allgemeine Literatur-Zeitung 1 (December 1843), 1–17.
Wellhausen, Julius, *Prolegomena zur Geschichte Israels* (Berlin: De Gruyter, 2001).

5. Secondary Literature

Adorno, Theodor W., and Max Horkheimer, *Dialektik der Aufklärung* (Amsterdam: Querido, 1947).
Allen, Chris, *Islamophobia* (Farnham: Ashgate, 2010).
Améry, Jean, "Rasende Verbrecher" (Anhang zu *Jenseits von Schuld und Sühne*), in Gerhard Scheit, ed., *Jean Améry. Werke*, vol. 2 (Stuttgart: Klett-Cotta, 2002), 505–513.
Anchel, Robert, *Napoléon et les Juifs* (Paris: Les presses universitaires de France, 1928).
Arndt, Martin, "Hegel und das Judentum", Hegel Jahrbuch 19, 1 (2013), 28–35.
Avineri, Shlomo, *Moses Hess: Prophet of Communism and Zionism* (New York: NYU Press, 1985).
Baumann, Ulrich, *Zerstörte Nachbarschaften: Christen und Juden in badischen Landgemeinden 1862–1940*, Studien zur jüdischen Geschichte 7 (Hamburg: Dölling und Galitz, 2004).
Behm, Britta L., "Moses Mendelssohn und die Frage der 'bürgerlichen Verbesserung' der Juden – Ansätze zur jüdischen Integration zwischen 'Gleichheit' und 'Mannigfaltigkeit'", in idem, ed., *Jüdische Erziehung und aufklärerische Schulreform: Analysen zum späten 18. und frühen 19. Jahrhundert*, Jüdische Bildungsgeschichte in Deutschland 5 (Münster: Waxmann, 2002), 269–289.
Berding, Helmut, *Moderner Antisemitismus in Deutschland* (Frankfurt am Main: Suhrkamp Verlag, 1st edition, 1988).
Berlin, Isaiah, "The Life and Origins of Moses Hess", in Philipp Rief, ed., *On Intellectuals: Theoretical Studies, Cases Studies* (Garden City, NY: Doubleday, 1966), 125–166.

Binnenkade, Alexandra, *Kontaktzonen: Jüdisch-christlicher Alltag in Lengnau*, Industrielle Welt 75 (Köln: Böhlau, 2009).
Birnbaum, Pierre, *L'Aigle et la Synagogue : Napoléon, les Juifs et l'Etat* (Paris: Fayard, 2007).
Blaschke, Olaf, "Die Anatomie des katholischen Antisemitismus. Eine Einladung zum internationalen Vergleich", in Olaf Blaschke and Aram Mattioli, eds., *Katholischer Antisemitismus im 19. Jahrhundert: Ursachen und Traditionen im internationalen Vergleich* (Zürich: Orell Füssli, 2000), 3–56.
Blaschke, Olaf, *Katholizismus und Antisemitismus im Deutschen Kaiserreich* (Göttingen: Vandenhoeck & Ruprecht, 1997).
Blau, Lucien, "Antisémitisme au Grand-Duché de Luxembourg de la fin du XIXe siècle à 1940", in Laurent Moyse and Marc Schoentgen, eds., *La présence juive au Luxembourg: Du moyen âge au XXe siècle* (Luxembourg: B'nai Brith 2001), 57–70.
Boch, Volker, *Juden in Gemünden: Geschichte und Vernichtung einer jüdischen Gemeinde im Hunsrück* (Konstanz: Hartung-Gorre, 2003).
Bouretz, Pierre, "Messianism and Modern Jewish Philosophy", in Michael L. Morgan and Peter Eli Gordon, eds., *The Cambridge Companion to Modern Jewish Philosophy* (Cambridge: Cambridge University Press, 2007), 170–191.
Bourgeois, Bernard, "Judaïsme", in idem, *Hegel à Francfort ou Judaïsme, Christianisme, Hegelianisme* (Paris: Vrin, 1970), 35–55.
Brämer, Andreas, *Leistung und Gegenleistung: Zur Geschichte jüdischer Religions- und Elementarlehrer in Preussen 1823/24 bis 1872*, Hamburger Beiträge zur Geschichte der deutschen Juden 30 (Göttingen: Wallstein, 2006).
Brandt, Peter, Martin Kirsch, and Arthur Schlegelmilch, eds., *Handbuch der europäischen Verfassungsgeschichte im 19. Jahrhundert*, vol. 1: *Um 1800* (Bonn: Dietz, 2006).
Brechenmacher, Thomas, *Der Vatikan und die Juden: Geschichte einer unheiligen Beziehung vom 16. Jahrhundert bis in die Gegenwart* (München: Beck, 2005).
Brentano, Margherita von, *Akademische Schriften* (Göttingen: Wallstein, 2010).
Brocke, Michael and Julius Carlebach, eds., *Biographisches Handbuch der Rabbiner*, vol. 1: *Die Rabbiner der Emanzipationszeit in den deutschen, böhmischen und großpolnischen Ländern 1781–1871*, arranged by Carsten Wilke (München: K.G. Saur, 2004).
Brumlik, Micha, *Deutscher Geist und Judenhaß: Das Verhältnis des philosophischen Idealismus zum Judentum* (Munich: Luchterhand, 2000).
Brumlik, Micha, *Hegels Juden. Reformer, Sozialisten, Zionisten* (Berlin: Neofelis Verlag, 2019).
Bühler, Marianne, "Die jüdische Gemeinde Triers zur Zeit der Franzosen", in Elisabeth Dühr and Christl Lehnert-Leven, eds., *Unter Der Trikolore: Trier in Frankreich, Napoleon in Trier* (Trier: Städtisches Museum Simeonstift, 2004), 437–459.
Bumb, Christoph, *Luxemburgs Weg zur parlamentarischen Demokratie* (Berlin: VS-Verlag für Sozialwissenschaften, 2011).
Bunzl, Matti, *Anti-Semitism and Islamophobia: Hatreds Old and New in Europe* (Chicago: Prickly Paradigm Press, 2007).
Bürge, Alfons, *Das französische Privatrecht im 19. Jahrhundert: zwischen Tradition und Pandektenwissenschaft, Liberalismus und Etatismus*, Ius commune, Sonderhefte, Studien zur Europäischen Rechtsgeschichte 52 (Frankfurt a.M: V. Klostermann, 1995, 2nd edition).
Burnotte, Angélique, "La communauté juive d'Arlon au XIXe siècle", Bulletin trimestriel de l'Institut archéologique du Luxembourg 81, 3/4 (2005), 72–82.

Calmes, Albert, *Der Zollanschluss des Grossherzogtums Luxemburg an Deutschland (1842)*, 2 vol. (Luxemburg: J. Beffort, 1919).
Calmes, Albert, *Histoire Contemporaine du Grand-Duché de Luxembourg*, vol 1: *Naissance et débuts du Grand-Duché (1814–1830)* (Luxembourg: Saint-Paul, 1971, 2nd edition).
Calmes, Albert, *Histoire Contemporaine du Grand-Duché de Luxembourg*, vol. 2: *Le Grand-Duché de Luxemburg dans la Révolution Belge (1830–1839)* (Bruxelles: L'Édition Universelle, 1939).
Calmes, Albert, *Histoire Contemporaine du Grand-Duché de Luxembourg*, vol. 3: *La Restauration de Guillaume Ier, Roi des Pays-Bas (l'Ère Hassenpflug) (1839–1840)* (Bruxelles-Luxembourg: L'Édition Universelle, Saint-Paul, 1947).
Calmes, Albert, *Histoire Contemporaine du Grand-Duché de Luxembourg*, vol. 4: *La création d'un état (1841–1847)* (Luxembourg: Saint-Paul, 1954).
Calmes, Albert, *Histoire Contemporaine du Grand-Duché de Luxembourg*, vol. 5: *La Révolution de 1848 au Luxembourg* (Luxembourg: Saint-Paul, 1982, 2nd edition).
Calmes, Christian, and Danielle Bossaert, *Geschichte des Großherzogtums Luxemburg* (Luxemburg: Saint-Paul, 1996).
Cassirer, Ernst, "Die Idee der Religion bei Lessing und Mendelssohn", in *Festgabe zum zehnjährigen Bestehen der Akademie für die Wissenschaft des Judentums* (Berlin: Akademie-Verlag, 1929), 22–41.
Central-comité der allgemeinen israelitischen Allianz, *Die allgemeine israelitische Allianz: Bericht des Central-comités über die ersten Fünfundzwanzig Jahre 1860–1885* (Berlin: Kauffman in Comm., 1885).
Cerf, Paul, "Les Juifs de Mondorf", in Martin Gerges, ed., *Mondorf, son passé, son présent, son avenir* (Luxembourg: Publications mosellanes, 1997), 309–312.
Cerf, Paul, and Isi Finkelstein, *Les Juifs d'Esch / Déi Escher Judden. Chroniques de la communauté juive de 1837 à 1999* (Luxembourg: Editions des cahiers luxembourgeois, 1999).
Claussen, Detlev, *Aspekte der Alltagsreligion: Ideologiekritik unter veränderten gesellschaftlichen Verhältnissen* (Frankfurt am Main: Verlag Neue Kritik, 2000).
Claussen, Detlev, *Grenzen der Aufklärung: Die gesellschaftliche Genese des modernen Antisemitismus* (Frankfurt am Main: Fischer, 2005, expanded new edition).
Claussen, Detlev, *Vom Judenhaß zum Antisemitismus. Materialien einer verleugneten Geschichte* (Darmstadt: Luchterhand, 1988, 2nd edition).
Cohen, Hermann, "Charakteristik der Ethik Maimunis", in Wilhelm Bacher, et al., eds., *Moses ben Maimon. Sein Leben, seine Werke und sein Einfluß*, vol. 1 (Leipzig: Buchhandlung Gustav Fock, 1908), 63–134, reprinted in Hermann Cohen, *Jüdische Schriften*, vol. 3 (Berlin: Schwetschke & Sohn, 1924), 221–289.
Cohen, Hermann, "Die Bedeutung des Judentums für den religiösen Fortschritt der Menschheit", in idem, *Hermann Cohens Jüdische Schriften*, vol. 1 (Berlin: Schwetschke, 1924) 18–35.
Cohen, Hermann, "Die Messiasidee" (1892), in idem, *Hermann Cohens Jüdische Schriften*, vol. 1 (Berlin: Schwetschke, 1924), 105–124.
Cohen, Hermann, *Religion der Vernunft aus den Quellen des Judentums* (Frankfurt: Kauffmann, 1919).
Cohen, Joseph, *Le Spectre juif de Hegel* (Paris: Galilée, 2005).

Daltroff, Jean, "L'histoire des communautés juives rurales de Moselle", Cahiers des pays de la Nied: Revue des recherches spécifiques aux pays de la Nied 11, 24 (1994), 12–26.

Daltroff, Jean, *Les Juifs de Niedervisse: Naissance, épanouissement et déclin d'une communauté* (Strasbourg: self-published, 1992).

Daum, Werner, ed., *Handbuch der europäischen Verfassungsgeschichte im 19. Jahrhundert*, vol. 2: *1815–1847* (Bonn: Dietz, 2012).

Debus, Karl Heinz, "Das Verhältnis zu den christlichen Religionsgemeinschaften", in Landesarchivverwaltung Rheinland-Pfalz, ed., *Dokumentation zur Geschichte der Juden in Rheinland-Pfalz und im Saarland*, vol. 4: *Das Verhältnis der Juden zu den christlichen Religionsgemeinschaften* (Koblenz: Landesarchivverwaltung Rheinland-Pfalz, 1974), 227–242.

"Den ale Juddekürfech", Ons Stad 1, 2 (1979), 10–12.

Dienemann, Max, "Die jüdischen Gemeinden in Elsaß-Lothringen 1871–1918", Zeitschrift für die Geschichte der Juden 7, 2 (1937), 77–85.

Dietrich, Tobias, *Konfession im Dorf: Westeuropäische Erfahrungen im 19. Jahrhundert*, Industrielle Welt 65 (Köln: Böhlau, 2004).

Dondelinger, Will, "200 Jahre Marktgeschehen", in idem, ed., *1780–1980: 200 Jahre Marktgeschehen* (Ettelbrück: Gemeindeverwaltung, 1980), 47–109.

Dondelinger, Will, and Arthur Muller, "Jüdische Bevölkerung in Ettelbrück: Zum Gedenken an eine einst blühende Religionsgemeinschaft", De Reider. Informatiounsblad vun der Gemeng Ettelbréck, part II, 11, 24 (1998), 23–28; part III, 12, 25 (1999), 24–37.

Driver, Samuel Rolles, and Adolf Neubauer, *The Fifty-Third Chapter of Isaiah – According to the Jewish Interpreters* (New York: Ktav, 1969).

Eliav, Mordechai, *Jewish Education in Germany in the Period of Haskalah and Emancipation* [Hebrew] (Jerusalem: Jewish Agency, 1960).

Erlewine, Robert, "Resolving Contradictions: Samuel Hirsch and the Stakes of Modern Jewish Thought", AJS Review 44, 2 (2020), 317–344.

Erlewine, Robert, "Samuel Hirsch, Hegel, and the Legacy of Ethical Monotheism", Harvard Theological Review 113, 1 (2019), 89–110.

Fackenheim, Emil L., "Samuel Hirsch and Hegel", in idem, *Jewish Philosophers and Jewish Philosophy*, ed. Michael L. Morgan (Bloomington, IN: Indiana University Press, 1996), 21–40.

Fackenheim, Emil L., *Samuel Hirsch and Hegel* (Cambridge: Cambridge University Press, 1964).

Fleischmann, Jacob, *The Problem of Christianity in Jewish Thought from Mendelssohn to Rosenzweig, 1770–1929* [Hebrew] (Jerusalem: Magnes Press, 1964).

Flies, Joseph, *Ettelbrück: Die Geschichte einer Landschaft* (Luxemburg: Imprimerie St. Paul, 1970).

Florence, Ronald, *Blood Libel: The Damascus Affair of 1840* (Madison, WI: University of Wisconsin Press, 2004).

Fraisse, Ottfried, ed., *Modern Jewish Scholarship on Islam in Context: Rationality, European Borders, and the Search for Belonging* (Berlin/Boston: De Gruyter, 2018).

Franco, Paul, *Hegel's Philosophy of Freedom* (New Haven: Yale University Press, 1999).

Frankel, Jonathan, *The Damascus Affair: 'Ritual Murder', Politics, and the Jews in 1840* (Cambridge and New York: Cambridge University Press, 1997).

Franz, Norbert, "Assistance municipale des pauvres de la ville de Luxembourg dans la deuxième moitié du XIXe siècle: le Bureau de Bienfaisance luxembourgeois (1850–1880)", in Henri Wehenkel, ed., *Luxembourg – Paris – Luxembourg. Migrations au temps de la Commune. Études d'histoire économique et sociale accompagnant l'exposition*, Publications scientifiques du Musée d'Histoire de la Ville de Luxembourg, vol. 8 (Luxembourg: Musée d'Histoire de la Ville de Luxembourg, 2001), 33–42.

Franz, Norbert, *Die Stadtgemeinde Luxemburg im Spannungsfeld politischer und wirtschaftlicher Umwälzungen (1760–1890). Von der Festungs- und Garnisonsstadt zur offenen multifunktionalen Stadt*, Trierer historische Forschungen, vol. 40 (Trier: Kliomedia, 2001/Diss. phil. Univ. Trier 1998).

Franz, Norbert *Durchstaatlichung und Ausweitung der Kommunalaufgaben im 19. Jahrhundert. Tätigkeitsfelder und Handlungsspielräume ausgewählter französischer und luxemburgischer Landgemeinden im mikrohistorischen Vergleich*, Trierer historische Forschungen, vol. 60 (Trier: Kliomedia, 2006/Habilitationsschrift Univ. Trier 2005).

Franz, Norbert, "Luxemburg", in Werner Daum, ed., *Handbuch der europäischen Verfassungsgeschichte im 19. Jahrhundert. Institutionen und Rechtspraxis im gesellschaftlichen Wandel*, vol 2: *1815–1847* (Bonn: Dietz, 2012), 543–573.

Franz, Norbert, "Nation oder Partikularismus: Die Revolution von 1848/49 in Luxemburg", in Elisabeth Dühr, ed., *"Der schlimmste Punkt in der Provinz". Demokratische Revolution 1848/49 in Trier und Umgebung* (Trier: Selbstverlag des Städtischen Museums Simeonstift Trier, 1998), 644–661.

Friedland, Eric L., "Marcus Jastrow and Abodath Israel", in Michael A. Fishbane and Paul R. Flohr, eds., *Texts and Responses. Studies Presented to Nahum N. Glatzer on the Occasion of His Seventieth Birthday by His Students* (Leiden: Brill, 1975), 186–200.

Frishman, Judith, "Good Enough for the Goyim? Samuel Hirsch and Samuel Holdheim on Christianity", in Marcel Poorthuis, Joshua Schwartz, and Joseph Turner, eds., *Interaction between Judaism and Christianity in History, Religion, Art and Literature* (Leiden and Boston: Brill, 2009), 271–287.

Frishman, Judith, "On Religion, Humanity and Tolerance. Samuel Hirsch's Addresses to the Freemasons Lodge in Luxemburg", in Norbert Franz and Jean-Paul Lehners, eds., *Nationenbildung und Demokratie. Europäische Entwicklungen gesellschaftlicher Partizipation*, Luxemburg-Studien / Études luxembourgeoises, vol. 2 (Frankfurt am Main: Peter Lang Edition, 2013), 157–170.

Frishman, Judith, "The Pitfalls of Counterhistory: Abraham Geiger and Samuel Hirsch on Rabbinic Judaism", in Christian Wiese, Walter Homolka, and Thomas Brechenmacher, eds., *Jüdische Existenz in der Moderne: Abraham Geiger und die Wissenschaft des Judentums* (Berlin and Boston: De Gruyter, 2013), 341–358.

Frishman, Judith, "True Mosaic Religion. Samuel Hirsch, Samuel Holdheim and the Reform of Judaism", in Judith Frishman, Willemien Otten, and Gerard Rouwhorst, eds., *Religious Identity and the Problem of Historical Foundation. The Foundational Character of Authoritative Sources in the History of Christianity and Judaism*, Jewish and Christian Perspectives Series 8 (Boston and Leiden: Brill, 2004), 195–222.

Funkenstein, Amos, *Perceptions of Jewish History* (Berkeley, CA: University of California Press, 1993).

Galas, Michał, *Rabbi Marcus Jastrow and His Vision for the Reform of Judaism* (Boston: Academic Studies Press, 2013).

Geller, Jay, *The Other Jewish Question. Identifying the Jew and Making Sense of Modernity* (New York: Fordham University Press, 2011).

Girard, Patrick, *Les Juifs de France de 1789 à 1860: De l'émancipation à l'égalité* (Paris: Calmann-Lévy, 1976).

Godchaux, Fabien, "Activités sociales", https://godchaux-fe.pagesperso-orange.fr/page-7.html.

Godchaux, Fabien, "Barrage à Ettelbruck", https://godchaux-fe.pagesperso-orange.fr/page-13.html.

Goedert, Joseph, "L'émancipation de la communauté israélite luxembourgeoise et l'administration du culte dans la première moitié du 19e siècle (1801–1855)", Galerie: Revue culturelle et pédagogique 11, 3 (1993), 345–384.

Goosens, Aline, "Mourir pour sa foi au temps des réformes dans les Pays-Bas méridionaux", in Wim Blockmans and Nicolette Mout, *The World of Emperor Charles V.*, Koninklijke Nederlandse Akademie van Wetenschappen, Verhandelingen, Afd. Letterkunde, Nieuwe Reeks, 188 (Amsterdam: Royal Netherlands Academy of Arts and Sciences, 2004), 227–245.

Gotzmann, Andreas, "The Dissociations of Religion and Law in Nineteenth-Century German-Jewish Education", Leo Baeck Institute Yearbook 43 (1998), 103–126.

Gotzmann, Andreas, *Jüdisches Recht im kulturellen Prozeß: Die Wahrnehmung der Halacha im Deutschland des 19. Jahrhunderts* (Tübingen: Mohr-Siebeck, 1997).

Graetz, Michael, *Les Juifs en France au XIXe siècle: de la Révolution française à l'Alliance israélite universelle* (Paris: Éd. du Seuil, 1989).

Graetz, Michael, "The New Schools", in Michael A. Meyer and Michael Brenner, eds., *German-Jewish History in Modern Times*, vol. 1 (New York: Columbia University Press, 1996), 367–368.

Greenberg, Gershon, "The Historical Origins of God and Man: Samuel Hirsch's Luxembourg Writings", Leo Baeck Institute Yearbook 20, 1 (1975), 129–148.

Greenberg, Gershon, "The Messianic Foundations of American Jewish Thought: David Einhorn and Samuel Hirsch", World Congress of Jewish Studies 6 (1975), 115–226.

Greenberg, Gershon, *Modern Jewish Thinkers: From Mendelssohn to Rosenzweig* (Brighton, MA: Academic Studies Press, 2011), 171–204.

Greenberg, Gershon, "The Reformers' First Attack upon Hess' Rome and Jerusalem: An Unpublished Manuscript of Samuel Hirsch", Jewish Social Studies 35 (1973), 175–197.

Greenberg, Gershon, "Religion and History According to Samuel Hirsch", Hebrew Union College Annual 43 (1972), 103–124.

Greenberg, Gershon, "'Religionswissenschaft' and Early Reform Jewish Thought: Samuel Hirsch and David Einhorn", in Andreas Gotzmann and Christian Wiese, eds., *Modern Judaism and Historical Consciousness: Identities – Controversies – Perspectives* (Leiden and Boston: Brill, 2007), 110–144.

Greenberg, Gershon, "Samuel Hirsch, Jewish Hegelian", Revue des études juives 129 (1970), 205–215.

Greenberg, Gershon, "Samuel Hirsch's American Judaism", American Jewish Historical Quarterly 62 (1973), 362–382.

Greenberg, Gershon, "The Significance of America in David Einhorn's Conception on History", American Jewish Historical Quarterly 63, 2 (1973), 160–184.

Greenberg, Gershon, "Zur Verteidigung Formstechers", Judaica 29 (1978), 24–35.

Grégoire, Pierre, *Das Luxemburger Wort für Wahrheit und Recht: Die Geschichte einer Zeitung in der Geschichte eines Volkes* (Luxembourg: Sankt Paulus, 1936).
Grözinger, Karl Erich, "'Schaddaj' – Hüter der Türen Israels: Jüdische Frömmigkeit in Alltag und Schabbat im 19. Jahrhundert", in Haus der Geschichte Baden-Württemberg, ed., *Nebeneinander – Miteinander – Gegeneinander? Zur Koexistenz in Süddeutschland im 19. und 20. Jahrhundert*, Laupheimer Gespräche 1 (Gerlingen: Bleicher, 2002), 65–79.
Guttmann, Julius, *Die Philosophie des Judentums. Mit einer Standortbestimmung von Esther Seidel und einer biographischen Einführung von Fritz Bamberger* (Berlin: Jüdische Verlagsanstalt, 2000).
Guttmann, Julius, *Philosophies of Judaism: The History of Jewish Philosophy from Biblical Times to Franz Rosenzweig* (Philadelphia: Holt, Rinehart and Winston, 1964).
Hannick, Pierre, and Jean-Claude Muller, "Juifs de passage dans les duchés de Luxembourg et de Bouillon, avant leur émancipation en 1808", Annales de l'Institut archéologique du Luxembourg 136 (2005), 241–254.
Hellinghausen, Georges, *Kampf um die Apostolischen Vikare des Nordens J. Th. Laurent und C.A. Lüpke: Der Hl. Stuhl und die protestantischen Staaten Norddeutschlands und Dänemark um 1840* (Rome: Pontificia Università Gregoriana, 1987).
Henne, Alexandre, *Histoire de la Belgique sous le règne de Charles-Quint*, vol. 3 (Bruxelles: Rozez and Paris: Borrani, 1865).
Hentges, Gudrun, "Das Janusgesicht der Aufklärung: Antijudaismus und Antisemitismus in der Philosophie von Kant, Fichte und Hegel", in Samuel Salzborn, ed., *Antisemitismus – Geschichte und Gegenwart* (Gießen: Netzwerk für politische Bildung, Kultur und Kommunikation, 2004), 11–32.
Herres, Jürgen, *Städtische Gesellschaft und katholische Vereine im Rheinland 1840–1870* (Essen: Klartext, 1996/Diss. phil. Univ. Trier 1991).
Heschel, Susannah, *Abraham Geiger and the Jewish Jesus* (Chicago, IL: University of Chicago Press, 1998).
Heschel, Susannah, "German Jewish Scholarship on Islam as a Tool for De-Orientalizing Judaism", New German Critique 117 (2012), 91–207.
Heschel, Susannah, *Jüdischer Islam. Islam und jüdisch-deutsche Selbstbestimmung* (Berlin: Matthes & Seitz, 2018).
Hilgert, Romain, *Zeitungen in Luxemburg 1704–2004* (Luxembourg: Service information et presse du gouvernement luxembourgeois, 2004).
Hirsch, Erhard, "Das für ihre Nation wiedergefundene Land! Erziehung zur Toleranz: Erfolg der Aufklärung: 'Judenemanzipation' von Anhalt-Dessau aus", in Giuseppe Veltri and Christian Wiese, eds., *Jüdische Bildung und Kultur in Sachsen-Anhalt von der Aufklärung bis zum Nationalsozialismus* (Berlin: Metropol, 2009), 67–114.
Hirsch, Erhard, *Die Dessau-Wörlitzer Reformbewegung im Zeitalter der Aufklärung: Personen, Strukturen, Wirkungen* (Tübingen: Niemeyer, 2003), 151–172.
Hirsch, Erhard, "Fürst Franz und die anhalt-dessauischen Juden: 'Von der Dessauer Gemeinde ging die Emanzipation der deutschen Juden aus'", in Evelien Goodman-Thau, ed., *Zwischen Wörlitz und Mosigkau*, Dessau-Wörlitzer Beiträge 8 (Dessau: Museum für Stadtgeschichte, 1998), 11–18.
Hortzitz, Nicoline, "Die Sprache der Judenfeindschaft", in Julius H. Schoeps and Joachim Schlör, eds., *Bilder der Judenfeindschaft: Antisemitismus – Vorurteile und Mythen* (München: Piper, 1995), 19–40.

Hyman, Paula E., *The Emancipation of the Jews of Alsace: Acculturation and Tradition in the Nineteenth Century* (New Haven: Yale University Press, 1991).

Hyman, Paula E., *The Jews of Modern France,* Jewish Communities in the Modern World, vol. 1 (Berkeley, Los Angeles: University of California Press, 1998).

Ittenbach, Elmar P., *Samuel Hirsch: Rabbiner – Religionsphilosoph – Reformer / Rabbi – Philosopher – Reformer* (Berlin: Hentrich & Hentrich, 2014).

Jaeschke, Walter, "Staat aus christlichem Prinzip und christlicher Staat: Zur Ambivalenz der Berufung auf das Christentum in der Rechtsphilosophie Hegels und der Restauration", Der Staat 18 (1979), 349–374.

Jeck, Marc, "De 'simples tisserands' aux 'barons de drap': Les Godchaux", Die Warte: Kulturelle Wochenbeilage des Luxemburger Worts 55, 17 (2003), 1.

Job, Francoise, *Les Juifs à Lunéville aux XVIIIe et XIXe siècles* (Nancy: Presse Université de Nancy, 1989).

Jospe, Alfred, Eva Jospe, and Raphael Jospe, eds., *To Leave Your Mark: Selections from the Writings of Alfred Jospe* (New York: KTAV, 2000).

Kaiser, Marcel, "Der alte Judenfriedhof in Clausen", Luxemburger Tageblatt 81, 171 (1993), 3.

Kajon, Irene, "Hegel, la Wissenschaft des Judentums et Samuel Hirsch", in Gérard Bensussan, ed., *La philosophie allemande dans la pensée juive* (Paris: Presses Univ. de France, 1997), 115–127.

Kasper-Holtkotte, Cilli, *Im Westen Neues: Migration und ihre Folgen: Deutsche Juden als Pioniere jüdischen Lebens in Belgien, 18./19. Jahrhundert,* Studies in Jewish History and Culture, vol. 0 (Leiden and Boston: Brill, 2003).

Kasper-Holtkotte, Cilli, *Juden im Aufbruch. Zur Sozialgeschichte einer Minderheit im Saar-Mosel-Raum um 1800* (Hannover: Hahn, 1996).

Kastner, Dieter, ed., *Der Rheinische Provinziallandtag und die Emanzipation der Juden 1825–1845: Eine Dokumentation*, vol. 1 (Köln: Rheinlandverlag, 1989).

Katz, Jacob, "Samuel Hirsch – Rabbi, Philosopher and Freemason", Revue des études Juives 125 (1965), 113–126.

Kaul, Leo, *The Story of Radical Reform Judaism* (Los Angeles: Leo Kaul, 1951).

Kavka, Martin, *Jewish Messianism and the History of Philosophy* (Cambridge: Cambridge University Press, 2004).

Kayser, Simone, *La lutte contre la pauvreté au Grand-Duché de Luxembourg 1839–1880* (Luxembourg: Unpublished typescript 1996 located in the Bibliothèque Nationale du Grand-Duché de Luxembourg).

Kluback, William, "The Jewish Response to Hegel: Samuel Hirsch and Hermann Cohen", The Owl of Minerva 18 (1986), 5–12.

Klüber, Johan Ludwig, *Acten des Wiener Congresses in den Jahren 1814 und 1815*, vol. 6 (Erlangen: J. J. Palm and Ernst Enke, 2nd edition 1836), 12–96.

Kocka, Jürgen, *Arbeitsverhältnisse und Arbeiterexistenzen. Grundlagen der Klassenbildung im 19. Jahrhundert,* Geschichte der Arbeiter und der Arbeiterbewegung in Deutschland seit dem Ende des 18. Jahrhunderts, vol. 2 (Bonn: Dietz, 1990).

Kohler, George Y., ed., *Der jüdische Messianismus im Zeitalter der Emanzipation: Reinterpretationen zwischen davidischem Königtum und endzeitlichem Sozialismus*, Mar'ot: Die jüdische Moderne in Quellen und Werken, vol. 2 (Berlin and Boston: De Gruyter and Oldenbourg, 2014).

Kohler, George Y., "Einleitung: Die Wiederentdeckung des Messianismus in der jüdischen Reformtheologie der ersten Hälfte des 19. Jahrhunderts", in idem, ed., *Der jüdische Messianismus im Zeitalter der Emanzipation: Reinterpretationen zwischen davidischem Königtum und endzeitlichem Sozialismus*, Mar'ot: Die jüdische Moderne in Quellen und Werken, vol. 2 (Berlin and Boston: De Gruyter and Oldenbourg, 2014), 1–91.

Koltun-Fromm, Ken, *Abraham Geiger's Liberal Judaism: Personal Meaning and Religious Authority* (Bloomington, IN: Indiana University Press, 2006).

Koltun-Fromm, Ken, "Public Religion in Samson Raphael Hirsch and in Samuel Hirsch's Interpretation of Religious Symbolism", Journal of Jewish Thought and Philosophy 9 (1999), 69–105.

Koltz, Jean-Pierre, *Baugeschichte der Stadt und Festung Luxemburg* (Luxembourg: Saint-Paul, 1972).

Korn, Bertram W., *American Jewry and the Civil War* (Philadelphia: Jewish Publication Society of America, 1957).

Kratz-Ritter, Bettina, *Salomon Formstecher: Ein deutscher Reformrabbiner* (Hildesheim, Zurich, and New York: Olms, 1991).

Kraut, Benny, *From Reform Judaism to Ethical Culture: The Religious Evolution of Felix Adler* (Cincinnati, OH: Hebrew Union College Press, 1979).

Krier, Emile, "Les Juifs au Grand-Duché au XIXe siècle", in André Neuberg, ed., *Le choc des libertés: L'église en Luxembourg de Pie VII à Léon XIII (1800–1880)* (Bastogne: Musée en Piconrue, 2001), 119–128.

Kronenberger, Friedrich L., *Die jüdischen Vieh- und Pferdehändler im Birkenfelder Land und in Gemeinden des Hunsrücks*, Schriftenreihe der Kreishochschule Birkenfeld 8 (Birkenfeld: Kreisvolkshochschule, 1983).

Lang, Jean-Bernhard, and Claude Rosenfeld, *Histoire des Juifs en Moselle* (Metz: Edition Serpenoise, 2001).

Lascombes, François, *Chronik der Stadt Luxemburg 963–1795*, vol. 1–3 (Luxemburg: Saint-Paul, 1968, 1976, 1988).

Lässig, Simone, "Bildung als kulturelles Kapital? Jüdische Schulprojekte in der Frühphase der Emanzipation", in Andreas Gotzmann, Reiner Liedtke and Till van Rahden, eds., *Juden, Bürger, Deutsche: Zur Geschichte von Vielfalt und Grenzen in Deutschland* (Tübingen: Mohr Siebeck, 2001), 263–98.

Lassner, Jacob, "Abraham Geiger: A Nineteenth Century Jewish Reformer on the Origins of Islam", in Michael Kramer, ed., *The Jewish Discovery of Islam* (Tel Aviv: The Moshe Dayan Center for Middle Eastern and African Studies, 1999), 103–136.

Lebrun, François, *Histoire des catholiques en France du XVe siècle à nos jours* (Paris: Hachette, 1985).

Leff, Lisa Moses, *Sacred Bonds of Solidarity: The Rise of Jewish Internationalism in Nineteenth-century France* (Stanford: Stanford University Press, 2006), 154–164.

Lefkovits, Maurice, *Samuel Hirsch* (New York: Central Conference of American Rabbis, 1915).

Lehrmann, Charles, and Graziella Lehrmann-Gandolfi, *La Communauté Juive du Luxembourg dans le passé et dans le présent* (Esch-sur-Alzette: Luxembourg cooperative printer, 1953).

Lenhard, Philipp, "Ein lebendiger Organismus: Der jüdische Hegelianismus", in idem, *Volk oder Religion? Die Entstehung moderner jüdischer Ethnizität in Frankreich und*

Deutschland 1782–1848, Religiöse Kulturen im Europa der Neuzeit, vol. 4 (Göttingen: Vandenhoeck & Ruprecht, 2016), 283–316.

Leopold, David, "The Hegelian Antisemitism of Bruno Bauer", History of European Ideas 25 (1999), 179–206.

Levinas, Emmanuel, "L'actualité de Maïmonide", Paix et Droit 15, 4 (April 1935), 6–7, reprinted in Traces 5 (Automne 1982), 142–144.

Lewis, Bernard, "Pro-Islamic Jews", in idem, *Islam in History: Ideas, People, and Events in the Middle East* (Chicago: Open Court, 1993), 144.

Liberles, Robert, *Religious Conflict in Social Context: The Resurgence of Orthodox Judaism in Frankfurt am Main, 1838–1877* (Westport, CT.: Greenwood Press, 1985).

Liebeschütz, Hans, *Das Judentum im deutschen Geschichtsbild von Hegel bis Max Weber* (Tübingen: Mohr Siebeck, 1967).

Loetsch, Klaus, "Zwischen vielen Stühlen. Geschichte des Protestantismus in Luxemburg", in Forum, Luxemburg 254 (March 2006), 33–40, http://www.forum.lu/pdf/artikel/5440_254_Loetsch.pdf.

Loewenstein, Steven M., "Anfänge der Integration 1780–1871", in Marion Kaplan, ed., *Geschichte des jüdischen Alltags: Vom 17. Jahrhundert bis 1945* (München: Beck 2003), 125–224.

Lorig, Wolfgang H., and Mario Hirsch, eds., *Das politische System Luxemburgs. Eine Einführung* (Wiesbaden: VS-Verlag für Sozialwissenschaften, 2008).

Löwith, Karl, *Von Hegel zu Nietzsche. Der revolutionäre Bruch im Denken des neunzehnten Jahrhunderts* (Zürich: Europa Verlag, 1941).

Ludyga, Hannes, *Die Rechtsstellung der Juden in Bayern von 1819–1918: Studie im Spiegel der Verhandlungen der Kammer der Abgeordneten des bayerischen Landtags* (Berlin: Berliner Wissenschafts-Verlag, 2007).

Luxembourg city tourist office, *Der Godchaux-Rundweg: Auf den Spuren der industriellen Revolution* (Luxemburg: city tourist office, n.d.).

Mak, Michael, "The Metaphysics of Eating. Jewish Dietary Law and Hegel's Social Theory", Philosophy and Social Criticism 27, 5 (2001), 59–88.

Mannes, Gast, "Charles Théodore André", *Luxemburger Autorenlexikon,* http://www.autorenlexikon.lu/page/author/766/766/DEU/index.html

Marcus, Jacob Rader, *United States Jewry 1776–1985*, vol. 3: *The Germanic Period*, part 2 (Detroit: Wayne State University Press, 1993).

Marx, Claude, "Jüdisches Leben in Luxemburg", in Antoinette Reuter, ed., *Ansichten jüdischen Lebens zwischen Maas, Mosel und Rhein im Spiegel alter Postkarten (vom Ende des 19. bis Anfang des 20. Jahrhunderts): Eine Ausstellung des Centre de documentation sur les migrations humaines* Düdelingen (Dudelange: Centre de documentation sur les migrations humaines, 2005), 42–43.

Marx, Hubert, "Die Tuchfabrik auf der Schleifmillen: Entstehung, Entwicklung, Untergang", in Klaus Schneider and Jan Nottrot, eds., *Schläifmillen: Geschichte und Gegenwart* (Luxembourg-Schläifmillen: Inter-Actions 2007), 31–61.

Mattioli, Aram, "'So lange die Juden Juden bleiben…': Der Widerstand gegen die jüdische Emanzipation im Grossherzogtum Baden und im Kanton Aargau (1848–1863)", in Olaf Blaschke and Aram Mattioli, eds., *Katholischer Antisemitismus im 19. Jahrhundert: Ursachen und Traditionen im internationalen Vergleich* (Zürich: Orell Füssli, 2000), 287–315.

Mechin, Colette, "Fêtes et saisons", in Jean Lanher, ed., *Encyclopédie Illustrée de la Lorraine*, vol. 4: *La vie traditionnelle* (Metz: Edition Serpenoise, 1989), 83–126.

Mendel, Pierre, *Les Juifs de Bionville en pays messin: Du 17e siècle à nos jours* (Metz: Association Mosellane pour la Conservation du Patrimoine Juif, 1995).

Meyer, Michael A., "Alienated Intellectuals in the Camp of Religious Reform: The Frankfurt Reformfreunde, 1842–1845", AJS Review 6 (1984), 61–86.

Meyer, Michael A., "German Jewish Thinkers Reflect on the Future of the Jewish Religion", Leo Baeck Institute Yearbook 51 (2006), 4–10.

Meyer, Michael, A., *Judaism Within Modernity: Essays on Jewish History and Religion* (Detroit: Wayne State University Press, 2001).

Meyer, Michael A., "'Most of My Brethren Find Me Unacceptable': The Controversial Career of Rabbi Samuel Holdheim", in Christian Wiese, ed., *Redefining Judaism in an Age of Emancipation: Comparative Perspectives on Samuel Holdheim (1806–1860)* (Leiden and Boston: Brill, 2007), 3–22.

Meyer, Michael A., *Response to Modernity: A History of the Reform Movement in Germany* (Detroit: Wayne State University Press, 1995).

Meyer, Michael A., "Should and Can an 'Antiquated' Religion Become Modern? The Jewish Reform Movement in Germany as Seen by Jews and Christians", in idem, *Judaism Within Modernity: Essays on Jewish History and Religion* (Detroit, MI: Wayne State University Press, 2001), 209–222.

Meyer, Michael A., "Universalism and Jewish Unity in the Thought of Abraham Geiger", in Jacob Katz, ed., *The Role of Religion in Modern Jewish History* (Cambridge, MA: AJS, 1975), 91–107.

Meyer, Michael A., and Michael Brenner, eds., *German-Jewish History in Modern Times*, vol. 2 (New York: Columbia University, 1996).

Meyer, Thomas, "Salomon Formstechers 'Religion des Geistes' – Versuch einer Neulektüre", Aschkenas 13 (2003), 441–460.

Mic, Albert, "Plazen, Gaassen, Weeer a Pied", in Vic Molitor, ed., *Fanfare Miedernach 1930–2005* (Mersch: Faber, 2005), 221–247.

Mignon, Laurent, "Le défi de l'altérité religieuse: Samuel Hirsch, le judaïsme et l'islam", in Alberto Ambrosio and Laurent Mignon, eds., *Penser l'islam en Europe: Perspectives du Luxembourg et d'ailleurs* (Paris: Hermann, 2021), 247–267.

Mignon, Laurent, "Of Moors, Jews and Gentiles", Journal of Turkish Studies 35, 1 (2011), 65–83.

Mignon, Laurent, *Uncoupling Language and Religion: An Exploration into the Margins of Turkish Literature* (Boston: Academic Studies Press, 2021).

Molitor, Hansgeorg, "La vie religieuse populaire en Rhénanie francaise, 1794–1815", in Bernard Plongeron, ed., *Pratiques religieuses: Mentalités et spiritualités dans l'Europe Révolutionnaire (1770–1820)* (Turnhout: Brepols 1988), 59–68.

Monz, Heinz, "Samuel Hirsch (1815–1889). Ein jüdischer Reformator aus dem Hunsrück", Jahrbuch für westdeutsche Landesgeschichte 17, 1 (1991), 159–180.

Morais, Henry Samuel, *The Jews of Philadelphia: Their History from the Earliest Settlements to the Present Time* (Philadelphia: Levytype Company, 1894).

Moyse, Laurent, *Du rejet à l'integration. Histoire des Juifs du Luxembourg des origines à nos jours* (Luxembourg: Édition Saint Paul, 2011).

Moyse, Laurent, "Les cimetières juifs", in Claude Geudevert, Micheline Gutmann and Laurent Moyse, eds., *Les Juifs du Luxembourg* (Paris: Association de Généalogie Juive Internationale, 1999).
Muller, Arthur, "Jüdische Bevölkerung in Ettelbrück", in Administration Communale d'Ettelbruck, ed., *Ettelbruck: 100 Joer Stad 1907–2007* (Ettelbruck: Administration communale, 2008), 267–272.
Myers, David N., *Resisting History. Historicism and its Discontents in German-Jewish Thought* (Princeton: Princeton University Press, 2003), 132.
Novak, David, *Jewish Social Ethics* (Oxford: Oxford University Press, 1992).
Nussbaum, Martha, *Cultivating Humanity: A Classical Defense of Reform in Liberal Education* (Cambridge, MA: Harvard University Press, 1997).
Pasto, James, "Islam's 'Strange Secret Sharer': Orientalism, Judaism and the Jewish Question", Comparative Studies in Society and History 40, 3 (July 1998), 437–474.
Patai, Raphael, *The Messiah Texts* (Detroit: Wayne State University Press, 1988).
Pauly, Michel, *Geschichte Luxemburgs* (München: C.H. Beck, 2011).
Pauly, Michel, *Luxemburg im späten Mittelalter*, vol. 1: *Verfassung und politische Führungsschicht der Stadt Luxemburg im 13.–15. Jahrhundert*, Publications de la Section historique de l'Institut grand-ducal 107 (Publications du CLUDEM 3) (Luxembourg: Saint-Paul, 1992).
Pauly, Michel, *Luxemburg im späten Mittelalter*, vol. 2: *Weinhandel und Weinkonsum*, Publications de la Section historique de l'Institut grand-ducal 109 (Publications du CLUDEM 5) (Luxembourg: Saint-Paul, 1994).
Petuchowski, Jakob, "Manuals and Catechisms of the Jewish Religion in the Early Period of Emancipation", in Alexander Altmann, ed., *Studies in Nineteenth-Century Jewish Intellectual History* (Cambridge: Harvard University Press, 1964), 47–64.
Philipson, David, *The Reform Movement in Judaism* (New York: Macmillan, 1931).
Pies, Christof, *Jüdisches Leben im Rhein-Hunsrück-Kreis*, Schriftenreihe des Hunsrücker Geschichtsvereins 40 (Simmern: Hunsrücker Geschichtsverein, 2003).
Reform Congregation Keneseth Israel: Its First 100 Years 1847–1947 (Philadelphia: Elkins Park, 1950).
Readings, Bill, *The University in Ruins* (Cambridge, MA: Harvard University Press, 1996).
Reupke, Beate, *Jüdisches Schulwesen zwischen Tradition und Moderne* (Berlin/Boston: De Gruyter, 2017).
Reuter, Antoinette, "Présence juive dans les forteresses louis-quatorziennes, l'exemple de Luxembourg", Conférence donnée le 19 janvier 2006 dans le cadre de l'exposition "Présence juive en Pays d'Arlon" organisée par le Musée Gaspar d'Arlon, www.cdmh.lu, n.d., https://www.cdmh.lu/resources/pdf/_base_3/9781683124009.pdf?ac=1400484551.
Richarz, Monika, "Die Entdeckung der Landjuden. Stand und Probleme ihrer Erforschung am Beispiel Südwestdeutschlands", in Karl-Heinz Burmeister, ed., *Landjudentum im süddeutschen und Bodenseeraum: Wissenschaftliche Tagung zur Eröffnung des Jüdischen Museums Hohenems 1991*, Forschungen zur Geschichte Vorarlbergs 11 (Dornbirn: Vorarlberger Verlagsanstalt, 1992), 11–21.
Roemer, Nils, *Jewish Scholarship and Culture in Nineteenth-Century Germany: Between History and Faith* (Madison: University of Wisconsin Press, 2005).

Rohrbacher, Stefan, *Gewalt im Biedermeier: Antijüdische Ausschreitungen in Vormärz und Revolution (1815–1848/49)*, Schriftenreihe des Zentrums für Antisemitismusforschung 1 (Frankfurt a. M.: Campus-Verlag, 1993).
Romeyn, Esther, "Anti-Semitism and Islamophobia: Spectropolitics and Immigration", Theory, Culture & Society 31, 6 (2014), 77–101.
Roos, Gilbert, *Les Juifs de France sous la monarchie de juillet*, Bibliothèque d'études juives 30 (Paris: Champion, 2007).
Roos, Gilbert, *Les relations entre le gouvernement royal et les Juifs du nord-est de la France au XVIIe siècle*, Bibliothèque d'études juives 10 (Paris: Champion, 2000).
Rose, Flemming, "Why I Published Those Cartoons", The Washington Post (February 19, 2006).
Rose, Sven-Erik, *Jewish Philosophical Politics in Germany, 1789–1948* (Waltham, Mass.: Brandeis University Press, 2014).
Rosenak, Michael, *Commandments and Concerns: Jewish Religious Education in Secular Society* (Philadelphia: The Jewish Publication Society, 1987).
Rosenthal, Gilbert, "Messianism Reconsidered", Judaism 40, 4 (1991), 552–568.
Rosenzweig, Franz, *Der Stern der Erlösung* (Frankfurt a. M.: Kauffmann, 1921).
Rotenstreich, Nathan, "For and Against Emancipation: The Bruno Bauer Controversy", Leo Baeck Institute Yearbook 4 (1959), 3–36.
Rotenstreich, Nathan, *Jewish Philosophy in Modern Times: From Mendelssohn to Rosenzweig* (New York: Holt, Rhinehart & Winston, 1968).
Runnymede Trust Commission on Antisemitism, *A Very Light Sleeper: The Persistence and Dangers of Antisemitism* (London: Runnymede Trust, 1994).
Runnymede Trust Commission on Islamophobia in the United Kingdom, *Islamophobia: A Challenge for Us All* (London: Runnymede Trust, 1997).
Said, Edward, *Orientalism* (New York: Vintage Books, 2004 [1979]).
Schacter, Rory, "Hermann Cohen's Secular Messianism and Liberal Cosmopolitanism", Jewish Political Studies Review 20, 1–2 (2008), 107–123.
Schlesier, Stephanie, "Grenzüberschreitend. Juden in Luxemburg, ihre Kontakte in die Nachbarregionen und ihre Einbindung in das luxemburgische Leben im 19. Jahrhundert", in Norbert Franz and Jean-Paul Lehners, eds., *Nationenbildung und Demokratie. Europäische Entwicklungen gesellschaftlicher Partizipation*, Luxemburg-Studien / Études luxembourgeoises, vol. 2 (Frankfurt am Main: Peter Lang Edition, 2013), 171–192.
Schneemelcher, Wilhelm, "Carl Immanuel Nitzsch, 1787–1868", in *Bonner Gelehrte. Beiträge zur Geschichte der Wissenschaften in Bonn, 150 Jahre Rheinische Friedrich Wilhelms-Universität zu Bonn, 1818–1968*, vol. 1: *Evangelische Theologie* (Bonn: Bouvier, 1968), 15–30.
Schoentgen, Marc, "Die jüdische Gemeinde in Medernach. Einwanderung, Integration und Verfolgung", in Vic Molitor, ed., *Fanfare Miedernach. 1930–2005* (Mersch: Faber, 2005), 299–366.
Schoeps, Hans Joachim, *Die Geschichte der jüdischen Religionsphilosophie in der Neuzeit*, vol. 1 (Berlin: Vortrupp-Verl., 1935).
Schoeps, Julius H., Anja Bagel-Bohlan, Margarete Heitmann, and Dieter Lohmeyer, eds., *"Philo des 19. Jahrhunderts": Studien zu Salomon Ludwig Steinheim* (Hildesheim, Zurich, and New York: Olms, 1998).

Scholem, Gershom, "Redemption through Sin", in idem, *The Messianic Idea in Judaism and other Essays* (New York: Schocken, 1971), 78–141.
Scholem, Gershom, "Toward an Understanding of the Messianic Idea in Judaism", in idem, *The Messianic Idea in Judaism and other Essays* (New York: Schocken, 1971), 1–36.
Schorsch, Ismar, "Emancipation and the Crisis of Religious Authority: The Emergence of the Modern Rabbinate", in Werner Mosse, Arnold Paucker and Reinhard Rürup, eds., *Revolution and Evolution: 1848 in German-Jewish History* (Tübingen: J.C.B. Mohr, 1981), 205–247.
Schreiber, Jean-Philippe, *L'immigration juive en Belgique du moyen âge à la Première Guerre mondiale* (Bruxelles: Édition de l'Université de Bruxelles, 1996).
Schröder, Bernd, "Jüdische Katechismen in Deutschland am Beispiel eines Katechismus aus der Feder von Samuel Hirsch (1815–1889)", in Klaus Herrmann, Margarete Schlüter, and Giuseppe Veltri, eds., *Jewish Studies Between the Disciplines – Judaistik zwischen den Disziplinen: Papers in Honor of Peter Schäfer on the Occasion of His 60th Birthday* (Leiden and Boston: Brill, 2003), 456–477.
Schulte, Christoph, *Die jüdische Aufklärung* (München: Beck, 2002), 15–16.
Schumann, Henri, *Mémoire des communautés juives de Moselle* (Metz: Édition Serpenoise, 1999).
Schwarz, Samuel, *Die Messias-Zeit: Erläuterungen der Talmudstellen, die Bezug auf Israels Zukunft haben, mit Rücksicht auf unsere Zeit* (Lemberg: Piller, 1865, 3rd edition).
Schweitzer, Friedrich, "Kirche als Thema der praktischen Theologie: Carl Immanuel Nitzsch, sein wissenschaftstheoretisches Programm und dessen Zukunftsbedeutung", Zeitschrift für Theologie und Kirche 90 (1993), 71–86
Scuto, Denis, "1848 – Die erste Revolution des industriellen Zeitalters: Zum Geburtsakt der Luxemburger Arbeiterbewegung", Forum fir kritsch Informatioun iwer Politik, Kultur a Relioun 13, 185 (1998), 42–47.
Seeskin, Kenneth, "Judaism and the Idea of a Better Future", in Jonathan A. Jacobs, ed., *Judaic Sources and Western Thought: Jerusalem's Enduring Presence* (Oxford: Oxford University Press, 2011), 49–70.
Shear-Jashuv, Aharon, "Hadatiut shel avraham befilosofiyat hadat shel shemuel hirsh", in Mosheh Halamish, Hannah Kasher, and Yohanan Silman, eds., *Avraham avi hama'aminim: Demuto birei hehagut ledoroteha* (Ramat Gan: Bar Ilan University, 2002), 281–294.
Shear-Jashuv, Aharon, *The Theology of Salomon Ludwig Steinheim* (Leiden: Brill, 1986).
Shereshevsky, Esra, "Rashi and Christian Interpretations", Jewish Quarterly Review 61 (1970), 76–86.
Sorkin, David, "Preacher, Teacher, Publicist: Joseph Wolf and the Ideology of Emancipation", in Frances Malino and David Sorkin, eds., *From East and West: Jews in a Changing Europe, 1750–1870* (Cambridge, MA: B. Blackwell, 1991), 107–128.
Sorkin, David, *The Transformation of German Jewry, 1780–1840* (Detroit: Wayne State University Press, 1987).
Stern, Malcolm H., "National Leaders of Their Time: Philadelphia's Reform Rabbis", in Murray Friedman, ed., *Jewish Life in Philadelphia* (Philadelphia: Institute for the Study of Human Issues, 1983).
Strauss, Leo, *Philosophie und Gesetz. Beiträge zum Verständnis Maimunis und seiner Vorläufer* (Berlin: Schocken, 1935).

Taubes, Jacob, *Abendländische Eschatologie* (München: Matthes und Seitz, 1991).
Theurich, Henning, *Theorie und Praxis: Die Predigt bei Carl Immanuel Nitzsch* (Göttingen: Vandenhoeck & Ruprecht, 1975).
Thewes, Guy, "Das Leben der Arbeiter der Schleifmillen im 19. Jahrhundert", in Klaus Schneider and Jan Nottrot, eds., *Schläifmillen: Geschichte und Gegenwart* (Luxembourg-Schläifmillen: Inter-Actions 2007), 12–30.
Thewes, Guy, *Les gouvernements du Grand-Duché de Luxembourg depuis 1848* (Luxembourg: Édition Guy Binsfeld, 2003).
Thilman, Daniel, *La présence juive à Mondorf-les-Bains et à Mondorff: Des origines à 1953* (Nancy: self-published, 2005).
Thulin, Mirjam, "Experience and Epistemology: The Life and Legacy of Marcus M. Jastrow (1829–1903)", European Judaism 45, 2 (Autumn 2012), 32–58.
Tomba, Massimiliano, "Exclusiveness and Political Universalism in Bruno Bauer", in Douglas Moggach, ed., *The New Hegelians. Politics and Philosophy in the Hegelian School* (Cambridge: Cambridge University Press, 2006), 91–113.
Toury, Jacob, *Soziale und politische Geschichte der Juden in Deutschland 1847–1871: Zwischen Revolution, Reaktion und Emanzipation*, Schriftenreihe des Instituts für deutsche Geschichte 2 (Düsseldorf: Droste, 1977).
Trausch, Gilbert, "Comment faire d'un état de convention une nation", in Gilbert Trausch, ed., *Histoire du Luxembourg. Le destin européen d'un "petit pays"* (Toulouse: Éditions Privat, 2003), 201–274.
Trausch, Gilbert, *Histoire du Luxembourg* (Paris: Hatier, 1992).
Trausch, Gilbert, *Le Luxembourg sous l'Ancien Régime (17e, 18e siècles et débuts du 19e siècle)*, Manuel d'histoire luxembourgeoise, vol. 3, (Luxembourg: Bourg-Bourger, 1986, 2nd edition).
Trausch, Gilbert, "Les Luxembourgeois devant la Révolution française", in Raymond Poidevin and Gilbert Trausch, eds., *Les relations franco-luxembourgeoises de Louis XIV à Robert Schuman: Actes du colloque de Luxembourg, 17–19 novembre 1977* (Metz: Centre de recherches Relations internationales de l'Université de Metz, 1978), 83–117.
Turner, Bryan S., *Religion and Social Theory* (London: SAGE Publications, 1983).
Ulbrich, Claudia, *Shulamit und Margarethe: Macht, Geschlecht und Religion in einer ländlichen Gesellschaft des 18. Jahrhunderts*, Beiheft Aschkenas: Zeitschrift für Geschichte und Kultur der Juden 4 (Wien: Böhlau, 1999).
Ulrich, Bernd G., "Samuel Hirsch als Rabbiner in Dessau", Mitteilungen des Vereins für Anhaltinische Landeskunde 16 (2007), 104–132.
Van Werveke, Nicolas, *Kurze Geschichte des Luxemburger Landes mit besonderer Berücksichtigung der Kulturgeschichte: Urgeschichte bis Ende des XIV. Jahrhunderts* (Luxemburg: Worré-Mertens, 1909).
Vogel, Manfred, "Does Samuel Hirsch Anthropologize Religion?", Modern Judaism 1 (1981), 298–322.
Volkov, Shulamit, *Antisemitismus als kultureller Code: Zehn Essays* (Munich: Beck, 2000, 2nd edition).
Volkov, Shulamit, *Die Juden in Deutschland 1780–1918* (München: Oldenbourg Wissenschaftsverlag, 2000, 2nd corrected edition).
Volkov, Shulamit, "Inventing Jewish Tradition: On the Formation of Modern Jewish Culture", Jewish Studies at the Central European University 3 (2002–2003), 211–227.

Volkov, Shulamit, "Moses Hess: Problems of Religion and Faith", Zionism 3 (1981), 1–15.
Wagener, Renée, *Die jüdische Minderheit in Luxemburg und das Gleichheitsprinzip. Staatsbürgerliche Emanzipation vs. staatliche und gesellschaftliche Praxis vom 19. bis zum Beginn des 21. Jahrhunderts* (Hagen: FernUniversität in Hagen, 2017), available online https://ub-deposit.fernuni-hagen.de/receive/mir_mods_00001049.
Weber, Josiane, *Familien der Oberschicht in Luxemburg. Elitenbildung & Lebenswelten 1850–1900* (Luxembourg: Édition Guy Binsfeld, 2013).
Wehler, Hans-Ulrich, *Deutsche Gesellschaftsgeschichte*, vol. 2 (München: C.H. Beck, 1987).
Westerkamp, Dirk, "Platon in Moses. Hegels Kritik der Substanzmetaphysik und die 'Philosophia Haebraeorum'", Hegel-Jahrbuch 7, 1 (2005), 106–113.
Wiehn, Erhard Roy, ed., *Interessante Zeitgenossen: Lebenserinnerungen eines jüdischen Kaufmanns und Weltbürgers* (Konstanz: Hartung-Gorre, 1998).
Wiener, Max, "The Concept of Mission in Traditional and Modern Judaism", YIVO Annual of Jewish Social Science 2–3 (1947/1948), 9–24.
Wiese, Christian, "Inventing a New Language of Jewish Scholarship: The Transition from German 'Wissenschaft des Judentums' to American-Jewish Scholarship in the 19th and 20th Centuries", Studia Rosenthaliana 36 (2003), 273–304.
Wiese, Christian, "The Philadelphia Conference (1869) and German Reform: A Historical Moment in a Transnational Story of Proximity and Alienation", in Christian Wiese and Cornelia Wilhelm, eds., *American Jewry: Transcending the European Experience?* (London and New York: Bloomsbury, 2017), 136–158.
Wiese, Christian, ed., *Redefining Judaism in an Age of Emancipation: Comparative Perspectives on Samuel Holdheim (1806–1860)* (Leiden and Boston: Brill, 2007).
Wiese, Christian, "Samuel Holdheim's Most Powerful Comrade in Conviction: David Einhorn and the Debate Concerning Jewish Universalism in the Radical Reform Movement", in idem, *Redefining Judaism in an Age of Emancipation: Comparative Perspectives on Samuel Holdheim (1806–1860)* (Leiden and Boston: Brill, 2007), 307–373.
Wiese, Christian, "Struggling for Normality: The Apologetics of Wissenschaft des Judentums in Wilhelmine Germany as an Anti-Colonial Intellectual Revolt against the Protestant Construction of Judaism", in Rainer Liedke and David Rechter, eds., *Towards Normality: Patterns of Assimilation and Acculturation in German Speaking Jewry* (Tübingen: Mohr-Siebeck, 2003), 77–101.
Wiese, Christian, "Von Dessau nach Philadelphia: Samuel Hirsch als Philosoph, Apologet und radikaler Reformer", in Giuseppe Veltri and Christian Wiese, eds., *Jüdische Bildung und Kultur in Sachsen-Anhalt von der Aufklärung bis zum Nationalsozialismus* (Berlin: Metropol, 2009), 363–410.
Wiese, Christian, Walter Homolka, and Thomas Brechenmacher, eds., *Jüdische Existenz in der Moderne: Abraham Geiger und die Wissenschaft des Judentums* (Berlin and Boston: De Gruyter, 2013).
Wynants, Paul, *Autres Cultes (1598–1985)* (Namur: Fondation Meuse-Moselle, 1986).
Yante, Jean-Marie, "Heurs et malheurs des établissements juifs dans le Luxembourg (XIIIe siècle – début XVIe)", in Laurent Moyse and Marc Schoentgen, eds., *La présence juive au Luxembourg: du moyen âge au XXe siècle* (Luxembourg: B'nai Brith, 2001), 11–20.
Yante, Jean-Marie, "Les Juifs dans le Luxembourg au Moyen âge", Bulletin trimestriel de l'Institut archéologique du Luxembourg 62, 1–2 (1986), 3–22.

Yovel, Yirmiyahu, *Dark Riddle: Hegel, Nietzsche, and the Jews* (University Park, PA: The
 Pennsylvania State University Press, 1998).
Zittartz-Weber, Susanne, *Zwischen Religion und Staat: Die jüdischen Gemeinden in der
 preußischen Rheinprovinz 1815–1871*, Düsseldorfer Schriften zur Neueren
 Landesgeschichte und zur Geschichte Nordrhein-Westfalens 64 (Essen: Klartext-Verlag,
 2003).

Contributors

Norbert Franz received his doctorate in 1998 and habilitated in 2006 in contemporary and modern history at the University of Trier. He taught European history at the Universities of Trier and Luxemburg and the *Institut d'Études Politiques de Paris*. His research is focused on the history of cities, rural communities, nation building, migration and agriculture as exemplified by *Durchstaatlichung und Ausweitung der Kommunalaufgaben im 19. Jahrhundert. Tätigkeitsfelder und Handlungsspielräume ausgewählter französischer und luxemburgischer Landgemeinden im mikrohistorischen Vergleich (1805–1890)* (Trier: Kliomedia, 2006) and, with Andreas Fickers and Stephan Laux, eds., *Repression, Reform und Neuordnung im Zeitalter der Revolutionen. Die Folgen des Wiener Kongresses für Westeuropa*, vol. 15 (Berlin: Peter Lang, 2019).

Judith Frishman is Professor emerita of Judaism at Leiden University where she headed the Leiden University Centre for the Study of Religion. Her main interests are religious diversity, minority-majority relations, and religious reform in Western Europe in the 19th-21st centuries. She has published widely on Samuel Hirsch and will soon commence on a project editing, translating and interpreting Hirsch's correspondence located in the Hirsch-Einhorn family archive.

Thorsten Fuchshuber is a research associate at the *Centre interdisciplinaire d'Etude des Religions et de la Laïcité* (CIERL) at the Université libre de Bruxelles (ULB). He received his PhD in philosophy at the Leibniz University Hannover. His main interests are critical theory, legal philosophy and the critique of antisemitism. His latest book is *Rackets: Kritische Theorie der Bandenherrschaft* (Freiburg/Wien: ça ira Verlag, 2019).

Gershon Greenberg is based at American University in Washington D. C., where he serves as Professor of Philosophy and Religion. He has been a long-term visiting professor in the history of Jewish religious thought through the Holocaust at Hebrew University in Jerusalem and Bar Ilan University in Ramat Gan. Early on he discovered the importance of Samuel Hirsch and subsequently published a wealth of articles on Hirsch's philosophy. Other research interests include America-Holy Land studies. Among his notable publications are: *Mishpatekha tehom rabbah: Teguvot hagutiot ortodoksiot lashoah*, with co-editor Assaf Yedidyah (Jerusalem: Mossad Harav Kook, 2016) and *Modern Jewish Thinkers: From Mendelssohn to Rosenzweig* (Brighton, Mass.: Academic Studies Press, 2011).

Irene Kajon is professor emerita of Moral Philosophy at Sapienza – University of Rome. She has also taught Jewish Religion and Thought at Pontificia Università Lateranense (Rome) from 2009 to 2020. Her recent research in the field of philosophical anthropology, in dialogue with Jewish and Christian sources and with art and literature, concerns the idea of humanism today. Among her books are: *Fede ebraica e ateismo dopo Auschwitz* (Perugia: Assisi, 1993); *Contemporary Jewish Philosophy. An Introduction* (London: Routledge, 2010, 2nd edition); *Ebraismo laico. La sua storia e il suo senso oggi* (Assisi: Cittadella Editrice, 2012).

George Y. Kohler is Associate Professor for modern Jewish religious thought at Bar Ilan University's department for Jewish philosophy. He is also the current director of the Joseph Carlebach Institute at Bar Ilan. His academic interests focus on German Jewish thought in the 18th and especially the 19th century, on Jewish Christian theological debates and on the philosophy of Hermann Cohen. His latest book rediscovered the achievements of nineteenth century *Wissenschaft des Judentums* scholars in their pioneering research of Kabbalah and Jewish Mysticism.

Ken Koltun-Fromm is Professor of Religion at Haverford College. His research focuses on Jewish and religious conceptions of identity, authority, authenticity, and materiality. Koltun-Fromm's publications include *Imagining Jewish Authenticity: Vision and Text in American Jewish Thought* (Bloomington, IN: Indiana University Press, 2015) and most recently, *Drawing on Religion: Reading and the Moral Imagination in Comics and Graphic Novels* (University Park, PA: Pennsylvania State University Press, 2020).

Michael A. Meyer is the Adolph Ochs Professor of Jewish History emeritus at Hebrew Union College-Jewish Institute of Religion in Cincinnati, Ohio. His chief academic interest lies in modern Jewish religious and intellectual history in Germany and the United States. Among his numerous works are *Response to Modernity: A History of the Reform Movement in Judaism* (New York: Oxford University Press, 1988), the co-edited four-volume series *German-Jewish History in Modern Times* (New York: Columbia University Press, 1996–1998), and most recently *Rabbi Leo Baeck: Living a Religious Imperative in Troubled Times* (Philadelphia, PA: University of Pennsylvania Press, 2020).

Laurent Mignon is Associate Professor of Turkish language and literature at the University of Oxford, a Fellow of St Antony's College and Affiliate Professor at the Luxembourg School of Religion & Society. His research focuses on the minor literatures of Ottoman and Republican Turkey, in particular Jewish literatures, as well as the literary engagement with non-Abrahamic religions in Turkey. He is the author most recently of *Uncoupling Language and Religion: An Exploration into the Margins of Turkish Literature* (Boston: Academic Studies Press, 2021) and co-editor of *Penser l'islam en Europe: Perspectives du Luxembourg et d'ailleurs* (Paris: Hermann, 2021).

Stephanie Schlesier is an academic staff member of the German Federal Archive's Repository of Stasi Documentation, Department of Communication and Knowledge. Her dissertation *Bürger zweiter Klasse? Juden auf dem Land in Preußen, Lothringen und Luxemburg* (Köln: Bohlau Verlag, 2014) and more recently "Am Rand, dazwischen oder etwas Eigenes? Chancen und Probleme bei der Erforschung von Grenzräumen/ Grenzregionen", in Francesca Brunet and Florian Huber, eds, *Vormärz. Eine geteilte Geschichte Trentino-Tirols* (Innsbruck: Universitätsverlag Wagner, 2017) 35–52, reflect her research interests, which include the history of European Jewry in the 19th century, especially Jewish-Christian relations in Prussia, France and Luxembourg and the history of the construction of borders.

Renée Wagener is a Luxembourger historian. Her PhD thesis treated the history of Judaism and antisemitism in Luxembourg. Her research areas are Jewish history, women's and emancipation movements and suffrage history in 19th and 20th century Luxembourg. She is currently collaborating on a research project on intellectual and material practices of historians at the University of Luxembourg. Her recent publications include *Fighting Hunger, Dealing with Shortage. Everyday Life under Occupation in World War II Europe: A Source Edition*, 2 vol. (Leiden: Brill, 2021) jointly edited with Tatjana Tönsmeyer and Peter Haslinger, and "'Crowning of the democratic edifice'? – Public discourses on referendums in Luxembourg since the First World War", Topos 1 (2021), 32–54.

Christian Wiese holds the Martin Buber Chair in Jewish Thought and Philosophy and is director of the Buber-Rosenzweig-Institute for Modern and Contemporary Jewish Intellectual and Cultural History at Goethe University, Frankfurt am Main, Germany. His research is devoted to modern Jewish history, Jewish philosophy, and the history of Jewish-Christian relations. Recent publications include the edition of Martin Buber's biblical writings (*Martin Buber Werkausgabe*, vol. 13 (Gütersloh: De Gruyter 2019)) and *Jews and Protestants from the Reformation to the Present*, co-edited with Irene Aue Ben-David, Aya Elyada, and Moshe Sluhovsky (Berlin/Boston: De Gruyter 2020).

Index of Names

Abrabanel, Isaac 141
Abraham 3, 22, 67, 70–72, 74, 79, 90, 96, 176
Achilles 287
Adam 83, 92, 116
Adames, Nicolas, apostolic pro-vicar, Bishop of Luxembourg 201
Adler, Cyrus 297
Adler, Samuel 287
Adorno, Theodor W. 85
Allgemeine Zeitung des Judenthums 31
Alliance Israélite Universelle 46, 253, 298
Anchel, Robert 219
André, Charles Théodore 263–264
Apostolic Vicariat(e) 186, 200
Archbishop of Cologne 259
Archives israélites 56
Aristotle 87–88
Athanasius 269
Avineri, Shlomo 57

Baeck, Leo 12
Banque Internationale à Luxembourg 196
Bar Kochba 166
Bauer, Bruno 1, 2, 4, 33, 49, 56, 61, 73, 106–107, 110, 113, 115, 127–128, 130, 132, 134, 138, 144, 257
Bendavid, Lazarus 162
Benjamin, Walter 166
Berlin, Isaiah 57
Besslinger, Jacob, cantor 242
Biren, Louis 235
Bishop of Luxembourg 201
Blaschke, Olaf 259, 274, 279
Blochausen, Friedrich Georg Baron von 260
Blumenstein, Isaac, rabbi 247, 252
Brentano, Margherita von 270
Brunswick rabbinical conference 1844, protocols of 281
Bürge, Alfons 216
Bureau de Bienfaisance 199

Cahen, Léon 242, 246–247

Charakteristik der Ethik Maimunis 89
Charles V 208–209
Christ 134, 137, 143
– archetype of the sublime and divine 266
Clausen, Detlev
Cohen, Hermann 12, 89, 167, 169–170, 172
Concordat of 1801 200
Congregation Beth-El 53
Conseil d'État 217, 219
Counter-reflections to Bonnet's Palingenesis 161
Courrier du Grand-Duché de Luxembourg 190–191, 237, 261, 277, 279–280
Cum nimis absurdum 209

Davidic Redeemer King 163
Deborah, Die 46, 283, 287, 292
Décret Infâme 6, 207, 217, 219, 222, 224–225, 234
de Lagarde, Paul 278
de Thiennes, Charles 234
Députation du collège électoral 222
deputies 213
– chamber of 191
Derenbourg, Josef 175
Descartes, René 91
Deutscher Bund (German Confederation) 257
Diekircher Wochenblatt 190
Directoire 213
Dohm, Christian Wilhelm von 138, 236
Drumont, Édouard 234
Duke Leopold Friedrich, see: Leopold Friedrich

Echtermeyer, Ernest Theodor 83
Echternachter Grenzbote 190, 269
Einhorn, David 2, 44, 46, 50–51, 282, 286
– elitist 287
– lack of philosophical depth 288
– scepter of autocracy 287
– tyrant 287
Eisenmenger, Johann Andreas 136

Elements of the Philosophy of Right 100
Elias, Mordechai 148
Engels, Friedrich 138
Entdeckte Christentum, Das 136
Essence of Christianity, The 60, 109, 111
europäische Triarchie, Die 57
Ezra and Nehemiah 288

Felsenthal, Bernhard, rabbi 291, 293, 294–295, 298
Feuerbach, Ludwig 1, 4, 60
Fichte, Johann Gottlieb 277
Flemming, Rose 130
Formstecher, Salomon 17, 164, 281
Fould, family 285
Fränkel, David 282
Frankfurt National Assembly 261, 263
Frankfurt rabbinic conference 43
French
– Republic 189, 200
– Revolution 1, 6, 60, 185, 190, 207–208, 211, 213, 224, 225, 260, 267, 277
Freund, Wilhelm 132
Friede, Freiheit und Einheit 17
Funkenstein, Amos 54, 153
Fürst, Julius 32

Geiger, Abraham 1, 5, 17, 22, 51, 62, 132, 143, 145–154, 157–160, 175, 297
Geiger, Ludwig 152, 175
German
– Confederal Fortress 189
– Confederation 185–186, 188–189, 191–194, 224, 258, 261–262, 267–268, 276
– Federal Convention 187
Godchaux
– Cerf 247
– family 232
– Louis 251
– Pinhas 214
– Samson, mayor of Hamm 248, 250
Goldziher, Ignác 143
Goosens, Aline 209
Görres, Joseph 269
Gospel(s) 80, 83, 95, 97, 115
– of John 80, 83, 97
– of Matthew 80

Gottlieb, Sara 14
Graetz, Heinrich 59, 170
Grand Duke of Luxembourg 32, 185–188, 191, 224, 241, 257
Greenberg, Gershon 2–3, 46
Guide for the Perplexed 89–90, 97
Guttmann, Julius 63

Hannick, Pierre 210
Hebrew Union College in Cincinnati 46, 290
heilige Geschichte der Menschheit, Die 57
Heine, Heinrich 293
Heintz, tobacco manufacturer 201
Hess, Mendel 41, 55–61
Hess, Moses 55, 58
Herz
– family 248
– Henriette 231
Hirsch
– Edward 282
– Emil G. 289, 296
– Salomon 14
– Samson Raphael 68
Holdheim, Samuel 15, 17, 23, 43, 51, 74, 132, 174, 284–285, 289, 291–292
Hollerich, Jean-Claude 202
Horkheimer, Max 85
House of Orange-Nassau 185, 190
Humanität als Religion, Die 39, 49, 55, 61, 70
Humboldt, Wilhelm 150
Hyman, Paula 213, 224

Imperial Council of the Crown of Bavaria 276
Intolerance and Tolerance 267
Isaac 71–72, 176
Israel, Adèle and Albert 253

Jastrow, Marcus, rabbi 290–293, 299
Jellinek, Hermann 114
Jesse 170, 175
Jerusalem (oder über religiöse Macht und Judentum) 161–162
Jesuit(s) 7, 44, 267, 292
Jesus 15–16, 36–39, 58–59, 72, 74, 79–84, 105, 111, 120–123, 133, 137, 175, 295

– quest for the historical Jesus 175
Jewish Edict of 1812 207
Jewish Times, The 46, 49
Joseph II 212
Jourdan, André Joseph 220, 222
Journal de Luxembourg 191
Judenfrage, Die 14, 70, 106, 114–115, 127–128, 130–132, 140
Judenthum, der christliche Staat und die moderne Kritik, Das 34, 110, 114, 124
Jüdische Religion im Zeitalter der Emanzipation 23, 63
Jyllands Posten 130

Kasper-Holtkotte, Cilli 210, 214
Katechismus der israelitischen Religion 152
King William I 185
King-Duke William II 32, 187, 259
King-Duke William III 188, 191
Klëppelkrich or *Peasants' War* 215
Kohler, Kaufmann 53, 62, 288, 290
Krauskopf, Joseph 290

Lacoste, Jean-Baptiste 220
Laqish, Resh 172
Laurent, Theodor, apostolic vicar 259
Lazare, Isaac 214
Leben Jesu, Das 83, 175
Leiden University Institute for Religious Studies 1
Leopold Friedrich Franz, Duke of Dessau 13, 75, 82
Leopold Friedrich, Duke 14
Lessing, Gotthold Ephraim 162
Letters on Israel's Mission in the History of Humankind 56, 59
Letzebuerger Nationalunio'n 233
Levi, Lazarre 221
Levinas, Emmanuel 89–90
Levita, Elias 141
Levy
– Henriette 237
– Isaias 245
– Lazarus 239–240
Lewis, Bernard 143
Lippmann, family 230
Literaturblatt des Orients 114

London Conference 186
Louis XIV 210
Lorraine and Luxembourg's Central Association of Jewish Migrant Welfare 252
Löwith, Karl 85
Luria, Isaac 141
Luther, Martin 74, 81, 84
Luxemburger Wort für Wahrheit und Recht 32, 190, 258–259

Maccabees 290
Maimonides, Moses 3, 98–90, 139–140, 161, 163, 176–177
March Revolution 259
Marr, Wilhelm 278
Martha, Nicolas 190
Marx, Heinrich 207, 217
Marx, Karl 1, 130, 138, 217
Marx, Samuel, Chief Rabbi 223
Maskilim 162
Masonic lodge(s) 33, 39, 124, 191, 251
Matthew, Gospel of 80, 81, 174
Mayer, Jacob, rabbi 291
McIlvaine, Mr. 286
Memorandum on the 1808 Law of Exception Against Jews 207
Mendelssohn, Moses 14, 22, 139, 141, 161, 174
Messiah 5, 38, 41, 121, 123, 161–180, 269
– concept, foundation of Judaism 112
– concept 171
– King 171, 177–178
– King, highest judge on earth 175, 177
– adviser 175
– as God's representative on earth 78
– as role model 175–176, 179
– collective 167, 170
– custodian of the kingdom 179
– end of salvation 171
– enlightened monarch 177–178
– exclusively human 172
– guarantor of the preservation of the kingdom 171, 175
– in Talmud 170
– Israel's savior 170
– king of all peoples 178
– miracle-working 173

- moral compass 175
- passive interpretation 171
- person of 169, 171
- personal 123, 169–170, 180
- preservation of ideal, future kingdom 22
- proclaim universal moral law 175
- pseudo 162
- supernatural 5, 172, 175
- violent 172
- worldly power 170

Messianic Doctrine of Judaism, The 164
Messiaslehre der Juden in Kanzelvorträgen, Die 25
Metaphysics 88
Meyer Wise, Isaac 288, 290, 294
Meyer, Miss 286
Michelet, Karl Ludwig 15
Michelis, Eduard 259–260
Minister of State Simon 195
Minister Servais 195, 219
Montalivet, Jeanne Pierre de 218, 222
Mortara Affair 237
Muller, Jean-Claude 210

Napoleon I (Bonaparte) 6, 185, 207, 215–219, 257
Napoleon III 188
Napoleon, defeat of 224
New Christians 209
New Testament 80, 115, 272
Nitzsch, Carl Immanuel 14, 70

Oberndörfer, prayer leader 242
On the Jews' Belief in a Future Messiah 162
Orient, Der 32

Partei Metz 191
Pasto, James 129
Paul (of Tarsus) 22, 79–81, 84, 95–96, 295
Peasants' or Klëppelkrich War 215
Persians 94
Philadelphia rabbinical conference, presidency of 299
Philippson, Gustav 132
Philippson, Ludwig 42
philosophia prima 90

Philosophie des Geistes, Die 92
Philosophie des Judentums, Die 63
Picard, Salomon 202
Pope Paul IV 209
Prince Leopold III Friedrich Franz of Anhalt-Dessau see: Leopold Friedrich Franz, Duke of Dessau
Protestant Evangelical congregation 187

Reform Advocate, The 62
Reformfreunde, see: Society of Friends of Reform
Reform Congregation Keneseth Israel 2, 282
Reformation 181, 119
Regeneration of the Israelites, report 218
Religion within the Limits of Reason Alone 107
Religionsphilosophie der Juden, Die 3, 17, 20–22, 25, 28, 69–70, 77–79, 86, 97, 110, 122, 142, 283
Renan, Ernst 52
Republic 88, 90
Reuter, Antoinette 210
Revolution of 1848 186, 188, 194, 204, 234, 258, 277
Riesser, Gabriel 132
Rohling, August 234
Rome and Jerusalem 55–56, 58–59
Rosenak, Michael 158–159
Rosenzweig, Franz 61, 85
Rousseau, Jean-Jacques 67
Ruge, Arnold 83
Ruth 288

Said, Edward 129
Salomon, Gotthold 132
Salvador, Joseph 141
Schleiermacher, Friedrich 14, 148
Scholem, Gershom 166
Schou, Pierre-Anton 191
Schreiber, Jean-Philippe 212, 218
Schrobilgen, Mathieu-Lambert 191
Schulte, Christoph 129
Schuster, day laborer 248
Schuster, Nathan 241
Schwarz, Samuel 167

Seelhof, Joseph   191, 262
Servais, Emmanuel, minister   188
Simonis, Charles   191
Society for the Promotion of Arts and Trades among the Israelites of Metz   252
Society of Friends of Reform   41, 49
Solis-Cohen, Solomon   297
Spinoza, Baruch de   139, 141
Stahl, Friedrich Julius   37, 83
Ständeversammlung   189
Steinheim, Solomon Ludwig   68
Strauss, David Friedrich   89–90, 175
St. Sophie congregation   201
Systematischer Katechismus der israelitischen Religion   152
Szold, Benjamin   283, 290

Taubes, Jacob   166
Theodicy of World History   168
Thoughts of a Sleepwalker (Gedanken eines Nachtwandlers)   266
Tornaco, Victor von   188
Toury, Jacob   278
Toussenel, Alphonse   234
Trausch, Gilbert   224
Trendelenburg, Friedrich Adolf   14–15
Turner, Bryan S.   129

Über das Geldwesen   58

Vienna, Congress of 1814/1815   185
Vital, Hayyim ben Joseph   141
Volkov, Shulamit   54, 57, 274
Volksfreund, Der   7, 190–191, 257–262, 269–270, 272–277

Wagner, Adolph   193
Wagner, Nicolas   232
Wagner, Richard   277
Was hat Mohammed aus dem Judenthume aufgenommen?   143
Wellhausen's *Prolegomena*   296
Wiener, Max   63
William I   185, 207, 224
William II   32, 187, 259
William III   188, 191
Wise, Isaac Mayer   46, 283, 288, 290–291, 294
Wolf, Joseph, rabbi   15
Worms, Aron   14
Writings on the French Revolution   277
Wynant, Paul   214

Yahweh   113

Zeitgeist, Der   46, 296
Zunz, Leopold   20, 68, 75, 114, 283
Zvi, Shabbatai   166
Zwé Judden als Schmoggler   235

Index of Places

Echternach
– Abbey of   201
Albany, New York   291
Alsace   213, 216–217, 221–222, 227
America   7, 44–50, 53, 67, 280–284, 289, 292–299
Anhalt   75
Anhalt-Dessau   13, 15
Arlon   215
Arrondissement Dickrich (Diekirch)   223
Austrian Netherlands   185

Baltimore   283, 290
Bavaria   276
Belgian departments   215, 220
Belgium   185, 190, 196, 225, 241
Berlin   14–15, 57, 69, 161, 193, 291
– University of   14
Bohemia   212
Bonn   14, 55, 70, 132
– University of   20
Bordeaux   216
Braunschweig   43
Breslau   43, 146–147, 151, 157, 289
Brussels   212

cemetery
– Jewish   127
– Clausen (Luxembourg City)   240
– Ettelbruck   240
– Grevenmacher   240
– Esch-sur-Alzette   240
Charleroi   212
Charleville   210
Chicago   1, 11, 46, 62, 283, 286, 289
Cincinnati   46, 291
Cobreville   213

Denmark   130
Département des Forêts   6, 185, 213, 215, 218, 220–222, 225
Department(s)
– Bas-Rhin   220

– Belgian   215
– French   213
– Gironde   216, 218
– Landes   216, 218
– Montenotte   218, 222
– Rhône   218, 222
– Rome   218, 222
– Saar   214–216
– Sambre-et-Meuse   215, 218
Dessau   1–2, 12–20, 22, 25–26, 29–32, 35, 40, 46, 53, 63, 67–68, 74–75, 82, 84, 99–100, 257, 281, 284
Duchy Anhalt-Dessau   15
Duchy of Holstein   186
Duchy of Luxembourg   6, 184–189, 192–193, 196–197, 204, 208, 210, 213, 229, 235, 239, 245, 249, 251, 253, 257–258
Dudelange   228

Eich (Luxembourg City)   202
Esch-sur-Alzette   228, 239–240, 259
– ritual bath remains   241
Ettelbruck   215, 228, 231–232, 236–242, 244, 246–247, 250–253
Europe
– Central   186, 197, 203
– Eastern   137, 211, 253

Fez   253
fortress City   185, 197, 204
France   119, 121, 185, 189, 213–214, 219, 221, 225, 237, 258, 285
– eastern   217, 228, 243, 253
Frankfurt   41, 43, 49, 136, 163, 187, 261, 263

Galicia   137
garden of bliss   154
Grevenmacher   221, 223, 239–240, 243–244
Grund (Luxembourg City)   197

Hamburg Temple   162, 164
Heiliggeistplateau   199

Hollerich (Luxembourg City)   202
Hungary   263, 276
Hunsrück   14

Jerusalem   23, 55–59, 143, 291

Krefeld   225

Leipzig (University of)   15–16
Limpertsberg (Luxembourg City)   197
Lorraine   214, 228–229, 232, 237–238, 248–249, 252
Lower Austria   212
Luxembourg   215, 238–242, 245–247, 249, 252
Luxembourg
– University of   1, 8
– City   183, 187, 196–198, 203, 239
– Crisis of 1867   188
– Sovereign state of   185

Medernach   201, 230–239, 243, 248
Metz   14, 210, 214, 215, 252
Mondorf-les-Bains   239
Montenotte, department of   222
Mosel area   227

Namur   212
Neufchâteau, arrondissement   220
New York   44, 53, 291
North Africa   140

Ostend   212

Palestine   28, 41, 45, 137, 284, 292
Passerelle (Luxembourg Viaduct)   199–200
Petrusbachtal (Luxembourg City)   197
Pfaffenthal (Luxembourg City)   197
Philadelphia   1–2, 7, 12, 44, 46, 50, 63, 281–282, 285–286, 288, 290–291, 293, 297–299 Poland   137, 186, 217
Portugal   209
Pressburg (Bratislava)   262
Prussia   76, 128, 189, 207

Remich   243

Rhine Province, Prussian   229
Rhineland   127, 190, 211
Rome   55–56, 58–59, 88, 218, 222, 260
Rosehill Cemetery, Chicago   11, 283
Ruwer   216

Saar Basin   229
SaarLorLux   249
Salonica   209
Sambre-et-Meuse   215, 218
Saxony-Weimar   41
Schleiden   213
Schleifmuhl   228
Schwerin   70
Siechenhof   197
Sierck   210
Sinai   76, 89, 283
Spain   86, 97
Strassen (Luxembourg City)   237, 238, 248
synagogue
– Esch-sur-Alzette   239
– Ettelbruck   215, 239, 241–242, 246–247, 252
– Grevenmacher   223, 239–240
– Medernach   239
– Mondorf-les-Bains   239

Tavern(s)   6, 230, 238, 253
– Kieffer tavern   238
Thalfang   1, 14–15, 127, 131, 144
Thionville   214
Trier   1, 207, 210, 212, 215, 218–219, 223, 225, 239–242, 245
Turkey   209

United Kingdom of the Netherlands   185–186
United States   2, 7, 12, 17, 44–46, 62–63, 160, 178, 282–283, 289, 293, 296
USA   1–2

Vatican   200

Willmar   194

Zion   29–30, 55, 77, 163, 170, 285

Index of Topics

a-historical 33, 73, 107, 138–139
absolute 22, 25, 71–74, 80, 84, 100, 104, 110, 113–114, 117, 122, 128, 168, 283, 297
– existence 69
– ground of freedom 67
– religion 22, 97, 103, 105, 108, 115, 123
absolutist 283
academic 25, 33, 49, 119, 121, 134–135, 139, 140, 144
– establishment 134
– hierarchies 134
– institution 134
acceptance 72, 78, 116, 227, 248, 292
acculturation 165
active religion 70, 122
actualization 3, 70, 82, 104
administrative work 200, 234
affective (religion) 154
age of reaction 188
Age of Tolerance 211
agrarian 196, 217
agricultural property 196, 216
agriculture 136, 198, 201
alienation 26, 58, 103
All Saints' Day 244
Alsatian 213
alterity 144
America(n)
– *golus* 48, 284
– patriotism 284, 292
– Revolution 190
– setbacks 299
Americanizing 282
amphibians 285
Ancien Régime 199–200, 208, 233, 249
Anstaltsstaat 198
anthropologization 49, 111
anti-clerical 191
anti-historical 73
anti-immigration 4, 128
anti-Islamic 4, 128–129, 131
– attacks 131

anti-Jewish
– articles 273–274
– attacks 2, 22, 33, 253, 273
– attacks in Fez 253
– citations 273
– pogrom(s) 262, 265, 269
– practices 268
– riots 136, 213
– stereotypes 235
anti-Judaism 2, 4, 7, 113, 138, 143, 249, 263
anti-liberal 260, 279
anti-liberal ideology 269
antireligious measures 215
antinomian 166
antiquity 29, 140, 216
antisemitic codes 273
antisemitism 4, 7, 129, 131, 233, 268, 270, 277–279
– as explanatory model of the world 278
– as failed Enlightenment 270
apocalyptic 164, 166
apostolic pro-vicar 201
Aqedah 71, 176
Arab 87, 90, 119, 143, 209
archaic 129
archives 56, 208, 228
argumentation 4, 35, 38, 136, 140, 165, 257–258
armed forces 189, 193–194
army 43, 210, 220
– personally serve 216
art(s) 179, 200
– and sciences 73, 178–179
– as Jewish strategy 269
Ashkenazic 214, 217, 225
Ashkenazic Jewry 214, 108, 178
assembly of congregations 288
assimilation 37, 52, 56, 58, 213
association(s) 192, 251–252
– ecclesiastical 254
– Jewish 254
– *Chevrah Kaddishah* 251
– *chevrot* 252

– chorus 251
– funeral costs 252
– gymnastics 251
– Jewish women's 252
– meetings 238
– secondary school parents' 251
– secular 251
– shooting clubs 251
– theater 251
atheism 132
atonement 72, 81, 172–173
Ausbildung 77
authenticity 91, 148
authoritarian 246
auto-emancipation 77
autonomy 100, 108, 117, 203, 213, 241
avarice 274
aversion 227

bakers 201, 230
baptized 209, 237
baptizing, of Jewish girl 237
bath(s) 240–241
beauty 19, 45, 103, 108, 111
Bekenntniß 156
Belgian Revolution 186, 199
Bewusstsein, religiöse 92–93
Bible, not revelation
biblical 43, 93, 96, 118, 154–155, 162–163, 166–167, 169–170, 172, 176–177, 179, 274, 289
– criticism 49, 173, 296
– figures 138
– history 145, 175, 242
– scholar 41, 129, 134
– scholarship 129
– studies 146
Bildung 13, 18, 20, 26, 31, 35, 45, 75–78, 82, 150
birth registry, Christian witnesses 248
bishop 120, 153, 261
blood 38, 52, 259
body tax 264
book and printing 201, 288
boundary maintenance 145
bourgeois-capitalist structures 258
boycott 233

Brabant Revolution 213
Breslau rabbinical conference 43, 289
breviary 285
brides and grooms 229
brokering 214
brotherhood 158, 252
Buddhism 94, 130
building 1, 6, 13, 183, 189. 194, 195–196, 204–205, 266, 291
burden 27, 193, 218, 295
bureaucratic character 271
business 6, 141, 149, 191, 196, 202, 208, 227, 232, 243–249
– life 230
– networks 229
– practices 233
– relations 233, 235
– butchers 230

cadaver 267
Calvinist leaders 190
cantor 241–242
capital investment 201, 203
capitalist mode of production 271, 272, 278
caprice 76
Capuchin monk 293
care of the poor 194, 199
career 1–2, 7, 259, 281, 282, 293
caricature(s), caricatured 130, 136, 139
casino 251
casuistic 119
casuistry 35, 292
catechism 5, 146, 151–159, 243–244, 267, 293
Catholic 76, 190, 204, 259–260, 264, 269, 274, 279
– agrarian circles 217
– resistance 208
– schools 237
Catholicism 76, 190, 204, 259–260, 264, 269, 274, 279
– political 190, 204, 265
cattle merchants 238
celebration 43, 141, 227, 231, 243, 247, 249–250, 253–254
censorship 135, 190, 259–260

ceremonies   15–16, 25, 33, 42, 48, 171, 231
– and customs, essential to preserving Jewish uniqueness   297
chamber   192
– of deputies   191
Chancellor   260
Charakterbildung   149–150
charity, for Jewish beggars and vagabonds   223
chief editor   259
Chief Rabbi   1, 32, 135, 187, 190, 194, 202, 223, 275
Chief Rabbinate   187
chimerical   33, 107, 128, 132, 140
Chinese   94
choir   247
cholera epidemics   199
chosenness   16
– particularizing concept   296
Christian
– accept fundamental doctrine   295
– buried in Jewish cemetery   294
– clients   232
– employees   232, 247
– lifestyle   231
– missionaries   294
– state   38–39, 67, 81, 106, 114, 120, 124, 127–128, 133, 165, 277
– supernatural revelation   294
– workforce   234
Christians, affairs   262–264
Christian-Jewish relations   68, 240, 249
– (religious) celebrations   249
– Easter   231, 249
– funerals   127
– furor of prejudice   249
– gifts   249
– Passover   231
– police investigation   249
– synagogue consecration   246–247, 249
– verbal abuse   249
– weddings   238
Christianity
– renounce   101, 285
– revealed supra-rational religion   294

church   7, 39–40, 45, 56, 77 81–82, 84–88, 105, 116, 124, 127, 142, 176, 187, 194, 200–201, 244, 249–250, 280
– and State   4, 213, 276, 279
– and State, separation of   4, 213, 260, 272, 279
– buildings   194
– Catholic   79, 84, 176, 187, 257–258, 260–261, 270, 272, 279
– construction of   200
– Protestant   120
– related events   227
– subjugation of   271
circumcision   28, 30, 42–43, 51–52, 71, 288, 297
– adult   288
– no intrinsic value   297
citizen(s)   75, 102, 105, 150, 157–158, 236, 262
– useful   213
– honorable   262
citizenship   5, 78, 142, 149–150, 164, 212, 250
– limited   212
city government   198
civic   6, 29, 127, 143, 162, 165–166, 174
– and moral calling   165
– duties   162
– emancipation   143, 162, 166, 174
– relations   127
– rights   162
civil liberties   213
civil list   187, 193–194
civil marriage(s)   248
Civil War   44
civilization, lowest ranks   246
class distinctions   152
clergy   194–195, 201, 236, 254, 258, 264, 267, 275, 285
clerical politics   267
coexistence, social   4, 227
collective patents   223
collective people of Israel   68
Cologne dispute   259
colonial   37, 140
colonialist   140

commandment(s)
– *Commandments and Concerns* 158
– sanctifying power 297
– symbolic 297
– yoke of the 173–174
commerce 223, 230, 234, 236, 258
commercial sector 230
commodities, production of 271–272
common faith 294
common good 103
communal 150, 152, 158–159
– education 150
– needs 159
communication 53, 194–195
competition 233
comprehensive religiosity 71
compromise 54, 81, 84, 101, 271, 281, 291
– intellectual 281
– religious 281
conatus essendi 85
confession 22, 30, 40, 132, 156–157
conform 6, 46, 86, 93, 95, 195, 222, 225, 244, 291
Congregation of Jacob 176
congregation, Rodeph Shalom 291
congregation, state subsidy 241
Congress of Vienna 1, 185
conquests 207
conservative-liberal 190–191, 196
consistories, integrated or excluded Jews into/from one community 225
conspiracy 113, 265
conspiratorial power, of Jews 271
constituent assembly 187
Constitutio Criminalis Carolina 209
constitution(s) 7, 186–192, 213, 224, 259, 272, 280, 284, 298
– constitution 1841 187, 189
– constitution 1848 187, 190, 272
– constitution 1868, revised 188
– of the Consulate 189
– of the Directory of the French Republic 189
– of the first French Empire 189
– Belgian 1830 186
– Dutch 1814, revised version 1815 189
– French 189, 213

– *landständische* 188
constitutional
– policy 189
– state 120–121, 190, 274
– status 224
contemporaneity 128
contextualize 136–137, 141
controversies 12, 32, 47
core knowledge 159
coreligionists 221, 223, 225, 229, 239–241, 262–253
cosmopolitanism 59
counter-history 36
counter-pressure 138
coup d'état 215
Covenant of pieces 71
create 229
creatio ex nihilo 68
creator 70, 117, 120, 161, 174
criminal offense 218
Critical Criticism 130
Crusades 86, 144
cultural 12–13, 20–21, 24, 33, 35, 37–38, 54–55, 63, 135, 141, 143
– non-sedentariness 210
– sector 194, 200
curriculum 46, 145
customs duties 198

daily lives 6–7, 227, 235
Damascus Affair 13
dance 147, 151
Danish 130
Day of Atonement 72, 172–173
de la Fontaine administration 193
debt, national 196
decision-making process 189, 193
Declaration of Principles 50
defamation 274
defortification 197, 204
degenerate 269
dehistoricization 137–138
Deism 15
deliverance from evil 180
demarcation 174
democracy 1, 7, 47–48, 177–178, 284
democratization 132, 191

demographic development   197–198, 227
depravity   121, 269, 295
dialectic process of development   168
dialectical   82
dialogue   11, 18, 64, 142
Diaspora   18–19, 48, 55
dietary   28, 30, 42–43, 48, 102, 135, 238, 297
– laws   28, 30, 42–43, 48, 102, 135, 297
– regulations   238
diocese   186, 200 of
discourse(s)   4, 17, 33, 35, 51, 74, 128–129, 131, 139, 142–143, 153, 204, 219
discrimination   27, 47, 137
dishonorable treatment   207
disloyalty   292
disregard for   138, 210, 290
distinctiveness   12, 25, 52, 55, 160
diversity   105, 140–141, 144
divine
– envoy   162
– image   99
– intervention   295
– purpose (for mankind)   167
– spirit   47, 71
– divine-human   42, 266
divinity   49, 59, 70, 73–74, 81, 103
divinization   111
divorce, civil law   285
doctrine
– Christian   116, 295
dogma(s)   14–15, 18, 33, 51, 68, 86–87, 135, 148, 153–154, 157
dogmatic(s)   14, 41, 60, 119, 151–152, 155, 259
dominating   12, 55, 278
– influence (Jewish) 272

Easter   231, 249
– eggs   231
Eastern Jews   211
economic competition   233
edicts   210
edifies   148
education   4–5, 13, 26, 30, 32–33, 141, 145–152, 154–162, 171, 179, 194–203, 236, 242, 245, 264, 272, 286, 290, 298

– public   194
educational   13, 33, 152, 154, 157–158, 160, 196, 200, 236, 272
– program   5, 146–149, 151, 157, 159
– school   145
egalitarian
– principles   207, 217, 266
– project   207

ego cogito   85
Egyptian   94
elderly   199
election(s)   19, 50, 187, 193, 229, 270
elite(s)   150, 189, 191, 203, 240, 243, 245
emancipation
– Jewish   1, 4, 6–7, 11–13, 34, 78, 81, 101, 129, 207, 224, 257, 268, 276, 279–280
– rescinded   224, 257
– worthy of   19, 223
emigration   197, 229, 237
Emperor   120, 209, 212, 221–223
end of time(s)   30, 163, 173
enemy within   276
English   8, 11, 49, 197, 282, 289
enlightened   11, 13, 18, 146, 150, 177–178, 245, 265, 276
– badly   265
– men of the community   245
Enlightenment   11, 13, 16, 18, 26, 28, 36, 50, 56, 129, 131, 141, 149, 262, 264–270
enlightens, someone who   245
enslavement   44, 116–117, 284
equal rights   37, 77, 121, 213, 216, 268
equality
– principle of   6, 213–214, 217, 219, 225
eschatological   157, 162–163
eschatology   161, 177
essence
– of Judaism, resting once a week   289
– oriental   128, 132
– reclamation of   165
essentialization   137
eternal   3, 24, 29, 47–49, 52, 76, 80, 85, 93–95, 103, 110, 116, 161–162, 173–175
– peace   161
– principle   48
eternity   26, 30, 80, 84

ethical   3, 54–55, 59, 85–86, 88–97, 105, 161, 166, 174–175
– development   73
– monotheism   55, 167
ethics   20, 22, 60, 89–90, 119, 145–146, 173–174
– humanist   174
ethnic   24, 52, 129
Europe/European
– baggage   281
– culture   2–3, 11, 20, 60, 85–86, 95, 108, 145
– Central   185, 203
– Eastern   211
evolution   107, 135, 140–141, 204
exchange village news   231
exclusion   40, 79, 81, 84, 107, 119, 131, 139, 196, 207, 254
– categorical   211
exclusionist   4, 131
exemption
 applications for   218–219
 decree(s) of   218
exile   29, 50, 52, 61, 72, 74, 142, 162, 170, 284
exile-Isaiah   170
expectation(s)   130, 133, 162, 165, 171, 173
experiences   5, 47, 112, 137, 145
explicit paradigm, of Jewish educational theory   158–159
expressive religion   154
expulsion(s)   208, 217
extensive religiosity   71
eyesore   138

fabric industry   196
factory dam   232
familial
– events   227
– relations   92
family
– celebrations, Christian participation   153
– pew   291
– seating   7, 291–292
fate   39, 56, 93–94, 121–122, 264, 288
fatherland   12–13, 18, 25–26, 29, 60, 83, 99–100, 166, 262

Feast of Tabernacles   72
Feast of Weeks   72
feeling(s)   94–95, 110
feudal   258
figurative analogy   104
finite-infinite   3
fire department   198
food trades   201
foreign
– campaigns against Jews   235
forest management   194
forgiveness   172
Franco-German War   229
fraternization   264
free
– choice   72
– subjectivity   82
Freemasonry   55–56, 124, 266
Freemasons   8, 260–261, 265, 269, 272
Freiheit   17, 99
French
– constitution   189, 212
– department   213
– Empire   189
– law system   6
– national identity   225
– rule   1, 227, 229
– Republic   189, 200
– Revolution   1, 6, 60, 185, 190, 207–208, 211, 213, 224, 225, 260, 267, 277
fulfillment   16, 28, 38, 40, 116, 120, 162, 219, 242
funerals   127, 238, 247

garden of bliss   154
Gemeindearmenschule   236
gendarmerie   187
German
– Confederal Fortress   189
– Confederation   185–186, 188–189, 191–194, 224, 258, 261–262, 267–268, 276
– customs union   186
– Federal Convention   187
– friendly   261
– language   20, 134, 139, 146–147, 153, 170, 283, 289, 297
geographic mobility   211

ger toshav 286–287
ghetto(s) 20, 62, 77, 141, 214, 264
glovemakers 201
goal (on earth) 30, 154
God
– freedom itself 296
– personal 291, 293
– universal recognition of the one God 176
golden wedding anniversary, wedding jubilee 247–248
government expenditure 193–199
governmental activity 6, 184, 193–194, 198
grain 52, 199, 229
Greek(s) 19, 87–88, 94, 102, 108–109, 119, 122, 142, 216

halachah 47, 86
halachic tradition 47
harmony, original 5, 177
Haskalah 12, 129, 146, 162
hate(ful) 106, 109, 128, 136, 176, 260
head covering 48, 262
health care ministration 198
healthcare 195
heart
– of flesh 174
– of stone 175
heathenism 16, 22
Hebrew
– grammar 298
– importance of teaching and using 297
– language 43, 134, 145–146, 297–298
– prayers 145, 298
– service 292
– terminology 134, 179
hell 114
heretic(s) 209
Herzensangelegenheiten 174
heteronomous, see: heteronomy
heteronomy 49, 103, 118
Hinduism 94, 130
historical
– circumstances, changing 290
history
– sacred history 59, 168, 294
historiosophy 3, 70
holiness 26–27, 52, 80, 93–95, 296

hollow 270
Holy Catholic Church 176
Holy Days, business on 243–244
Holy Grave 143
Holy Scripture(s) 87, 121
homemaking 146
homo religiosus 96
hope of return, meaningless babble 284
horse-trading 210
horseradish 231
hostility 2, 257, 270, 276–278
human
– progress 161
– flourishing 145
humankind, moral 59, 171
Hungarian uprising 276

I consciousness 67, 69
idolatry 93–94
idols 166
image 12, 22, 24–25, 57, 78, 80, 99, 114, 117, 174, 266–267, 288
– of divine freedom 102
– of God 81
immediate
– religion 103
immigration 2, 4, 128, 131, 211, 228–229
immorally mingling the sexes 292
immortality of the soul 168
imperial
– dynasty 178
– ideology 225
impersonal 63, 169, 271
implicit model, of Jewish educational theory 158
improvement(s), contemporary 246
incarnate 80
incarnation 22, 103, 110–111
income 187, 194, 221, 261, 274, 299
individualism 59, 295
industrialists 230
industrialization 6, 183, 201–202, 204
industry 196, 198
inequality
– social 198
inflation 199
injustices, class and creed 298

innovate   245
Inquisition   83, 209
institutional anarchy   213
integration
– social   63
intemperance   291
intemperate   7
intensive religiosity   71
interior minister   218, 220–222
Interior Ministry   220, 222
intermarriage, viewed negatively   248–249
interreligious   4, 64, 131, 248
– couple(s)   248
intolerance   45, 113, 267–268
iron industry   196
iron producer   6, 183
irrational   18, 258
Isaac   72, 176
Islam   4, 128–131, 142–144
Islamophobia   129, 131
Israelite Congregation   25, 31

Jesuit Catechism   44, 264, 267
Jesuitism   264, 292
Jew
– buried in Christian cemetery   294
– by birth   295
– exemplary model   18
Jewishness   36, 45, 55, 60, 139, 141, 278, 297
Jewish
– consistory   215
– debts, moratorium on   216
– distinctiveness   18, 25, 52, 55, 160
– education   147, 149–150, 160
– educational practice   147, 152, 158
– emancipation, unconditional   207
– Germans   235
– identity   1, 5, 23, 26, 33, 47, 50, 56, 60, 145–146, 152
– issues   257
– literati   273
– merchants   223, 233, 243
– newspapers as   273
– petition   242
– notables   216, 249
– occupations   210, 229
– organizational projects   298
– people, grubs and locusts   219
– presence   116, 210
– Question   33, 106, 127, 279–280
– rabbis   32, 262, 264–265, 269
– school(s)   236–237, 242
– solidarity   225
– standpoint   272
– strategy   269
– studies   147
– views   155
– youths   265
– wandering beggars   211
Jews
– American   63, 284, 286
– Ashkenazic   214
– contempt for   218
– Dutch   207
– improvement of   119
– profiteering   235
– Russian   298
– Sephardic   213, 217
– social classification of   6, 207
Josephinism   260
journalist(ic)   7, 259–260, 269
Judaism(s)
– antithesis of Catholicism   279
– divinely ordained mission to the nations   294
– everything great, noble and beautiful   295
– future rooted in unconstrained moral choice, love and tolerance   295
– *golus*   48
– medieval   246
– religion of progress   45
– religion of the present   45
– religion of the future   48
– sacred history of the people of Israel   294
– teaching not law   297
Juddeglieser   238
Judentumswissenschaft   67
judgment, free   177
judicial system   193
jüdische Aufklärung, Die   129
juste milieu   109
justice   2–3, 5, 13, 19, 22, 36, 48, 60, 67, 88–89, 96–97, 123, 171, 175–179, 222

Kabbalah 119
kabbalistic 162
kashrut 135, 154, 297
Keneseth Israel, Reform Congregation 2, 282
king 7, 26, 74, 76, 81, 100–101, 163, 188, 191, 224, 283–284
– of the Netherlands 32, 224, 257
– true shepherd of humanity 283
kingdom 5, 22, 40, 80, 82, 121, 163, 170–171, 174–177, 179–180, 185–186, 190
– moral 5
knavishness (Jewish) 265, 269
knowledge 22, 48, 141, 147–148, 151–152, 154–159, 161, 168, 173, 177, 180, 208, 243, 245, 282, 297–298
– evolving 217
– of God 48
– production of 141
– secular 282
Konfession 284
kosmos 90

labor 118, 120, 124, 136, 160, 203–204, 271, 289
– imperative for mission of Israel 290
laity 41, 146, 285–286, 298
language of the heart 45, 153, 156–157
laundry 231
law
– abrogation 174
– before the 267–268
– of God 299
– of the state is law 284
– of the state, God's law 7
– of the state, sacrosanct 284
lawsuits 233
leather industry 196
Lebensanschauungen 152, 155
Left Hegelian 257
legalism 27
Leistungsverwaltung 194
Leitkultur 129
liberalism 273, 278
life contract 282
liturgy 163, 282, 291
livestock 14, 229, 235, 243

Logos 80, 91
loneliness 299
losers 210
lost brothers 165
loving-kindness 3, 88, 97
lower class(es) 190–193, 202
Lutherans 81–82, 119, 136

majority, tyrannous 284
manual laborers 201–202
manufactured goods 214
manufacturers 232, 234
marginalization 211, 278
marginalized 130
marriage 51–53, 229, 248, 249, 285, 292, 287, 288–290, 299
– and divorce 285
– children born outside of 248
– mixed 51–53, 259, 285–290, 299
– partners 229
– religious ceremony no legal effect 285
– sanctified 285
martyr 42, 73
mass murder 264
mass poverty 194, 197–198, 204
massacred 264
material constraints 271
materialism 53, 282, 299
materialist 109, 124
materiality 72
matzah 231
media, transnational 237
mediation 74, 81, 84, 114, 170
medieval 49, 76, 97, 166, 246, 267
– intolerance 267
– Judaism 245
mercantile expeditions 211
merchant(s) 201–202, 209, 221, 223, 229, 232–232, 235, 238, 243
Messianic 15–17, 22–25, 28–29, 38, 40 42, 45, 50, 52–54, 59, 77, 80, 84, 97, 122–123, 133, 163, 283–284
– age, as monarchy 5
– era 5, 60, 71, 123, 164–165, 168–169, 174, 176–178
– idea, theological reinterpretation 165
metal engraver 214

metaphor(s)   90, 104, 170, 174
metaphorical language   27
metaphysical   88–89
metaphysics   3, 86
Middle Ages   87–88, 90, 100, 119–120, 124, 170, 236
middle class   202–203
Midrash   21, 92
migration   216, 264
mikvah(s)   240
military
– service, compulsory   215
militia   193, 202
mimetic representation   153
minority, subservient   284
miracles   15, 113, 123, 172, 175
misanthropy   107, 275
misrepresentation(s)   110
mission
– disabusing non-Jews of belief in Original Sin   296
– Jewish   60, 170
– priestly   45, 294
missive, open   263
mixed marriage   51–53, 259, 285–290, 299
– nail for the coffin of Judaism   287
– officiation   299
– sanctify   285–286
modernization   8, 12, 34, 40, 51, 63
monarch   4–5, 7, 34, 76, 107, 123, 177–179, 185, 187–194, 204, 259, 283–284
– partyless   178
monarchism, enlightened   177
monarchist   5, 7, 76, 177, 283
monarchy   40, 76, 177, 189, 191, 283
money   68, 136, 239, 153, 271–272, 274
moneylending   213–214
monolithic   4, 129, 141–142
monotheism   15, 37, 55, 68, 79, 108, 113, 117, 120, 133, 140, 162, 167, 169, 296
Moor   140
moral
– authority, in individual conscience   296
– improvement   253
– responsibility   22, 168
morality   16, 52, 107, 114, 161, 167, 216, 270, 292, 294

mortality   3, 86, 168
mortgages   221
Mosaic religion   41–42
Mosaism   41, 132, 141, 179
mourning, Christian public   247
muckraking   262
Muhammad cartoons   130
multicultural   4, 131
mundus sensibilis   93
municipality   6, 183, 200, 203–204, 236–237, 239, 249
music   147, 201, 247, 250
musical accompaniment   247, 250
Muslim(s)   86, 129–130, 140, 142, 144, 253
mystical   73, 171
mysticism   59, 119

nabobs   264
name
– family   217
– first   217
Napoleonic   218, 234
– Empire   215
– policies   225
– system   225
– rule   257
nation building   6, 183, 189, 196, 204–205
nation of Israel   74
national character   25, 33, 150
nationality   22, 28, 52, 142, 266
– spiritual   284
naturalism   90
need of the human heart   153–156, 159, 172
neighborhoods   230
Neo-Platonist   87
New Year   72
newspaper(s)   7, 190, 235, 257, 259–263, 265, 272–273, 275, 283
nihilism   85
nihilistic-anarchist revolution   166
non-Jews, rights of seat-holders   286
nothingness   72, 94
numerology   162
nuns   236–237

objective   5, 68, 79, 104, 132, 135, 167, 178, 266, 279

observance of law 168
occupational 214, 228, 233
– distribution 227
– structure 201–202, 204
occupations, service 201
Offenbarungsphilosophie 92
omnipotence 89, 117
omnipotent 117
ontological 89, 91
oppressed 26, 35, 54, 73, 87, 119, 134, 141, 253
Orangists 191
ordinances revoking privileges 209
organ 45, 92, 247
oriental 14, 33, 48, 62, 94, 132, 137, 143
Orientalism 129
orientalization 128, 137, 140
Original Sin 15, 120, 295
– Jew not redeemed from 295
– inherited human depravity 295
orphans 46, 199, 298
Orthodox 14–15, 47, 116, 246, 284–285, 288–289
Orthodoxy 47–48, 50, 141, 287, 291
othering 129
otherness 128, 232
otherworldliness 38, 117
otherworldly 37, 59, 111, 119, 124
outward forms 119

pagan(s) 22, 70, 72, 82, 94–95, 118, 122, 140
paganism, inequality of 267
papacy 209
papal bull 209
Paradise, fall 175
parasitic existence, Jewish 274
pariahs 261, 264
parish vicars 200
parliament 189, 191–193, 275–276
participation 1, 2, 19–20, 26, 39, 96, 145, 184, 188, 191–193, 196, 248, 250, 253, 265, 268, 270, 275, 279
particular manifestation, of a universal category of religion 153
party, the Catholic party 263–264

passionate 30, 90, 132, 257, 263
– commitment 148
– convictions 148
passions 93, 95
passive 70, 72, 74, 94, 122, 137, 171, 286, 294
– membership 286
– religion(s) 70
Passover 72, 74, 99, 231
pastor 201, 250
Patent of Toleration 212
Pauline 22, 37, 73, 78–79, 83, 95, 174, 295
– burden 295
– doctrine 83
paupers 210
pawn broking 136
payments 194
– back 233
– late 233
pedagogical 145, 148, 150–151, 156–157, 159–160
– approach(es) 145, 148, 152, 159
– ideals 145
– reversal 156
peddlers 210, 220, 240
pensions 194–195, 201
Pentateuch 134, 145
people
– apart 219
– of Israel, as challenger of evil 177
persecution 18, 47, 72, 165–166, 211, 260, 262, 265, 274, 284
personal 14, 31, 57–59, 80, 107, 123, 135, 147–149, 151–154, 157, 159, 169–170, 175, 186, 216, 246, 261, 266, 271, 275, 277, 281, 286, 290–293
– commitment 159
– meaning 145, 147, 151
– Messiah 169–170, 180
– sentiment 145, 148, 153
– union 186
philanthropy 266
pilpul 119, 136
pilpulism 288
Pittsburgh Platform 62
Platonic ruler 284
plurality 141

pogroms 208, 262, 265, 269, 279
polemical writings 282
police 83, 150, 198, 249
police supervision 267
Polish 36, 86–87, 204, 211, 268
political
– ambition 251
– authority 291
– emancipation 34, 128, 133
– liberation 166
– participation 8, 26, 184, 190–191, 196, 205, 250
– systems 93, 207
– theology 105
– views, un-American 292
polytheism 15, 140
poor 89, 178–189, 194, 199, 223, 225, 235–236, 244, 282
poor relief 199
populace 196–197, 202
population, rural 198
post office 194
post-Hegelianism 85
poverty aid 194–195
practical egoism 111–112
prayer(s) 45, 96, 145, 215, 239, 246, 284, 289, 297–298
– efficacy 291
– leader 242
– service, contemporary 245
prayerbook 162, 286, 288, 291
– Einhorn's Reform 282
– Szold 291
preach 31, 75, 99, 127, 164–165, 175, 242, 246, 264, 275, 282, 296
prefect(s) 216, 219–220, 222
preparation 116, 121, 231
press, hostile 260
priest(s) 16, 19, 24, 41, 45, 50–53, 59, 74, 81, 127, 201–202, 237, 250
prince 14, 62, 71
principle(s)
– of Judaism 3, 16, 22, 67, 84
– of faith 151
private property 271
privilege 36, 106, 108–109, 111, 119–120, 130, 209, 221

privy council 212
privy secretary 259
profanation of God's name 292
profane 58, 60, 72, 82
professional advancement 146, 149
promised land 29, 44, 168
proof texts 154–155, 159
prophetic messianism 161, 167, 169
prosecution 210
proselytism 16, 135
proselytize 135
Protestantism 36–37, 59, 105
providence 60, 72, 89–90, 161
Prussian 14, 40, 83, 128, 132, 135, 185–188, 190, 197, 227, 229, 237, 246, 259, 283
– garrison 186–188
– king 283
– policy of tolerating Jews 283
– regions 227
pseudo-messiahs 162, 166
psychological 68, 84, 222
public
– administration 194, 201
– assistance 197
– *Public Company Theater Society of Luxembourg* 251
– education 194, 196
– enterprise 194–195
– health 199
– office 212
– schools 221
– service(s) 100–101, 193–195, 198, 201, 203, 205, 245
– structures 194
publicist 7, 274
purchasable souls 294
pure egoism 112
purpose, of religious practice 168

qualification, 190–192, 284
quarrel 281

rabble-rousing 276
rabbi
– appointment of 240
– associate 282

– request for   241
– subsidy for   241
rabbis
– and laity, non-existent division   298
– of yore   245
rabbinical
– certificate   31
– colleagues   281, 283
– literature   27, 41, 49
race   51, 56, 161, 274
radical Reform congregation   2, 7, 33, 44, 63, 246, 281, 283, 289–290
railroads   195
rational
– administration   224
– contemplation   111
– principles   152
– truth   152
rationalism   59, 97, 296
reactionary   257, 260
reason
– universal laws of   162
recipes, exchange   231
reclamation (of the essence of Judaism)   165
reconciliation   31, 58, 62, 70, 81, 116, 179
Redeemer   162–163, 172
redemption   56, 59, 80, 83, 89, 95, 97, 162–163, 173
reform(s)
– aesthetic   40
– moderate   246, 287
– radical   41, 63, 299
Reform Judaism, radical extreme   289
reform party   245
reform, liturgy and customs   282
rejection of, hollow   270
relationship Judaism – Christianity   50–53
religion
– active   70, 122
– ancient   49, 94
– as anthropology   109
– as humbug   293
– classes   243
– consummate   104, 110, 115
– of the heart   153–158
– of tolerance   39, 124
– passive   70

– true   114
Religionslehre   153–155
Religionsunterricht   154
religiosity
– extensive   71
– intensive   71
religious
– affiliations   236
– character   153
– communities   4, 6, 144, 184, 213, 224, 242, 272
– customs   238, 244
– decision-making   288
– dogma   153–154
– edification   148
– expression   153, 156
– immediacy   157
– institutions   239, 241
– knowledge of   159
– otherness   232
– passion   148
– practice(s) (purpose of)   168
– principles   152
remarriage
– refuse officiation   285
renunciation, of Judaism   165
repair of churches   200
repentance   93, 172, 174
republicanism   46, 299
residency, temporary   210
resident alien   286
response strategies   131
resurrection
– of the dead   299
– spiritual interpretation   299
Restoration   29, 177, 276, 292
restricted participation   189
retirement   201, 203, 299
revelation
– divine   12
– un-Jewish, Christian doctrine   295
revocation of rights   207
revolutionary calendar   216
rhythms of life   243
right-wing circles   233
rishus   292
rite, meaning of   297

ritual(s)
– abandonment of 297
road construction 194, 199, 204
robberies 223
Roman(s) 19, 94
royal dynasty 179

Sabbath 7, 28, 30, 42–43, 99, 136, 243–246, 289, 298–299
sacred 59, 81–82, 121, 168, 264, 270, 294
sacrifice(s) 95, 100, 104–105, 172, 176, 266
salaries, of cleric 194–195
salary 31, 194, 241, 288
Salonmensch 147
salonnières 147
salons 149
salt monopoly 194
salvation 5, 58–59, 79, 83, 86, 111, 120, 143, 171, 175–176, 266
Satan 80
satire 130
Saturday 232, 245, 289–290
scandal 287
Schmutzblätter 269
scholasticism 35, 86
scholastics 93–94
school(s)
– according to faith 237
– building 194
– Catholic 236–237
– higher education 200
– Jewish 236
– moral improvement 253
– primary 272
– secondary 191
– village 237
schooling, mandatory 238
Second Temple 50
second-hand goods 214, 229
secularism 82
secularization 53, 63, 224, 260, 269, 272–273, 279
secularizing state 171–172
segregation 132, 138, 209
self
– actualization 104
– betterment 167

– consciousness 15, 69, 71, 82, 84, 100, 104, 121
– preservation 104
– restraint 114
– sacrifice 104–105
– sufficiency 89
selfishness 113, 274
seminary 201, 259, 291
sensibilities 5, 14
– modern 147
sensuousness 142
sentiment(s) 18, 145, 147–149, 151–154, 258, 264
separatist tendencies 165
Sermon on the Mount 80
servants 102, 195, 201
– Christian 230–231
– domestic 201
settlement 6, 210, 215, 225, 230, 249
– ban 228
– prohibition 208
sewing workroom 236
shochet 241–242
shofar 72
sickness of the spirit 172
sign language 48
sin(s) 26, 72, 80–81, 84, 113, 117, 120, 172, 295–296
– forgiving of 172
– Original
sinfulness 50, 116, 118, 172, 176
six days 145
– creation in 155, 289
– of labor 289
slave(s) 35, 76, 103, 178, 264
slavery 7, 44, 76, 99, 102, 121
social
– abuses 298
– advancement 151
– classification 207
– contract 100
– control 239
– emancipation 146, 270
– gaps 233
– inequality 198
– peace 234
– relations 3, 92, 95, 97

– secularization 272
– spending 196, 199
– stratification 202
– transformation 204, 257
– transitions 184
– reformist 190
socialist systems 267
socialization 271
socioeconomic 184, 197–200
sociopolitical 257
sovereign ruler 120
sovereignty (of the state) 188
Spanish 87–88
– regiment 210
Speichellecker 283
spending, social 195, 199
spies, Jewish 276
spiritual
– identity 142
Staat vor Ort 198
stagnation 204
State, religious sanctity of 284
statehood 6, 184–185
stereotypes, anti-Jewish 235
stewards 103
stigmatization 257
stolen goods 234
stratification, social 6, 202–203
stubbornness 4, 33, 113
subjectivity 82, 103–104, 112, 117
subjugation 272
sublimity 103
suffering 25, 30, 50, 80, 104, 107–108, 111, 116, 176, 274, 295
– servant 170
suffrage 191
Sunday 7, 43, 243–244, 289–290
superiority 23, 37, 54, 56, 58, 61, 104, 119, 135
supernatural 5, 48, 163, 171–175, 294
supersede(d) 86, 96, 133, 272, 297
survival 53, 108, 165, 210
symbolic 6, 16, 28, 48, 260, 297–298
synagogue
– attendance 238
– consecration 247
– contributions 239

– donations 239
– government grant money 239
– grant from municipality 239
– honors, auctioning of 245
– reserved seats 239
symbolism 42, 110
systematic treatment (of the Jewish religion) 153

Talmud, outlook superseded 57
Talmudism 47
tax(es) 186, 190–192, 198, 210, 212, 214–215, 264, 275
tefilin 297
Temple 13, 45, 50, 74, 162, 164, 245, 282, 283, 291
Ten Commandments 134
Ten Words 134
tenets 11, 135, 153, 293
tension 12, 89, 159, 232
terror 213
textiles 201
theocratic (state) 267
theological-spiritual defense, of Judaism's continued existence 164
Theresian-Josephinian era 211
thieves 211
Thorgeld (body tax) 264
throne and altar 260
tobacco 201
topos 268, 273
Torah 18, 27, 72, 87, 134, 168, 242, 296
– new 173
– reading of 242
trade guild(s) 211–212, 214
– abolition of
trade(s)
– authorizations 234
– cattle 238
– horse 210
– intermediary 214
– itinerant 211
train stations 195
transcendence 3, 93, 100, 112
transcendent 95, 112, 117
transcendental 103

transformation 33, 46, 48, 58, 68, 104, 171, 174, 184, 195, 214, 257–258, 268, 271, 278–279
transnational 8, 63, 237, 252
transportation 194–201, 203
treason, Jewish 263
Treaty of London 196
trust 19, 26, 235
tsitsit 297
Turkish 129
typeset 155–156, 200
typology 105

ultramontane 2, 259, 274, 279
ultramontanism 259, 279
ultramontanist 190
un-freedom 67, 83
uncircumcised 174
unemancipated consciousness 112
unhappy consciousness 112
unhistorical 140
unification (of all humanity) 5, 50
Union of American Hebrew Congregations 290
universalism 1, 12, 22–28, 51–52, 54–55, 58, 61, 128, 296
universalized ethical life 166
university (universities) 8, 11, 14–16, 70, 132, 134–135, 150, 162, 275
unmediated consciousness 68
unprincipled 271, 290
unworthy practices 290
upper class(es) 202–204, 230, 247, 251–252
urban development 184
urban population 202
upbringing , Jewish 268
usury 216–218, 220–221, 234, 274
utilitarianism 113
utopia 5, 177, 267

vagabonds 210, 223
violation of proper morality 292
violence 86, 97, 262, 278
violent rule 166

virtue 16, 18, 22, 38, 89, 111, 113, 116, 121, 133, 149, 241
virtuosos 147
vita activa, vita contemplative 90
vocational training 298
Volksgeist 33, 35
Voraussetzung 115–116, 120
Vorstellung(en) 104–105, 110
voters 191–193
voting rights 190, 261

wage labor 271
wage(s) 195, 271, 264–265
watered-down 262, 265
weddings 238, 286
welfare 99, 111, 121, 199, 234, 252, 259, 298
– Mosaic social welfare laws 298
– of civil society 298
– paternalistic welfare considerations 234
Weltbürgerlichkeit 5, 158
whole and real 287
Wissenschaft des Judent(h)ums 11, 36, 54
witness 28, 40, 158, 248, 284
women and girls, gossip 292
woodworking 201
workers' movement 263
working class 130, 264
world
– citizenship 5
– -consciousness 69
– domination 265
World War I 204, 303
world-historical vocation 296
worldliness 38, 117, 142
Wucher 234
xenophobic 217

yellow badge 264
yeshivah 12, 14
Young Hegelian(s) 2, 4, 33, 83–84, 110, 123, 127–128, 134–135, 137–138, 140

Zeitbildung 68
Zeitgeist 41, 68
Zionist 55, 62, 169

Biblical and Rabbinic Sources

Hebrew Bible

Genesis 92, 112, 117–118, 155
Gen 1:3 112
Gen 2:15 103
Gen 12:1 71
Gen 15:10 71
Gen 17:23–27 71
Gen 18:19 71
Exodus 99, 168
Lev 16 172
Deut 30:20, 32:46–47 154
2 Sam 7:14 80
Isa 11:1 170
Isa 11:9 168
Jer 31:23 122
Ezek 36:26 174
Ps 24:1 103
Prov 21:1 78

New Testament

Matthew 80, 81, 174
John 80, 97
– 8:32, 34 83
– 15:15 83
Epistle to the Romans 174

Rabbinic Texts

bGit 10b 74
bSan 56b 74
bYoma 38b 172
BerR
– 39:11 71
– 56:5 72
– 51:9 72
yBer 9:24 70

www.ingramcontent.com/pod-product-compliance
Lightning Source LLC
Chambersburg PA
CBHW020219170426
43201CB00007B/257